Godroads

The book aims at studying processes of religious change in India. The focus lies neither on any particular religious tradition, nor is it the aim to provide an encyclopaedic overview of conversion in different religious traditions. Instead, the studies presented here investigate the different modalities of religious change across and within religious traditions. In order to understand the different patterns involved, diverse cases are scrutinised. The cases are diverse in different ways. First, they discuss different religious traditions (Hindu traditions and sects, Christianity, Islam and indigenous religions). Second, they cover most regions of India. Third, the chapters discuss historical as well as contemporary examples. Finally, the different cases involve micro, meso and macro dynamics of religious change in different ways, dealing with large-scale political processes of colonialism and nationalism, dimensions of social structure in relation to conversion and subjective meanings of and motives for conversion. In this way, the book seeks to do justice to the complexity of the phenomenon under study, a complexity that is also reflected in the multivalence and multidirectionality of the trope of Godroads, which is introduced here as a heuristic metaphor. Studying modalities of conversion means for the authors of this volume to identify patterns of the processes studied. To this aim, the comprehensive introduction provides, next to an overview of the relevant literature, a thorough discussion of theoretical approaches that attend in particular to structures in these (sudden or continuous) dynamics of religious change. The afterword by the Brazilian anthropologist Aparecida Vilaça, a specialist on conversion in the Amazon region, extends the comparative scope beyond India.

Peter Berger teaches anthropology of Indian religions in the Department of Comparative Study of Religion, Faculty of Theology and Religious Studies, University of Groningen, the Netherlands.

Sarbeswar Sahoo teaches sociology in the Department of Humanities and Social Sciences, Indian Institute of Technology Delhi, India.

Godroads
Modalities of Conversion in India

Edited by
Peter Berger
Sarbeswar Sahoo

CAMBRIDGE
UNIVERSITY PRESS

University Printing House, Cambridge CB2 8BS, United Kingdom

One Liberty Plaza, 20th Floor, New York, NY 10006, USA

477 Williamstown Road, Port Melbourne, vic 3207, Australia

314 to 321, 3rd Floor, Plot No.3, Splendor Forum, Jasola District Centre, New Delhi 110025, India

79 Anson Road, #06–04/06, Singapore 079906

Cambridge University Press is part of the University of Cambridge.

It furthers the University's mission by disseminating knowledge in the pursuit of education, learning and research at the highest international levels of excellence.

www.cambridge.org

Information on this title: www.cambridge.org/9781108490504

© Cambridge University Press 2020

This publication is in copyright. Subject to statutory exception and to the provisions of relevant collective licensing agreements, no reproduction of any part may take place without the written permission of Cambridge University Press.

First published 2020

Printed in India by Nutech Print Services, New Delhi 110020

A catalogue record for this publication is available from the British Library

ISBN 978-1-108-49050-4 Hardback

Cambridge University Press has no responsibility for the persistence or accuracy of URLs for external or third-party internet websites referred to in this publication, and does not guarantee that any content on such websites is, or will remain, accurate or appropriate.

Contents

Foreword   vii
Piers Vitebsky

Acknowledgements   xi

Introduction   1
Peter Berger and Sarbeswar Sahoo

1   **The Rise, Growth and Significance of Shudra Conversion Movements in the Methodist Mission, Hyderabad, 1925–1947**   47
Geoffrey A. Oddie

2   **Communism and the Cross: A Caste–Class Trajectory of Religious Conversion in South India**   68
Ashok Kumar Mocherla

3   **Religious Conversion as Ethical Transformation: A Study of Islamic Reformism in Rural West Bengal**   85
Fernande W. Pool

4   **Conversion versus Unity: The Basel Mission among the Badaga on the Nilgiri Plateau, 1845–1915**   109
Frank Heidemann

5   **Identity Change and the Construction of Difference: Colonial and Postcolonial Conversions among the Sumi Naga of Nagaland, Northeast India**   129
Iliyana Angelova

6   **Conversion to Christianity and Healing: The Naga of Northeast India**   155
Vibha Joshi

7   **Reshaping the American Evangelical Conversion Narrative in Nineteenth-Century North India**   179
Arun W. Jones

vi   *Contents*

8   **Cultural Transformations through Performance Arts in Early Twentieth-Century South India** 199
Rajalakshmi Nadadur Kannan

9   **Reservation and Religious Freedom: Understanding Conversion and Hindu–Christian Conflict in Odisha and Rajasthan** 222
Sarbeswar Sahoo

10   **Rupture and Resilience: Dynamics between a Hindu Reform Movement and an Indigenous Religion in Highland Odisha** 246
Peter Berger

Afterword: India Seen from Amazonia 272
Aparecida Vilaça

About the Contributors 285

Index 289

Foreword

Piers Vitebsky

This is an important and original collection. Scholarly approaches to conversion generally focus on Christianity, seeing conversion as a distinctive feature of that religion in accordance with its own rhetoric. Christianity then appears as something one converts *to* from something else, often tracing a trajectory from polytheism to monotheism with an apparent teleological inevitability.

Numerous historical and anthropological studies, from early Europe (Brown 1995; Burke 1978) to modern Africa (Meyer 1999) and Papua New Guinea (Robbins 2004), confirm that this kind of shift does indeed happen. But the chapters in this collection show that it is not the only possible journey. Western Europe is the point of origin of much colonialism and many missionaries, yet today people there are turning away from Christianity, which is in serious decline across the region. For India, this volume shows clearly how conversion is not only a story about Christianity – or even about conversion as such. Religious change takes place across Islam, Hinduism and Buddhism, as well as in India's numerous tribal religions. One of this book's important contributions, both theoretical and ethnographic, is to show how the same kinds of shifts can also occur right inside what is considered to be one and the same religion, where they manifest themselves as reformist movements. And Chapter 7 explores a deeply spiritual figure who moves between Muslim, Hindu and Christian devotional forms. Such situations are not so much examples of conversion, as of something that could perhaps be called religious adjustment.

Many religious discourses talk of a road or path. In religious terms, these seek a destination so other-worldly that it can perhaps never be reached. The roads in the title of this book refer to journeys with no end point, but for a different reason. They are also a historical and sociological metaphor. For a while, sometimes for generations, a community may feel static, with little change. Then, the pressure for change will build up, and the metaphor of a journey will again seem appropriate.

viii *Piers Vitebsky*

The chapters in this collection survey a wide range of historical and contemporary situations across the country. The picture that emerges is highly interactive, as local situations are impinged upon by a range of influences, triggering reactions and counter-reactions: missionaries, communists, Dalit liberationists and prophets emerge from or are met by the agency, agendas and cultural depth of diverse populations. Contributors see these changes as process, as movements rather than moments, which in some situations can even lead to deconversion or 'retroversion', as different religious styles fail to face up to moral and existential questions of their time. In Chapter 4, some members of a community move to a more individualised Protestant Christian self, while others in the same community hold on to communal values for the sake of village unity and collective rights. Chapters 3 and 8 give us a move towards purification associated with a rising middle class. In Chapter 3, this move is towards reformist Islam as a protest against Western, rather than Hindu, dominance, and aims at the development of a modern ethical self which is both religious and secular. This contrasts with the process in Chapter 8, where Western dominance is resisted by performers through the development of a new *habitus* while their audience develops a new taste, both sides together intensifying an already existing Hindu tone. This Chapter 8 shows a Hindu elite resistance to colonialism, in contrast to Chapters 1 and 2, where low-caste resistance takes advantage of new possibilities opened up *by* colonialism. Several chapters also show protest against the conversion of others away from Hinduism (especially Chapter 9), as well as a move towards forms of Hinduism among tribes who may perhaps be regarded as not yet Hindu (Chapter 10). The enlightening juxtaposition of Chapters 5 and 6 explores the long history of Christian conversion among Naga groups from the quite different perspectives of identity formation and healing.

In her Afterword, Vilaça gives a thoughtful response from the perspective of a specialist on Amazonia, contrasting the hierarchical and totalising nature of Indian society (and one could add the essentialism of caste ideology) with Amazonia's egalitarianism, as well as with that region's ready transformations and reversals of identities between human and animal, kin and affine.

It is true that such Amazonian modes of being and becoming are strikingly un-Indian. But for me as an Indianist, these chapters also offer another lesson: that there is an almost infinite variety in what people do with the distinctive elements which the Indian cultural universe does provide. Against a background of these principles of hierarchy and holism, imperfectly realised or cleverly subverted, there is so much more going on than can be encompassed even by this collection. The Sora of southern Odisha are close geographically, linguistically and culturally to Berger's Gadaba (Chapter 10). Yet my own experience of studying them since the 1970s shows them to be travelling in a different set of directions. All younger Sora are abandoning their parents' unique shamanistic dialogues with the dead (Vitebsky 1993). But while some turn to Baptism and other Christian churches, others turn to indigenised versions of reformist Hindu movements (Vitebsky 2017). These are not the Olek Dormo of the Gadaba but range from nationalist Hindutva-inspired versions to the cult of a unique Sora script revealed to a prophet in a dream, somewhat like the Ol Chiki script of the Santal (Carrin 2014).

All of these may be regarded as new Sora religions. While Hindu forms keep some strands of the old religion but bring them into line with national orthodoxy, Baptists reject everything that came from their ancestors. This reinforces the point that conversion need not be about Christianity as such since in political terms these new Christian and Hindu Sora religions are functionally equivalent. The old tribal religion, for all its subtleties and fulfilments, was rooted in a feudal regime of oppression and humiliation which has become unacceptable. Young Sora are not so much converting *to* something, as *from* an archaic local cosmology which has become too small and humiliating for the aspirational world of literacy and government jobs which they now inhabit. It is not that the structure of society has changed, but rather that they are now able to re-position themselves within the wider structures and values that encompass them. Various aspects of modernity and democracy had long been visible, but had not been available *to them*. What has changed is that they are no longer victims of a one-way extractive economy, but recipients of effective government programmes and participants in the nation-state as voters and political party candidates. Outside authorities – whether kings previously or politicians today – are no longer oppressors, but have become answerable and responsible as patrons (Piliavsky 2014). Where the Naga in Chapters 5 and 6 became Christians in order to resist the Indian state, the Sora do so in order to join it on better terms than before.

My own comparison outside the region would be, not with Amazonia, but with Arctic Siberia, where I have also done fieldwork (Vitebsky 2005). The comparison would reveal another distinctive feature of India which this collection brings out strongly: the intensely religious idiom of even the most political process. It would not be so in Russia. From the 1920s to the 1980s, the Soviet state strove to abolish religion altogether and create a population of atheists. Among the Russian majority it suppressed Christianity; among indigenous Siberian tribes it imprisoned or murdered their shamans (after the end of the Soviet regime in the 1980s, there has been a resurgence everywhere of religiosity in a variety of new or supposedly old forms). The Soviet revolution was a conversion to un-religion or anti-religion, in which religion featured as an inferior form within a spectrum of other, secular ideologies. But in the Andhra Pradesh of Chapter 2, the communists do not diminish religion, but facilitate a change

x Piers Vitebsky

that is itself religious. Similarly among the Sora, the escape from feudal oppression has come not through political movements as such but by turning to an array of alternative religions.

There are some great recent edited collections of papers which rethink an important topic comparatively across South Asia, such as Piliavsky's volume on patronage (2014). But there is nothing else like this volume, which will become a landmark reference point on the hugeness and restlessness of religion in India. No specialist on the region can afford to ignore it, while those who study any other region of the world will find fascinating echoes, reflections and contrasts.

BIBLIOGRAPHY

Brown, Peter. 1995. *Authority and the Sacred: Aspects of the Christianisation of the Roman World*. Cambridge: Cambridge University Press.

Burke, Peter. 1978. *Popular Culture in Early Modern Europe*. London: Temple Smith.

Carrin, Marine. 2014. 'The Santal as an Intellectual.' In *The Politics of Ethnicity in India, Nepal, and China*, edited by Marine Carrin, Pralay Kanungo, and Gérard Toffin, 77–99. Delhi: Primus Books.

Meyer, Birgit. 1999. *Translating the Devil: Religion and Modernity among the Ewe in Ghana*. London: University Press for the International African Institute.

Piliavsky, Anastasia, ed. 2014. *Patronage as Politics in South Asia*. Delhi: Cambridge University Press.

Robbins, Joel. 2004. *Becoming Sinners: Christianity and Moral Torment in a Papua New Guinea Society*. Berkeley: University of California Press.

Vitebsky, Piers. 1993. *Dialogues with the Dead: The Discussion of Mortality among the Sora of Eastern India*. Cambridge: Cambridge University Press and Delhi: Foundation Books.

———. 2005. *Reindeer People: Living with Animals and Spirits in Siberia*. Boston: Houghton Mifflin and London: HarperCollins.

———. 2017. *Living without the Dead: Loss and Redemption in a Jungle Cosmos*. Chicago: University of Chicago Press; Indian edition 2018 Delhi: HarperCollins.

ACKNOWLEDGEMENTS

Most of the chapters of this volume were first presented at the European Conference on South Asian Studies held at the University of Warsaw, Poland, in 2016.

Our individual contributions to this volume are based on research conducted in the context of a project titled 'Modalities of Conversion in India' funded by the Gratama Foundation. We thank the Gratama Foundation for its unbureaucratic and flexible support.

We would also like to thank Qudsiya Ahmed and Sohini Ghosh at Cambridge University Press for their cooperation and careful work during the publication process.

Peter Berger
Sarbeswar Sahoo

Introduction

Peter Berger and Sarbeswar Sahoo

A road is only a simple thing at first sight, as has been previously noted (Miller 2001: 183). On second look, however, it reveals its dazzling complexity, as well as a profound and deep connection with human endeavours that it entails, for instance, with the human desire to escape from one place or to reach another. Movement, change and transformation are intrinsic to roads, to the experiencing subjects who travel along them and the environment they traverse, which they connect as much as divide. As the epitome of modernity, the road is a symbol of violence, colonialism, conquest, oppression and exploitation, as well as an icon of hope, protest and freedom.

Roads are connected to religion in manifold ways, not only in the sense that religions offer certain 'paths' to salvation (Sting 1997). Some of our readers and most of our authors will know what it feels like to be squeezed between narrow rows of a crowded bus in India, the vehicle coming to a sudden stop, the bus driver (or one of his team) jumping off to quickly offer a coconut at a small shrine on the side of the road, before diving back into the bus, hoping that the gods will hear him and give their blessing. Obviously, not only in India, but definitely there, roads are places of worship and of pilgrimage. They may represent 'mythographies' (Masquelier 2002), imaginations of an indigenised modernity which also involve ideas about the anger of those spirits whose dwellings have suffered destruction in the very construction of the road. They are also sites of reflection, a moral geography in relation to which loss of traditions and moral anomie can be contemplated (Luning 2009). They are liminal spaces and, as such, dying on the road – or rather on the path – may be considered a particularly 'bad death' (P. Berger 2015: 276f.). Being on the road may be associated with potential transgressions of embodied local moral orders and codes, and, as such, they may be a powerful tool restricting movement and reproducing asymmetrical relationships in terms of caste, class and gender (Miller 2001).

As with roads, conversion might also initially be perceived as a simple movement from one religion to another; however, as in the previous case, this

2 *Peter Berger and Sarbeswar Sahoo*

assessment will not hold up on closer examination. We have chosen a connection with the road and coined the term 'Godroads' because the metaphor of the road helps us to capture the complexity of the phenomenon of conversion. When concerned with the different modalities of conversion, as is the case in this volume, the properties of the road facilitate their visualisation and reflection on them. Godroads, then, is not understood here as a one-dimensional movement towards or away from a god or religion, but stands for the complex, conflict-ridden and at times contradictory processes of engaging with religious traditions.

In this introduction, we intend to outline and elaborate on a few of the themes that run throughout the volume. However, we hope to not merely point out cross-connections between the different contributions but to stimulate reflection on modalities of conversion that go beyond the present volume and also beyond India (see Vilaça, this volume). The introduction begins by situating this volume in relation to some of the main contributions to the study of conversion in India, without aiming to provide an exhaustive overview.[1] We then discuss Godroads in relation to protest, the changing of religious affiliation as the expression of protest and as an attempt to break free from oppression and exploitation, as well as the protest against conversion, especially voiced by Hindu nationalists. It is in this political arena that the metaphor of Godroads coagulates into a concrete materiality, when roads, shrines, mosques, churches and temples become part of a topography of conversion which often entails violence. We briefly touch on this aspect once more later in the introduction when discussing conversion and urban spaces. Subsequently, we take up the widely debated issue of conversion and its relation to modernity, in its material as well as ideological dimensions, and its relatedness to colonial discourses and institutions.

A longer section follows, subdivided into four parts that, attempts to explore some of the dimensions and implications of the terms 'process', 'event', 'continuity' and 'change'. Like travelling on a road, the process of conversion can be fast or slow, there may be obstacles on the way, a street may turn out to be a dead end, and even if this is not the case, one may decide to turn around and return to where one started (but perhaps revisiting later). While we thus emphasise the multifaceted, potentially irregular *processes* of Godroads, the significance of *events* is not underestimated, accidents can occur that significantly alter the mode of the journey or even its aims, or may motivate a return. However, even if a decision to return is taken, one usually brings home some of the things one had collected on the journey – if not material objects, then memories. Even if one decides to return, one is no longer the same as when one started, as common travel wisdom suggests; yet one is not completely different either, still recognisably a certain person.

Travelling along the road thus highlights the ambivalence and complexity in remaining the same yet becoming different, of continuity and change. This is a multilayered and complicated dynamic that concerns the old and the new, which we wish to discuss here. We focus on this intricate relationship between rupture and resilience in distinguishing and understanding different modalities of conversion. In a first step, this section thus outlines different patterns of continuity and change. In a second step, it introduces several analytical frameworks – needless to say that there are others – that help to theorise such patterns in a structural manner, thereby not merely considering the process as entailing increase or loss, of *more* of this religion or *less* of this worldview. The third step consists in identifying locations in the processes of conversion that are particularly relevant for either continuity or change. In no case are all aspects of a culture equally relevant in producing resilience or facilitating change, and we want to point towards some particularly significant locations. As a consequence of thinking about locations of conversion, in the final part of this section, we ask whether conversion, and the relationships of continuity and change that it entails, actually *means* something different and *works* differently in different kinds of society. No doubt, we cannot come to any kind of definitive conclusion in this regard, but we think it is important to ask the question. The introduction finishes with a consideration of the value of the term 'conversion' on the basis of the contributions to this volume.

STUDYING CONVERSION IN INDIA

A major part of the scholarly work on conversion in India has been historical. These writings have primarily focused on the nature of missionary organisations and their relationship with the colonial state. According to Frykenberg (2005), the relationship between Christian missionaries and the colonial state in India was ambiguous in nature. While the colonial authorities initially opposed conversion and did not permit missionaries to operate freely, fearing that their activities might disturb the religious sensibilities of the majority Hindus, later, based on the conditionalities of the Charter Act of 1813, they actively encouraged Christian missionary activities. Broadly speaking, historians were interested in analysing the mutually enabling relationship between missions and the Empire, especially how the Empire facilitated missionisation and how missionaries helped consolidate the colonial Empire through their civilising missions (Fischer-Tine and Mann 2004; Porter 2004; Watt and Mann 2011).

In contrast to these historical texts, sociologists and anthropologists working on Christianity and conversion in India have mainly focused on caste and identity issues. For them, the central question has been: what implications does conversion have for caste and systems of hierarchy, and how does it transform identity-formation processes? In this regard, the work of Chris Fuller (1976) and David Mosse (2012) has been very significant. While Christian missionaries presented Christianity as 'casteless' and argued that conversion would result in the end of the caste hierarchy (Mallampalli 2004: 159), based on his study of Kerala Christians, Fuller shows how caste hierarchies and practices continue to govern the everyday social life and relationship of converts in Kerala. Even long after conversion, low caste converts continue to experience economic and social marginalisation and are very often discriminated against by high caste Christians. As Fuller (1976: 61) argued, 'the various Protestant churches in Kerala are regarded as low in status because almost all of their members are converted Harijans'. He also noted that inter-caste marriages were strictly prohibited between high caste and low caste Christians: 'there are no marital unions between the Syrians and Latin Christians or New Christians, nor are there unions between the latter two groupings. Such a marriage would be as unthinkable for a Syrian as would a marriage to a Harijan be for a Nayar' (Fuller 1976: 56–57).

Following on from Fuller and drawing on historical and anthropological research, in his book, *The Saint in the Banyan Tree*, Mosse (2012) shows how Christianity has accommodated caste over centuries. According to Mosse, Christian missionaries disliked caste and criticised caste practices as 'pagan' and 'superstitious'. However, in order for caste to be 'tolerated among converts', Jesuit missionaries attempted to reform and secularise caste (Mosse 2012: 8). With this, caste was denied its religious significance and practised only as a civil institution. Even when caste was socially or politically permitted, it was denied its rank. The secularisation of caste allowed converts to retain their caste practices, and as Catholicism became indigenised, caste continued to influence the structure of relationships within it. In addition to Fuller and Mosse, Bauman (2008) and Robinson and Kujur (2010) have also recently discussed the relationship between caste and Christianity by analysing the ways in which conversion has transformed the subaltern identity and marginality of Dalits and tribals in India.

Although most anthropological contributions have dealt with the caste question, they have rarely examined conversion theoretically or conceptually. With the exception of work by Robinson (2003) and Robinson and Clarke (2003), very little has been written about continuity and rupture; meanings, motivations and modalities or issues of modernity in conversion. Combining theoretical and empirical insights, contributors to this volume attempt to conceptualise conversion in multiple ways (as protest, as process, as modernity, as ethical transformation) and examine its implications, not only for the everyday

Introduction **5**

lives of the individuals involved but also for the community and greater societal structures and processes. Bringing together both experienced and young scholars from different disciplinary backgrounds and drawing on empirical insights from different parts of India, this book intends to combine theoretical and empirical insights, paying attention to the micro, meso and macro levels of the social context and processes, investigating questions of caste and identity on the one hand and issues of continuity/rupture and modernity on the other. The following sections of the introduction discuss these aspects and highlight the multiple ways in which conversion can be encountered and conceptualised in India.

CONVERSION AS PROTEST AND PROTEST AGAINST CONVERSION

B. R. Ambedkar, the architect of India's Constitution, once famously declared, 'Though, I was born a Hindu, I solemnly assure you that I will not die as a Hindu.' The oppressive social hierarchy of Hinduism, organised according to the principle of purity and pollution and institutionalised through the caste system, treated a large section of India's population as 'slaves'. As Rupa Viswanath (2013: 125) notes, in south India, the names of some of the 'untouchable' castes, such as Pariah and Palla, were used interchangeably by Tamils with the terms 'al' and 'atimai', which literally meant slave. The low caste untouchables were dehumanised and denied basic human dignity and respect. Ambedkar argued that under the caste system, the untouchable Dalits had 'their very persona confiscated' (cited in Rao 2009: 118). For him, since caste constituted an integral part of Hinduism, escaping caste discrimination necessarily involved a change of religion or conversion from Hinduism. In 1935, Ambedkar announced before a large crowd that 'because we have the misfortune to call ourselves Hindus, we are treated thus. If we were members of another faith, none dare treat us so.... We shall repair our mistakes now' (cited in Rao 2009: 118).

While it was thus clear to Ambedkar that he would convert from Hinduism, the question was which religion to choose. Ambedkar deliberated on the cosmologies of various religious traditions and found that there were many similarities between the cosmologies of Hinduism on the one hand and Christianity and Islam on the other (Barlingay 1974: 145). All of these religions believed in various 'customs' and 'superstitions'. For Ambedkar, it was only Buddhism which would entail a 'massive revolt' (ibid.)[2] against the 'superstitious' beliefs and practices of Hindus. As Heredia (2011: 95) notes, Ambedkar's Buddhism was 'cleansed of the Brahmanic interpolations of the doctrines of Karma and rebirth'. Gail Omvedt (2003) also notes that it is Buddhism which has, over a period of 2,500 years, been engaged in a struggle against Brahmanical Hinduism and caste hierarchy. Considering this, Ambedkar converted to

6 Peter Berger and Sarbeswar Sahoo

Buddhism in Nagpur on 14 October 1956 as a mark of 'social revolt' or protest against the existing Hindu religious and social order.

Conversion was thus articulated by members of the low castes and marginalised communities not only as a form of protest against the caste system and the Hindu social hierarchy, but also as a quest for equality, human dignity and social justice. In a sense, it was considered a 'personal and collective accomplishment' (Strauss 1979: 158). Along with Ambedkar, almost 500,000 Dalits converted to Buddhism on the same day. Anupama Rao (2009: 118) argued that Ambedkar's public conversion from Hinduism became 'the symbolic core of a liberated Dalit identity' and 'emphatically affirmed a defining characteristic of Dalit emancipation'. Ambedkar's conversion moment not only marked a rejection of Hindu religious ideology but also a moment of liberation. After his conversion, he declared: 'I feel as if I have been liberated from Hell' (cited in Rao 2009: 119). Ambedkar's conversion constituted a pivotal moment in India's postcolonial history and the significance of this can be imagined based on the scale of today's neo-Buddhist movement which, according to Heredia (2011: 94), is 'the largest mass conversion of the twentieth century'.

Conversion from Hinduism was considered the basis for restructuring society and achieving Dalit dignity. Although Ambedkar converted to Buddhism, Christianity and its association with a modern Western egalitarian value system has also been attractive to the Dalits for a long time. As Louis Dumont (1980) has pointed out, while Indian social structure and ideology was marked by the principle of 'homo hierarchicus', the Christian West was represented through the principle of 'homo equalis'. The Christian missionaries played a significant role in highlighting this contrast between India and the West, and worked actively with the low castes to convert them to Christianity. For example, having been exploited and oppressed by Hindus and Muslims, the whole of the Paravar, or the Fisherman caste on the Fishery Coast, approached Portuguese missionaries and converted to Roman Catholicism. According to Forrester (2017 [1980]: 15), between 1535 and 1537, about 20,000 people were baptised. Similarly, the Pariah (Dalits) of Tamil Nadu also converted to Christianity to escape caste-based and economic exploitation. Discussing the case of Pariah conversion in colonial south India, Rupa Viswanath (2013: 121) argued that conversion of the Pariahs to Christianity not only significantly transformed their relationship with their masters, but also changed 'the balance of power and distribution of authority'. Furthermore, Sanal Mohan (2015), in his recently published *Modernity of Slavery*, shows how the low caste Dalits in Kerala, who comprised one-sixth of the population, were 'owned' by upper castes and Europeans, and how Christian missionary work transformed their collective self-identity and deeply impacted the emergence of Dalit consciousness and modernity in Kerala.

Introduction **7**

Escaping caste oppression has also been a key motivating factor in low caste conversion to Islam in India. According to Sikand and Katju (1994: 2214), the vast majority of India's Muslims 'are descendants of low caste Hindus who converted to Islam to escape the oppression of the higher castes and in search of equality and dignity'. Some scholars, however, have pointed out that conversion to Islam in the Indian subcontinent was in many cases achieved only by force (see Mathew 1982: 1029), with Hindus converting to Islam to 'save their lives' (Patvardhan, 1994: 2566). Although this is true, what is important is that in many cases conversion to Islam did indeed involve the rejection of the caste system. In one of the most recent and talked about cases, we witnessed the Dalits of Meenakshipuram village in Tamil Nadu converting to Islam on a mass scale, renaming their village Rahmatnagar (Wright Jr, 2007: 239). In this case, the Dalits of Meenakshipuram had striven for equality with the higher ranked Thevar castes of the village, but the Thevars had mistreated them. In 1981, when two Thevars from the nearby village of Mekkarai were found dead, the Dalits were suspected of being involved and the police came down heavily on the community. Enraged by the attitude of the police, the Dalits of Meenakshipuram converted to Islam as a symbol of protest, as well as a means of achieving equality and dignity.

Conversion as protest has thus been imagined by people of low caste and marginalised communities as an important 'event' symbolising a break with their past identities and experience of exploitation. Through conversion, low caste communities attempt to consciously construct a non-Hindu identity, which is perceived to be empowering and emancipating. As Heredia (2011: 90) argued, 'conversion becomes a passage to a new identity that empowers and frees the group. The converts do not attempt to reform the old; they have lost hope in this regard. Their choice is a social protest directed not to reform the old, but to reject it, inspired by hope for a better future elsewhere'.

Many of the chapters in this book reflect on how caste and tribal communities have used conversion as a sign of protest or revolt against the existing dominant religious and social order. For example, Geoffrey Oddie's and Ashok Kumar's chapters highlight the feudal oppression of the Shudra and the untouchable Mala and Madiga in the Telugu-speaking region of south India, respectively. Oddie argues that the Shudra considered conversion to Christianity as an opportunity to escape the exploitation and oppression of the feudal landlords. The successful work of the British Methodists among the outcaste Mala and Madiga in the region also facilitated the conversion process. The Shudra's conversion to Christianity severely undermined the authority of the local landlords, who unleashed a period of 'savage persecution' in an attempt to stop the conversion and missionary activities. This, however, could not deter the Shudra from

8 *Peter Berger and Sarbeswar Sahoo*

converting. Oddie argues that in addition to their ambition to achieve material progress, what mainly inspired the Shudra's conversion to Christianity was their desire for 'freedom' from forced labour and protection from oppression by the upper caste feudal landlords.

Similarly, discussing the relationship between caste, communism and Christianity in coastal Andhra, Kumar considers how communist activism played a major role in creating caste consciousness among the outcaste Mala and Madiga and helped them to not only resist caste inequality and dominance but also prepare the ground for their conversion to Lutheran Christianity. For Kumar, Christianity was at the forefront of advancing an alternative Dalit liberation agenda, which enabled them to not only attain political power, but also economic independence. Kumar concludes that the village church and religious celebrations are used today by Dalit Christians as platforms to reassert their power and strength in the local political context.

While the Shudra and outcastes used conversion as a form of protest against caste hierarchy and oppression, the upper castes and feudal lords protested against conversion because it posed a threat to their power and dominance. Frank Heidemann's contribution to this volume clearly brings out this aspect in his discussion of how the conversion of the Badaga met with fervent resistance from co-villagers and relatives. Heidemann argues that what drove Badaga resistance to conversion was not opposition to a religious orientation but identity politics. Some villagers and relatives believed that conversion violated ethnic boundaries and threatened the 'unity' of the village. It also posed a threat to endogamy and landed property of the village, as well as violated principles of purity and commensality. Although the Badagas who converted were motivated by the idea of 'forgiveness of sins', according to Hindu Badaga villagers, by converting to Christianity their fellow villagers committed even greater sins. As a consequence, the Christian Badaga were excommunicated and excluded from the village social structure in the Nilgiri regions of Tamil Nadu.

Similarly, in his contribution, Sahoo discusses how the upper caste Hindu nationalists perceived conversion as a threat to their idea of a 'Hindu nation'. They believed that conversion from Hinduism, especially to Christianity and Islam, would increase their enemies, make Hindus a minority in their own nation, and endanger their agenda of making India a Hindu nation. Resisting tribal conversion to Christianity, the Hindu nationalists argued that the missionaries were using material incentives to lure the 'poor tribals' to Christianity, which was a violation of the constitutional right to freedom of religion. Furthermore, they argued that tribal Christians were taking undue advantage of the affirmative action (reservation) policies of the government and depriving the 'Hindu tribals', for whom the policies were originally formulated, of their rights.

Discussing caste–tribe relations and the politics of conversion in the context of Odisha and the freedom of religion and inducement in the context of Rajasthan, Sahoo shows how Hindu nationalists politicised the issue of conversion and mobilised people against it, often resulting in violent clashes between the two communities involved.

Fernande Pool's, Iliyana Angelova's and Vibha Joshi's contributions go beyond the caste factor and examine conversion as a form of protest against political dominance and the socio-religious status quo. In her chapter, Pool conceptualises conversion to reformist Islam as an alternative form of modernity that offers resistance to Western cultural and political dominance. According to Pool, conversion defies the existing power structure, particularly the hegemonic secularity of the Indian nation that has engendered a substantial moral void in people's lives, and offers new modes of cultivating the religious and secular self. Similarly, discussing the case of the Naga ethno-nationalist movement in northeast India, Angelova shows how conversion to Baptist Christianity was used by Sumi Naga as a form of resistance against the Indian nation-state. For Angelova, conversion to Christianity has helped the Naga construct a distinct collective cultural identity and strengthened their nationalist movement (Nagaland for Christ) for autonomy and political independence from the Indian state. Taking Angelova's argument further, Joshi shows how revival churches emerged between the 1950s and 1970s as a mark of protest against the Indian government's attempt to intensify security operations in Nagaland. In fact, their response to increasing persecution by the Indian armed forces was an intense desire to convert. As Joshi writes, 'the more that they persecuted, the more that Naga sought refuge in religion. Within a few decades Nagaland became almost entirely Christian'.

CONVERSION TO MODERNITIES

Several of the chapters in this volume also discuss conversion in the context of what Peter van der Veer (1996) theorised as 'conversion to modernities'. The relationship between conversion and modernity is widely discussed in the anthropological and sociological literature (Comaroff and Comaroff 1997; Hefner 1993; 2013; Pelkmans 2009; van der Veer 1996; Washburn and Reinhart 2007). While secularisation theory of the 1960s discussed the incompatibility of religion and modernity and predicted the decline or privatisation of religion with the growing modernisation of society, anthropologists have convincingly demonstrated the co-existence of religion and modernity in contemporary societies (Hefner 1998; Joas 2009). In fact, several major sociological and anthropological works have demonstrated how the conversion of a single

10 *Peter Berger and Sarbeswar Sahoo*

individual or entire community is often motivated by desires and dreams of modernity (Martin 1995; P. L. Berger 2010).

In his book *The Protestant Ethic and the Spirit of Capitalism*, Max Weber (2005 [1904/5]) described modernity as a process of rationalisation and individualisation. He distinguished the 'universality' of major world religions from the 'irrationality' of primitive religions built around magic, and analysed the role of Protestant Christianity, in particular, in the making of European modernity. Peter van der Veer (1996: 3) argued that, in the Indian context, missionaries and the colonial ruling authorities believed Christianity to be superior to Hinduism. For them, what distinguished Christianity and made it attractive for people to convert was its unique emphasis on rationality (reason) and freedom (free will), in contrast to the irrationality and immorality of Hinduism. In particular, van de Veer pointed out that Christian missionaries and colonial authorities supported their argument by citing examples of the 'authoritarian irrationality' of India's priests (van der Veer 1996: 3) and the immorality of Hindu practices such as widow burning (*sati*). Given the prevalence of such 'backward customs' in Indian religious and social life, colonial authorities strongly believed that there was a need for the colonised to be converted to modernity.

The conversion to modernities project was thus intimately attached to the civilising mission of Christianity and British colonialism in India. Carey Watt (2011: 1) has argued that in addition to bringing the benefits of free trade and capitalism, as well as law, order and good government, at its core, 'the civilizing mission was about morally and materially "uplifting", "improving", and later "developing" the supposedly "backward" and "rude" people of India to make them more civilized and more modern'. In particular, Christian missionaries advanced scathing attacks on India's caste system and offered an alternative and egalitarian socio-religious order through conversion to Christianity. As Nicholas Dirks (1996) argued, missionaries fiercely criticised the immorality of the Hindu caste system, especially the Brahman, and presented the low caste Dalits and tribals as 'non-Hindus' to facilitate their conversion project. In a sense, Christianity offered a new individualised notion of self, personhood and citizenship, to which Europe's Others were to be converted (van der Veer, 1996: 9).

Similar accounts of conversions to Christian modernity are also found in the African context. For example, Comaroff and Comaroff (1997) have provided in-depth ethnographic narratives on how the civilising project of the colonial missionaries reshaped and reconfigured the mundane, ordinary and everyday social world of the ethnic subject in South Africa. Specifically, the Comaroffs argued that the colonial modernity project in Africa was not confined to 'material' improvements but also concerned the discourse on 'individual rights' (ibid.: 366). The creation of 'stable, discrete persons [individuals] and properties' (ibid.: 337)

Introduction **11**

was a major objective of the colonial modernity project. In order to thus create discrete individuals, the evangelists played a significant role by intervening in the people's material domain and ultimately transforming the food they ate, as well as their clothing, health, hygiene and other aspects of social and religious life. While the creation of the rational subject continues to be a major missionary objective around the world today, material progress or utilitarian aspects also occupy a major place in the conversion discourse across religious and faith traditions.

The relevance of these aspects of modernity resonate in many of the chapters of this book. For example, drawing on historical and archival materials from the period between 1910 and 1947, Oddie argues that the successful work of the British Methodist missionaries among the outcaste Mala and Madiga impressed the caste above, the Shudra. In particular, the Shudra were impressed by the material progress, especially improvements in education, lifestyle, attitude and the aspirations of the outcaste converts, and thus decided to convert to Christianity themselves. In addition to teaching Christian moral values, the missionaries also taught the converts 'how to speak with [upper] caste people' (Oddie, this volume) and provided them with knowledge of modern practices in areas such as health and medicine, first aid, vaccination and agricultural technologies. Access to education and a modern knowledge system helped the low caste converts to not only dissociate themselves from 'superstitious' beliefs (for example, smallpox and cholera being associated with the displeasure of the village deity) but also to exercise their 'autonomous agency' and articulate their demands through the language of rights, freedom and citizenship. Similarly, Ashok Kumar's contribution illustrates how conversion to Lutheran Christianity helped the Dalits assert their rights and organise their protest against upper caste oppression through modern discourses of self-respect, human dignity and social justice. Furthermore, Kumar argues that Dalit conversion to Christianity in Andhra was motivated by people's deep-seated desire for greater social mobility and material prosperity.

Although material progress and social mobility constituted major motivations for conversion across religious traditions in many parts of India, it was not always the case. As Frank Heidemann shows, drawing on archival and ethnographic data, 'utilitarian' factors played a minor role in the Badaga conversion to Christianity in the Nilgiri Hills of south India. In fact, Heidemann argues that due to their conversion, the Badaga lost their homes, property and employment, and even faced severe difficulties in finding marriage partners for their children. The question then is: what motivated the Badaga to convert to Christianity? As mentioned earlier, Heidemann argues that early Badaga conversions to Christianity were largely motivated by a strong desire for 'forgiveness of sins' and

12 *Peter Berger and Sarbeswar Sahoo*

such desires were cultivated over time through the Badaga's continuous contact with the British. At the same time, British knowledge of modern medicine and smallpox vaccination also played an important role in facilitating Badaga conversion to Christianity.

Among other factors, one reason that motivated the marginalised castes and tribes of India to convert to Christianity, rather than Buddhism or any other religion, was that Christianity was perceived to be superior because of its association with colonialism, European modernity and the dominant power structure of the time. Examining this aspect of modernity, Vibha Joshi and Iliyana Angelova discuss how the Angami and Sumi Naga tribes, respectively, associated Christianity with Western modernity, technological advancement and moral superiority. Discussing healing practices among the Angami Naga, Vibha Joshi shows how traditional healers perceived the modern biomedical healing of the missionaries to be superior to their own systems of healing. This not only contributed to the acceptance of modern medicine in the community but also the missionaries themselves. According to Angelova, the Sumi Naga also viewed their own indigenous spirit-centred faith system as 'backward' in comparison to Christianity, which they associated with prestige and high status. They considered Christianity superior because of its monotheistic traditions and belief in 'one true God'. Such perceptions of Christianity, Angelova argues, played a major role in facilitating the conversion of the Sumi Naga to Christianity. Angelova further shows that conversion to Christianity also provided access to mission education, which offered new ways of understanding the world, new opportunities and new forms of social mobility.

Similarly, Nadadur Kannan's contribution discusses the perceived superiority of the West and the Western language of modernity and demonstrates how such language was used by colonial Indian elites to 'standardise' and produce 'pure' forms of performance art, not only to restore the sacrality of art but also to reconstruct a purified national cultural identity. What is especially significant about Kannan's chapter is that it is not about 'religious' conversion (conversion from one religion to another) as such but about how religion was used in the production of a modern Hindu cultural identity. According to Nadadur Kannan, in a sense, conversion refers to a 'process of purification' within the same religious and cultural tradition, but brought into the British colonial framework.

Expanding on this idea of conversion as purification within the same religious tradition, Fernande Pool describes it as a process of 'ethical transformation'. Drawing on long-term ethnographic fieldwork in rural West Bengal, Pool discusses the conversion of nominal Muslims to a more pious and reformist form of Islam. In contrast to the scholarship that presents reformist Islam as the 'antimodern antithesis' to liberal, secular modernity, Pool argues that reformist

Islam is inherently modern. In fact, Pool provides a detailed ethnographic narrative to show how conversion is motivated by modern, liberal values related to ethics, order and social justice. Moreover, Pool argues that conversion to Islamic reformism could be considered as a 'technology of creating the modern moral subject' (Pool, this volume), where the converts undergo the process of religious and secular self-cultivation. What makes Pool's paper particularly relevant is that, for her, conversion is not about 'religious change' from one tradition to another; rather, it is about ethical transformation within the same religious tradition, and it is primarily aimed at cultivating both a religious and secular self to bring about a 'holistic' transformation of society.

In summary, the chapters in this volume highlight two dimensions of conversion to modernities. While one aspect of modernity refers to missionary education, modern medicine, advanced agricultural technologies and the prospect of material progress and social mobility, the other dimension is represented through enlightenment value systems, such as increasing rationalisation and individualisation, the quest for equal rights and human dignity, freedom from oppression and humiliation and the establishment of law, order and social justice.

CONTINUITY, CHANGE, PROCESS, EVENT

The four terms that form the title for this section describe a conceptual and heuristic field, a set of problems and questions, as well as an area of investigation with which most contributors to this volume wrestle. In the title, the terms simply follow each other; there is no indication of their interrelationship. Usually, of course, continuity is contrasted to change, and process is opposed to event. Although semantically related, the two pairs differ in their meaning. Continuity and change refer to the outcome of either processes or events, either the persistence of cultural forms or their transformation. Not only are continuity and change contrasted, they are also commonly thought to exclude each other; there is either continuity or change, brought about through a gradual process or sudden events. However, scholars have long questioned such dichotomies and pointed out that in order to persist, cultures have to change (for example, Bourdieu 1991; Locher 1978; Sahlins 1999). The question of the relationship between the four terms, and the extent to which they exclude each other or perhaps even condition each other, is now acknowledged to be much more complex.

Most contributors to this volume are critical of a view of religious transformation as a rupture, as a 'complete break with the past' (Meyer 1998) with a concomitant radical change (Robbins 2004; 2009), as proposed by a number of scholars with reference to their ethnographic fields. In his study of

14 *Peter Berger and Sarbeswar Sahoo*

Methodist missionary activities in Hyderabad before Indian Independence, Oddie (this volume), for instance, rejects the notion of rupture in the case he examines, and with it, the notion of conversion itself. He describes rather an unfolding and gradual process, a 'Christward movement', which is not a moment on the road to Damascus. Not only do many authors in this volume observe continuity and change, they also discern processes and identify significant events. Despite important moments in the revival of Christianity among the Sumi Naga of northeast India in the 1950s and 1970s, Angelova (this volume), for example, argues that conversion should be regarded as an ongoing process that is crucially related to change in the broader political context of colonialism and postcolonial nation-building. One of the most striking claims in this connection is provided by Jones (this volume). With reference to his analysis of the autobiography of Zahur-al-Haqq, he argues – thereby inverting the above-mentioned statement that cultures persist because they change – that from al-Haqq's personal perspective, conversion was possible and enduring because of the continuities with his cultural background and his previous and continuing adherence to religious traditions. While joining a devotional Hindu sect, al-Haqq remained a Muslim, and he also considered that it was Islam that helped him understand Jesus when he converted to Christianity. Change is thus predicated on continuity.

It should be clear that neither continuity nor change, neither processes nor events, are self-explanatory or somehow 'natural' phenomena. Discussing hierarchy and equality over the years with students, there are often several who initially assume that hierarchy is a historical product while equality is a natural condition (and a value). Examining the efforts that South African bands undertake to avoid status difference (Woodburn 1982) – efforts which are at least as intensive as those of Indian Brahman engaging in maintaining hierarchy – usually helps them to problematise the question of 'naturalness' and to recognise the cultural conditionality of both hierarchy and equality, as with the phenomena under discussion here. However, Robbins has argued that anthropologists on the whole have failed to theorise change and also to even consider continuity as an object of explanation and inquiry, regarding it as a given, a 'null hypothesis' (2014: 12). He certainly has an important point here, reminding us of the academic biases of 'continuity thinking' (Robbins 2007) that informs or restricts scholarly endeavours.

While acknowledging that there is much more to be done, we do not think that the situation is as bleak as that depicted by Robbins – not least due to his own fruitful efforts to theorise change. Moreover, we think that a considerable number of anthropologists and sociologists have been explicitly concerned with the analysis of continuity from different perspectives, for instance, by investigating

Introduction **15**

the workings of traditional authority (Bloch 1989), the ritual constitution of moral obligations (Rappaport 1999) and authenticity (Geertz 1973a), or the formation and reproduction of the habitus (Bourdieu 1990).

This volume recognises that it is important to investigate both the processes and events that generate change and those that produce persistence. Heidemann's contribution to this volume, for instance, not only aims at understanding why some Badaga of the Nilgiris converted to Christianity, but also provides a clue as to why the majority did not, choosing reproduction and continuity, not innovation and change. Much more important than any particular 'belief' was the value of village unity, closely associated with communal rituals. Most villagers feared that conversion would affect local integration and strongly opposed conversion on these grounds. However, given the topic of conversion, in this volume, there remains an emphasis on understanding the dynamics of change.

In this section of the introduction, we want to approach the problematic of continuity/change, process/event from four angles, thereby pointing to cross-connections between the contributions in this volume, while also going beyond the contributions collected here and beyond India as well in the hope of providing a new stimulus for the study of conversion in general. Below, we will first draw attention to two older contributions to the field that pointed out patterns in the interaction between old and new religious traditions and how this affects continuity or change, or both. Subsequently, we focus on what we think are fruitful avenues for theorising conversion and highlight the theoretical contributions of Dumont, Sahlins and Bourdieu in particular to the study of cultural and religious change. As Dumont and Sahlins have already been recognised as important for the study of cultural change, we discuss the potential of Bourdieu's work in a little more detail. In the third subsection, we address the question of the locations of the processes of religious transformation and persistence; in other words, we ask: what are the crucial cultural domains that can be analytically distinguished when investigating conversion? Finally, we will link the questions of continuity and change to society more broadly, that is, we will ask whether different societal types deal with issues of conversion in different ways.

Identifying Patterns of Continuity and Change

Stating that our aim is to study continuity and change, processes and events is one thing. Explaining how we actually intend to do this analytically speaking – thus going beyond a general and vague 'as well as' approach – is more difficult. However, there are a number of theoretical frameworks and analytical tools already available, some of which we mention here, also indicating how

16 *Peter Berger and Sarbeswar Sahoo*

contributors to this volume have addressed some of them, or how, in our view, their research can be linked to such tools.

To begin with, although religious change, or conversion more specifically, can occur as an internal process (based on 'endogenous events' in Sahlins' terms, 2000: 301), in most cases, change occurs in relation to another worldview – Christianity, colonialism, capitalism, for instance – that appears on the social horizon of the community in question, along with institutional structures and practices. As we are concerned with continuity and change, we thus focus not only on the emergence of the new or the disappearance of the old, but on the forms of interaction between the two (or more) traditions. There have been important contributions to the study of such dynamics, with one of the most influential and well known being the work of Sahlins and its partial reformulation by Robbins, to which we will return below. However, there are also older contributions that provide important avenues and inspiration for further research, and also new questions, two of which we will briefly mention here. Both deal with the conversion of an indigenous community to Christianity, one in West Africa (Baum 1990) and the other in India (Sahay 1968), and both are rarely mentioned in the contemporary literature on conversion.

In his analyses of the conversion of the Oraon (Sahay 1968, who spells the name as 'Uraon') of central India, Sahay distinguishes five 'cultural processes', which he also regards as possible successive phases of conversion, although he does not argue that this sequence is inevitable. The initial phase of 'oscillation' is described as often unstable and crisis-ridden due to a dual allegiance to two religious systems (he often speaks of 'values, beliefs and practices', see, for example, 929), with the new system only superficially understood. When the new belief is sufficiently embedded (for example, in the following generation), a process of 'scrutinisation' occurs, with elements of the indigenous religion either eliminated or retained, depending on whether they contradict the new religion or not. Subsequently, there is a period of the 'combination' of elements from the old and new traditions, a special case of which Sahay calls 'indigenisation', by which he means 'a replacement of a Sarna [indigenous] belief or practice by functionally similar Christian elements fulfilling indigenous needs' (1968: 936). As an illustration of this process, Sahay mentions that the belief that women are subject to attacks from evil spirits during childbirth remained constant, but images of Jesus and Mary replaced the formerly used objects of protection, such as an axe or fishing net. 'Retroversion', finally, refers to the process of reintroducing elements from the indigenous religion that had earlier been discarded. Of course, while we might want to discuss the suitability of some of his terms, what is important from our point of view is that Sahay's processual model emphasises the ongoing nature of the interaction between the old and the new religions.

Conversion does not mean closure, as the Oraon and others continue to return to and draw on their old religion, bringing various elements back in modified forms.

This point is also explicitly made by Baum (1990: 370): 'Diola religion has not withered away; it has remained an independent and dynamic faith. Furthermore, it has helped to shape the worldview of an emerging Diola Christianity.' Probably unaware of Sahay's contribution, Baum also attempts to capture the interaction between the indigenous Diola religion and Christianity by outlining five patterns of dialogue and conflict (see Berger in this volume). The first is a 'sudden and far-reaching conversion' (1990: 375), resembling what Robbins understands to be radical change; however, Baum argues that such cases would rarely be encountered. In the second model – and, for Baum, these may also be subsequent phases – a new religious authority has been accepted and ideas of the new tradition have settled in the community. During this phase, hostility towards the old ideas and practices is great. Baum also refers to one pattern as 'indigenisation' but means something quite different from Sahay. For Baum, this is also a period in which real interaction between the new and the old religions occurs, but unlike Sahay's description, it is not about new ideas or practices replacing the old in functional terms, but rather that 'moral and spiritual questions' (ibid.: 376) from the old religion are put to the new faith. As I understand it, here the old religion gains recognition and relevance once more after a period of straightforward rejection, and questions that the new religion left unresolved are brought up again. While in some respects the new religion provides the basic religious orientation, in some respects even a 'continued inadequacy' (ibid.: 392) may be experienced, with some questions not being answered or not persuasively so. The aspect of indigenisation here thus refers to the fact that the new religion is adapted and brought back into relation with older concerns. This is akin to Sahay's phase of retroversion, when features of the old religion regain currency and significance.

'Syncretism', Baum's fourth pattern, is similar to his view of indigenisation, describing a situation in which there is an acceptance of two valid religious systems, each one feasible or insufficient in some domains but not in others. In contrast to the situation described by Oddie (this volume), where missionaries actively followed a strategy of indigenisation to enable the conversion of the locals to their faith, at around the same time (during the interwar period), apparent syncretic practices among the Diola were rejected and opposed by some of the missionaries. As a result of unresolved tensions between the two systems, when a syncretic mode cannot be maintained, 'reconversion' may be another option, the reverse of the first pattern, excluding dialogue and interaction. One aspect that we want to highlight with reference to Baum's model is his emphasis on conflict. He argued that not only does the interaction between the old and the

18 *Peter Berger and Sarbeswar Sahoo*

new continue, but that it is consistently characterised by a struggle between the new and the old, a point that is also made by Robbins (2004: 327).

Theorising Religious Continuity and Change

When described in a summary manner, as we did above, the models of Baum and Sahay may seem schematic. However, in our view they may provide important reference points in the study of conversion, as they analytically identify certain aspects and patterns in the process of conversion and the ongoing negotiations between the old and the new religion. While they thus enable scholars studying conversion to see more nuances in the dynamics they investigate, they do not provide specific theoretical tools to study these dynamics. Moreover, we agree with Robbins' (2009: 67) sceptical view of what he calls an 'elemental approach' to cultural change, that is, a focus on isolated aspects of the old or new religion – such as the images of Jesus replacing the fishing net in Sahay's example – that have been rediscovered, replaced or rejected, depending on the situation. Terms such as hybridity or syncretism would simply refer to a mix of such elements without any attention being paid to the structural aspects of cultural change (Robbins 2004: 328f.; 2009: 66).

Robbins can be credited for recognising the potential of Dumont's theory of value for the structural study of cultural change, integrating it with some important ideas of Sahlins – to which we will return below – to formulate his own model of religious conversion on the basis of his research with the Urapmin of Papua New Guinea (2004; 2009; 2014). While Dumont himself worked more as a historian of ideas, studying long-term transformations of systems of cultural categories in a Maussian manner (see Dumont 1986; 1994), Robbins showed how Dumont's framework could be fruitfully applied to more down-to-earth and short-term processes of change. Robbins argued that when key values that structure relationships between other cultural categories are transformed or adopted, this has implications for the culture (understood as a system of cultural categories) as a whole and one can thus speak of radical change. Significantly, Dumont's distinction of different empirical situations ('contexts') and analytically distinct domains within any particular system of values ('levels') enable a nuanced, dynamic and relational analysis of changing relationships between categories and values. Robbins shows how conversion was 'radical' for the Urapmin, in the sense that the new Christian value of individualism came to play a key role in Urapmin culture, only allowing the restricted elaboration of traditional values (for example, with regard to spirits) in subordinate contexts (2009). Importantly, therefore, Robbins also recognises transformation and continuity, and, in his view, it is precisely the ongoing tensions between traditional and Christian values – even when hierarchically ranked – that produce a moral dilemma for the Urapmin about how to live a good life (2004: 298, 314, 332).

For the Gadaba of central India who 'converted' to a Hindu reform movement called Olek Dormo, the value of 'happiness-peace' acquired a key place in their worldview and ethos, permeating all aspects of their life, especially with regard to alcohol and meat consumption, from which the converts abstain, but which the Gadaba generally enjoy (Berger, this volume). While ritual contexts among the Gadaba are highly marked in terms of ideas concerning 'proper action', everyday contexts are left morally unelaborated. The indigenised Hindu reform movement thus enables Gadaba converts to morally articulate their lifestyle in a new way. This is not regarded by the non-Olek Gadaba as problematic in any way; in contrast, differences between the Olek Dormo movement and the indigenous religion are not recognised. This explains how it was possible to select a recent convert to Olek Dormo to be the village priest and sacrificer.

The situation was quite different among the Badaga of the Nilgiris, as described by Heidemann in this volume. In this case, 'village unity' remained a key value, usually manifested in collective ritual practices and worship. Early converts to Christianity faced fierce opposition because it was suspected that their conversion would undermine village solidarity. As long as the new religious orientation did not contradict this central value of village unity and the converts publicly showed acceptance (in Rappaport's sense; Rappaport 1999: 119f.) of the key value in the context of village rituals, no one was concerned.

While Dumont's theory provides a useful theoretical tool to analyse transformations in value systems, the agency of actors plays little or no part in this framework, at least not in his formulation. In Sahlins' theory of the event, in contrast, the agency of actors and practice is embedded in the structural analysis of change (Sahlins 1985; 2000; see Golub, Rosenblatt, and Kelly 2016). As Sahlins' describes it, cultural change is always a possibility when actors give meaning to happenings, thus turning them into 'events' – happenings that are interpreted. Under normal conditions, cultural categories serve to make conventional sense of any empirical situation and even new phenomena can be 'assimilated' (Robbins 2004: 10) to the cultural structure. While the result of this is the continuation of cultural structures, different kinds of encounters and events can produce a change in the relationships between categories. Actors explicitly come into play with regard to what Sahlins calls 'subjective risk', that is, when actors – often those in positions of power – making strategic use of the ambiguities of signification, manage to have their interpretation of events accepted, with new meanings thus becoming objectified.

Although Angelova's contribution to this volume does not describe this process in detail, one can imagine that the chiefs who first opposed Christianity

20 *Peter Berger and Sarbeswar Sahoo*

and then supported conversion among the Sumi Naga were actually manipulating such subjective risks, using their power to define the new faith, either as a threat to their traditional authority or, later, as a vehicle to articulate opposition to the Hindu Indian state. The same may have been the case in the change of mind of the village headmen (Patels) in Telangana, who first opposed the missionaries and new adherents but later supported conversion or even converted themselves (Oddie, this volume). Of course, this is speculative, and one would need to have detailed descriptions of particular events in order to unravel the situation à la Sahlins. Events are crucial in understanding both continuity and change, but as we emphasised above, and as Berger argued in relation to the study of death (P. Berger 2016), both processes and events are crucial in the investigation of conversion.

Despite the fact that he is more of a power theorist and that his theory is informed by a sometimes distressing economic rationality, Bourdieu's work on habitus in general and on the 'religious field' in particular (see McCloud 2012; Verter 2003) significantly overlaps with Sahlins' theoretical interests, complementing the latter's approach in important ways. One commonality is that both regard actors as part of relational confluences, of structural situations within which they operate and attempt to pursue their interests according to the 'pragmatics of their interaction' (Sahlins 2000: 341), rather than seeing the power of actors as being due to inherent personal charisma, as does Max Weber (Bourdieu 1991). As such, similarly to Sahlins, Bourdieu speaks of 'structured interests' (Bourdieu 1987). Moreover, actors compete with each other: chiefs and priests compete in the signification processes with regard to Captain Cook in Sahlins' (1985) example, while Bourdieu (1991), following Weber, focuses on the dynamics between priests, magicians and prophets. Due to the contingency of situations, in Sahlins' framework any actor can have a decisive role to play in the process of turning a happening into a specific event. For Bourdieu, who focuses on institutionalised and bureaucratic 'world religions' with distinct social classes, priests are the custodians of continuity, while prophets (who follow a calling rather than fulfil an office, and engage with people emotionally, not normatively) are agents of change; 'they cause moments of discontinuity every time they enter the religious field' (Deploige 2004: 7).

Prophets, 'petty independent entrepreneur[s] of salvation [or rather, "religious goods" in general]' (Bourdieu 1991: 24), are generative of change in various ways. First, by unravelling the unarticulated religious *doxa* – the implicit opinions, conventions, ideas that appear as 'natural' – revealing them to be contingent and thus changeable, the prophet is 'an unveiler of the doxic mechanisms of domination' (McCloud 2012: 5) and thus an instigator of alternative religious forms. This unveiling potential of patterns of oppression and exploitation may

Introduction **21**

have played an important role in the processes of low caste and Dalit conversion to Christianity, as described by Oddie and Kumar in this volume. Although missionaries only conform to some features commonly attributed to prophets, we argue that they often work in similar ways, for instance, in assuming a subversive function as far as caste hierarchies are concerned.[3] Moreover, the way some Badaga of the Nilgiris – similar to Zahur-al-Haqq (Jones, this volume) – were 'impressed' by the way the missionaries behaved, being friendly, devout and approachable, which contrasted considerably with the behaviour of other Europeans they had previously encountered, also leads us to assume that it was the charismatic nature of the missionaries-cum-prophets which was the basis of their great attraction to the Badaga converts and which tied them closely to the mission. This was so much so, in fact, that they protested when, during the Second World War, Wesleyan missionaries, displaying a very different kind of attitude, took over from the Basel Mission (Heidemann, this volume).

Second, the prophet has appeal and incites people to see the world differently because 'he puts words, meaning, and structure to that which the members had previously only felt and experienced in a non-reflective way' (McCloud 2012: 5). According to Berger (this volume), concerning the 'conversion' of the Gadaba to the Olek Dormo Hindu reform movement, such a situation occurred when the ascetic *baba*s first came to the Koraput hills in the 1970s. They articulated a lifestyle ethic that enabled those who cared to listen to perceive alcohol consumption in a new light. All of a sudden it was a 'problem' in the religious sense, and not an aspect of social and ritual life that was taken for granted. Domestic conflict and violence had been perceived socially but not ethically before. The ascetics articulated these problems in a new way and offered a new explanation and lifestyle that seemed to provide a permanent solution. They thus 'displaced the boundary between the ... thinkable and the unthinkable' and 'symbolized in [their] extraordinary discourse and behavior that which ordinary symbolic systems [here: indigenous Gadaba religion] are structurally incapable of expressing' (Bourdieu 1991: 34).

Another commonality between Bourdieu and Sahlins is that they pay attention to situations that are 'out-of-tune', ambivalent situations in which things 'do not fit', or where they are ambiguous, or 'risky' in Sahlins' sense, and thus provide fertile ground for the new. While Sahlins focuses in particular on the mismatch of categories in the 'structure of the conjuncture' (2000: 341), as pointed out earlier, Bourdieu notes situations of disjunction of the habitus. Much like Sahlins' view of the 'normal' conditions of social life, when categories serve to make sense of situations and thus reproduce the cultural order, the conventional dispositions also work well if the habitus operates in the fields that produced it. However, actors can occupy contradictory social positions that may lead to

22 *Peter Berger and Sarbeswar Sahoo*

tensions and suffering because of the in-between status of habitual dispositions. This can be well illustrated with reference to converts to Deobandi reformist Islam, as described by Pool in this volume. Here, the change in lifestyle entails the total ethical transformation of the self and of society; it should turn members into educated participants in secular civil society. However, parts of the explicitly religious habitus of these converts seem to contradict the habitus required by secular modernity, as Pool writes, partly quoting Osella and Osella (2008: 251):

> The reformist aesthetics and practices of Deobandi Islam and Islamic Mission Schools raise more suspicion rather than less, are associated with violent extremism rather than peace, and further alienate the Muslim from the Indian nation. As a result, many Muslims in Joygram find themselves in 'an impossible double-bind: faced with a choice between being charged as 'bad Muslims' if they ignore the call to reform or as 'bad Indians' if they choose to follow reform.

The case of a Gadaba adherent to a Hindu reform movement abstaining from alcohol, meat and bloody sacrifice, who at the same time was also chosen as the village sacrificer, whose 'job description' exactly requires all of this, might also have led to the habitual disjunction to which Bourdieu refers. That it did not, is related to the particular circumstances outlined by Berger (this volume).

We can identify another kind of out-of-tune situation when changes in a social environment mean that habitual dispositions no longer work in relation to the changing societal field (McCloud 2012: 4). One is reminded here of Geertz' (1973b) famous example of the Javanese funeral, where the political situation drastically changed the conditions of the actors' participation in the ritual, which led to the failure of the performance. Nadadur Kannan's argument concerning the *devadāsi*s of south India in this volume might also be understood in this light. Representing womanhood in a way that was no longer appropriate to the new nationalist elite's understanding of the performing arts, which heavily borrowed from Victorian and reformed high caste ideas of femaleness, the *devadāsi*s – traditional female dancers – were marginalised and excluded. At the same time, the male Brahmanical elite constructed Hindu middle-class 'new women', adopting an appropriate habitus to take over the role of the *devadāsi*s.

Nadadur Kannan is the only contributor to this volume who explicitly refers to the work of Bourdieu in her analysis of how south Indian elite Brahmans reconceptualised and standardised the performing arts between 1927 and 1947, thus in the context of emergent nationalism and anti-colonialism. In this endeavour, the performing arts were selected as a means to 'sacralise' the nation, which meant to sacralise the arts as such, 'purifying' them of supposedly degraded or low practices, such as those of the *devadāsi*s. Inventing a new code not only required that the performers adopt a new habitus, but also that the consumers had to develop a new 'taste', being transformed into 'connoisseurs'. In Bourdieu's terms, as claimants of religious authority, localised in privileged positions in the social structure, elite Brahmans increased their own religious capital by inducing a certain religious habitus in performers and consumers alike (Bourdieu 1991: 22).

Although only Nadadur Kannan refers explicitly to Bourdieu, the latter's theoretical framework has relevance to the understanding of the processes dealt with in several other chapters in this volume, as we indicated above. One important aspect in this regard is the link between conversion and crisis (see Hefner 1993). Certainly, not all conversion occurs in situations of crisis; however, often it is precisely such moments of disjuncture and misfit that spark processes of conversion. It is not by chance that Bourdieu regards the prophet as 'the man of crisis situations, in which the established order see-saws' (Bourdieu 1991: 34). Missionaries often also operated in such structural crisis situations. This can be argued with respect to the conversions to Christianity that Oddie and Kumar are concerned with in colonial south India, where political and economic disjunctions take the form of oppression and exploitation. In his new book about the Sora, Vitebsky (2017) has also described how Christianity was a means for the Sora to emancipate and empower themselves, overcoming decades of oppression by colonial agents, moneylenders and headmen.

A broader historical crisis situation was most likely also relevant to Zahur al-Haqq's conversion to Christianity, analysed by Jones in this volume. Al-Haqq converted to Christianity in 1858, a year after the 'Mutiny', and his silence on this aspect in his autobiography may itself be significant. Historical situations of crisis, which are themselves productive of 'generic moments' (Meinert and Kapferer 2015), may thus be important triggers for religious conversion. The study of conversion, therefore, may still gain much by paying close attention to the risks in the related processes of signification, the disjunctures of the habitus, as well as the characteristics of liminality, communitas and effervescence that accompany crisis and events (see P. Berger 2016; Willey 2016).

A significant aspect of such crisis situations often are experiences of 'humiliation'. This concept, developed by Sahlins (2005 [1992]), which has been adopted by a number of scholars working on cultural change in different contexts (see Robbins and Wardlow 2005), helps to understand how such profound experiences of cultural self-depreciation may trigger strong reactions in various directions (see Vilaça, in this volume). Sahlins does not speak of conversion specifically, but about the process of cultural change experienced by indigenous peoples who come into contact with global capitalism. He regards 'humiliation' as one important phase in the process of change, which, significantly, is not simply the result of the power of the dominant forces representing capitalism and

24   Peter Berger and Sarbeswar Sahoo

Western modernity, but what could be called mechanisms of desire: they 'first learn to hate what they already have, what they have already considered their well-being. Beyond that, they have to despise what they are, to hold their own existence in contempt – and want, then, to become someone else' (Sahlins 2005 [1992]: 38).[4] On the one hand, this experience can lead to a community actively seeking to abandon its culture and religion, to fully endorse the 'superior' worldview offered to them as surrogate, for instance, to embrace Christianity as a morally superior way of life. However, humiliation can, on the other hand, also have an inverse effect in 'provoking a self-consciousness of the indigenous culture' (ibid.: 39). Rather than wanting to become someone else, they want to remain who they are, or rather, discover their 'culture' for the first time in an objective and explicit way. Indigenisation, in Sahlins' terms – different from both Baum and Sahay, discussed above – refers to this form of culturalism and self-confidence, the 'active appropriation' (Sahlins 2000: 48) of external elements, be they material or conceptual, to pursue indigenous ends. A consequence of humiliation may thus be an emphasis on and reformulation of traditional values and practices and a decided rejection or 'cultural appropriation' (Sahlins 2000: 47) of the opposing culture. Needless to say, this process of reassertion also involves cultural change, albeit in a different way.

In India, the situation regarding humiliation is complex. Low caste, Dalit and tribal communities have been subject to 'local' humiliating practices and discourses for a long time. Another reaction to humiliation – not mentioned by Sahlins – that has been employed by Indian subaltern groups is withdrawal, either into the forest (Gardner 1972) or into an underworld cosmology (Vitebsky 2017). The advent of Europeans, among them colonial officers and missionaries, only added new dimensions to and variants of debasement strategies, which have metamorphosed into ongoing discourses of development. However, the new worldview and lifestyle offered by missionaries, for example, in many cases enabled a break away from earlier forms of degradation and exploitation. As mentioned earlier, for the low caste and Dalit communities discussed in Oddie and Kumar's contributions to this volume, Christianity was understood as a way to escape humiliation and assert a Dalit identity. It might be argued that in the case described by Nadadur Kannan, different experiences of humiliation are related to one another. The 'sacralisation' initiatives of Brahmans who 'converted' both the consumers of and performers involved in the performing arts were directed explicitly against the colonisers and the West, albeit also informed by the latter's discourse. In a sense, it was an elite response to the humiliating experiences of colonialism, a form of culturalism, as described by Sahlins, and a reinvention of the performing arts tradition. In the course of their reform, these elites in turn humiliated and marginalised the *devadāsi* dancers. In other processes of conversion, humiliation was not an incentive to seek religious transformation. The cases discussed by Pool, Berger, Heidemann and Jones in this volume show that although humiliation may be a significant element of experience in processes of conversion, it is certainly not a necessary part of them.

Locations of Religious Continuity and Change

Looking at the contributions to this volume, it is apparent that the authors identify different locations[5] of conversion and of the processes that lead to change or result in continuity. Most authors take different levels of these processes into account: the micro level of personal experience of religious change, the meso level of social relationships, or the macro level of larger political and economic contexts. However, in each of the processes described in the book, there are certain 'areas' that are particularly relevant to the transformation or the persistence of cultural patterns. Therefore, we will take a closer look at these locations, which entails the following questions: Where, or in which social or cultural domain, does the process of conversion occur in particular? Which locations do converts select to effect continuity or change? Which dimensions of a local culture resonate with the new worldview and which aspects of it? Or, conversely, where might we locate contradiction rather than resonance? Which domains of the local culture further or hinder religious transformations? And how can we account for all this? The patterns of conversion identified by Sahay and Baum summarised earlier describe modes of interaction between the old and the new religions, but they say little about the locations of these processes.

Pursuing the question 'How do religions end?' Robbins (2014) distinguished between different processes that he considered crucial for understanding how the Urapmin dismantled their old religion. His ideas may serve as a starting point for our reflection. He mentions three aspects – social relations, material erasure, and concepts and practices – and describes these as part of a sequence in the process of deconstruction (2014: 6). Initially, the problem was that most of the young men for whom the initiation rituals were performed, which characterised the Urapmin as a community (and also regionally), were no longer available, either because they had already converted and refused to participate or because they were away undertaking waged labour. The second step that followed was the material deconstruction of the traditional religion, for example, the removal of ancestral bones. Finally, there was a substitution and displacement of concepts and practices, for instance, traditional performance was replaced with prayer, while previously held ideas about 'taboos' were addressed through the notion of Christian 'law'. By taking such measures, the Urapmin successively dismantled their old religion. Robbins emphasises that his contribution is experimental in nature, and he does not claim that there are no other dimensions that could be considered, nor that these aspects are crucial in all cases of 'ending' a religion. However, he focuses attention on the processes of how this is done and invites us to consider these questions with regard to other ethnographic (or historical) fields.

Such dimensions are not only distinguishable and scrutinisable in the process of deconstructing a religion, of course, but can also be identified in the process of building a new one. Moreover, these two movements of destruction and construction usually go hand in hand. Communities usually do not decide to first do away with their religion and then subsequently start building a new one. The patterns outlined by Sahay and Baum show how communities wrestle with these movements at the same time, and Robbins (2004) also described and analysed these processes of negotiation and conflict. It is also evident that distinguishing such domains is an analytic operation and, as such, is also arbitrary to some extent. Nevertheless, this contrasting of the material with concepts and practice does not deny the fact that the former is closely related to the latter.

That said, we want to take up Robbins' invitation in two steps. First, we will briefly consider some of the different locations of religious transformation and continuity that we can identify in the cases discussed in this volume. We do not aim to be exhaustive, but rather intend to show that this is a relevant question and, moreover, that it is important to consider additional dimensions that are relevant. In a second step, in the following section, we will consider the domain of the 'social', but in an extended way. We will also rephrase the initial question, shifting the focus somewhat from asking about the significant locations of continuity and change, towards the question of the nature of the social itself and how this may be connected to specific locations relevant to conversion. In other words, we ask what the 'social' means in the different cases. Is the way conversion occurs and is brought about or avoided related to the specific kind of society under consideration?

While, in the first step, the different locations are considered to be separate – social relations, material and so on (though they are connected, as pointed out earlier) – in the second step we also want to indicate a different, more holistic, perspective that does not reduce 'society' to social morphology but considers forms of subsistence and ideology as necessarily integrated parts, or as Bird-David argues with reference to gatherer-hunters, and against the compartmentalisation of society (ecology, society, economy, and so on), we are dealing with 'a total life form' (Bird-David 2010: 233). Thus, the societal conditions for the processes of continuity and change as such are at stake. Not only do different societies transform their religions in different ways, selecting different locations for construction and deconstruction, but the basic terms may be different. On the basis of specific 'historicities' (Sahlins 1985: xf.), some societies are inclined to pursue or prevent change, or, if it occurs, ignore it culturally. Some ideological constructions, usually anchored in lasting social structures, are intended to be eternal, while other religions are 'not made to last' (Vilaça 2014: 18; this volume) in the first place.

One location that is significant for processes of continuity and change, which Robbins mentions in particular, is the politico-economic domain. Robbins points out that 'the coming of colonialism and modernization' (2014: 7) was crucial to making it impossible to recruit young men for the initiation rituals in the first place, but he does not consider this as a location in its own terms. We assume that the reason why he does not explicitly consider this dimension is because he is interested in the inner workings of the culture that are bringing about the end of their religion, not so much in the external forces that triggered them. However, while we acknowledge that the politico-economic domain can in some cases be considered outside of the community that orchestrates its own transformation, we prefer to consider it as a crucial location in its own terms because of its significant impact on these processes. For instance, while the colonial power framework, its institutions and discourses, did not determine how a community shaped its religious transformations, it provided an important stimulus for transformation – for example, through the process of humiliation mentioned above – and also served as a constant point of reference, a background against which changes were pursued or prevented. In the case described by Nadadur Kannan in this volume, for instance, colonialism not only served as a trigger for transforming the performing arts in south India – the political other in a struggle for independence – but also provided a discourse that shaped the way these transformations were brought about, as it informed ideas about 'proper womanhood' that stood in contrast to the independence of traditional female dancers (the *devadāsi*). Conversion among the Naga, as Angelova argues in this volume, also cannot be understood without reference to the broader political context of the colonial and the postcolonial state. Pool's contribution to this volume similarly holds that the ethical transformation that some Muslims strove for by joining the Deobandi Islamic reform movement has to be seen in the context of the structural violence and discrimination in West Bengal, under which the Muslim population suffered in particular.

While some locations are of crucial importance to most of the cases discussed in this volume, some other locations are little considered. Practices and ideas have, unsurprisingly, a central place in the analyses of most of the chapters, and we need not elaborate on this point. Shrine worship is rejected by followers of a reformist Islamic movement (Pool, this volume), dietary practices are transformed, meat and alcohol abandoned and, related to these practices, ideas about *dharma*

28 *Peter Berger and Sarbeswar Sahoo*

and 'happiness-peace' are modified, extended or introduced (Berger, this volume).

One location of conversion that does not receive much attention in the chapters that follow is the material dimension. While Berger, for example, does mention the ochre clothes that conspicuously separate the adherents of Olek Dormo from the others, this aspect does not receive much attention and is not considered key with respect to the processes under discussion. This does not mean, however, that the material dimension is irrelevant to the cases described here, but rather that the authors chose a different focus in their analysis. Discussing Sahlins' theory, Sewell (2005: 213f.) rightly pointed out the significance of the material – what he calls 'resources' – for processes of change in or between cultural categories, emphasising independent dynamics and the constraints of the material domain. He asks us to take Sahlins' dictum that 'ideas are burdened with the world' more literally (Sewell 2005: 118), and argues that

> the risk of transformations of cultural categories arises above all from the fact that the things marked as resources in an initial action may be subject over time to other determinations, natural and sociocultural, that will cause them to change significantly in content, in quantity, in value, and in relations. (Ibid.: 217)

One of the effects of 'conversion' to the Olek Dormo Hindu reform movement can be mentioned in this respect. In material terms, sacrifices provide an important resource for the management of social relations. Especially when larger animals are killed, such as cows or buffaloes, an abundance of meat is available that is distributed among agnates and affines. Moreover, different parts of the animals (legs, chest, head) are particularly associated with particular types of relationships. With the abandonment of animal sacrifices, adherents of Olek Dorma no longer have the resources to maintain their relationships as before and, as a result, the relationships are no longer as visible and active as they had been.

Another location that is important but barely discussed might be called the 'aesthetic' dimension, which is clearly related to Bourdieu's notion of habitus and his focus on embodied schemas and tastes. For example, Zahur-al-Haqq's attraction to the Pranami devotional order and to Christianity was significantly linked to the 'musical element in worship' in both traditions (Jones, this volume). Thus, his spiritual quest appeared to have been mediated to a significant degree by aesthetic inclinations and preferences. This aesthetic location is often considered an epiphenomenon in the study of religion, as Meyer (2010) laments. She demands that more attention should be paid to what she calls 'sensational forms',[6] which deal in particular with the ways religious practices generate and orchestrate the senses and the emotions. Confirming Jones' point about the role of music in his processes of conversion, Meyer also states that such sensational forms are 'an excellent point of entry into processes of religious transformation' (Meyer 2010: 751). Of course, such sensational forms, the organisation of the 'atmosphere', can serve different ends, alongside religious transformation, ritualised forms of political agitation or the reproduction of social and cultural patterns (Heidemann 2014).

Conversion and Society

After commenting on some relevant locations in the study of processes of religious continuity and transformation, we now want to turn to the question of the relationship between such locations and particular kinds of society, especially those commonly referred to as band, tribal and peasant societies. In his important and widely read introduction to the volume *Conversion to Christianity*, Hefner (1993) discussed the relationship between 'world religions' and 'traditional religions' at length, mainly in the context of Weberian arguments and questions. In doing so, he especially focused attention on the dimensions of world religions and how they manage to thrive and endure and the basis of their 'world building' capacities. Traditional religions, however, were scrutinised with much less nuance and rigour. They were not differentiated internally and the question of what might account for the very different kinds of responses to Christianity was not systematically addressed. This seems to be a pertinent question, however. The particular features of a world religion *and* the specific characteristics of traditional religions, including their societal correlates, as well as the actual conditions of the historical situation, are all relevant to the understanding of processes of conversion. Therefore, we must pay more attention to patterns of indigenous religions and societies. Revisiting the different notions of gatherer-hunter, tribal and peasant societies is certainly only a small and preliminary step in this direction.

Moreover, such an endeavour is potentially open to various criticisms. First, it may be understood as an undesirable reification of such classifications; second, it may be accused of ignoring the fact that gatherer-hunter or tribal societies around the globe share some features but not others; third, it may be argued that it is an anachronistic endeavour, as all such communities are parts of modern nation-states anyway or, finally, it might be argued that it bespeaks a sociological determinism that assumes religion would directly mirror social conditions. To these objections, we can respond by saying that we are interested first of all in posing a question about conversion and the locations of related processes and possible connections to societal types. Does conversion mean something different, and does it 'work' differently, in different kinds of societies? We do not

30 *Peter Berger and Sarbeswar Sahoo*

claim to have the answers. Moreover, we are well aware that bands, tribes and peasants are sociological ideal-types used for the purpose of analysis, and we are not particularly dedicated to any of these terms. However, even as part of modern nation-states, different forms of society – of *Vergesellschaftung* – continue to exist, and although one can argue about the feasibility of any of these terms, the term 'tribe'[7] probably being the most controversial, as scholars we have to take these differences into account, for instance, in relation to the topic at hand, conversion. We will also see that even the examples we are referring to here do not all fit squarely into the classifications of band/tribe/peasant, but that a comparative perspective, nevertheless, has added value for understanding religious continuity and change.

Finally, we do not restrict the notion of society to the level of social structure. 'Society' not only refers to social morphology, but also, as Durkheim already pointed out, society is 'above all [constituted] by the idea it has of itself' (1995: 425). Economy, social structure and ideology (or worldview, religion) together usually characterise a certain type of society and, although none of the aspects determines the others, they are all correlated and correspond to each other in specific ways. As Sahlins (1968: 96) notes: 'When we were pastoral nomads, the Lord was our shepherd.... When we were serfs and nobles, the Lord was our king.... Finally, we are businessmen – and the Lord is our accountant.' What conversion means, which shape it takes and which locations are ultimately relevant certainly depend on the agency of actors; however, in turn, they are members of specific social formations that inform, enable and restrict the range of possibilities for transformation and continuity.

In this volume, the Naga, Gadaba and Badaga are examples of Indian tribal societies that feature enduring structures of affinity and descent, and there is a strong emphasis on the social unit of the village in all three cases. Their religious ideas and practices are closely interwoven with these social structures and their idea of their society as a totality. The Naga's struggle for independence against the Indian state may well be understood to be related to the common value of tribal (thus collective, not individual, as with gatherer-hunter bands; Gardner 1972: 439) autonomy. According to Angelova in this volume, conversion to Christianity has to be first understood in relation to this political context.

Moreover, speaking of social structure, missionaries soon realised the relevance of Naga chiefs to their conversion projects, and rightly so, as the chiefs first obstructed and only later facilitated conversion in their communities. Similarly, in this volume, Heidemann describes the initially strong resistance to conversion among the Badaga, based on the fear that Christianity might jeopardise village unity, which is above all expressed in collective rituals. The case of the Gadaba (Berger, this volume) points to a different aspect of tribal society: the lack of religious specialists and centres, the segmented nature of religious life and the corresponding fact that there is little in the sense of dogma (certainly no written canon) and nothing comparable to the idea of 'salvation' or 'sin'. Gadaba tradition, *niam* (a term also common in the northeast), is based on orthopraxis, but also open to new aspects. The Gadaba do not cautiously protect their religion, as it is hardly objectified as such. This openness enabled the unproblematic introduction of a Hindu reform movement in the highlands – even allowing the selection of a 'convert' as village sacrificer – despite the fact that, viewed from the outside, this tradition stands in contrast to some key elements of the indigenous religion. The embeddedness of religion in enduring social structures is certainly an important point to consider when investigating processes of conversion.

This aspect becomes clear when one considers gatherer-hunter societies and the ways they deal with religious change. Of course, this is not to say that gatherer-hunters in Siberia are the same as those in southern Africa; however, this type of society does feature some particular characteristics. Again, also in relation to these societies, ideology, modes of subsistence and social organisation have to be jointly considered – gatherer-hunters cannot be defined as such simply because they gather and hunt (Lee and Daly 1999: 3; see Pfeffer 2002; 2016). Significantly, their social system, usually referred to as a band, is characterised by a high degree of mobility and flux. In contrast to tribal societies, enduring structures of affinity and descent are often lacking. Individuals are dependent on one another but not on 'specific others' (Woodburn 1982: 439). The Jenu Kurumba of south India, for example, do not follow what Demmer calls a 'group model' of their own society, conceiving it as a totality, but rather understand it as a moral community based on 'interpersonal sociality' (Demmer 2011: 381). An ethic of sharing (rather than a morality of reciprocity) is closely linked to values of equality and individualism and ideas about being part of a 'giving environment' (Bird-David 1990). In such societies, animism and shamanism are usually the cornerstones of indigenous worldviews, often predicated on the interaction with and classification of humanity and animality; anything resembling 'gods' is often conspicuously absent.

Although the Wari' of southwestern Amazonia are not a gatherer-hunter society,[8] their 'approach' to conversion introduces some relevant comparative aspects (see Vilaça, this volume). In the discussion of 'How do religions end?' Vilaça argues that Wari' religion 'was not made to last' (2014: 18). This is a highly significant statement, as it points towards 'flux', not only on the level of morphology, but concerning a particular dynamics on the level of worldviews as well (see Guenther 2010: 430). Within a period of roughly 60 years, the Wari' more or less *en bloc* converted to Christianity, then deconverted, and then – after

32 *Peter Berger and Sarbeswar Sahoo*

the significant event of the World Trade Center attack of 2001 – converted again. Vilaça acknowledges the significance of the political and economic dimension we have referred to above in relation to conversion, namely the devastated situation of the Wari' as the result of the violent, disruptive, disease-bringing contact with Europeans. Conversion to Christianity enabled the Wari' to find a place for themselves in this 'new social order' (1997: 108). However, Vilaça argues that the Wari' were not forced to adopt Christianity, but rather adopted it on their own terms, that is, on the basis of Wari' society and their conceptualisations of it.

Throughout their different 'conversions', there have been significant continuities, at least in two related ways: first, what Vilaça calls a 'meeting of sociologies' (1997: 99); and, second, in the pervasive idea and attitude of 'opening to the Other', an idea developed by Lévi-Strauss that found widespread resonance among anthropologists working in this region (see Vilaça 2015: 204). Affinity for the Wari' is connected with enmity, fighting and funeral cannibalism, it is fraught with aversion; only after death is a world without affines achieved. The Christian doctrine of universal brotherhood, Vilaça (1997) argues, matched this indigenous ideal perfectly and the Wari' sought to establish generalised consanguinity (realised especially though generalised commensality effecting consubstantiality) in life by adopting Christianity. The second location for conversion relates to their precarious vision of humanness, common in the Amazon region. As Viveiros de Castro (1998) pointed out in relation to the hunting mode of subsistence, humans are animals and vice versa, predator or prey, depending on the perspective. For the missionaries, Vilaça writes (1997: 98), divinity might have been the problem; for the Wari', it was humanity. Their relational view of humanity assumed a 'coexistence of different worlds' (2015: 205) and the above-mentioned 'opening to the Other' entailed the appropriation of alterity, whether animal or white European (2009: 115). The appropriation of the Christian perspective enabled the Wari' to consolidate their status as humans (and predators), making it unequivocal and permanent. What informed their indigenised view of Christian 'Hell', conversely, was the idea that those unfortunate enough to end up there would become eternal prey, roasted over a fire forever. The fundamental stance of appropriating Otherness as part of one's own being makes 'conversion' nothing special and, accordingly, Vilaça argues that 'the conversion to Christianity was not the first conversion experienced by the Wari''(2009: 119).

The specific features of gatherer-hunter societies – among them mobility and flux – in connection with the nature of the encounter with representatives of other religions (for example, missionaries) and the specificities of the particular denominations involved (for example, Mennonite or Anglican Christians, see

Mendoza 2003: 205f.), should be relevant to the process of conversion and the question of continuity and transformation of worldviews. However, in contrast to other regions, there seems to be little to no scholarly work on religious transformation in general, let alone conversion in particular, on gatherer-hunter communities in India. While there is also no contribution in this volume that offers a step in the direction of filling this lacuna, we at least want to briefly refer to two south Indian communities – the Paliyan and the Nayaka – and their forms of interaction with the surrounding Hindu peasant society.

With reference to the Paliyan one could also say that their religion was not made to last. Gardner describes their society and their worldview as being fluid, 'an atmosphere of constant change and adjustment' (1972: 439). As the most characteristic feature of their lifestyle, he identifies their individualism and individual autonomy as a key value. Standardisation is neither sought nor valued and, accordingly, rituals are optional, irregular, ad hoc performances. However, Gardner makes an important observation, namely that the Paliyan would have developed a parallel and alternative set of cultural practices that could be situationally applied. In intracommunal contexts, Paliyan ritual is unelaborated and fluid, as indicated above, in extracommunal contexts – in contact with lowland culture – they adopt the elaborate Tamil ritual (and kinship) forms, especially with regard to lifecycle rituals. These two patterns are continuously kept distinct, and the Paliyan oscillate between the two depending on the situation (Gardner 1972: 437). Most of the time, the lowland pattern is adopted as a kind of superficial mimicry that enables the Paliyan to gain easy access to lowland resources. This camouflage is yet another response to exploitation and humiliation, a play to facilitate the interaction of the Paliyan with their social environment. However, at times, Gardner also detects an assumption of the actual superiority of lowland culture, whose gods have told the Paliyan to stay away from beef and leather. Nevertheless, at the time of Gardner's fieldwork (1960s and 1970s), the Paliyan do not seem to have adopted lowland culture in intracommunal contexts.

This dual mode of existence has still another dimension. On the one hand, the Paliyan experience humiliation from lowlanders, whom they mimic and at times perhaps actually regard as superior. On the other hand, these lowlanders, on the basis of their own worldview, associate the Paliyan with Hindu ascetics, due to their assumed lifestyle of austerity, with some Paliyan even being integrated into Hindu cults as temple officiants (Gardner 1982). From the Paliyan perspective, this may merely be an extension of the mimicry strategy that allows the Tamil lowlanders to 'see' in them pure ascetics eligible to perform temple worship. This cultural parallelism of outward formal mimicry – even to the extent of assuming the role of a 'Hindu' priest – and inward ritual inconstancy and flexibility may be

34 *Peter Berger and Sarbeswar Sahoo*

reminiscent of the Wari' assumption of the coexistence of different worlds; although, in the case of the Paliyan, presumably, multiculturalism lies at its basis and not – as in Amazonia – multinaturalism.[9]

Something similar to the 'openness' referred to above may thus also be detected with reference to Indian foragers. Bird-David (1994), for instance, has shown that the Nayaka of south India readily extend their ethos of sharing and their generalised idea of kinship to 'others' of all kinds, whether foreigners, anthropologists, Hindu deities or icons. In the process of this indigenisation, foreigners, anthropologists and gods become kin, while icons of Hindu deities do not become objects of worship but indices of persons who used them. The Nayaka thus integrate these elements into their own worldview so that what looks like a Hindu *puja* is actually an extension of sharing among kin within the domestic sphere. Thus, while the elements are foreign, the pattern is local (see Hardenberg 2010; Sahlins 1999).

It might thus be supposed that, based on this societal form, Christian ideas of brotherhood, Jesus and equality could be easily integrated into the gatherer-hunter ethos, and it would be this location in particular on which the study of continuity and change could focus. It is conceivable, for instance, that just like Christian missionaries in Papua New Guinea, who in some cases managed to established the Church as a mediator of competitive exchange practices and modified the indigenous tribal exchange system from 'gifts to men' to 'gifts to God' (Gregory 1980), missionaries might become mediators of the giving environment or otherwise become engaged in a 'cosmic system of sharing' (Bird-David 1992: 39).[10] However, this is a conjecture, an informed guess at best, and only future research will be able to offer greater understanding.

The modalities of conversion are no less related to society – in the comprehensive, holistic sense described above – in the case of peasants.[11] Peasants are also partial societies, like gatherer-hunters, but in a different way (see Pfeffer 2002). While the latter are part of the environment, the former are part of encompassing social orders (Wolf 1966). As is well known and thus requires no further discussion here, in India a particular form of social stratification (caste) is intimately intertwined with Hindu religious beliefs and practices, in which the idea of purity is crucial for the hierarchical order (Dumont 1980; Fuller 2004). While it has been argued that 'untouchables' share the ideology of the higher castes (Moffatt 1979), missionary activity has been particularly successful among lower castes and Dalit communities who aimed to overcome oppression and discrimination based on caste ideology (Kumar and Oddie, this volume). Caste has been a significant location for conversion, not only because the missionaries recognised early on that proselytisation among high castes and Brahmans in particular would probably be less fruitful band that caste would rather provide incentives for conversion for those at the bottom. Caste also proved to mark the limit of the missionaries' willingness to pursue a strategy of indigenisation – of accepting that Christianity would be indigenised according to local patterns. While they accepted and promoted the inclusion of local forms of worship in Christian practice, such as the *jatra* or procession, missionaries refused to accept distinctions on the basis of caste (Oddie, this volume).

We would like to close our reflections by briefly addressing the question of conversion and the city. As early as 1960, Pocock criticised the general idea that villages and cities would in principle be different, that 'rural' and 'urban' would refer to different kinds of facts, such as 'rural religion' or 'rural people' in contrast to urban forms (Pocock 1960: 80). Instead, he argued that one should not be misled by the enormous architectural difference to assume different types of society; ultimately, we could speak of the '*Indian* city' and the '*Indian* village' and we would not require two separate sociologies (1960: 81). We agree with Pocock that the city does not need to be constructed as a distinct societal type. It is widely known that caste is also crucial in cities and, moreover, members of gatherer-hunter or tribal communities also populate urban streets. At the same time, however, cities do have their own social and cultural dynamics, which makes them markedly different from rural contexts. It may, therefore, not be out of place to ask whether conversion and the processes of religious continuity and change take different forms in Indian cites, although none of the contributors to this volume explicitly discusses the relationship between conversion and the city. Here, we wish to briefly point to two locations of conversion that do take specific forms in cities and that are connected to some of the chapters of this volume; one concerns ethics, the other materiality. We will start with the latter.

Thus far, we have discussed the conversion of people, but urban spaces, in particular, demonstrate the conversion of places. Such material transformations often occur in relation to sometimes violent confrontations between 'religious groups',[12] as discussed by Sahoo in this volume in relation to affirmative action benefits in Rajasthan and Odisha. With regard to Ahmedabad, Ghassem-Fachandi (2012) argued that in moments of violence, the 'Hindu–Moslem divide has been the default mode of all division' (Ghassem-Fachandi 2012: 13). It is particularly in relation to religious communalism and competition that he describes the 'mushrooming' of Hindu temples and how sacred places become 'sites of conversion' (2012: 16, 13). Not only has the Bharatiya Janata Party (BJP) built numerous standardised Hindu temples to appropriate and convert city space, asserting and signalling Hinduness, but former Muslim sites have also been 'reconverted' into Hindu temples. Such places become nodal points, as well as dividing lines demarcating community affiliation, in situations of communal violence. Obviously, place-making and the politics of space are not confined to cities (see Sahoo, this volume), but they do seem to assume particular forms related to the specific materiality of the city, with its bridges, crossroads and junctions.

The second aspect concerns efforts to achieve ethical reformation. As Blom Hansen (2014) points out – in line with Pocock – while the 'traditional' need not be linked to the village and the 'modern' to the city; nevertheless, urban religious movements exhibit a particular quest for universalism and moral transformation for 'modernity' in their view (2014: 374f.). Hindu, Muslim and evangelical reform movements all condemn 'traditional' practices as backward, impure and decadent, among other terms. In this connection, Ghassem-Fachandi (2012: 19) noted that both the reformist Muslims and the Hindu nationalists held similar positions, although on different grounds, in their rejection of Muslim shrines following traditional worship practices. The former objected to the kind of worship that would not conform to 'true Islam', while the latter held that places where Hindus and Muslims worship (as is often the case in such places) must be originally Hindu and only converted to a Muslim shrine.

The contributions by Nadadur Kannan and Pool in this volume both relate to such efforts and discourses of ethical reform. As a centre of colonial power, Madras was an appropriate place for the Brahman elite both to oppose the Raj and to strive for an aesthetic – and at the same time ethical – regeneration of the performing arts. This was a purifying exercise that eliminated secularity and amorality, returning to religion, while at the same time, it dispelled the 'polluted' practices of the *devadāsi*s. In this sense, the elite did not perceive it as a move forward – towards modernity, as it were – but as reconversion and re-sacralisation (Nadadur Kannan, this volume). The Islamic reform movements discussed by Pool also developed in relation to British colonial power and strove towards a complete ethical regeneration of lifestyle, faith and religious practice.

CONVERTING 'CONVERSION'?

The scholarly debates about conversion discuss, on the one hand, how the phenomenon should be understood and defined and, on the other, whether the term 'conversion' is appropriate at all. It has been repeatedly pointed out that the term is particularly problematic with regard to Indian religions, and Hinduism in particular. Hinduism, or Hindu religions, is a heterogeneous category, comprising very different religious traditions. Moreover, religious practitioners can easily be affiliated with a number of devotional or ascetic movements – in addition to their religious affiliations through caste, kinship and locality – that often do not require exclusive membership. In joining such a tradition (*sampradaya*), a person does not 'convert', but is initiated (see Robinson and

Clarke 2003; Sharma 2014; Young and Seitz 2013). Taking account of this particular situation, Robinson and Clark (2003: 8) retain the term 'conversion' but define it in a broad way – 'as a fluid process of changing affiliations of religious beliefs and traditions' – so as to include a change of religious relatedness to Hinduism. Young and Seitz also argue for the continued use of the term, as long as its Christian heritage is acknowledged and the dimensions of 'suddenness and interiority' (2013: 15) removed, as they consider that 'conversion is not an event but a process' (2013: 18).

Among the authors of this volume, there is a general agreement about the need to understand conversion as a process – and we have argued in this introduction that this should not lead to ignorance regarding the significance of events. However, there are very different opinions about whether or how the term should be used. Some contributors suggest abandoning the term, while others retain it with qualifications. With reference to the affiliation sought by some Gadaba of Odisha to the Olek Dormo Hindu reform movement, Berger considers 'conversion' to be an inadequate term. This is because, first, it does not sufficiently capture the complex dynamics of religious and cultural change involved, while, second, the actors themselves do not recognise any process of conversion to be involved. Berger argues that only in cases of an explicit acknowledgement of the transformation of religious affiliation can 'conversion' be properly applied. In their contributions, Angelova and Oddie also prefer the term 'religious transformation' rather than 'conversion', precisely because the former does not connote the idea of rupture but of a gradual, possibly uneven, process. Oddie quotes a Methodist missionary in this regard, who speaks of a 'Christward movement', bringing out this point very well.

In contrast to the above-mentioned authors, in her contribution, Pool does not reject the term 'conversion' in principle, but rather considers the focus on *religious* conversion (or transformation) as problematic. With reference to Islamic reformism in West Bengal, she argues that conversion not only relates to religion but is part of a more encompassing process of ethical renewal, including personhood and society. For Pool, conversion is 'a diagnostic of power' (a term she borrows from Abu-Lughod), by which she means that choices of conversion signify hegemonic discourses, for instance, those within the Indian state that allow 'ethical renewal only within the constraints of the depoliticized "cultural" community' (Pool, this volume). The hegemonic secularity of the Indian state excludes Muslim forms of modernity as part of the secular state and confines it to a renewal within 'religion'. This argument resonates with the contribution of Nadadur Kannan, who also prefers to think about 'conversion' with regard to her case in a wide sense. The transformation of the performing arts propagated by elite Brahmans entailed a 'conversion to a religious, Hindu ideology' (Nadadur

38 *Peter Berger and Sarbeswar Sahoo*

Kanan, this volume), insofar as 'religion' was used as a hegemonic category redefining and re-sacralising dance practices as well as music, thereby excluding and marginalising certain groups.

Other contributors to the volume are not particularly concerned about the term as such, merely attempting to spell out what conversion means in their specific cases. To us, this also appears to be a feasible approach, that is, deciding on the basis of particular ethnographic or historical contexts what conversion means without intending to use it as a general and comparative category. If conversion is intended as a comparative category, we agree with those scholars mentioned above that it should not be narrowly defined, either being restricted to religion (for example, in the form of belief) or to ethics. The metaphor of Godroads introduced here is not meant as a substitute category for conversion, although it has been used as a synonym in some places in this introduction. However, it may be 'good to think' in this way when studying conversion, as it is a metaphor that invites a consideration of the multilayered events, as well as processes related to changing religious affiliations that we have identified above, which entail transformation and continuity in different, perhaps unexpected, locations.

NOTES

1. For a very competent overview of the scholarship on conversion generally, see Rambo and Farhadian (2014). For an overview of modes of – and motivations for – religious conversion in the Indian context, see Robinson and Clarke (2003).

2. Barlingay (1974: 145) notes that according to some scholars, prior to Buddha, it was Carvaka who was the first to 'revolt' against the superstitious beliefs and practices of Hinduism.

3. In contrast to prophets, missionaries are part of an institution and are not part of the local religious system but outsiders. Moreover, they do not oppose priests. However, a number of similarities between missionaries and prophets can be identified: they offer new 'religious goods', are subversive and heterodox in relation to the existing local religious system and are charismatic. Furthermore, missionaries also often 'occupy places of structural tension' (Bourdieu 1991: 35) and are ambivalent figures, on the verge of being rejected or admired. Although institutionally embedded, like prophets, missionaries often act individually in the remote places where they work. Weber only mentioned the missionary in relation to one aspect of the prophet, namely with regard to their non-profit orientation (Weber 1976 [1921]: 269).

4. Robbins (2004: 20f.; 2005) has pointed out that, in order for humiliation to be really effective, the debasing strategies of the representatives of the West, be they missionaries or colonialists of other kinds, have to somehow resonate with certain aspects of the traditional culture. Humiliation, he argues, initially has to be understood in traditional terms.

Introduction **39**

5. In their important analysis of anthropology and colonialism, Pels and Salemink (1999) also use the term 'location' in relation to other analytical terms (such as 'préterrain', 'ethnographic occasion' and 'ethnographic tradition') to create a framework for distinguishing various fields of influence on anthropological practice. By taking up Appadurai's notion of 'location', they indicate fields of influence on anthropology as a discipline and especially ethnography as a practice. The locations they identify, however, are all expressions of power or are power-driven (military, administration, missionary observation, settlers, slaves and workers). In contrast, we do not restrict the idea of location to power techniques but extend it to cultural domains in general.

6. 'Sensational forms are authorized modes for invoking and organizing access to the transcendental that shape both religious content (beliefs, doctrines, sets of symbols) and norms' (Meyer 2010: 751).

7. As is well known, the Indian situation is special, as here 'tribe' is an administrative category with its own history and political implications (see Pfeffer 1997; 2002; 2016: 272f.; Skoda and Otten 2013; Weisgrau 2013; Xaxa 2003).

8. As far as subsistence is concerned, the Wari' also engage in the slash-and-burn cultivation of maize. However, they share some aspects with this kind of society: their social relations show a high degree of flexibility, they formally move villages every few years – although they are not strictly peripatetic, they return to their places of maize cultivation as appropriate soils are rare (Vilaça, personal communication) – they have a pronounced ethos of equality, and value hunting most as a form of subsistence (Conklin 1995: 78).

9. Regarding conversion to Christianity, Gardner (2010: 264) only reports: 'Workers at a Jesuit coffee estate are exposed to Christianity. Some have been baptized with little instruction and few changed practices except for avoiding *caami* ["gods and ancestral spirits", 2010: 263] rituals.'

10. Roland Hardenberg 'shared' this latter idea concerning the missionaries' potential role as mediators of the 'giving environment' with me in a personal communication.

11. See Skoda (2005) for a detailed ethnography of peasant/tribal patterns with reference to the Aghria of western Odisha.

12. 'Religious groups' has been put in inverted commas here, as they usually do not exist as eternal units but, as Blom Hansen (2014: 370) has pointed out, rather appear as effects of violence.

BIBLIOGRAPHY

Barlingay, W. S. 1974. 'Dr Ambedkar and Conversion to Buddhism.' *Indian Philosophical Quarterly* 1(2): 144–153.

Baum, Robert M. 1990. 'The Emergence of a Diola Christianity.' *Africa: Journal of the International African Institute* 60(3): 370–398.

40 *Peter Berger and Sarbeswar Sahoo*

Bauman, C. M. 2008. *Christian Identity and Dalit Religion in Hindu India, 1868–1947.* Michigan: W.B. Eerdmans Publishing.

Berger, P. 2015. *Feeding, Sharing, and Devouring: Ritual and Society in Highland Odisha, India.* Berlin: de Gruyter.

———. 2016. 'Death, Ritual, and Effervescence.' In *Ultimate Ambiguities: Investigating Death and Liminality*, edited by Peter Berger and Justin Kroesen, 147–183. New York: Berghahn.

Berger, Peter L. 2010. 'Max Weber Is Alive and Well, and Living in Guatemala: The Protestant Ethic Today.' *The Review of Faith and International Affairs* 8(4): 3–9.

Bird-David, Nurit. 1990. 'The Giving Environment: Another Perspective on the Economic System of Gatherer-Hunters.' *Current Anthropology* 31(2): 189–96.

———. 1994. 'Puja or Sharing with the Gods? On Ritualized Possession among the Nayaka of South India.' *The Eastern Anthropologist* 49(3–4): 259–276.

———. 2010. 'Introduction: South Asia.' In *The Cambridge Encyclopedia of Hunters and Gatherers*, edited by Richard. B. Lee and Richard Daly, 231–237. Cambridge: Cambridge University Press.

Bloch, Maurice. 1989. 'The Disconnection between Power and Rank as a Process: An Outline of the Development of Kingdoms in Central Madagascar.' In *Ritual, History and Power: Selected Papers in Anthropology*, edited by Maurice Bloch, 46–88. Oxford: Berg.

Blom Hansen, Thomas. 2014. 'Religion.' In *A Companion to Urban Anthropology*, edited by Donald M. Nonini, 364–380. Chichester, West Sussex: Wiley-Blackwell.

Bourdieu, Pierre. 1987. 'Legitimation and Structured Interests in Weber's Sociology of Religion.' In *Max Weber, Rationality, and Modernity*, edited by Scott Lash and Sam Whimster, 199–136. London: Allen and Unwin.

———. 1990. *The Logic of Practice.* Cambridge: Polity Press.

———. 1991. 'Genesis and Structure of the Religious Field.' *Comparative Social Research* 13: 1–43.

Comaroff, J. L. and J. Comaroff. 1997. *Of Revelation and Revolution: The Dialectics of Modernity on a South African Frontier.* Chicago: The University of Chicago Press.

Conklin, Betha A. 1995. '"Thus Are Our Bodies, Thus Was Our Custom": Mortuary Cannibalism in an Amazonian Society.' *American Ethnologist* 22(1): 75–101.

Demmer, Ulrich. 2011. 'Social Representations "In Between": Concepts of Society and Community in Orissa and Beyond.' In *Centres Out There? Facets of Subregional Identities in Orissa*, edited by Hermann Kulke and Georg Berkemer, 373–387. New Delhi: Manohar.

Deploige, Jeroen. 2004. 'The Priest, the Prophet, and the Magician: Max Weber and Pierre Bourdieu vs Hildegard of Bingen.' In *The Voice of Silence: Women's Literacy in a Men's Church*, edited by Thérèse de Hemptinne and María Eugenia Góngora, Vol. 9, 3–22. Turnhout, Belgium: Brepols.

Dirks, N. 1996. 'The Conversion of Caste: Location, Translation, and Appropriation.' In *Conversion to Modernities: The Globalization of Christianity*, edited by P. van der Veer, 115–136. New York: Routledge.

Dumont, Louis. 1980. *Homo Hierarchicus: The Caste System and Its Implications*. Chicago: The University of Chicago Press.

———. 1986. *Essays on Individualism: Modern Ideology in Anthropological Perspective*. Chicago: University of Chicago Press.

———. 1994. *German Ideology: From France to Germany and Back*. Chicago: University of Chicago Press.

Durkheim, É. 1995 [1912]. *The Elementary Forms of Religious Life*. New York: The Free Press.

Fischer-Tine, H. and M. Mann, eds. 2004. *Colonialism as a Civilizing Mission: Cultural Ideology in British India*. London: Anthem Press.

Forrester, D. B. 2017 [1980]. *Caste and Christianity: Attitudes and Policies on Caste of Anglo-Saxon Protestant Missions in India*. London: Routledge.

Frykenberg, R. E. 2005. 'Christian Missions and the Raj.' In *Missions and Empire*, edited by Norman Etherington, 107–131. New York: Oxford University Press.

Fuller, C. J. 1976. 'Kerala Christians and the Caste System.' *Man* 11(1): 53–70.

———. 2004. *The Camphor Flame: Popular Hinduism and Society in India*. Princeton, NJ: Princeton University Press.

Gardner, Peter M. 1972. 'The Paliyans.' In *Hunters and Gatherers Today: A Socioeconomic Study of Eleven Such Cultures in the Twentieth Century*, edited by Marco Giuseppe Bicchieri, 404–447. New York: Holt, Rinehart and Winston.

———. 1982. 'Ascribed Austerity: A Tribal Path to Purity.' *Man* 17(3): 462–469.

———. 2010. 'The Paliyan.' In *The Cambridge Encyclopedia of Hunters and Gatherers*, edited by Richard B. Lee and Richard Daly, 261–264. Cambridge: Cambridge University Press.

Geertz, Clifford. 1973a. 'Religion as a Cultural System.' In *The Interpretation of Cultures*, 87–125. New York: Basic Books.

Geertz, Clifford. 1973b. 'Ritual and Social Change: A Javanese Example.' In *The Interpretation of Cultures*, 142–169. New York: Basic Books.

Ghassem-Fachandi P. 2012. 'The City Threshold: Mushroom Temples and Magic Remains in Ahmedabad.' *Ethnography* 13(1): 12–27.

Golub, A., D. Rosenblatt and J. D. Kelly. 2016. *A Practice of Anthropology: The Thought and Influence of Marshall Sahlins*. McGill: Queens University Press.

Gregory, Christopher A. 1980. 'Gifts to Men and Gifts to God: Gift Exchange and Capital Accumulation in Contemporary Papua.' *Man* 15(4): 626–652.

Guenther, Mathias. 2010. 'From Totemism to Shamanism: Hunter-Gatherer Contributions to World Mythology and Spirituality.' In *The Cambridge Encyclopedia of Hunters and Gatherers*, edited by Richard. B. Lee and Richard Daly, 426–433. Cambridge: Cambridge University Press.

42 *Peter Berger and Sarbeswar Sahoo*

Hardenberg, Roland. 2010. 'A Reconsideration of Hinduization and the Caste-Tribe Continuum Model.' In *The Anthropology of Values: Essays in Honour of Georg Pfeffer*, edited by Peter Berger, Roland Hardenberg, Ellen Kattner and Michael Prager, 89–103. New Delhi: Pearson.

Hardiman, D. 2003. 'Assertion, Conversion, and Indian Nationalism: Govind's Movement among the Bhils.' In *Religious Conversion in India*, edited by Rowena Robinson and Sathianathan Clarke, 255–284. Delhi: Oxford University Press.

Hefner, Robert W. 1993. *Conversion to Christianity: Historical and Anthropological Perspectives on a Great Transformation*. Berkeley: The University of California Press.

———. 1998. 'Multiple Modernities: Christianity, Islam and Hinduism in a Globalising Age.' *Annual Review of Anthropology* 27(1): 83–104.

———. 2013. 'Introduction: The Unexpected Modern – Gender, Piety and Politics in the Global Pentecostal Surge.' In *Global Pentecostalism in the Twenty-First Century*, edited by Robert W. Hefner, 1–26. Bloomington: Indian University Press.

Heidemann, Frank. 2014. 'Objectification and Social Aesthetics: Memoranda and the Celebration of "Badaga Day".' *Asian Ethnology* 73(1–2): 91–110.

Heredia, R. C. 2011. 'Interrogations from the Margins: Conversion as Critique.' *History and Sociology of South Asia* 5(2): 83–102.

Joas, H. 2009. 'Society, State and Religion: Their Relationship from the Perspective of the World Religions – An Introduction.' In *Secularization and the World Religions*, edited by Hans Joas and Klaus Wiegandt, 1–22. Liverpool: Liverpool University Press.

Lee, Richard B. and Richard Daly. 2010. 'Introduction: Foragers and Others.' In *The Cambridge Encyclopedia of Hunters and Gatherers*, edited by Richard B. Lee and Richard Daly, 1–19. Cambridge: Cambridge University Press.

Locher, G. W. 1978. 'Transformation and Tradition.' In *Transformation and Tradition and Other Essays*, 169–184. The Hague: Martinus Nijhoff.

Luning, Sabine. 2009. 'The Chief' of Fatal Car Accident: Political History and Moral Geography in Burkina Faso.' In *The Speed of Change: Motor Vehicles and People in Africa, 1890–2000*, edited by Jan-Bart Gewald, Sabine Luning, and Klaas van Walraven, 232–252. Afrika-Studiecentrum Series, vol. 13. Leiden: Brill.

Mallampalli, Chandra. 2004. *Christians and Public Life in Colonial South India, 1863–1937*. London: Routledge.

Martin, Bernice. 1995. 'New Mutations of the Protestant Ethic among Latin American Pentecostals.' *Religion* 25(2): 101–117.

Masquelier, Adeline. 2002. 'Road Mythographies: Space, Mobility, and the Historical Imagination in Postcolonial Niger.' *American Ethnologist* 29(4): 829–856.

Mathew, G. 1982. 'Politicization of Religion: Conversions to Islam in Tamil Nadu.' *Economic and Political Weekly* 17(26): 1068–1072.

McCloud, S. 2012. 'The Possibilities of Change in a World of Constraint: Individual and Social Transformation in the Work of Pierre Bourdieu.' *Bulletin for the Study of Religion* 41(1): 2–8.

Mendoza, Marcela. 2003. 'Converted Christians, Shamans, and the House of God: The Reasons for Conversion Given by the Western Toba of the Argentine Chaco.' In *The Anthropology of Religious Conversion*, edited by Andrew Buckser and Stephen D. Glazier, 199–208. Lanham: Rowman & Littlefield.

Meinert, Lotte and Bruce Kapferer, eds. 2015. *In the Event: Toward an Anthropology of Generic Moments*. New York: Berghahn.

Meyer, Birgit. 1998. '"Make a Complete Break with the Past." Memory and Post-Colonial Modernity in Ghanaian Pentecostalist Discourse.' *Journal of Religion in Africa* 28(3): 316–349.

———. 2010. 'Aesthetics of Persuasion: Global Christianity and Pentecostalism's Sensational Forms.' *South Atlantic Quarterly* 109(4): 741–763.

Miller, Cynthia J. 2001. 'Landscapes of Encounter: Gender and the Morality of the Road in South India.' *Women's Studies Quarterly* 29(1/2): 183–192.

Moffatt, Michael. 1979. *An Untouchable Community in South India: Structure and Consensus*. Princeton, NJ: Princeton University Press.

Mohan, S. P. 2015. *Modernity of Slavery: Struggles against Caste Inequality in Colonial Kerala*. New Delhi: Oxford University Press.

Mosse, D. 2012. *The Saint in the Banyan Tree: Christianity and Caste Society in India*. Berkeley: University of California Press.

Omvedt, G. 2003. *Buddhism in India: Challenging Brahmanism and Caste*. New Delhi: Sage Publications.

Osella, F. and C. Osella. 2008. 'Introduction: Islamic Reformism in South Asia.' *Modern Asian Studies* 42(2–3): 247–257.

Patvardhan, V. S. 1994. 'Mass Conversion of Muslims.' *Economic and Political Weekly* 29(40): 2566.

Pelkmans, M., ed. 2009. *Conversion after Socialism: Disruptions, Modernisms and Technologies of Faith in the Former Soviet Union*. New York: Berghahn Books.

Pels, P. and O. Salemink. 1999. 'Introduction: Locating Colonial the Subjects of Anthropology.' In *Colonial Subjects: Essays on the Practical History of Anthropology*, edited by P. Pels and O. Salemink, 1–52. Ann Arbor: The University of Michigan Press.

Pfeffer, Georg. 1997. 'The Scheduled Tribes of Middle India as a Unit: Problems of Internal and External Comparison'. In *Contemporary Society: Tribal Studies, Vol. 1: Structure and Process*, ed. G. Pfeffer and D. K. Behera, 3–27. New Delhi: Concept Publishing.

———. 2002. 'Debating the Tribe.' Unpublished paper presented on the European Conference of Moderns South Asian Studies in Heidelberg, pp. 1–16.

44 *Peter Berger and Sarbeswar Sahoo*

———. 2016. *Verwandtschaft als Verfassung: Unbürokratische Muster öffentlicher Ordnung.* Baden-Baden: Nomos.

Pocock, D. F. 1960. 'Sociologies – Urban and Rural.' *Contributions to Indian Sociology* 4: 63–81.

Porter, A. 2004. *Religion vs. Empire: British Protestant Missionaries and Overseas Expansion, 1700–1914.* Manchester: Manchester University Press.

Rao, A. 2009. *The Caste Question: Dalits and the Politics of Modern India.* Berkeley: University of California Press.

Rappaport, Roy A. 1999. *Ritual and Religion in the Making of Humanity.* Cambridge: Cambridge University Press.

Robbins, Joel. 2004. *Becoming Sinners: Christianity and Moral Torment in a Papua New Guinea Society.* Berkeley, CA: University of California Press.

———. 2005. 'Humiliation and Transformation: Marshall Sahlins and the Study of Cultural Change in Melanesia.' In *The Making of Global and Local Modernities in Melanesia. Humiliation, Transformation and the Nature of Cultural Change*, edited by Joel Robbins and Holly Wardlow, 3–21. Aldershot: Ashgate.

———. 2007. 'Continuity Thinking and the Problem of Christian Culture.' *Current Anthropology* 48(1): 5–17.

———. 2009. 'Conversion, Hierarchy, and Cultural Change: Value and Syncretism in the Globalization of Pentecostal and Charismatic Christianity.' In *Hierarchy: Persistence and Transformation in Social Formations*, edited by Knut M. Rio and Olaf. H. Smedal, 65–88. New York: Berghahn.

———. 2014. 'How Do Religions End? Theorizing Religious Traditions from the Point of View of How They Disappear.' *Cambridge Anthropology* 32(2): 2–15.

Robbins, Joel and Holly Wardlow, eds. 2005. *The Making of Global and Local Modernities in Melanesia: Humiliation, Transformation, and the Nature of Cultural Change.* Aldershot: Ashgate.

Robinson, R. 2003. *Christians of India.* New Delhi: Sage Publications.

Robinson, R. and S. Clarke. 2003. 'Introduction: The Many Meanings of Religious Conversion on the Indian Subcontinent.' In *Religious Conversion in India: Modes, Motivations, and Meanings*, edited by R. Robinson and S. Clarke, 1–21. New Delhi: Oxford University Press.

———, eds. 2003. *Religious Conversion in India: Modes, Motivations, and Meanings.* New Delhi: Oxford University Press.

Robinson, R. and J. M. Kujur, eds. 2010. *Margins of Faith: Dalit and Tribal Christianity in India.* New Delhi: Sage Publications.

Sahay, Keshari N. 1968. 'Impact of Christianity on the Uraon of the Chainpur Belt in Chotanagpur: An Analysis of Its Cultural Processes.' *American Anthropologist* 70(5): 923–42.

Sahlins, Marshall D. 1968. *Tribesmen.* Engelwood-Cliffs: Prentice-Hall.

———. 1985. *Islands of History*. Chicago: University of Chicago Press.

———. 1999. 'Two or Three Things That I Know About Culture.' *The Journal of the Royal Anthropological Institute* 5(3): 399–421.

———. 2000. 'The Return of the Event, Again.' In *Culture in Practice: Selected Essays*, 293–351. New York: Zone Books.

———. 2005 [1992]. 'On the Anthropology of Modernity, or, Some Triumphs of Culture over Despondency Theory.' In *Culture and Sustainable Development in the Pacific* edited by Antony Hooper, 44–61. Canberra: ANU Press.

Sewell, W. H. 2005. 'Historical Events as Transformations of Structures: Inventing revolution at the Bastille.' In *Logics of History*, 225–262. Chicago: University of Chicago Press.

Sharma, Arvind. 2014. 'Hinduism and Conversion.' In *The Oxford Handbook of Religious Conversion*, edited by Lewis R. Rambo, 429–440. Oxford: Oxford University Press.

Sikand, Y. and M. Katju. 1994. 'Mass Conversion to Hinduism among Indian Muslims.' *Economic and Political Weekly* 29(34): 2214–2219.

Skoda, Uwe. 2005. *The Aghria: A Peasant Caste on a Tribal Frontier*. New Delhi: Manohar.

Skoda, Uwe and Tina Otten. 2013. 'Odisha: Rajas and Prajas in a Multi-Segmented Society.' In *The Modern Anthropology of India: Ethnography, Themes and Theory*, edited by Peter Berger and Frank Heidemann, 208–226. London: Routledge.

Sting, Stephan. 1997. 'Straße.' In *Vom Menschen. Handbuch Historische Anthropologie*, edited by Christoph Wulf, 202–211. Weinheim: Beltz.

Strauss, Roger A. 1979. 'Religious Conversion as a Personal and Collective Accomplishment.' *Sociological Analysis* 40(2): 158–165.

van der Veer, P. 1996. 'Introduction.' in *Conversion to Modernities: The Globalization of Christianity*, edited by P. van der Veer, 1–21. New York: Routledge.

Verter, Bradford. 2003. 'Spiritual Capital: Theorizing Religion with Bourdieu against Bourdieu.' *Sociological Theory* 21(2): 150–174.

Vilaça, Aparecida. 1997. 'Christians without Faith: Some Aspects of the Conversion of the Wari' (Pakaa Nova).' *Ethnos* 62(1–2): 91–115.

———. 2009. 'Conversion, Predation and Perspective.' In *Native Christians: Modes and Effects of Christianity among Indigenous Peoples of the Americas*, edited by Aparecida Vilaça and Robin Wright, 113–127. Farnham, Surrey, UK: Ashgate.

———. 2014. 'What if a Religion Is Not Made to Last?' *Cambridge Anthropology* 32(2): 16–18.

———. 2015. 'Dividualism and Individualism in Indigenous Christianity: A Debate Seen from Amazonia.' *HAU: Journal of Ethnographic Theory* 5(1): 197–225.

Viswanath, Rupa. 2013. 'The Emergence of Authenticity Talk and the Giving of Accounts: Conversion as Movement of the Soul in South India, ca. 1900.' *Comparative Studies in Society and History* 55(1): 120–141.

Viveiros de Castro, Eduardo. 1998. 'Cosmological Deixis and Amerindian Perspectivism.' *Journal of the Royal Anthropological Institute* 4(3): 469–88.

Vitebsky, Piers. 2017. *Living without the Dead: Loss and Redemption in a Jungle Cosmos.* Chicago: The University of Chicago Press.

Washburn, D. and Kevin A. Reinhart, eds. 2007. *Converting Cultures: Religion, Ideology and Transformation of Modernity.* Leiden: Brill.

Watt, C. A. (2011) "Introduction: The Relevance and Complexity of Civilizing Missions c 1800-2010.' In *Civilizing Missions in Colonial and Postcolonial South Asia*, edited by Carey A. Watt and Michael Mann, 1–34. London: Anthem Press.

Watt, C. A. and M. Mann, eds. 2011. *Civilizing Missions in Colonial and Postcolonial South Asia: From Improvement to Development.* London: Anthem Press.

Weber, Max. 1976 [1921]. *Wirtschaft und Gesellschaft: Grundriss der Verstehenden Soziologie.* Tübingen: J.C.B. Mohr.

———. 2001 [1904/5]. *The Protestant Ethic and the Spirit of Capitalism.* New York: Routledge.

Weisgrau, Maxine. 2013. 'Rajasthan: Anthropological Perspectives on Tribal Identity.' In *The Modern Anthropology of India: Ethnography, Themes and Theory*, edited by Peter Berger and Frank Heidemann, 242–259. London: Routledge.

Willey, Robin D. 2016. 'Liminal Practice: Pierre Bourdieu, Madness, and Religion.' *Social Compass* 63(1): 125–141.

Wolf, Eric R. 1966. *Peasants.* Upper Saddle River, NJ: Prentice Hall.

Woodburn, James. 1982. 'Egalitarian Societies.' *Man* 17(3): 431–451.

Wright, T. P. Jr. 2007. 'The Movement to Convert Harijans to Islam in South India.' *The Muslim World* 72(3–4): 239–245.

Xaxa, Virginius. 2003. 'Tribes in India.' In *The Oxford India Companion to Sociology and Social Anthropology*, edited by Veena Das, 373–408. New Delhi: Oxford University Press.

Young, Richard Fox and Jonathan A. Seitz. 2013. 'Introduction.' In *Asia in the Making of Christianity: Conversion, Agency, and Indigeneity, 1600s to the Present*, edited by Richard Fox Young and Jonathan A. Seitz, 1–26. Social Sciences in Asia, vol. 35. Leiden: Brill.

1

The Rise, Growth and Significance of Shudra Conversion Movements in the Methodist Mission, Hyderabad, 1925–1947

Geoffrey A. Oddie

Any discussion of the nature of Shudra or other conversion movements towards Christianity in Hyderabad, or elsewhere, raises the question of what is meant by 'a conversion movement'.

In line with the discussion of terminology in Christopher Harding's recent book, *Religious Transformation in South Asia: The Meanings of Conversion in Colonial Punjab* (2008), we intend to place the emphasis not on a movement normally involving some kind of dramatic or sudden type of emotional conversion experience among those involved (Bebbington 1989: 5–10) – though, in some cases, this may have occurred – but on the idea of an initial attraction to the movement, adherence and gradual transformation. This emphasis on a slower and less dramatic process coincides with many descriptions of the spread of Christianity in early modern Europe. It also reflects the language of C. G. Early, an experienced Methodist missionary based in Hyderabad, and a close observer of the Shudra's increasing involvement in Christianity, who referred to it, not as a 'conversion', but a 'Christward' movement.[1]

While the idea of 'conversion' among evangelicals in Britain and the United States echoes St Paul's description of his own experience, implying a dramatic or sudden 'turning' from old ways to new, the turning, in the case of many new followers of Christianity in the Indian and Hyderabad context, was often a slow, gradual and unsteady process. As in the case of other missions, and under the supervision of Charles Posnett, who arrived in India in 1896 and became and remained the effective head of the mission until 1939 (Sackett 1951), baptism was regarded not as an end in itself, but as part of an ongoing process of changes in understanding, lifestyle and behaviour. This view closely accords with the editors' description of 'Godroads' involving approaches to God, including 'movement, change and transformation' (see the editors' introduction to this volume).

Enquirers (who were largely outcastes prior to the reception of the Shudra) were expected to learn and observe the basic precepts of Christian faith and

48 *Geoffrey A. Oddie*

conduct. After perhaps nine months or a year's preparation and teaching by a resident Indian pastor and his wife, those candidates asking for baptism were expected (amongst other things) to have learnt 'passages of Scripture, the Lord's Prayer, the Commandments, and some hymns of praise' (Sackett 1926: ch. 3). After their baptism, the pastor and his wife were required to remain with their congregation to give them further support, encouragement and advice.

This process of learning and gradual growth and transformation took place within the familiar context of family and caste allegiance. This was in spite of the fact that the Methodists did as much as they felt they could to discourage traditional views of caste separateness, pollution and hierarchy. As noted in other accounts of Christian 'conversion' in south India elsewhere, it was family and caste structures which facilitated many Christian movements in the first place, and it was the retention of many other traditional cultural practices in worship, dancing and celebration that strengthened Christian movements, especially in rural areas.

This chapter begins with introductory and general comments on Shudra movements towards Protestant Christianity across the Telugu-speaking regions of southern India from about 1910 to 1947. Following this discussion is a more detailed analysis of the situation in Telangana – a distinctive geographic and Telugu-speaking region in the eastern part of what was formerly the Nizam's domain or Hyderabad. Much of this territory was then a largely rural, heavily forested area with poor communications, and somewhat isolated from the main centres of the Nizam's administration. As the census of 1921 suggests, the city of Hyderabad in the south of the mission was, at that time, the only suburban area in Telangana with a population above ten thousand. It was in this essentially rural (or 'jungle') context that the Shudra movements towards Protestant Christianity in Hyderabad first developed.

The main focus of our argument is on the condition and plight of the lower caste Shudra who were seeking protection from the oppressiveness of landlords and the landed system. We point out that they were especially impressed with the changes they noted in the lifestyle and attitude of the outcaste converts, who seemed to benefit from contact with the mission and used its educational and other advantages to progress and aspire to something better in their way of life. While some landlords, feeling threatened by the movement, unleased savage persecution, others joined the movement and helped lead the way. This chapter also emphasises the effectiveness of some missionary policies, for example, the Methodist stress on the importance of training large numbers of pastors and 'bible women' (their wives) for work in the countryside, the establishment of special sensitively conducted summer schools for Shudra enquirers, and a strong emphasis in the mission on building Christianity, as far as possible, on indigenous roots. Our final section includes comments on the prevalence of illness and disease, on the introduction of modern Western forms of treatment through the mission and on the possible impact this had on the Shudra's views of Christianity. We conclude by raising some further questions about developments in the Hyderabad mission compared with the Shudra movements towards Christianity in other Protestant missions in British territory.

SHUDRA MOVEMENTS TOWARDS CHRISTIANITY IN ANDHRA PRADESH – HYDERABAD AND ELSEWHERE

Data provided by Christian leaders of various Protestant missions in the Telugu-speaking regions in the early 1930s shows that developments in Hyderabad were part of a broader and more widespread movement of the Shudra towards Christianity across the region.

Tables published in the *National Christian Council Review* suggest that by 1932, the total number of individuals, drawn from Shudra communities and baptised in the Wesleyan Methodist Missionary Society (WMMS) in Hyderabad (in present-day Telangana), was the third highest in the seven Protestant missions operating in Andhra: the total number of Christians from these communities in Hyderabad being exceeded only by the number of caste converts in the neighbouring CMS Dornakal Diocese and American Baptist Mission (Table 1.1).

These figures show the outcome of a movement that gained momentum, continued and, in the case of the Hyderabad mission, began to decline a few years

TABLE 1.1 Estimated number of Christians from Shudra communities in Protestant churches in the Telugu country, 1931

Canadian Baptist	500
London Missionary Society	400
American Baptist Mission	7,500
Dornakal Diocese	7,100
SPG Telugu	52
Wesleyan Mission, Hyderabad	6,000
American Evangelical Lutheran Church	5,000
Total	26,552

Source: *The National Christian Council Review*, New Series, X (January 1932), p. 32.

50 *Geoffrey A. Oddie*

TABLE 1.2 Caste background of new additions to the English Wesleyan Methodist Church, Nizams Dominions, 1921–1931

Caste	Number
1 Mala	21,763
2 Madiga	13,856
3 Gond	305
4 Brahmin	7
5 Kapu	2,948
6 Fishermen	730
7 Weavers	966
8 Dhobi	282
9 Potters	146
10 Shepherds	317
11 Barbers	93
12 Lambada	37
13 Other Hindus	446
Total	41,896

Source: Census of Hyderabad, Part 1, 1933, p. 242.

prior to Indian independence in 1947. The specific castes, including Shudra, joining the Hyderabad movement from 1921 to 1931, appearin Table 1.2.

According to these tables, 85 per cent of new recruits who joined the mission during the ten-year period (from 1921 to 1931) were the outcaste Mala and Madiga. Slightly over 1 per cent were tribals (Gond and Lambada) normally placed at the bottom of the social hierarchy, while a few Brahman were also included as new additions. But what is also apparent, and a new element in the situation, is that 13 per cent were Shudra – the most prominent among them being the Kapu, weavers and fishermen.

According to Hassan's detailed report on castes and tribes in the Nizam's dominions, published in 1920 (ul Hassan 1920), the Kapu were 'the chief landholding and cultivating caste' – rearing cattle and engaged in agricultural operations. Though described as 'Kapu', they included Reddi, Kamma and other middling caste groups. While having their own specific customs, they, together with Hindu weavers, fishermen and other Shudras, also participated with 'outcastes' (in this case, the Mala and Madiga) in many of the more popular religious events (ibid.: 318).[2]

A METHODIST MISSIONARY 'AWAKENING': POSSIBILITIES OF WORK AMONG THE SHUDRA

The British Methodists, who began work in Hyderabad in 1879, were firmly focussed on work among the outcastes. Like many other Protestant missionaries of that period, they had no expectation of much success in working among Brahman or other elites. Furthermore, the Methodist movement in Britain itself had been a movement strongest and especially popular among the common people. Hence, it is hardly surprising that from the time of the foundation of the Hyderabad mission, at least up until the 1920s, the missionaries' focus (with the consent of their mission society) was almost exclusively on the welfare of the outcaste Mala and Madiga, and on progress among them.

However, there had long been Shudra students in Methodist elementary schools[3] and presumably among those given medicine or treated in one of several mission dispensaries. But while this was happening, apparently without further results, there were promising signs of Shudra interest in Christianity elsewhere, including in the neighbouring CMS and Lutheran missions which bordered Methodist territory to the southeast. Methodist workers, aware of these developments, debated the possibility of work among the Shudra, but nothing further was done until events within Methodist mission territory itself prompted changes in the Methodist policy and their first positive steps towards working among the Shudra.

In 1914, 30 Waddars, lower caste Shudra, described in the census as earth workers and stone dressers (ul Hassan 1920: 645), were baptised in the mission at Aler. This was in the southeastern portion of the mission, in close proximity to Shudra movements towards Christianity elsewhere, and almost certainly a result of caste and family connections. According to the resident European missionary, the Rev. Edwin Lance, the leader of the movement was Vellepu Ramaswamy 'chief of the Vaddara caste' who led the way for 20 of his relatives 'to come into the fold of Christ'.[4] Like the Waddar, in some other parts of the region, the family had long given up the life of a wandering and/or 'criminal tribe', settling into the more respectable and stable conditions of village life. Ramaswamy, a chief of the local police, together with his six sons, their wives and children, continued to live in the village and on the produce of family land.

However, despite Ramaswamy taking up evangelistic work after baptism, there appeared to be no further Shudra expressions of interest in Christianity in that part of the mission for the next few years. Nevertheless, the issue of Shudra conversion had been raised and was widely discussed, a survey conducted by the

52 Geoffrey A. Oddie

local synod in 1926 showing that 'there was hardly a centre among the thirty written down as circuits where caste enquirers were not known'.

THE SUMMER SCHOOL INITIATIVE AND ITS IMPACT

Heartened by these findings, the missionaries finally took steps to encourage further Shudra conversions. They organised in Medak in 1926, the first of a number of summer schools for the Shudra wanting more information about Christianity and what was involved in joining the Christian movement (Sackett 1930: 234–237).[5] A special feature of these meetings was that instead of ignoring or even challenging caste distinctions (an aspect of the more traditional confrontational British Protestant approach), organisers chose to respect caste taboos in relation to eating and drinking. This more sensitive approach was reflected in the employment of a caste cook and the provision of water from a caste well.[6]

Though personal invitations were sent to no more than 70 individuals on the first occasion, 150 men arrived and remained as special guests of the mission for five days of lectures, discussion, prayer and reflection. At the end of the meeting, and to show their expression of gratitude, heads of the various castes represented gave to each and everyone alike *prasatham* (coconut and sugar) as a token of goodwill.

At the close of the meeting, 15 men from villages bordering the Godavery River (to the north of the mission) asked for immediate baptism. However, they were advised to return home, bearing witness to their new-found faith with family and friends, and promised that, if after long thought and prayer, and so on, they still wanted baptism 'we would come to their villages and baptize them, and their people, in public' (Sackett 1930: 236). Following on from this event, there were several large-scale public baptisms of Shudra converts in the Godavery River and subsequently Christian leaders, inspired by the success of the summer school model, continued to organise similar events for the Shudra in different parts of the mission at least up until 1947.[7]

The effect of these meetings was not only to clarify the nature and implications of the Christian message, but to consolidate trust and challenge delegates to a deeper commitment and understanding of what was expected and involved in Christian life. Lastly, meetings such as these gave enquirers an opportunity to meet each other, as well as hear Shudra Christians from other parts of the mission, or even from outside the Hyderabad region. For example, during the first experiment in Medak, several converts from the Lutheran mission in Andhra nearby gave their testimony – making it quite clear that Shudra Hindus, not only those in Hyderabad, were already participating in Christian movements.

The holding of the initial Shudra summer school of 1926 was both a symptom of and stimulus to further Shudra interest in Christianity in Hyderabad. For the missionaries it was clear evidence that these castes were affected by many of the same problems and aspirations that were influencing the Shudra in other parts of the Telugu region.

THE INFLUENCE OF THE OUTCASTE MALA AND MADIGA CHRISTIANS ON CASTES ABOVE

A second and more fundamental factor in arousing and sustaining Shudra interest in Christianity (and one which helps to explain the success of Shudra summer schools) was the preceding outcaste conversion movements – a phenomenon noted in other parts of the Telugu region.[8] J. W. Pickett, appointed director of a large-scale detailed study of Christian mass movements in India by the National Christian Council in 1929, conducted enquiries into Shudra movements into Christianity in the Telugu-speaking areas, including the northern districts of the Hyderabad Methodist mission. Referring to findings of the commission's report (based on interviews), Pickett expressed his conviction that the Shudra movements in Hyderabad, as well as in many other parts of Andhra, were largely a result of the influence of preceding outcaste movements into the Christian fold.

These views, with reference to the situation in Hyderabad, were verified independently by both Posnett and Frank Whittaker – (the latter appointed to an educational position in 1922 and chairman of the district in 1947).[9] Both agreed that it was the change in the lives of outcastes which had a great effect – especially, in Posnett's view, as seen in changes in the lives and characters of 'our Indian ministers'.[10] Indeed, an early decision by Posnett (resident at Medak) to raise up and train an indigenous ministry of Indian Christian pastors and their wives (the latter known as bible women) – all of them of outcaste origin – was crucial, and probably the single most important factor in encouraging the subsequent Shudra movements.

Indeed, the extent of the mission's dependence on the dedication and ministry of its outcaste workers is reflected in figures relating to staffing. Thus, in 1914, and even before the superintendents of the mission became aware of Shudra interest in Christianity, there were, at that time, 15 European missionaries working in the Hyderabad mission, 7 Indian ministers, 188 evangelists or catechists and 242 day school teachers – almost all of the Indian staff being of outcaste origin[11]. Furthermore, according to the missions report four years later, there were by then 'over two hundred young men' (Mala and Madiga) in the Medak seminary being trained to become pastors and teachers of village

54 *Geoffrey A. Oddie*

congregations, while the wives of many of them were receiving suitable instruction under 'Miss Posnett'.[12]

Bible study at Medak in 1924 included Posnett's *Outlines of Bible Characters* which followed the Indian method of telling stories to emphasise personalities, rather than doctrines or texts. And while knowledge of the Bible and the teaching of Christian moral values were regarded as the most important topics, subjects also included practical information – some of it dealing with relations with the Shudra. As evangelists and outcastes, students were, for example, expected to know 'how to speak with caste people', and to be able to read the best of their own literature that was in higher Telugu (Sackett 1926: 53). Posnett's programme also included practical subjects such as health, medicine and first aid, and also 'special subjects' such as agriculture, village social service and scouting – or, in other words, the acquisition of knowledge and special skills which would unite and benefit caste as well as outcaste communities.

Furthermore, and as Taneti has shown in his recent book, it was the Mala and Madiga bible women (usually married to pastors) who also played an important role in the extension of Christianity in the Telugu-speaking regions of southern India more generally (2013: esp. 89–93). Their teaching and practical skills (and, if married, their work which complemented their husband's ministry) helped gain trust and access to the homes of caste communities – especially those influenced by an increasing desire for social improvement. Indeed, Sackett, long-term missionary and historian of the Hyderabad mission, declared that the success of the Methodists in establishing an increasing number of elementary village schools, as well as in the founding of new and expanding village congregations, depended 'wholly upon the fidelity of the evangelist and his wife' (Sackett 1926: 32).[13]

However, it was not only the officially appointed representatives of Methodism who achieved important results. As well as a trained leadership, there were the more ordinary outcaste converts scattered in an ever-widening range of villages. Indeed, knowledge of what was involved in becoming Christian and how this might effect one's life, or the life of one's family, was not always confined to the official activities and teaching of pastors and bible women. It was also conveyed by converts directly and further facilitated through the operation of the traditional forms of social and economic interaction embedded in the local *jagmani* system operating in village society.

Of all the castes, lower caste Shudra were the most closely in touch with the Mala and Madiga. The new Christians might be beyond the pale, living in hamlets in the most polluted location just outside the main part of the village. However, their services were still required for all kinds of activity on behalf of the larger village community. Describing the system as it operated in a Telangana village in 1955, S. C. Dube pointed out:

> No caste alone is self-sufficient, for it requires the services of several other occupational castes which hold the monopoly of certain castes and professions. This system of co-operative labour, based on a pattern of inter-caste relations approved by tradition, is not confined only to economic activities but also to ceremonial and ritual life. (1967: 7)

Hence, while, in some respects, the Mala and Madiga lived separate lives, they collaborated with other castes (especially low caste Shudra) in various forms of agricultural activity and in the exchange or selling of leather, textiles and other goods.[14] Also significant was their participation (and even leadership) in village rituals – such as the sacrifice of a buffalo to the village deity Peddamma during epidemics, when it was believed that the goddess was angry and required propitiation.[15]

In these varied circumstances, especially through labour in the fields, the lines of communication between outcastes and lower caste Shudra were perhaps more open than between the outcastes and other castes in the village community. Hence, changes in the beliefs, attitude, behaviour and aspirations of newly won outcaste Christians, including changes in their habits and attitude to work, in their collaboration or otherwise in the worship of village deities, and in other activities, were more apparent and better understood by low caste Shudra than by others in the village hierarchy.

LANDLORD OPPRESSION AND INCREASING RURAL DISTRESS

Another factor in the situation in Hyderabad were radical changes in the state's socio-economic system during the period from 1920 to 1947 – changes that brought the lower caste Shudra (increasingly under- or unemployed) into closer touch with outcastes in similar distress. Thus, the official report on the mission in 1918 noted that 'there is a tendency to-day for the Patel, and bigger land-holder to swallow up all the rest'[16] – the tenants' loss of land and of traditional forms of employment on land creating an ever-expanding pool of landless labourers.

Indeed the unrestrained power and oppressiveness of local landlords was possibly greater in Hyderabad than it was in British India including in the other areas of Andhra where Shudra movements were taking place.[17] Furthermore, in his analysis of the origins of the communist uprising in Telangana in 1942, Ian Bedford, in a detailed analysis, has shown that throughout the early decades of

56 *Geoffrey A. Oddie*

the twentieth century leading up to the time of the revolt, there was an ever-increasing process whereby small holders were 'parted from their land' (Bedford 1967) and were forced to join the ranks of wage labourers or the unemployed. As one of the Hyderabad missionaries, referring to Shudra enquirers into Christianity, wrote in 1930, 'their first desire has been for some kind of millennium free from forced labour in all its forms and protection from the rapacity of the village headman'.[18]

Oppression and exploitation on an unprecedented scale was clearly driving the lower caste Shudra closer to other exploited classes in Hyderabad society. These long suffering people included outcaste Christians, many of whom welcomed the Shudra into their village churches. The formation of these new inter-caste and, at times, separate Shudra congregations inflamed the situation even further, as landlords, seeing the movement of people into Christian churches, began to fear they (the landlords) were losing control. Their apprehension and fear of what might be happening was described by C. G. Early, a missionary of many years' experience of work in and around Dadgaon in the northeast. Writing at the end of 1943, Early, who knew many of the local landlords, remarked:

> Already I have written of our concern for the village headmen. These men who are the petty representatives of the Nizam's Government in each village, have immense power. They own much of the land, and they are to a great extent dictators. Most of them are proud, unscrupulous men, and as the Christian movement spreads in their villages, they realise that the people are gaining a new kind of freedom, that new forces are being released which they do not understand, and they fear the consequences. Hence the persecution by which they seek to intimidate the Christian people.[19]

Missionary reports from as early as the 1920s' are indeed full of accounts of the persecution of Shudra as well as outcaste Christians.[20] Nevertheless, despite the attitude of landlords, there was a continuing though moderate growth in the number of Shudras becoming Christian. Exploitation brought the Shudra into an even closer contact with outcaste Christians who were also searching for work and a means of survival. Indeed, a growing sense of class solidarity was beginning to replace more traditional caste divisions and rivalry – the Shudra and outcastes together sensing a new commonality and perhaps even empowerment through the Christian movement. In this respect there can be little doubt that some pastors, supported by the padre Sahibs (missionaries such as Posnett), stood by their flocks, as is evidenced by the number of cases being conducted in country's courts of law. Not the least of these episodes was a missionary win in the case

The Rise, Growth and Significance of Shudra Conversion Movements **57**

involving the landlord known as 'the tiger' of Gumeralla – one of the most notorious of the persecuting landlords, and the subject of much discussion in missionary records.[21]

CHRISTIAN MOVEMENTS FROM THE TOP DOWN

While observers agreed that, in its earlier stages, the Christian movement arose from the bottom up, from among outcastes to the lower echelons of the caste communities, this model does not always seem to apply to the movement as it developed in the latter part of the 1930s. In its later years, the process began to look a little more like the pattern that developed in some parts of the Roman and Medieval world where, in some cases, Christianity appears to have moved from the bottom up, and then again, from the top downwards (Hillgarth 1986: 150–168).

Leading opponents of the Christian movement in the Telangana region were often the *patel*s (heads of villages) and other powerful village officials – all of them landowners and influential. For example, referring to this particular issue in October 1929, Colyer Sackett (a man of nearly 30 years' experience in the mission)[22] remarked: 'In one village I visited, a company of patels gathered to witness the baptism, and did all they could to influence adversely the Catechumens. The malas for the most part did not come, because of the threats of the Patels ... but the others – over 200 refused to be intimidated at all.'[23]

However, over time and by 1940, this type of landlord opposition appears to have gradually declined or, in some parts of the mission, disappeared. Alongside reports of continued savage persecution were also comments on the village authorities, including *patel*s, joining with Christians. Clearly, some *patel*s and their employees were changing their mind and attitude towards Christianity and local Christian movements. When the question of the number of *patel*s baptised was raised by the Methodist home office in 1940, Sackett (as noted earlier, a man of considerable experience in the region) replied that there were at least 11 *patel*s who had, by that time, been 'received into the Christian church'.[24]

In fact, the story of some of these men is reflected in other records. For example, in 1939, it was reported that one Kista Reddi, the *mali patel* (the revenue officer and head of the village),[25] realised that though Ramanuja taught them what is true *bhakti*, there was nothing in such teaching to show them the real saviour about whom they had heard. He surrendered himself to the Lord, and in order to proclaim his decision to the other people in his village he removed the idols from his puja room and 'has now set up the picture of our Lord in its place'.[26]

Writing to the general secretary of the WMMS in December 1937, Sackett described the activity of another *patel* who was active in promoting the Christian

58 *Geoffrey A. Oddie*

movement. Referring to his visit to villages around Sarjana, northwest of Medak and near the Manjira River, he wrote:

> In one, a caste village, we had about 60 to 70 baptisms. These were the direct result of the influence of Anthiah Patel of Sarjana whom you baptized when you were out last year – Anthiah was present and gave his own testimony before the whole congregation of catechumen and non Christian caste people.[27]

The same caste movement in the same area continued to spread and, referring to further baptisms, Posnett, wrote: 'Anthiah Patel ... was [again] there and brought with him another patel who had been prepared so that we have now two village chiefs who have cast in their lot with us. Great crowd on the river bank.'[28]

CONVERTS AND INDIGENISATION IN THE RURAL SETTING

While the peculiar and extreme circumstances of oppression and exploitation in Hyderabad (as distinct from other parts of Andhra) played a major role in encouraging the Shudra, as well as outcastes, to look to the Christian movement for some sort of relief, decisions by the missionary leadership were also important in encouraging further Shudra interest in the Christian movement.

As we have seen, the most important of these decisions was Posnett's resolve to train up converts (all of them outcastes) to become evangelists (pastors and bible women) in the villages – a strategy that proved to be of considerable importance in awakening and consolidating Shudra interest in Christianity. Another important decision, and one relating specifically to caste Hindus, was the decision to conduct summer schools for Shudra enquirers. A third decision, or series of decisions, also of importance to the Shudra, was the mission's ongoing strategy of what might be called 'indigenisation'. This policy helped, to some extent, to integrate Christian teaching and practice into the existing Telugu cultural milieu, and made it easier for the Shudra, as well as other enquirers, to develop their faith and understanding on the basis of what was already familiar to them in their own traditional practices and understanding.

But, as with missionary policies of this nature more generally, notions of indigenisation had limitations, not only in connection with the uniqueness of the 'swami' Jesus Christ, but also (in the Methodist view) with respect to caste practice.

The compilers of the Hyderabad Methodist *Mass Movement Commission Report* of 1918 declared that, in the event of caste conversions, the Methodists 'would not force a convert either to eat what he did not like or to marry one whom he did not choose' (p. 27) a policy also adhered to in the Dornakal diocese

The Rise, Growth and Significance of Shudra Conversion Movements **59**

(Harper 2000: 259), and it was this view, with respect to eating and drinking, which was (as we have seen) reflected in the preparations for and conduct of caste summer schools.

It was, however, one thing to respect caste taboos at summer school meetings and in connection with eating and drinking, but acceptance of caste discrimination generally among Christians (for example, between outcastes and Shudra) was, for Posnett and other leaders in the Methodist mission, anathema, and totally contrary to the spirit of the Christian gospel. While the pastor's or missionary's role was not to force a convert either 'to eat what he did not like or to marry one whom he did not choose', his role was also, quite clearly, to encourage mixing and collaboration between different castes, especially in Christian worship.[29] In the case of caste divisions generally, therefore, the missionaries were simply unable to build on indigenous foundations, and could hardly be expected to accept an indigenous practice which, in their view, contradicted the basic idea of love and fellowship as seen in the Christian gospel.[30]

However, apart from caste practices which were gently (and sometimes unsuccessfully) discouraged,[31] there were other traditional methods, customs or observances which could be used quite effectively as a basis for encouraging Shudra and others interested in joining the Christian movement. Posnett's stress on the importance of utilising and building on indigenous tradition is, as we have seen, reflected in the teaching methods he introduced in the training school at Medak where he favoured indigenous rather than European styles of learning. This meant that instead of placing an emphasis on the more abstract doctrines and statements of belief, his teaching included the narration and learning of Christian myths and stories and linking these with local festivals and other events (Sackett 1926: 53).

Among the Methodists, as in some other missions, there was also some emphasis on adhering, as far as possible, to local tradition in forms of worship. Writing in a book published in 1929, and with his Methodist neighbours as well as others in mind, Azariah, the bishop of Dornakal[32], declared:

> Everywhere the country is homogeneous and native, the town heterogeneous. This is true of the Church too. Surpliced choirs in Gothic edifices, with pews and benches, and organs and harmoniums, appear to be essentials of urban churches. Not so in the villages. The chapel architecture is natural and Indian. The singing is always to indigenous music, often accompanied, too, by Indian musical instruments. The seating and worship is in Indian style – all sit on the floor and worship, either kneeling as in south India, or prostrate upon their faces as in Chota Nagpur. The offertories are given and received in indigenous style – food grains, home-grown vegetables, first-fruits of all garden crops and of all of cattle and

60 *Geoffrey A. Oddie*

chickens come to the altar. The spontaneity and naturalness of the worship are often most refreshing and inspiring. (Cited in Mackenzie 1929: 29)

In addition to baptism in sacred rivers, the use of coconut and sugar as sacred elements in communion, as well as the practices as described above, the Methodists also developed the idea of a Christian *jathara* or pilgrimage which was in some ways modelled on the Hindu practice. Posnett, who often preached and distributed literature at Hindu *jathara*s or festivals on the banks of rivers, subsequently declared: 'We too must have our own Christian *Jathara*' (C. V. Rao 2008).[33] After revisiting the Doodgaon *jathara* on the banks of the Godavery River in 1937, Sackett reported that he had held a communion service for 300 people and that 'it was impossible to say which of the people were caste and which were outcastes'.[34] Writing in the *National Christian Council Review* 10 years later, E. L. Anantha Rao suggested that his readers might enjoy a visit to the annual *jathara*s of Doodgaon and Armoor (both in the northeast of the mission). He argued that these events not only encouraged a greater sense of unity among Christians, a deepening of spiritual life and Christian giving, but that one might also be surprised to see on these occasions 'the number of non-Christians displaying not a little eagerness to have a share in giving to Swami Jesus. Their motives and their ideas may not be altogether Christian, but here they see a celebration, a festival, so Indian that as Indians they feel that they cannot keep out of it' (E. L. A. Rao 1947: 490). Vasantha Rao, who has explored the history and nature of these festivals, has argued that they were a unique occurrence among Protestant missions in south India, and a special feature of the Medak diocese of the Church of South India. His detailed evidence suggests that at least seven Christian *jathara*s were established in different parts of the Methodist mission prior to 1947 – six of them taking place after the rise and continuation of Shudra involvement in Christianity and up to the time of India's independence in 1947 (C. V. Rao 2008: 75–82).

THE SHUDRA AND THE SPIRITUAL IMPLICATION OF MODERN MEDICINE

A further factor which attracted the Shudra and others to the Christian movement was its apparent association with healing. During the period under discussion, outbreaks of cholera (indigenous to India), plague and smallpox were common. For example, the Hyderabad census report of 1921 stated that, during the previous decade, 'plague and cholera carried off, on the whole, 194,325 and 42,246 persons respectively'.[35] While cholera originated in India, plague was a comparatively new phenomenon – the plague bacillus having arrived in India from Hong Kong in 1895.[36]

The Rise, Growth and Significance of Shudra Conversion Movements **61**

Outbreaks of smallpox also caused many deaths in Telangana during this period – the disease being associated, in the mind of many Hindus, with the displeasure of the local village deity. For example, according to the mission's report of 1934, in the village of Palde, it was only the Christians who consented to being vaccinated against smallpox. When the disease broke out, it was only the Christians who refused to participate in the puja to the local goddess Poshamma and, to the amazement of the non-Christians, only the Christians remained free from infection.[37]

While smallpox epidemics associated with village deities continued to cause concern throughout the mission, it was cholera (also associated with deeply held religious convictions) which caused the greatest terror among India's population. Writing in 1825, James Annensley, an authority on diseases in India, remarked that few diseases had excited 'more terror in the mind of the Indian community at large, than the epidemic cholera' (Arnold 1993: 159). Reporting from Aler in 1913, the Rev. Lant (of the Methodist mission) remarked that 'the very thought of cholera goes straight to the heart of the average Indian. It is the visitation of the goddess!'[38] At such times, wrote Sackett, 'the whole village is paralysed with fear' and rituals included the slaying of buffalo, sheep and goats, the beating of drums, and wild dancing and yelling to drive away the evil spirit (Sackett 1926: 43). Missionary sources suggest that while some Christians continued to join in these rituals, others, supported by their local pastor, stayed away.[39] Furthermore, and as Sackett remarked, whether it was the simple instruction the evangelist gave his people whereby they avoided infection, or the result of 'a little medicine bottle he kept hard bye', the fact remained that 'the percentage of deaths from cholera [was] lower among our Christian people than among those outside the circle' (Sakett 1926: 43–44).

Vaccination against smallpox, introduced in Bombay in 1802, was improved by the introduction of a new type of vaccine produced in the same city in 1907. A cure for cholera eluded British authorities until Koch's discovery of the bacillus in 1884, while practical preventative measures (not always successful) were gradually extended to minimise the possibilities of plague (Arnold 1993: 194–195). All of these cures and preventive measures were introduced and in operation in the Methodist mission during the period under discussion and almost certainly affected Shudra as well as outcaste attitudes towards Christians and the Christian movement.

Furthermore, increasingly available in the mission were simple modern remedies which staff were trained to administer. Compulsory courses at the training institute in Medak for pastors and wives included talks on health, *bazaar* (country) medicine and first aid (Sacket 1926: 55). Furthermore, reporting on the mission's resources in 1932, Posnett stated that there were then not only

62 *Geoffrey A. Oddie*

Christians in more than 600 villages 'shepherded by nearly 600 well-trained Indian evangelists, all of whom are married to well-trained Bible women' but also 'three large hospitals and 10 dispensaries – most of which have a few beds' and the Leper Hospital in Dichpali with 400 patients – 'one of the largest and finest in all India!'[40]

The effect on the Shudra and other Hindus of time spent in mission hospitals, and of modern medical treatments increasingly available through the mission in some of the villages, was the subject of some reflection on the part of one of the more prominent missionary women. In a letter in October 1937, Ethel Wilson remarked that, after discussions with the village women, she was again struck with the proximity in their minds of disease and worship: 'not one of the testimonies omitted to tell of some reference to worshipping idols during a time of disease, or of their being brave enough not to join in some village festival to idols, during some epidemic. So practically all their tests in faith come about in connection with disease.'[41]

While hospitals and dispensaries, as well mission schools,[42] were open to Shudra and other castes, relations between Christian outcastes and Hindu Shudra (increasingly brought together and consolidated through landlord oppression) were further cemented by village-level boy scout movements – encouraged by the mission and popular in the 1920s and 1930s. Among other activities, the scouts sought to improve village-level environmental conditions. For example, among other activities at Medak and Sarjana, Christian and Hindu 'caste' scouts were working together, providing special diets and medicines for the sick, clearing refuse pits, destroying rats and cleansing streets.[43]

SLOWING DOWN OF THE MOVEMENT AND ISSUES INVOLVED IN FURTHER RESEARCH

Our story ends with the extraordinary disarray, upheavals and violence which affected Hyderabad in the 1940s and which ended with the annexation of 'the Nizam's dominions' by the government of India in 1948. The Methodist Missionary Society cut back on its financial commitments to the region during the Second World War – action which possibly affected Western-type institutions such as hospitals and some schools more than mission work in the countryside. There was famine in some parts of Hyderabad in 1942, while some parts of the country, especially Nalgonda and Warangal districts in the east, were also affected by the communist uprising (India's only communist rebellion) that lasted from 1942 to 1946. Lastly, there was the turmoil created by the Razakars, an Islamic paramilitary voluntary force that was organised to prevent Hyderabad's

The Rise, Growth and Significance of Shudra Conversion Movements **63**

absorption into the Indian union after the British withdrawal from India in 1947. This latter movement was finally terminated by the new Indian government's parachute drop and Hyderabad's integration into India.

How far these events affected the strength and continuance of the Christian-orientated Shudra movement is difficult to say. In their book based on the Rev. and Mrs Luke's research in the Jangarai section of the Wadiaram Pastorate undertaken in 1959, Luke and Carman claim that conversions among the lower Shudra castes 'gradually increased until 1940, decreased until 1947, and have since almost stopped' (Luke and Carman 1968: 19). Though they cite no evidence for these claims, there can be little doubt that there was a slowing down in the rate at which the Shudra were joining the movement in the early1940s. According to E. L. Anantha Rao, who had been actively involved with them from the very beginning, and whose comments were included in a paper on evangelism published in 1946, 'The caste movement in Hyderabad continues in certain areas among certain communities, though the pace has slowed down lately' (E. L. A. Rao 1946).

While this evidence suggests that the number of Shudra conversions in Hyderabad was already slowing down during the Second World War, space does not permit a full or adequate explanation as to why a loss of momentum in some parts of the mission was taking place.

Nor have we space to adequately compare the situation among the Shudra in Hyderabad with their position more generally and in British India. Certainly, excessive landlord oppression in Hyderabad compared with landlord behaviour in British India, the attractions of the communist movement in Hyderabad and the periods of violence, as a result of the communist and Razakar activity, suggest a different environment in Hyderabad compared with other parts of Andhra. How far these issues affected the Shudra response to the Christian movement in Hyderabad, making it different from the Shudra response to Christianity elsewhere, is therefore a matter for further consideration.

Alongside these issues are questions relating to differences in status, wealth and general condition among different grades of 'Shudra' in the different missions, and whether these differences among the Shudra were important in the growth of Shudra movements in different parts of Andhra. Last but not least is the issue of missionary policy. How different were missionary policies in the different missions, and how important were these different strategies in encouraging conversion? One factor here is that the leaders of the different Protestant missions in Andhra collaborated to an increasing degree[44] and possibly borrowed ideas increasingly from each other as the ecumenical movement expanded throughout the Telugu region.

64 *Geoffrey A. Oddie*

These and perhaps other issues might be further considered in any future comparative analysis of Shudra movements into Christianity in Andhra from the 1920s to the end of the Second World War.

NOTES

1. Early to Committee, July 1941, SOAS Archives, London, Wesleyan Methodist Missionary Society (WMMS) Hyderabad, Microform

2. For the possible origin of the term 'Dalit', which does not occur in the Hyderabad mission records during this period, see Mendelsohn and Vicziany (1998: xii).

3. SOAS, Hyderabad District, Annual Report 1913; see also reference to the caste boys day school in Nizamabad, Hyderabad District, Annual Report 1914.

4. WMMS, Hyderabad, 34th Report, 1914, pp. 66–70.

5. See also *In the Nizam's Dominions* (henceforth *Dominions*), 1926, p. 8, where it is noted that the meeting was told that the missionaries in Guntur already had 3,000 caste converts. For further comment on the emotional impact of this meeting, see *The National Christian Council Review*, October 1926, p. 587. Another school for caste Hindus was held at Medak in 1930 when, although 150 guests were invited, 640 were present at the opening (*Dominions*, 1931). See also reference to further caste summer schools at Luxettepet (*Dominions*, 1936) and to one at Karimnagar; D. N. Francis, to Sec. WMMS, between 8 September and 4 November 1940.

6. For further discussion of this type of approach, see the editors' introduction.

7. For example, Sackett, referring to a newly developing caste movement towards Christianity around Sarjana near Medak in 1937, remarked that he was persuaded that this was entirely due to (1) the work already done in Sarjana and (2) the Summer Schools that the Methodists had for caste people; Sackett to Noble, 12 November 1937, WMMS.

8. See especially Pickett (1938: 50–51) and Harper (2000: 276–277).

9. First Church of South India Bishop of Medak, 1947–1960

10. *WMMS Report*, 1930, p. 33 and Whittaker (1933: 520).

11. Report of the W. M. Mission, Hyderabad, 1914.

12. WMMS, *Mass Movement Commission Report*, 1918, p. 10.

13. For further comment on the contribution, or even pivotal role, of bible women in the spread of Christianity in Hyderabad, see *Dominions*, 1930, pp. 41–42.

14. One estimate in the *NCCR* was that 'ninety per cent of our Christians are said to be employed by the Sudras', 47 (February 1927): 589.

15. See especially Whitehead (1921: 48–70). Referring to the part played by outcastes in village festivals, Posnett, in a letter to Miss Bradford, WMMS (22 November 1921), told the story of village preparations for a big public puja 'on account of the prevalence of fever'. These proceedings were designed to propitiate the village deity through animal

The Rise, Growth and Significance of Shudra Conversion Movements **65**

sacrifice, but when the chief Madiga drummer (a Christian) refused to lead his men, the puja had to be abandoned.

16. WMMS, *Mass Movement Commission Report* (Hyderabad), 1918, p. 30.

17. For example, Bishop Whitehead, one of the best informed of commentators, and author of *The Village Gods of Hinduism,* during a visitation to a neighboring district in the Dornakal Diocese, remarked: 'In the Nizam's Dominions the Christians are perhaps more exposed to petty persecution from village officials than in British Territory'; see Oddie (1991: 101).

18. *Dominions,* 1930, p.16

19. Early to Committee, undated (between letters dated 1 November 1943 and 3 February 1944).

20. WMMS Reports, 1928, p. 34; Sackett to brethren, 16 October, 1929; *Dominions,* 1931, p. 17.

21. WMMS Reports, 1928–32; *Dominions,* 1931.

22. He joined it in 1901. See his *Vision and Venture* (1930: 247).

23. Sackett to Brethren, WMMS, 16 October 1929.

24. Sackett to Home Committee, WMMS, 22 April, 30 August and 3 September 1940.

25. See Dube (1967: 50).

26. *NCCR* 18 (1939): 267–268.

27. Sackett to WMMS, 2 December 1937.

28. Posnett to Noble, WMMS, 29 November 1938.

29. Posnett to Noble, 10 June 1934 and to Sec, 25 July 1934.

30. For the development of British Protestant missionary attitudes to caste, see especially Oddie (1969) and Forrester (1980: ch. 7).

31. Sackett to Noble, 13 July 1937.

32. For the Bishop of Dornakal's life, ideas and administration, see especially Harper (2000).

33. The earliest one was a Christian pilgrimage led by the Rev. Akula Titus (an Indian minister) in the Ramayampet Pastorate in 1914

34. Sackett to Noble, WMMS, 12 November 1937.

35. *Census of India,* 1921, Vol. 21, Hyderabad State, p. 6.

36. For these and other references to developments in medicine, see Arnold (1993).

37. *Dominions,* 1935.

38. Report 1913, p. 67.

39. Report, 1914, p. 79.

40. *Dominions,* 1932, p. 64.

41. Ethel Wilson to Mrs. Leith, 17 October, 1937.

42. *Hyderabad District Report,* 1913.

43. *Dominions,* 1931, p. 12; 1932, p. 15; Posnett to Noble, 9 June 1934.

66 Geoffrey A. Oddie

44. Especially after the formation of the National Christian Council of India, Burma and Ceylon in 1923.

BIBLIOGRAPHY

Arnold, David. 1993. *Colonizing the Body: State Medicine and Epidemic Disease in Nineteenth-Century India*. Delhi: Oxford University Press.

Bebbington, David William. 1989. *Evangelicism in Modern Britain. A History from 1730s to 1980s*. London and New York: Routledge.

Bedford, Ian. 1967. 'The Telengana Insurrection: A Study of the Causes and Development of a Communist Insurrection in Rural India, 1946–51.' Ph.D. thesis, Australian National University.

Dhangare, D. N. 1983. *Peasant Movements in India:1920–1950*. New Delhi: OUP.

Dube, S. C. 1967. *Indian Village*. Bombay: Allied Publishers.

Forrester, Duncan B. 1980. *Caste and Christianity: Attitudes and Policies on Caste of Anglo-Saxon Protestant Missions in India*. London and Dublin: Curzon Press.

Harding, Christopher. 2008. *Religious Transformation in South Asia: The Meanings of Conversion in Colonial Punjab*. Oxford: Oxford University Press.

Harper, Susan Billington. 2000. *In the Shadow of the Mahatma: Bishop V. S. Azariah and the Travails of Christianity in British India*. Michigan: Erdmans.

Hillgarth, J. N., ed.1986. *Christianity and Paganism, 350–750: The Conversion of Western Europe*. Philadelphia: University of Pennsylvania Press.

Luke, P. Y. and John B. Carman. 1968. *Village Christians and Hindu Culture: Study of a Rural Church in Andhra Pradesh South India*. London: Lutterworth Press.

Mackenzie, John, ed. 1929. *The Christian Task in India*. London: Macmillan & Co.

Oddie, G. A. 1969. 'Protestant Missions, Caste and Social Change in India, 1850–1914.' *The Indian Economic and Social History Review* 6(3): 259–291.

———. 1991. *Religion in South Asia*. Delhi: Manohar, 2nd rev. and enlarged ed.

Mendelsohn, Oliver and Marika Vicziany. 1998. *The Untouchables: Subordination, Poverty and the State in Modern India*. Cambridge: Cambridge University Press.

Pickett, J. W. 1938. *Christ's Way to India's Heart*. London: Livinstone Press.

Rao, E. L. Anantha. 1946. 'Evangelism.' in General Synod of the Methodist Church in India, Burma and Ceylon, Papers.

———. 1947. 'The Spiritual Growth of Rural Churches.' *The National Christian Council Review* (October).

Rao, Chilkuri Vasantha. 2008. *Jathara: A Festival of Christian Witness*. Delhi: CISRS/ISPCK.

Sackett, F. Colyer. 1926. *Out of the Miry Clay: The Story of the Haidarabad Mission to the Outcastes*. London: Cargate Press.

————. 1930. *Vision and Venture: A Record of Fifty Years in Hyderabad, 1879–1929*. London: The Cargate Press.

————. 1951. *Posnett of Medak*. London: Cargate Press.

Taneti, James Elisha. 2013. *Caste, Gender, and Christianity in Colonial India: Telugu Women in Mission*. Palgrave Macmillan.

ul Hassan, Syed Siraj. 1920. *The Castes and Tribes of H.E. the Nizam's Dominions*. Bombay.

Mendelsohn, Oliver and Marika Vicziany. 1998. *The Untouchables: Subordination, Poverty and the State in Modern India*. New York: Cambridge University Press.

Whitehead, Henry. 1921. *The Village Gods of South India*. London: Oxford University Press.

Whittaker, Frank. 1933. 'The Caste Movement towards Christianity.' *The National Christian Council Review* 53(9).

2

Communism and the Cross

A Caste–Class Trajectory of Religious Conversion in South India

Ashok Kumar Mocherla

Sometimes a road leads to unexpected destinations, for instance, from communism to Christianity. This chapter investigates the conditions and implications of this unforeseen journey as it explores the rather distinct trajectory of religious conversion to argue that communist activism indubitably nurtured the seeds of caste consciousness which, over time, contributed to the growth of Christianity in Andhra Pradesh. The arguments are developed in the light of ethnographic data collected from the Lutheran community of Dravidapuram village[1] in Guntur district of coastal Andhra, south India. To unfold this distinctive trajectory of conversion to Christianity, one needs to historically examine communist activism in coastal Andhra with special reference to local politics, especially politics of the lower castes. Often, local politics is seen as a significant platform wherein caste and class, as dominant categories of mobilisation, interact with and feed into each other in many ways. In this particular case, the local politics of coastal Andhra paved the way for the consolidation of class and caste consciousness. In turn, the Lutheran community produced syncretic Christian practices that in many ways communicate symbolic meanings from its own historical trajectory.

The idea of religious conversion is no longer viewed as a sudden shift from one belief system to another but as a complex process that accommodates converts' sociopolitical motives and aspirations. In the Indian context, perhaps the most viable and comprehensive academic explanation of conversion is that it is a fluid process of changing affiliations of religious beliefs and traditions, as it can then theoretically accommodate accounts of shifting sectarian affiliations within Hinduism as well as conversion to Islam and Christianity (Robinson and Clarke 2003). To understand these processes of changing affiliations of religious beliefs, one has to pay careful attention to the social, political and historical contexts of conversion. How fluid these processes are depend largely upon the historical trajectories it travelled through. In making sense of syncretic practices and contextual meanings, the trajectory of conversion – the multiplicity of factors affecting the journey down the *godroad* – is as significant as the individual act of conversion.

Since the nineteenth century, the lower castes, especially former 'untouchables' – who came to self-identify as Dalit[2] in modern India – have invariably been distinct in terms of their public protest against structures of caste discrimination allegedly legitimised by the Hindu religious faith. Despite overtones, Dalit scholars have long been arguing that caste discrimination is a direct result of a religiously sanctioned and legitimised social system, and hence for a better understanding of caste one must examine it with reference to Hindu religious faith (Ilaiah 1996; Aloysius 1998; Webster 1999). Contesting marginality or degradation sanctioned and imposed by religion is therefore quite obviously at the forefront of alternatives that the Dalit liberation agenda aspires to pursue. Their attempts to contest caste discrimination and regain self-respect and human dignity have led Dalit politics to dominate the narrative of conversion in modern India. In the course of time, Dalits have arrived at four interconnected options to pursue their agenda of liberation from the discriminatory caste system of India. Attain political power as an end in itself or as a means to attain specific goals: first, attain economic independence from upper castes; second, bring about internal social reforms; third, in the light of modern education, aim to reduce social prejudices and stereotypes within the Dalit community; fourth: the strategy of religious conversion to forge new religious identities and worldviews (Webster 1999: 12–13).

It is the fourth alternative, with its immense potential, that has generated much heated and long-standing national debate in modern India over religious freedom and an individual's constitutional right to follow and propagate any religion. The Dalit assertion generated religious awareness among community members across Indian states and promoted religious conversions as a mark of public protest against caste tyranny. The narrative of religious conversion and history of Dalit assertion in India is incomplete without referring to the mass conversion to Christianity.

In the following sections, I will first present, then argue how the mass movements to Christianity and the history of communism in Andhra together determined and guided the caste–class trajectory of the religious journey for Dalit Christians of Dravidapuram. Furthermore, the following sections will explore how the decline of class awareness, which had its own set of reasons, directly strengthened caste consciousness followed by the convergence of caste, class and religious articulations in Andhra Pradesh. I will also argue how important it is politically for Dalit Christians to demonstrate political ideologies in the religious domain given the complex relations they have been sharing with religion and politics of this region.

MASS MOVEMENTS TO CHRISTIANITY IN INDIA, 1840–1920

At different times in India, caste inequality and oppression have created unfavourable social conditions that made Dalits explore options to revive Hindu religious faith towards the formation of a new religious group or sect based on principles of equality and if necessary to go beyond the fold of Hinduism. Some examples of such movements are the Adi Dharam movement in Punjab (Juergensmeyer 1982), the Satnami movement in Chhattisgarh (Dube 1998; Bauman 2010), the Buddhist movement in colonial Tamil Nadu under the leadership of Pandit Iyothee Thass (Aloysius 1998), the mass conversion movement to Islam in Meenaskhipuram (Khan 1983), the conversion movement to Buddhism among Mahars in Maharashtra (Zelliot 1969) and the mass movements to Christianity in south India (Pickett 1993). While conversion has apparently long been a symbol of social protest and a compelling force among Dalit communities all over India, their political outlook has never been homogenous in terms of their choice of religion. Dalits converted to Christianity to escape caste tyranny and degradation, but it is well documented that – in the absence of ritual justification – caste exists among Indian Christians. Consequently, Dalits who converted to Christianity are twice-alienated – inside the Church and outside it (Wilson 1982). Forms of caste discrimination and presence of caste among Indian Christians today are important to investigate but fall outside the purview of this chapter, which aims to understand the very source of motivation for conversion among Dalits, as conversion movements highlight a pressing need for such an attempt.

Group conversions to Christianity between 1840 and 1920, what missionaries then termed 'mass movements', were among the most visible manifestations of caste consciousness demonstrated by lower castes, particularly Dalits, in modern India. These movements drastically changed the religious demographic landscape of south India and determined the course of Indian Christianity. Christianity in India, especially in south India, expanded hand in hand with the development of caste consciousness among Dalits. Embracing Christianity was part of the larger Dalit struggle against caste tyranny and discrimination, which has long been institutionalised in Indian society. The mass movements to Christianity, therefore, made the plight of Dalits a public concern in an organised fashion for the first time ever in the history of modern India (Webster 1992: 33–76). These mass movements were unique in many ways, but most notable was the shift from the conventional 'individual conversion' to 'group conversion' and that caste elders – not individuals, out of personal conviction – decided that a group would convert. Consequently, caste groups converted to Christianity *en masse* but retained social ties with their own former community vis-à-vis other communities they interacted with daily (Pickett 1933). Christian missionaries in India were seriously concerned that new converts retained pre-conversion social ties, and some questioned their motives. Clearly, their motives and motivations reflect a deep-seated desire for material prosperity and better social mobility and status (Kim 2003). Uniquely, the Lutheran community of Dravidapuram is an outcome of both mass movements to Christianity in the region and Dalit assertion against upper caste domination in the village. The Mala, one of the Dalit castes of this region, constitute the majority of the Lutheran community in Dravidapuram village. Notably, they were influenced by a strong communist wave that started in 1930 and significantly changed the political landscape of coastal Andhra.

HISTORY OF COMMUNISM IN ANDHRA, 1930–1960

In the 1930s, the ranks and cadre of the Indian National Congress (INC) – particularly the socialist-minded – felt a growing sense of neglect within the party. Consequently, in May 1934, the All India Congress Socialist Party (AICSP) was constituted. To expand their ideological base, the AICSP encouraged members to establish provincial parties in their respective states. To socialist-minded Congressmen, independence meant more than ending British rule in India; issues such as the liberation of the masses from economic exploitation and the removal of exploitation through the achievement of socialism had an equal stake in the independence movement. At that time, Andhra witnessed a strong wave of communist ideology propagated by diverse revolutionary organisations; one, the Hindustan Socialist Republican Party (HSRP), promoted the idea of attaining *swaraj* through revolutionary means. The British had declared the Communist Party of India (CPI) an unlawful organisation; for allegedly attempting to form a provincial committee of the CPI, Amir Haider Khan – a Moscow-trained Bolshevik propagandist – was imprisoned in 1934. Despite robust legal obstacles, some of his followers managed to form the Andhra Provincial Communist Party (APCP) and set up branches in Madras, Guntur, West Godavari and Krishna. The first-ever meeting of the APCP was held secretly at Kakinada, and Puchalapalli Sundaraiah was elected general secretary. Since the CPI was an unlawful association, the APCP could not conduct activities on its own; therefore, the CPI let communists in Andhra join the Andhra Provincial Congress Socialist Party (APCSP) to use it as a political platform for their activities.

There were three interconnected aspects of the growth of communism in Andhra. First, from the very beginning, the Left movement was subject to divergent influences: socialists, communists, Congressmen with socialist ideas and various other organisations and political parties. Second, the right-wing Congress leadership in Andhra raised serious concerns about the growing

72 Ashok Kumar Mocherla

influence of communists in the APCSP and tried its best to counteract it. Third, despite the open opposition of the APCSP's right-wing leadership, the communists maintained leadership over the agricultural labour associations, peasant organisations, labour unions and youth leagues (Adapa 1986: 34–36). According to N. G. Ranga, a prominent leader of the APCSP, its main objective was to convert the Congress to socialism. To realise this goal, many branches of the APCSP were established at Eluru, Guntur, Gudivada and Bezwada. Initially, they organised various political conferences to further the socialist propaganda. In the course of time, they organised tours of national leaders such as Jaya Prakash Narain, Y. Mehrauli, S. A. Dange and Jawaharlal Nehru, who addressed several public meetings. On such occasions, the peasantry, as well as the young people, expressed themselves explicitly in favour of these socialist ideas (Venkatarangaiya 1965: 668). Various resolutions were passed condemning the ban on the CPI and calling on socialist and communist organisations to protest the arrest of Amir Haider Khan and other political prisoners, and many committees were formed to propagate anti-imperialist ideas in Andhra.

To mark their political support of socialist ideology, the APCSP celebrated Anti-Imperialist Day and Russian Day. The communists successfully expanded their organisational and social base in Telugu districts in a short time. They secured a substantial number of seats in the Andhra Provincial Congress Committee (APCC) and also in the All India Congress Committee (AICC)[3] and became quite visible. By 1937, Andhra communists dominated the district and provincial committees of the APCSP and even its executive committee.[4] In their efforts to spread communist ideology, and to make the working class aware about the ongoing economic exploitation and the larger political economy of India, communist leaders organised peasant associations and peasant marches, agricultural labour unions, hunger marches and summer schools on politics and economics. During 1937–1939, a number of such summer schools were organised, one of their fundamental functions being to recruit local party cadre and consequently expand the organisational base in rural Andhra.

The Kothapatnam Summer School on Politics and Economics

In the summer of 1937, the colonial state alleged that the school organised at Kothapatnam in Guntur district taught revolutionary socialism under the leadership of Kameswar Rao, a Russian-trained communist. As per the colonial law, it was a punishable offence. The British government considered the school dangerous, declared it illegal and imprisoned organising members of the Kothapatnam summer school. The government alleged that these summer schools disseminated prohibited literature and began arresting their organisers –

all prominent communist leaders – to curb Leftist activism in Andhra. Communist organisations in Andhra considered the action unwarranted and condemned it as an attack on civil liberties, but the right-wing Congress leadership largely remained silent.[5] The school divided socialists and right-wingers in the Congress into two rival factions within the APCSP. The then Governor-General of India, C. Rajagopalachari, declared that while the government would not interfere in the lawful preaching of any political, social or economic doctrine, it would not tolerate the dissemination of class hatred or of ideas involving the use of violence and would take all steps necessary to prevent it.[6] In the next section, we look into the peasant marches in Andhra, which contributed immensely to the consolidation of class awareness.

Peasant Associations (Kisan Sabhas) and Peasant Marches in Andhra

During the Great Depression and its aftermath (1929–1939), the prices of agricultural products slumped, and this affected the cash income of peasants in Andhra. Peasants and agricultural labourers were the worst affected. Gradually, their inability to repay their debts produced complex forms of indebtedness and growing unrest. By 1940, peasant associations (*kisan sabhas*) were present in 11 of 12 Telugu-speaking districts in the erstwhile Madras Presidency and were popular in numerous villages. Peasant marches came to be one of the most popular ways to protest against growing agricultural unrest and economic exploitation; the ones in Andhra were said to be larger than the biggest in England.[7] Their demands included liquidation of agricultural indebtedness and substantial reduction of rent and revenue. Peasant associations viewed the *zamindari* class as their immediate exploiter in the social hierarchy and agitated against it. Between 1937 and 1939, they focused on anti-*zamindari* agitations over the issues of rent reduction, economic exploitation and ill-treatment. These agitations were held at various estates.[8] Agricultural labour unions were also organised to contest exploitation in the agriculture sector.

Agricultural Labour Unions

In organising agricultural labour unions, there seems to have been a clear shift in the focus of communists away from peasant associations. The Alaganipadu Agricultural Labour Union of Nellore is the first known agricultural labour union. Its central objectives were to standardise daily wages and annual salaries and to provide by means of legislation a minimum wage to agricultural labourers to facilitate a comfortable life.[9] During 1935–1937, agricultural labour unions organised several strikes in Guntur (under the leadership of J. Ramalingaiah),

74 *Ashok Kumar Mocherla*

Nellore, Krishna and West Godavari. They put forth a set of demands: wages should be doubled and paid by authorised means, advances should be interest-free, a two-hour lunch break should be allowed, twenty paid holidays per annum, sick leave and wages should not be docked if ill health prevents a labourer from working. Rich landlords and peasants strongly resisted these demands and at times broke the solidarity of unions at the village level. However, despite strong opposition from both the Congress and landlords, the Andhra communists persisted in organising agricultural labour unions. Between 1939 and 1944, the rural poor could not afford foodgrains or consumer goods; hoarding by merchants and the rich landed gentry raised the price of rice and paddy even further. Out of desperation, the rural poor, led by agricultural labour unions, resorted to looting rice mills, fire depots and cloth shops. In December 1942, it was reported that a crowd of 400 people in Guntur district looted grain shops and carried away rice and paddy. Nellore district also witnessed four such cases. There seems to have been a substantial rate of increase in crime, looting and housebreaking during this period.[10]

Hunger Marches in Andhra

During the Second World War, communists organised numerous hunger marches throughout Andhra. In May 1939, an estimated five thousand people participated in the first ever hunger march in Rajol *taluk* of East Godavari. In Narsapur *taluk* of West Godavari district, around ten thousand people staged a demonstration in front of the District Collector's office demanding work. Similar protests in other districts demanded employment, residential sites, a wasteland for cultivation and various reforms and amenities. The Governor of Madras worried over rising prices. There were reasons to believe that local communists instigated lootings and hunger marches; the government arrested several communist leaders and banned many agricultural labour unions.[11] Andhra communists organised labour protection leagues (LPL), and encouraged the production of popular literature through people's theatre and participated in the activity. This new art form of popular literature, modelled on folk traditions, was characterised by a new tone and tenor of literacy. The *karmika bhajanalu* (psalms of labour), which describe the hardships of workers and encouraged them to organise into unions to fight for their human rights, occupy a prominent place in the popular literature promoted by Andhra communists. Another prominent form of popular literacy was the Andhra Praja Natyamandali, in line with the Indian People's Theatre Association, which was largely seen as the epitome of people's expression of freedom, cultural progress and economic justice. These new platforms became significant avenues in developing class awareness among the rural masses. After the 1960s, the popularity of communism in Andhra started to fade away gradually, as did the fortunes of communists and socialist Congressmen. Through *kisan sabha*s, agricultural labour unions and hunger marches organised by the local communist leadership, that I have discussed here, the local communists made an attempt to sideline the real issues of caste and religion from public political articulations. Being indifferent to caste and religion in their political activism had cost them dearly and eventually weakened the discourse of class in Andhra Pradesh.

The Decline of Communism and Class Awareness

The coming of the INC party into power in Andhra Pradesh, as well as the political spectrum in the state, had acquired a different combination of caste, class and power relations that gradually left the communist activism/communism behind in the political contest. Many communist leaders joined the INC to pursue their own political and personal interests, which in turn weakened the communist party unit in Andhra. One of the most severe criticisms on the communist party in Andhra was regarding the social background of its leadership being overtly belonging to two dominant caste groups who are mostly landlords. The unconcealed presence of caste domination in the regional communist leadership by the Kamma and Reddy castes and the constant denial of caste being a predominant system of social stratification that determines patterns of social inequality amongst India had sent out inconsistent and dichotomous signals to its cadre. In other words, communists practiced the dichotomy of criticising caste politics, yet capitalising on the caste identity of its leadership. Examination of the political language used by communists of Andhra is invariably demanding and yet an exciting enterprise. By the late 1960s, as Sudipta Kaviraj rightly observes with regard to the contest of how radical socialist ideas translated into an Indian context, 'the most effective section of the Indian left became a party which was both impeccably Stalinist in its ideology and impeccably electoralist in its political practice' (2009: 176). One of the reasons for the gradual decline of the influence of communist ideology and activism on Indian politics is that even though Leftists were most deeply committed to an end of inequality in Indian society, they have been strangely indifferent to the primary form in which Indians experienced inequality in social life, that is, caste system. There is a strange absence of caste in their articulations of social inequality and power relations of India. Such articulations of inequality on the lines of the class eventually created a gap between the language of political ideas they promoted and caste realities experienced by its cadre in their social world (ibid.: 186).

76 Ashok Kumar Mocherla

It is evident in Marxist writings that class denotes the form of social stratification that is specific to modern capitalist economies and hence determined by their relation to mode of production. There is also a generic conception of class that does not view class as a historically regional form specific to European capitalism. Having said that, the conceptualisation of class in Indian context got translated into indigenous expressions and articulations that may not necessarily maintain correspondence with the conventional Marxist categorisations of class. In our present context, the concept of 'class' among communist Lutherans and the Mala of Dravidapuram by no means refers to the industrial working class; rather it denotes the agricultural labourers who are landless and survive primarily on daily wage labour. Therefore, political articulations of the class by the communist cadre/activism is mainly centred around narratives of labour exploitation, landlessness, politics of land ownership and feudal domination of landlords but oddly maintains a historical silence on caste and caste exploitation. This is where the dangers of articulating social inequality through class perspectives come into play when juxtaposed with the caste system, both today and historically. The translation of Marxism into Indian political scenario through articulations of class at the cost of caste seems to have not worked out quite the way communists have imagined it would. Occasionally, there were efforts to accommodate caste in communist articulations of class, but in terms of their presence, volume and influence on Andhra politics they are almost negligible.

This failure to attend to the issues of caste also showed its repercussions during a series of legislative assembly elections. The CPI suffered defeat in the assembly elections of Andhra held in 1955 despite having a huge cadre base which in course of time got eroded. Interestingly, the CPI contested for 169 seats out of the total 196 seats available against the INC that fielded candidates only in 142 seats. The INC managed to win 119 seats with 39.35 per cent of vote share, whereas the CPI won only 15 seats with 31.13 per cent of vote share.[12] On 1 November 1956, Andhra state was merged with Hyderabad state to form a single state called Andhra Pradesh under the States Reorganization Act of 1956. Subsequently, legislative assembly election was held in 1957 for 85 constituencies (20 two-member constituencies and 65 single-member constituencies) with a total of 105 seats. As per changing geopolitical dynamics, the communists of Andhra Pradesh contested elections under the banner of People's Democratic Front. It contested for 65 seats and managed to win only 22 seats. The INC managed to win the subsequent two legislative assembly elections of Andhra Pradesh held in 1962 and 1967, respectively, with a comfortable margin. In an interesting turn of events, Mr Damodaran Sanjivayya – a Dalit – became Chief

Minister of Andhra Pradesh from 1960 to 1962, a symbolic gesture, which marked a clear shift in lower caste vote base from the CPI to the INC.[13]

Subsequent erosion of the cadre base along with constant shifting loyalties of the local communist leadership further weakened the morale as well as the political future of CPI in Andhra Pradesh. In their attempt to consolidate the class-consciousness among the Telugus, communist ideology and activism failed to address the issue of caste that was pressing for many Dalits in their every-day struggles. Such willful negligence of caste in their political articulations by the local communist leadership and the Protestant missionaries' constant criticism of caste discrimination further weakened communist ideology and its chances of realising class-consciousness. As an unintended consequence, it, in turn, paved the way for new forms of caste consolidations and awareness that directly fed into the growth of Lutheranism among Dalits in Andhra Pradesh. Historical practices of caste, class and religion shaped the trajectory of religious conversion in coastal Andhra and converged in the contemporary religious practices of the Lutheran community in Dravidapuram. The next section deals with such convergences and makes a special reference to Lutheran religious celebrations. In their view, these are more than just religious celebrations.

A CONVERGENCE OF CASTE, CLASS AND RELIGION

The sociopolitical messages, motives and outcomes of religious celebrations at the level of both family and community are not confined to the domain of religion alone. In India, especially in rural India, religious celebrations are not quite separate from the domain of politics and so the actual consequences of religious celebrations on various social groups are more diverse than may appear. The scope of expected outcomes and unintended corresponding changes of religious celebrations may often not confine to the domain of religion. Therefore, the actual consequences of religious celebrations usually interact with and spill over to other domains of social life. In rural India, religious celebrations of any group closely correspond with local systems of power, social mobility, perceptions of social status and caste ranking. Chatterjee (1998: 282) rightly mentions that 'communities in post-colonial societies in India have come to be recognized as some of the most active agents of political practice'. The religious celebrations of Lutherans must be understood at two different levels. The first deals with the internal dynamics of the Mala with respect to their kinship groups. The second deals with caste politics at the village level by placing special emphasis on the collective strength of the Mala, issues related to changing social status and their claims for new social status. Religious celebrations are platforms for such kinship groups to demonstrate or reassert their strength. The Church facilitates all their

78 Ashok Kumar Mocherla

sociopolitical aspirations. Robinson (1998: 189) rightly points out in the context of southern Goa that 'the village church is at the center of relations of power and hierarchy'. Similarly, in Dravidapuram, the village Lutheran church is at the centre of both the Mala's village-level community politics and among the Mala themselves; it is rooted deeply in indigenous systems of social rank and, hence, its ceremonies and celebrations are important occasions to demonstrate kinship and individual rank as per changing social relations.

Demonstration of Political Ideologies on Religious Terrains

This section deals with divergent ways of demonstrating political ideologies on the religious terrain at the level of the village Lutheran community. As a greater number of people belonging to economically weaker sections follow Christianity in coastal Andhra, Christianity is viewed as the religion of the poor, and Christmas is the most popular festival of poor people, especially Dalits. The Malas of Dravidapuram celebrate Christmas collectively as a group and the Sangham[14] elders make sure that Ambedkar's statue is decorated well as part of the celebration.[15] The same decoration is continued until the first week of every January. This particular practice establishes that the Malas by no means neglect Ambedkar. Mala Lutherans strongly believe that religious celebrations are important occasions to demonstrate their political ideology in public; it is no surprise, then, that Jesus Christ and Ambedkar coexist in their symbolic world. It is clear from the ethnographic data that the Malas led the mass conversion to Christianity in this region in colonial India. They chose Christianity over Buddhism as it was the religion of the rulers and there was a substantial presence of western missionaries in the region.

As an organisation, the Lutheran church does not operate independent of caste and has never opposed the political leadership of Ambedkar for Lutherans. In the context of the religious practices of Syrian Christians and Paravas of southern Tamil Nadu, Bayly (1989: 453) mentions that religion cannot be situated in isolation; rather 'the domains of religion and politics have been inextricably intertwined'. In Dravidapuram, from the beginning, Lutheranism has gone hand in hand with Mala community politics, and Lutheran religious celebrations interact with several sociopolitical and economic aspects of both the Malas and other villagers. During Easter, many Lutherans pay tribute to their ancestors who were communists. On Easter Sunday, village Lutherans participate in the early morning worship service at the cemetery conducted in remembrance of Jesus Christ's victory over death. In preparation, Lutherans clean the cemetery and its surroundings, paint the gravestones white and place Christian religious symbols (the cross, the Bible and pictures of Jesus Christ) on them and also a few political symbols. In some cases, religious and political symbols coexist on a single gravestone. Most prominent among political symbols is the Communist Party of India (Marxist), or CPI (M), symbol.[16] Young people who decorate their ancestors' tombs make it a point to paint the gravestones every year. If their ancestors were communists, they paint the gravestones red or place the CPI (M) symbol at the centre, next to the image of Jesus Christ, or along with the Bible. Significantly, one can also see the political identity of communist Lutherans in the form of epitaphs that read: Comrade Mr John is resting in God's presence. However, among Lutherans, adherence to communism is not only demonstrated in death but in life as well.

The present-day communist Lutherans collectively view marriage ceremony as a rare and once-in-a-lifetime opportunity to demonstrate their political ideology, to foster a distinct identity of their own, which is different from other Lutherans, by way of choosing to go for what is called the 'party wedding' instead of 'church wedding'. Here the wording 'party' essentially refers to CPI. It is all about taking solemn vows of marriage in the auspicious presence of the communist party flag, local political leadership and fellow comrades. In fact, it is more than what meets the eye. The venue of the 'party wedding' is preferably the groom's residence. One needs to follow certain procedures before getting authorisation from the district secretary of the regional unit, CPI, who is authorised to conduct and oversee the 'party wedding' ceremony in that region. The eligibility criteria for 'party wedding' is clearly laid out: one must be an active member of the party locally, or personal involvement in party activities is necessary, or full-time staff working for the party or at least an evident supporter of party activities and political ideology.

Upon receiving the request from a family for 'party wedding', the village unit and divisional unit together provide comprehensive feedback to the district secretary on the family under consideration, over their degree of involvement in party activities locally and their overall political commitment towards communist ideology. In the event of positive feedback and favourable decision, the district secretary informs the same to the state committee members along with details of the wedding. Communists also take this as an opportunity to distinguish themselves from Hindu religious practices. The most important custom of a Hindu wedding ceremony is the tying of the *thali/mangalsutra* around the bride's neck (auspicious thread of goodwill and love, signifying the bond of marriage). In the party wedding, there is a strict policy of 'no Thali and no Priest'. Instead, what is required is the exchange of garland to each other in willingness to live an honest and responsible life, and to make genuine efforts/ contribution – materially and morally – towards the establishment of much envisaged 'classless society' in India. Even the marriage certificate issued by the

80 *Ashok Kumar Mocherla*

regional leadership categorically expresses such views in black and white undersigned by the newlywed as a constant reminder. Such epitaphs and marital practices show how political ideology and religious faith come together to offer unique symbolic meanings and a sense of belonging by way of retaining some aspects of their own past.

There seems to be an inseparable connection between the communist ideology and the growth of Lutheranism in Dravidapuram and among the Malas. This distinctive viewpoint offers us prominent historical insights on how local politics influenced religious discourse in the region. In the 1950s and 1960s, first-generation communists fought against the dominant caste and religious structures in Dravidapuram village and are respected by the Malas today. Communist activism generated caste consciousness among the Malas and, in an unintended consequence, contributed to the rapid growth of Christianity, that is, Lutheranism in our present context. Today, communism and Lutheranism coexist in Dravidapuram. All the communists among the Malas are Lutherans but not vice versa. The children and grandchildren of these first-generation communists remember their contribution and make sure to keep their ancestors' communist identity alive. But second-generation communists among the Malas today do not contribute to the ongoing Dalit movement against dominant caste structures, as they do not recognise caste as a fundamental category of social inequality in India. Even today, the second-generation communists hardly talk about questions of caste exploitation or discrimination despite their compelling significance since the local communist leadership project these issues as insignificant compared to political articulations of 'class' and 'class struggle' in Indian politics.

Therefore, the primacy of class over caste continues to be the most dominant pattern of communist political articulations adopted by Indian communists. That does not mean caste cease to exist among them. For the first-generation communists of Dravidapuram, dealing with caste discrimination and agriculture labour exploitation, had set the tone and tenor of their political activism. But interestingly, now the second-generation communists of Dravidapuram have clearly moved away from caste issues, giving more importance to class over other social categories. On the other hand, the Lutheran Christians who predominantly belong to Dalit social background engage themselves closely with the Dalit movement in Andhra Pradesh to deal with Dalit questions at the level of activism but continue to follow Christianity as their personal religion. It is to be noted here that not all the Lutheran Christians are communists, but all the communists are Lutherans. The second-generation communists, though small in number and follow Christianity (Lutheranism), feel uncomfortable with Dalit activists who speak the language of religion, caste and anti-caste politics without invoking the idea of class.

In more than one way, Dalit Lutheran Christians take the help of cultural resources to establish the Christian worldview amongst them. It is quite different from the Hindu worldview in many ways. For instance, Dalits themselves organise Christian rituals and celebrations in the village; if they were Hindus, they would have needed Brahmin priests. These Dalit Christians are not just followers and protagonists of Christianity but actual representatives in this region. In their struggle against caste structures in Andhra, the Lutheran church occupies centre stage in their politics and political activism. It is through and with the help of these religious festivals that Dalit Christians form and maintain their corporate identity.

CONCLUSION

Both caste and communist ideology continue to exist, in some form or the other, among Lutheran Christians of coastal Andhra in the absence of ritual justification (Roche 1984; Kooiman 1989; Mosse 1994). In other words, both caste and communist ideology actively present in their lived religion in the form of various social and political practices but their religious text does not support or provide justification for such practices. Lutheranism, although American in adoption, has largely been indigenised in practice. Conceptual tools, methodological techniques and theoretical frameworks that we prefer to study apart tend to merge and, to some extent, collapse boundaries in the context of Andhra Lutheran practices, which often shares a paradoxical relationship with their faith. Looking at the class–caste trajectory of religious conversion provides us nuanced/deeper insight into syncretic practices and lets us understand their meaning in context. In Dravidapuram, awareness – if not consciousness – of the class has certainly contributed to the consolidation of caste consciousness and in effect conversion to Christianity. The same class awareness could not sustain itself for long in the context of rather vividly expressed caste-based social relations in Andhra. Hence, class articulation had to take refuge in caste and religious terrains. Therefore, communist ideas and activism have undoubtedly prepared the ground for religious conversion. But it was not a simple journey from one religious faith to other. The conventional meaning of 'religious conversion' no longer captures the essence of Communist Lutheran practices with reference to their political ideology and caste politics.

Godroads captures the complexities of religious conversion in a highly diverse society like India. As Berger and Sahoo argue in the introduction, 'Godroads' – a metaphor to reflect on religious transformations and change – goes beyond one-dimensional movement towards or away from a god or religion and attempts to capture and accommodate diverse ideas and practices that have been (re)

82 *Ashok Kumar Mocherla*

shaping individual and group religious experiences. Similarly, religious and political ideas of communist Lutherans of Andhra gain contextually defined social meanings generated from their religious journey on the *Godroad* that does not denote a completed action or process rather a trajectory. The *Godroad* that communist Christians of Andhra are travelling right now speaks volumes about how the political ideology of a social group of yesteryear along with contemporary religious practices could produce, and in course of time strengthen, syncretic practices in the religious and political domain.

NOTES

1. Dravidapuram is a recognised major village panchayat bordering the Guntur and Krishna districts of Andhra Pradesh, south India. This region has historically been a bastion of communist ideology as well as Christian faith. In 2006 and 2007, I carried out ethnographic fieldwork in this village towards my doctoral dissertation. In 2015, I revisited Dravidapuram and gathered additional field data which I have used in this chapter. Dravidapuram is not the original name of this village; it is a pseudonym.

2. Originally, the word 'Dalit' meant oppressed, broken and crushed. In modern India, it refers to a diverse set of caste groups who shared the stigma of untouchability and are officially recognised as Scheduled Castes (SC). Their identity being Scheduled Castes is merely an administrate category used by the Indian government to undo the historical subjugation of these groups. On the other hand, the contemporary form of Dalit identity is truly an assertive one aimed to overcome their untouchable past.

3. In 1936, only 3 socialists were elected to the AICC and 23 to the APCC. By 1937, their strength went up, respectively, to 7 and 47.

4. *The Governor's Situation Report*, 2nd half of November 1937, clearly mentions the domination of communists in the APCSP. Their numerical strength stands at 3 in the working committee in 1934 but grew to 11 (out of 17) by 1937.

5. *Governor's Report*, 2nd half of April 1937, LJP/5/197; *Congress Socialist*, 5 June 1937.

6. *Congress Socialist*, 14 August 1937.

7. *National Front*, 24 April 1938.

8. Munagala, Venkatagiri, Khalipatnam, Challapalli, Guntupally, Talasamudram, Gampalagudem, Srikakulam, Visakhapatnam and Vizianagaram.

9. *Selections from Secret Files*, Andhra Pradesh State Archives, Hyderabad, p. 2584.

10. *Governor's Report*, 1st half of December 1942, LJP/5/205.

11. Ibid.; *Communist*, November 1940, p. 12.

12. Statistical Report on General Elections, 1955: To the Legislative Assembly of Andhra. The Election Commission of India.

13. Ibid.

14. Sangham is a customary body that represents their caste collective. It is nothing but a local expression and a successful replacement of caste *panchayat* that is meant to safeguard common interests of its caste group.

15. The statue of Dr B. R. Ambedkar is a symbol of their collective political assertion against caste discrimination and other forms of social inequality in this village. For them, Christmas celebration is no longer a personal religious matter but a community affair that actively interacts with local politics of caste and religion. The combination of these two aspects produced a fusion for the coexistence of Ambedkar and Jesus Christ in their politics. Hence, along with church, it is equally important for them to decorate the statue of Ambedkar on the occasion of Christmas.

16. Even though the strength of communist Christians is gradually declining, they take pride in the communist activism of their ancestors, the first-generation communists of this village, who fought against caste discrimination. Even today, Dravidapuram is considered a stronghold of communist ideology in this region. A few district-level office bearers of the CPI hail from here.

BIBLIOGRAPHY

Adapa, Satyanarayana. 1986. 'Rise and Growth of Left Movement in Andhra, 1934–1939.' *Social Scientist* 14(1): 34–47.

Aloysius, G. 1998. *Religion as Emancipatory Identity: A Buddhist Movement among the Tamils under Colonialism*. New Delhi: New Age International Publication.

Bauman, Chad. 2008. *Christian Identity and Dalit Religion in Hindu India, 1868–1947*. New York: Eerdmans Publishing.

Bayly, Susan. 1989. *Saints, Goddesses and Kings: Muslims and Christians in South Indian Society: 1700–1900*. Cambridge. Cambridge University Press.

Chatterjee, Partha.1998. *Possible India: Essays in Political Criticism*. New Delhi: Oxford University Press.

Dube, Saurabh. 1998. *Untouchable Pasts: Religion, Identity and Power among Central Indian Community: 1780–1950*. New York: State University of New York Press.

Forrester, B. Duncan. 1980. *Caste and Christianity: Attitudes and Policies on Caste of Anglo-Saxon Protestant Missionaries in India*. London: Curzon Press.

Ilaiah, Kancha. 1996. *Why I Am Not a Hindu: A Sudra Critique of Hindutva Philosophy, Culture, and Political Economy*. Kolkata: Samya Books.

Juergensmeyer, Mark. 1982. *Religion as Social Vision: The Movement against Untouchability in 20th Century Punjab*. Berkeley: California University Press.

Kaviraj, Sudipta. 2009. 'Marxism in Translation: Critical Reflections on Indian Radical Thought.' In *Political Judgement: Essays for John Dunn*, edited by Richard Bourke & Raymond Geuss, 172–200. Cambridge: Cambridge University Press.

84 Ashok Kumar Mocherla

Khan, Mumtaz Ali. 1983. *Mass-Conversions of Meenakshipuram: A Sociological Enquiry.* Chennai: The Christian Literature Society.

Kim, Sebastian C. H. 2003. *In Search of Identity: Debates on Religious Conversion in India.* New Delhi: Oxford University Press.

Kooiman, Dick. 1989. *Conversion and Social Inequality in India: The London Missionary Society in South Travancore.* New Delhi: Manohar Publications.

Mosse, David. 1994. 'Idioms of Subordination and Styles of Protest among Christian and Hindu Harijan castes in Tamil Nadu.' *Contributions to Indian Sociology* 28(1): 67–106.

Pickett, J. W. 1933. *Christian Mass Movements in India: A Study with Recommendations.* New York: The Abingdon Press.

Ramakrishna. V. 2012. 'Left Cultural Movement in Andhra Pradesh: 1930s to 1950s.' *Social Scientist* 40(1–2): 21–30.

Robinson, Rowena. 1998. *Conversion, Continuity and Change: A Lived Christianity in Southern Goa.* New Delhi: Sage Publications.

Robinson, Rowena and Sathianathan Clarke, eds. 2003. *Religious Conversion in India: Modes, Motivations, and Meanings.* New Delhi: Oxford University Press.

Roche, P. A. 1984. *Fishermen of the Coromandel: A Social Study of the Paravas of the Coromandel.* New Delhi: Manohar Publications.

Venkatarangaiya, Mamidipudi. 1965. *Freedom Movement in Andhra.* Vol. 4. Hyderabad: Andhra Pradesh State Committee Appointed for the Compilation of a History of the Freedom Struggle in Andhra Pradesh (Andhra) 1965–74.

Visvanathan, Susan. 1999. *Christians of Kerala: History, Belief and Ritual among the Yakoba.* New Delhi: Oxford University Press.

Webster, C. John. 1999. *Religion and Dalit Liberation: An Examination of Perspectives.* New Delhi: Manohar Publications.

Wilson, Kothapalli. 1982. *The Twice Alienated: Culture of Dalit Christians.* Hyderabad: Book links.

Zelliot, Eleanor.1969. 'Dr. Ambedkar and the Mahar Movement.' Ph.D. Diss., University of Pennsylvania.

3
Religious Conversion as Ethical Transformation
A Study of Islamic Reformism in Rural West Bengal
Fernande W. Pool

Masiruddin Khadim[1] was a relatively wealthy businessman in his early thirties who lived in Joygram, a village in West Bengal. He was a vocal proponent of the Deobandi reformist Islam and an occasional participant of the Tablighi Jamaat (TJ). One day I asked Masiruddin to tell me why he converted to reformist Islam and joined TJ. Masiruddin narrated that he was an ordinary boy, Muslim by name but did not give Islam much thought. He had been living the 'lifestyle', and although he was a tad embarrassed about his previously un-Islamic lifestyle, he showed me pictures to testify with a big smile on his face. Like many rural boys aspiring for urban masculinity, he had his pictures taken in a studio, wearing a transparent shirt, tight jeans, large sunglasses, and a clean-shaven chin.

At some point in his twenties, Masiruddin started on a quest for ethical guidance: despite how exciting his life was, he felt a moral void. Inspired by his Hindu friends he started to read the Hindu scriptures, and afterwards the Christian Bible. But he came to the realisation that the Quran, directly given by Allah, provided the most complete system for life, both scientific and ethical, and that he had to follow the 'right path' and immerse himself in Islam. Masiruddin spent four months at the global headquarters of TJ in Delhi and changed his lifestyle: he started wearing a white *kurta* and an untrimmed beard under a shaven upper lip, prayed five times a day, fasted during Ramadan and attended all important local Islamic congregations.

Masiruddin firmly believed that a better society begins with becoming a better person individually. For this reason, he spoke very highly of the Islamic Mission Schools. The most important and distinguishing aspect of these private boarding schools – the first of which emerged in Howrah in 1986 – is not its curriculum but its strict regimen and discipline, and the seamless inculcation of an Islamic disposition within the larger project of the making of the modern Muslim middle class.[2] For Masiruddin, it is important that the mission education would not only benefit the Muslims, but the entire country.

86   Fernande W. Pool

The Muslims lag behind, and thanks to the mission schools they will 'rise up' (*piche theke uṭhe yāy*). India is a democratic country, and I am a part of this country, so if I study better, if I can do a government job (*cākri*) well, then that's good for all of India. Muslims can't lag behind.

Masiruddin's narrative is but one example of conversion among Muslims in rural Bengal, which nonetheless exemplifies a trend. The Muslims in Joygram were previously non-denominational Islamic: they would follow the five pillars of Islam, but most would not identify with a particular school of thought apart from being Sunni as opposed to Shia; their practices would include syncretic local practices of worship (including Hindu and Shiite practices, such as shrine worship); and everyday habits and aesthetics were for the most part determined by Bengali culture rather than by Islamic norms or prescriptions. As in many Bengali villages, towns and cities, there is currently a wave of conversion to the reformist Islam of the Deoband, most clearly expressed in rhetoric, shifting aesthetics and practices, and active participation in the proselytising movement, the TJ.

The TJ and the Deoband are among the numerous South Asian Islamic reformist movements that originated around the turn of the nineteenth century in interaction with British colonialism, Christian missionaries and Hindu reformism (see, for example, Ahmad 2009; Hansen 1999; Metcalf 1989; van der Veer 2001). The Deobandi school of thought originates in the Darul Uloom Deoband Islamic seminary in northern India, founded in 1867 (Metcalf 1989). Its doctrine is spread mainly through its vastly expanding network of madrasas (Gupta 2009) and through the network of the TJ. The TJ is a transnational voluntary movement of lay preachers, whose activities are characterised as 'Deobandi *Da'wa*' (call towards god) (Masud 2000b: xlvii; see also Metcalf 1993; Sikand 2002), The presence of the TJ in West Bengal has been limited until recent decades but is rapidly growing and is crucial for the spread of Deobandi reformism. The imams in Joygram are nearly all educated at the Darul Uloom Deoband, but most of the TJ members in Joygram that I spoke to did not have an Islamic education at a madrasa; they had learned the Deobandi normativity from the frequent gatherings organised by the TJ.

Islamic reformism is usually studied within the context of the anthropology of Islam, and defined as 'projects whose specific focus is the bringing into line of religious beliefs and practices with the core foundations of Islam, by avoiding and purging out innovation, accretion and the intrusion of "local custom"' (Osella and Osella, 2008a: 247–248). However, this definition, and studying these projects within the anthropology of Islam, risks a kind of 'Islamic exceptionalism' (Osella and Osella 2008b: 320). In this chapter, I therefore look at reformism in the theoretical context of the anthropology of conversion. Analytical and theoretical approaches in the study of conversion give us new insights into the motivations for turning to Islamic reformism. In turn, I suggest that looking at Islamic reformism as a mode of conversion demonstrates that it may be useful to suspend 'religion' as an analytical category in the study of conversion, in favour of ethics.

Drawing on long-term ethnographic fieldwork,[3] I demonstrate that conversion to Islamic reformism in Joygram is part of a larger process of social renewal and moral regeneration deeply embedded in both local theories of personhood and the contemporary sociopolitical context. These insights are generated by proposing an alternative analysis of conversion, which takes conversion as a diagnostic of freedom and constraint. It concludes by arguing that if scholars analyse and theorise conversion in terms of 'religious' change, they not only fail to understand the full spectrum of factors involved in conversion, but they also reproduce the same exclusionary mechanisms as modern modes of categorisation and similarly constrain the potential for ethical transformation and modern aspirations among ordinary people seeking to live in a coherent ethical framework.

CONVERSION: A DIAGNOSTIC OF FREEDOM AND CONSTRAINT

Classic psychological accounts would consider conversion a change of beliefs inspired by an inner experience (James 1929 [1902]; Nock 1933). These accounts often reflect personal narratives of conversion but fail to take into account that conversion in the last centuries has been deeply embedded in a process of modernisation. This is certainly true for conversion to Islamic reformism. Although some scholarly work reproduces the common perception expressed in popular discourse and Western media that Islam, and in particular reformist Islam, is the 'antimodern antithesis' to liberal, secular modernity (Deeb 2006: 4; see, for example, Iqtidar 2011; Mahmood 2009), it has been emphasised that reformist Islam is inherently modern: in dialogue with modernity, Muslims have developed a 'heightened self-consciousness' of Islam as a religious 'system' (Eickelman and Piscatori 1996: 39) which demonstrates an increased rationality; an end to the authority of the past; a new emphasis on human will; growing individualism (Robinson 2008: 261–276); and an emphasis on modern tropes of development and progress (Osella and Osella 2008a).

A variety of approaches in the anthropology of conversion, encapsulated in what Gooren (2014) calls the 'modernity paradigm', have attempted to explain this kind of 'conversion to modernity' (van der Veer 1996a), with a focus on conversion to Christianity in particular and to world religions more broadly. A classic Weberian approach would consider conversion to world religions, which

88 *Fernande W. Pool*

display a higher level of rationalisation, as an integral part of the teleological modernisation thesis which postulates an inevitable process of rationalisation and 'disenchantment' (see Hefner 1993a; Meyer 1996; and Berger and Sahoo's introduction to this volume). Horton's (1971; 1975a; 1975b) 'intellectualist' approach argues traditional African religions are not less rational, but smaller in scope, and conversion to macrocosmic world religions allows people to live meaningfully in a changed, globalised world. This model still displays a Weberian bias towards 'meaning' and has been criticised for being Eurocentric (Asad 1993), reductionist (Fisher 1985) and for considering beliefs 'as instruments of explanation and control of actual time-space events' (Hefner 1993b: 102).

Instead, Hefner argues that in addition to phenomenological accounts, material conditions, historical processes and 'political mechanisms ... need to be integrated into a larger theory of conversion' (1993b: 119). Indeed, Islam has rationalised and modernised from within as a result of mass education, new media technologies and increased literacy (Eickelman 1992; Eickelman and Anderson 1999; Starrett 1998). The contributions in van der Veer (1996a) emphasise a variety of modern structural arrangements impacting motivations for as well as modalities of conversion: the complex political projects of colonisers and missionary societies, the formation of nation-states and questions of citizenship, to name a few (cf. Austin-Broos 2003; Viswanathan 1998). Moreover, conversions can result in 'multiple modernities' (Eisenstadt 2000; cf. Hefner 1998) due to a variety of political contexts, the encounter between coloniser and colonised, and the effect of impartial or syncretic conversions on the nature of modernity itself (van der Veer 1996b). In this vein, Islam modernised as a result of structural conditions yet, in the form of Islamic reformism, developed an alternative mode of modernity that offers resistance to Western cultural and political domination (see, for example, Iqtidar 2011; Janson 2013; Noor 2014; Mahmood 2005).

More structural accounts of conversion demonstrate that the onset of modernity is a crucial causal factor but risk losing sight of the ways in which local frameworks of understanding and agency exert influence on the particular mode of conversion: we still need to know why, under a given set of conditions, people choose to convert, and why people choose to convert to Islamic reformism specifically. 'Godroads' are processes interjected with events, often initiated by wilful actors in perhaps unexpected locations (see Berger and Sahoo, introduction to this volume). In the study of conversion, the typically anthropological challenge is 'to strike a balance between the two extremes of intellectual voluntarism and structural determinism' (Hefner 1993a: 23), that is, to try and determine where agency/freedom ends and structure/power begins. Power and freedom, however, are not easily located and hermeneutically related, as ideological power seems

Religious Conversion as Ethical Transformation **89**

increasingly hegemonic and is implicated in changing epistemic structures that themselves make possible new forms of agency and control (Asad 1996: 265).

I therefore propose an analytical move inspired by Abu-Lughod's (1990) work on resistance. She suggests using 'resistance as a *diagnostic* of power' (1990: 42): by analysing shifting modes of resistance, she diagnoses shifting hegemonic ideas of being and sociality. Similarly, I suggest that, instead of taking power as a given framework within which to analyse conversion, I take a particular mode of conversion as an ethnographic fact from which to analyse power and hegemonic ideas of freedom and constraint. This analysis is not limited to those cases where conversion is an obvious mode of resistance (see, for example, Dirks 1996; Viswanathan 1996) or protest (Berger and Sahoo, this volume); any mode of conversion can give us insights into structures of power and knowledge because of the intricate politics and disruptive nature of conversion. Taking conversion as a diagnostic of power allows me to foreground salient vernacular categories and reveal hegemonic ideas of being, sociality and governance present both in vernacular theories of personhood and in postcolonial structures of power.

The structure of the chapter reflects the analytical method. The first section of the chapter looks at narratives of conversion in its context. It seeks to answer the question why Muslims convert, why they embark on 'Godroads', looking at immediate motivations and consequences. As such, this section provides the ethnographic context, but it does more than only that. The immediate motivations and consequences demonstrate that a phenomenological account of conversion is not satisfactory, and that we need to take into account material conditions. A sense of moral responsibility for the corrupted social environment and structural inequality drives the cultivation of the moral self, which is by implication the cultivation of a moral society. Importantly, the aspiration for ethical renewal is not limited to the religious self but includes the creation of the modern subject and inclusion in the secular democracy. These aspirations transgress a religious/secular binary. Instead, they are embedded in *dharma*; *dharma* denotes an ethics of justice and order, rather than religion, as it is usually translated. Hence, this conversion is about ethical renewal rather than about religion as such; however, it does not explain why Bengali Muslims choose *this* mode of conversion that *does* seem to be religious. Why, for example, would they not choose a Marxist form of rebellion against the establishment?[4] This is particularly curious, given that claims for inclusion in the modern nation-state on the basis of an Islamic modernity are not considered legitimate in the Indian state, and, as such, Islamic reformism is counterproductive to its aims. We therefore need to take the particular mode of conversion as an indicator of hegemonic ideas that constrain the possibilities for ethical renewal. Exploring the question why Muslims choose

90 Fernande W. Pool

to convert to Islamic reformism leads me to explore two sets of hegemonic ethical relationships and power structures.

First, the emphasis on *dharma* among my interlocutors leads me to an exploration of the constraints and freedoms offered by vernacular theories of personhood and ethics. Among Muslims, *dharma*, and the ethical autonomy offered within this ethical framework, is essentialised in Muslim moral personhood, and they are therefore only free to revive *dharma* within the constraints of the Muslim moral community (*jāti*). So, whereas conversion to a more moral self and society is not about Islam per se, an emphasis on *dharma* is expressed in conversion within Islam. This is an important observation because although (post)colonial power is omnipresent in accounts of conversion (see Hefner 1993; van der Veer 1996a), much less attention has been paid to the freedoms and constraints afforded by indigenous ideas of the self and sociality. For instance, Asad's (1996) understanding of modernity's power seems at times entirely hegemonic, but by taking conversion as the analytical starting point for revealing hegemonic ideas I have been able to reveal vernacular ideas of freedom. Vernacular and modern ideas are hermeneutically related rather than in a zero-sum game.

Second, the observation that the emphasis on *dharma* is directed at holistic ethical renewal whilst being expressed in religious renewal leads me to an exploration of the constraints and freedoms offered by modern forms of categorisation and governance. This exploration demonstrates that the colonial invention of religious communities, and the ambiguous secularism of postcolonial India, offers the freedom of ethical renewal only within the constraints of the depoliticised 'cultural' community. Moreover, while my interlocutors are attempting to resist the hegemonic secularity, they are already implicated within it and end up reproducing the exclusionary mechanisms of the secular state by converting to Islamic reformism.

Taken together, these deeper and broader insights challenge the religious change narrative and offer possibilities of a different way of understanding conversion as ethical renewal. One of the key consequences of my analytical framework is that it suspends the need for religion as an analytical category and instead allows religion to emerge as a hegemonic cultural category. As Asad (1993; 2003) points out, our understanding of religion is itself a product of modernity and the concomitant project of secularisation. My interlocutors' enactment of their aspirations for holistic renewal and modern citizenship in the form of *religious* conversion is a reflection of their implication in secular modernity, which at once enables and constrains their mode of conversion.

In fact, it is not only unhelpful but also morally incorrect to consider conversion here as religious change. Whereas my informants convert to reformism as an act of both religious and secular self-cultivation, to call this mode of conversion 'religious change' is to limit their freedom and constrain them within the religious paradigm that has in fact already significantly constrained the modalities of conversion available to them.

CONTEXTUALISING CONVERSION

The narratives of conversion in Joygram, as exemplified by Masiruddin's story, often picture conversion as a 'leap of faith', a sudden change of heart and mind inspired by reading the Hindu, Christian and Islamic scriptures. Another convert in the village, Faizul, was inspired by a mystical experience (the appearance of an angel), alike the experiences that inspired St Paul and Augustine (James 1929 [1902]), to leave behind his sinful life as a Bollywood dancer and become a Deobandi proselytiser. The aspect that unites the stories of Masiruddin and Faizul, and of most other converts in Joygram, is a sense of moral failure or void, in which conversion arrives as a 'turning point that enables one to become a full person' (Hansen 2009: 14). Conversion plays a similar role in Tablighis' narratives in Gambia (Janson 2013) or Pentecostal testimonies in the United States (Luhrmann 2012).

The above are, however, phenomenological descriptions of the process as 'intellectual voluntarism'. I suggest that the sense of moral failure and the consequential leap of faith in these individual stories, and particularly their striking recurrence across Joygram, can only be properly understood if placed within the political context, and here we need to combine the psychocultural approach that favours agency with an acknowledgement of material conditions and historical processes.

MORAL FAILURE AND THE RECOVERY OF DIGNITY

Across India, the 'rural masses', and in particular the minorities, suffer from various forms of structural violence. West Bengal in particular has a history of oppressive communist rule and is currently tainted by corrupt realpolitik, vast economic inequality and widespread political violence. A coalition of communist parties called the Left Front has ruled West Bengal for 34 years, until 2011. Politics had over the years successfully permeated every aspect of life, and the current party in power, the Trinamul Congress (TMC), appears to have furthered the politiciation of Bengali society. Joygrami men and women would not cease to comment on the moral bankruptcy they experienced in their environment, and there was a constantly lingering sense of impending chaos. It was generally thought that politicians were involved with the accumulation of private wealth

92 *Fernande W. Pool*

and criminal activities and very little with bringing development to those who need it. The Muslims in particular faced discrimination and a lack of access to governmental institutions and opportunities and political representation (Sachar Committee 2006), while the Hindu *bhadralok* (gentlefolk) formed the intellectual and political elite ever since colonial times. Partly as a result of centuries of bigotry towards Muslims, partly as a result of lower levels of education and employment, Muslims were often considered 'dumb', uncivilised and prone to criminal activity. This was a perspective expressed not only by non-Muslims but equally adopted by Muslims themselves in a narrative of moral responsibility and failure.

In an essay on the 'moral and spiritual striving in the everyday', particularly regarding the physical proximity of Muslims and Hindus, Das (2010) observes that Hindus located themselves in 'a kind of natural history of morality' when explaining the ethical impossibility of their actions with reference to *kaliyuga* (time of moral decline). By contrast, Muslims took an active stance of moral responsibility for the time of *fitna* (equally meaning moral decline): 'the sense that the time of *fitna* was their own creation imbued their actions with a greater sense of moral disquiet, if not failure' (Das 2010: 242). The sense of personal moral failure, 'humiliation' (Sahlins 2005; see Berger and Sahoo, introduction to this volume) and responsibility for Muslim suffering among Joygrami Muslims inspired the idea that a better society would start with improving oneself.

The traction of this discourse is obvious if we listen to Anisul, who was himself not a TJ participant or particularly pious in everyday life, but slowly started identifying himself with Deobandi Islam. For him, politics meant trouble and violence, and he did not like it a bit. He particularly did not believe that politics was the way to a more just society. 'If you want to do good, and want a better society, then you first have to become a better person yourself, then the society will improve as well. That's what the [Tablighi] Jamaat people say.' Clearly, the sense of moral failure and individual responsibility did not only come from an antipathy to the violence in one's environment, but also because of one's own involvement. Politics is trouble, the economy is vicious; but when corruption has seeped into every corner of the politicised society, engagements with the immoral environment are inevitable. Joygrami Muslims used to blame themselves and other Muslims for engaging in violent party politics and failing to progress in education and employment. It was, at least in part, the responsibility of the Muslims themselves that the *bhadralok* (Hindu 'gentlefolk') still rules West Bengal, and that they suffer from exclusion. This narrative always concludes that Bengali Muslims have adopted a 'backward' culture and need to be reminded of the ethics and the ritual practices of Islam. Humiliation, caused by mechanisms of desire catalysed by capitalism and Western modernism, can inspire

Religious Conversion as Ethical Transformation **93**

abandonment of religion and culture, or the adverse – indigenisation (Sahlins 2005; see Berger and Sahoo, introduction to this volume). Among Joygrami Muslims, humiliation inspires, on the one hand, the rejection of what came to be seen as a backward culture and, on the other hand, the active improvement of the self and of religion from within.

The sense of moral failure was strongly related to a geographical moral hierarchy. Although scholars reject the idea of 'Great' and 'Little' traditions and centres and peripheries in world religions, this is how reformist Muslims in Joygram themselves perceived their situation. West Bengal was the periphery, far removed from the 'real Islam' in the centre of the Muslim world (Mecca) or the centre of the TJ (Delhi) and areas closer to the centre in geography and practice. Masiruddin and other Tablighis are stirred when talking about Uttar Pradesh (northern India): 'It looks like an Islamic place'; Muslims wear Islamic dress; the women are all in *purdah*; and the Islamic rules are obeyed. In Uttar Pradesh, the Deoband madrasa was founded, which instructs and spreads the 'real Islam' (*saṭhik Islām*). Whereas in West Bengal, Muslims have 'hinduised' and forgotten Islam because they used to lack access to madrasas and the TJ.

The sense of marginalisation, within India and within the Muslim world, and the involvement with morally degrading political and economic practices, has disenfranchised Muslims from their moral dignity and ethical autonomy. The TJ offers the opportunity for the personal construction of an ethical narrative and offers spaces of equality and solidarity that break down hierarchies associated with class or caste, wealth or descent. All Muslims, and not only those who have access to the *bhadralok* spaces of education and 'civilisation', have access to the potential to reform and transcend themselves, above their older 'inferior' self. As such, conversion to Islamic reformism fits perfectly within the idea of conversion as a 'civilising mission' not unlike the great reform movement in Europe from the fourteenth century (Taylor 2007) or worldwide conversions to Christianity in the context of colonialism (see Asad 2003; Hefner 1993; van der Veer 1996a). Importantly, as in other civilising missions, the cultivation of a pious self is not the ultimate end: it is only the first step in civilising society as a whole.

CULTIVATING MODERN CIVILITY

This last observation requires me to complicate the picture. First, I looked at the phenomenological differences one may observe in Joygram. I then demonstrated that material conditions (structural violence and inequality) are drives for the ethical cultivation of the self. However, I introduce another element: central to the reformist project of my interlocutors is the cultivation of the *modern* self, and the civilisation of society as a whole.

94 Fernande W. Pool

Joygramis were eager to be respected citizens of Indian democracy. Again, they took a moral responsibility for the image of the 'bad' Muslim: the Muslim whose allegiance to the Indian nation-state could never be entirely trusted, and who would fail to understand the secular and liberal values of the Indian democracy. Faizul would repeatedly emphasise that Muslims are not all terrorists, and with his white-starched Islamic dress, a symbol of cleanliness, wanted to prove the opposite. Moreover, Joygrami reformists wanted to demonstrate that Islam is not anathema to secularism. Secularity is an ethical disposition (see Asad 2003); in the Indian case, secularity denotes the value of equality of all Indian citizens irrespective of religious affiliation or identity. Part of the perceived moral degradation in society was the lack of secularity, which had degraded to mere vote-bank politics. As Masiruddin exclaimed, 'Secularism is great! But ... secularism isn't happening.' Muslims were among the victims of the lack of a proper implementation of secular policy. Taking responsibility for this political failure, they aimed to demonstrate that they deserved to be treated with equal respect, as a good secular citizen, and to imbue secularism with revived ethical content. To be a good secular citizen would denote a disposition of respect towards religious others as well as a willingness to abide by constitutional law and contribute equally to the Indian democracy. These were some of the key values expressed by Deobandi reformists in Joygram.

For Masiruddin, as for other converts in Joygram, Deobandi reformism offered the ethical content, aesthetics and status to cultivate himself as a moral secular citizen, who abides by the law, lives peacefully with others, and contributes to the democracy by educating himself and his son. For him, as for the other converts, the Islamic Mission School, which would aim to inculcate the Islamic piety and discipline associated with Islamic reformism as well as high quality modern education, would be the best education for becoming a respectable Indian citizen.

However, the reformist aesthetics and practices of Deobandi Islam and Islamic Mission Schools raised more suspicion rather than less, were associated with violent extremism rather than peace, and risked further alienating the Muslim from the Indian nation. As a result, many Muslims in Joygram found themselves in 'an impossible double-bind: faced with a choice between being charged as "bad Muslims" if they ignore the call to reform or as "bad Indians" if they choose to follow reform' (Osella and Osella 2008a: 251).

Nonetheless, the conversion to Islamic reformism was intended to overcome this opposition, as Islamic reformism became the expression of a revived *dharma*, which is a holistic ethics of order and justice. Moral failure and social degradation were the signs that there was a lack of *dharma*, and in turn evoked an emphasis on *dharma* in every aspect of life. The civilising mission was, as such, an individual spiritual project, a transformation in practices and beliefs, but also a collective political project, a transformation of society. For Joygrami converts, these were not two separate, but embedded processes. In order to understand why Islamic reformism became the expression of a revived *dharma*, I move into the analysis of conversion as a diagnostic of freedom and constraint. Why did Muslims choose to convert to Islamic reformism if the aims were broader than cultivating piety? What were the hegemonic ideas limiting this choice?

FREEDOM AND CONSTRAINT IN LOCAL THEORIES OF BEING AND SOCIALITY

The preceding section explains that conversion was motivated by a perception of social moral degradation and a sense of individual moral failure. Moral degradation and failure were considered due to a lack of *dharma* (ethics). *Dharma* is best understood as an all-encompassing, holistic ethics of justice and order. The Islamic *dharma* is one particular expression of this ethics, as is the Hindu *dharma*, or the Christian *dharma*. As I argue in detail elsewhere (Pool 2016), the Islamic *dharma* is both a processual, embodied Aristotelian virtue ethics and a macrocosmic ideal, and includes the Islamic normativity. This section discusses the Joygrami combination of Islamic and South Asian ideas of personhood and ethics. In this vernacular theory, there is no human being before the related person with *dharma*. Furthermore, due to local conceptualisations of personhood, the 'human person' with *dharma* is essentialised within a particular religious community (*jāti*). Therefore, holistic ethical transformation of conversion in Joygram took place *within* this religious community, that is, within Islam.

The category 'person' is a social construction with normative implications, varying in time and place. In South Asian ideology, the 'person' is a category constructed out of the exchange of bio-moral substances (see, for example, Bear 2007; Carsten 2000; Inden and Nicholas 1977; Marriott 1989). Due to the indivisibility of biological and moral substances, there is a fluid overlap between the biological construction of the human being and the social, moral construction of a person; the one does not precede the other, and humanity and personhood are not separate categories of understanding. I refer to the 'human person' to connote this conflation of the biological and the moral in personhood, and because it best reflects the vernacular term *mānuṣ*. When people in Joygram talk about raising a child, the language used is significant: they say 'mānuṣ karā', which has the double meaning of 'humanising', and 'making a person'. The human person is generated out of ritualised and everyday exchanges within networks of relations.

96 *Fernande W. Pool*

In Joygrami Muslim theology, the fundamental, sacred exchange behind the generation and regeneration of humanity/society (these categories are fundamentally the same) is the exchange with Allah: the gift of life from Allah, reciprocated with faith and submission to Allah. This cosmogonic idea is the first step in the essentialisation of the Muslim identity in the human person: one is already embedded in a moral relationship – and thus has a social identity (Muslim) – from the moment of conceiving life.

Thus, for my Muslim interlocutors, it would be only subsequent to the sacred exchange with Allah that one would enter the perpetual process of becoming through exchanges within social networks. These were networks of kin, but also neighbours, and foremost, the *jāti*. *Jāti* is the most important category through which to classify the social world in Joygram. Although conventionally translated as caste, *jāti* can carry manifold, historically produced meanings (Bear 2007: 287). Among Muslim Joygramis, *jāti* was commonly used to denote an entire religious community, and the pivotal social group to which my informants claimed to belong is the Muslim *jāti*.

The sacred exchange with Allah first places one within the Muslim *jāti*, and the *jāti* identity is subsequently essentialised within the human person, from the ritualised incorporation in the *jāti* at birth through to life cycle and funerary rituals. This may seem like a very essentialised conception of communal identity – but one has to understand this ideological essentialisation as a tendency to counter the perceived inherent instability of personhood: all bio-moral exchanges are precarious as they continually affect what kind of human person one is becoming. Moreover, rather than that the biological human precedes the socialised moral person, as it is commonly thought in Western ideology, here bio-moral forms of 'relatedness' (Carsten 2000) precede the bio-moral human person. Since relatedness is most fundamentally with the *jāti*, one is inevitably generated as a human person of a certain *jāti* – *jāti* membership does not come after one is a completed human being but allows the human person to become. To change as a human being, then, means to change as a human person with a particular *jāti* identity.

There is another important element in the vernacular theory of ethics that further constrains conversion to take place within Islam. The bio-moral substances that enable human persons to live according to the Islamic *dharma* – that is, the embodied ethical potential – are *jñān*, knowledge or 'practical judgement', and *imān*, an embodied habitus of faith. The capability to develop judgement and faith is first given by Allah (on the condition of reciprocal divine submission) and consequently engendered at the same time and inevitably during the process of 'becoming human' or 'making a person'. That is, the potential for *dharma* stands not in diachronic but in symbiotic relation to humanity/

personhood: just as much as humanity makes *dharma* possible, *dharma* makes humanity possible. Due to the essentialisation of the *jāti* identity within the human person, *dharma* necessarily has a *jāti* identity, even though every human person inevitably has a *dharma*.

Jñān is where ethical autonomy is located in the ethno-theology of Joygrami Muslims: Allah has given humans the capacity for *jñān* (practical judgement) in order to choose between the wrong and the right path. This element of freedom that emerges from divine submission is central to the reform project. The idea that Allah has given Muslims the capacity for virtuous judgement means that Muslims have a responsibility for their own choices and for the consequences of their judgement – and thus for their own moral failure. In the preceding section, we have seen that the sense of moral failure was one of the driving motivations for conversion. Again, because this ethical freedom afforded by *jñān* is located in *dharma*, which in turn is constrained by a particular *jāti* identity, ethical agency (the choice for conversion) is enacted from within the *jāti* identity. We can see here how agency and structure are hermeneutically related in local theories of personhood and ethics.

I cannot expound in more detail here the ways in which personhood is generated from within a *jāti* and how a person is inevitably and viscerally endowed with *dharma*. For the purpose of this chapter, what matters is that in the ethical imagination of my informants there is no conceivable self that exists before sociality organised by *jāti* and *dharma*. If there is no ideological distinction between the human and the moral person, the corollary is that there is no distinction between humanity and society. It follows that *dharma* is essential for ethical personhood, and for humanity itself. Having said that, to become a better human person means by implication to become a better Muslim, and becoming a better person implies creating a better society. It is only from within the particular positionality within a *jāti* and with a *dharma* that ethical self-fashioning and social renewal can take place to begin with. Significantly, a revival of *dharma* can be Islamic, yet it can also be Hindu, depending on the moral community (*jāti*) from which the ethical potential is generated. Only with *dharma* one can avoid living like an animal in a politically corrupt world.

Taking the observed mode of conversion as a diagnostic of hegemonic ideas, I have revealed that *jāti* is the element constraining the possible modalities of conversion, because ethical freedom (*jñān*) is located in *dharma*, and any particular *dharma* is constrained within a *jāti*. So, despite the fact that an emphasis on *dharma* denotes broader ethical and social transformations, the 'civilising mission' is a mode of intrareligious conversion. However, these theories of personhood and ethics do not stand in isolation from the wider social and political environment. The onset of modernity has in fact played a significant role in the essentialisation of the *jāti* and, in particular, in the essentialisation of *dharma* as related to a particular *jāti*. Moreover, the question remains: why was intrareligious conversion expressed in this particular kind of Islamic reformism? What did the TJ have to offer? Why did it take place now? The next sections will address these questions within the context of the postcolonial Indian state.

THE CONSTRAINTS OF MODERN CATEGORISATION

This section reveals the role that modern categorisations play upon modalities of conversion, by taking conversion as a diagnostic of freedom and constraint in the broader political environment.

As mentioned, Islamic reformism offered an opportunity for ethical self-cultivation in order to become a better Muslim and by implication a better modern citizen; these are embedded ideals of moral personhood. As one of my interlocutors pointed out to me, one needs *dharma* in order to obey the law – *dharma* is not an alternative to the law, but a sine qua non. Indeed, as *dharma* is a holistic ethics rather than a religion, it incorporates non-Islamic values and ideologies, such as liberal values, secularism and democracy. As *dharma* contains all ethical potential, secularity is a feature of *dharma*. So, reformism, as a particular expression of ethical transformation in India, is rooted in local theories of personhood and morality, yet it is simultaneously a creative response to the ambiguous modernity produced in the Indian nation-state, as modernity offers new constraints and freedoms for ethical transformation (see Asad 1996).

The onset of modernity in India, emerging from the colonial encounter, forced lived experience into predetermined dichotomies and frameworks. Chief amongst these is the translation of *dharma* to religion and the 'invention' of religious communities, clearly bounded and hierarchically ordered, set apart from the secular political society (Dirks 2001; van der Veer 2001). However, even *ideologically*, postcolonial India never displayed a seamless separation of the sacred and the secular: the morally neutral sphere of what increasingly became seen as 'dirty' politics was to gain value from the apolitical sphere of religion rendered a benign 'culture' (Hansen 1999). In the postcolonial ideology, the depoliticised 'cultural' communities are meant to be the harbourers of timeless, sacred morality and the source of public ethics. This also means that the 'irrational masses' are confined to their communities, supposedly unspoiled by politics, and denied the aspirations for modern personhood, which is the exclusive right of the enlightened members of the 'rational' political society. 'Religion' is the source of public ethics only insofar the latter consists of timeless cultural values, not claims to modern rights and duties. Moreover, as communities are hierarchically ordered, the Hindu religion/culture is valued higher than any other religion/culture.

In other words, the *jāti* is essentialised not only from within, to counter the inherent instability of the bio-moral substances that constitute the person, but also from without, as a cultural community to be regulated by political society. *Dharma* has become limited to the timeless cultural values and private religious practices of a particular community, losing its potential as a resource for broader social transformation. As such, the hegemonic ideological power of postcolonial secularism constraints possible modes of ethical transformation.

THE VERNACULARISATION OF MODERN CATEGORIES

To complicate the matter, the ambiguous binary of secular politics/religious culture has vernacularised within local frameworks of understanding. Islamic reformism can be considered a technology of creating the modern moral subject, in Joygram and elsewhere (see, for example, Janson 2013), only if this does not imply that before reformism they were stuck in tradition. My Muslim interlocutors most likely converted to Islam in the sixteenth and seveneenth centuries (Eaton 1996) and were subjected to colonial rule and incorporation in the modern nation-state in subsequent centuries. As mentioned in the introduction, these elements have been considered key to the 'conversion to modernities' (van der Veer 1996a). Hence, rather than this conversion to Islamic reformism being the initial creation of the modern subject, these Muslims were already operating within a framework of modernity. Modern categories have vernacularised in their ethical imaginaries. Their own ambivalence about the modern categories they operated with, in conjunction with vernacular categories of understanding, reflects the complex ways in which hegemonic powers shaped their personal and social self-understanding.

I recall a conversation with Fuaduddin, a Deobandi *maulānā*, and his brother Wasim. They said that taking money from the poor is not politics; it is *party*. Or, they corrected themselves, it is *kunīti*, a term more often used to describe the actual 'dirty' practice of politics. Fuaduddin and Wasim explained that '*kunīti* means bad work, it means they do the opposite of good politics'. They went on to describe what good, wise politics would be like (for instance, providing good education for all children and providing clean drinking water). Yet when I asked whether doing these good works would be like doing *dharma*, they resolutely rejected this idea. 'Politics is one thing, *dharma* another' (*rāj'nīti ālādā, dharma ālādā*), says Wasim, and Fuaduddin exclaimed: 'That's not *dharma*! That's politics!' (*aiṭā dharma nay! aiṭā rāj'nīti!*).

100 *Fernande W. Pool*

In this conversation, Fuaduddin and Wasim considered politics and *dharma* to be separately delineated realms of society. Similarly, Ruud observed that politics in his fieldsite in West Bengal was generally considered to be about worldly pursuits (*artha*): 'politics is about power and not morality' (2001: 134). This implies that people had become familiar with a legal model of society where politics and *dharma* are declared separate domains. The paradoxical role of the law in colonial power incited 'the fundamental reordering of epistemic constructions of social reality' (Dirks 1986: 309) – politics had become an amoral, 'dirty' realm 'increasingly adrift from its moral moorings in the religious realm of *dharma*' (Parry 2000: 30).

Nevertheless, the narrative of moral decay incited a dismay with this epistemic reordering. Politics was increasingly considered dirty *because* it was supposedly set apart from *dharma*. That a conception of politics without *dharma* was problematic is clear from the following conversation I had with Basir, a local TMC leader. Relating *dharma* to politics, Basir explicitly referred to politics as serving people, a practice embedded in *dharma* as an ethics of care. One day he lashed out at the local Communist Party of India (Marxist), or CPI(M), leader, talking to me in a conspiratorial whisper. 'He is a very bad man. He is a communist, right, so he doesn't have a god, he is an atheist. If you don't have a god, you don't have any values either, so how can you do good politics?' 'But is there not some separation between politics [*rāj'nīti*] and *dharma*?' I asked. 'Yes, we have that separation as well … it has become like that', he said a little flustered. 'Yet, doing politics is automatically doing *dharma*. Politics is taking care of people (*sebā karā*), isn't it? And that is *dharma*. And everything comes from god above [*uparoyālā*], so it wouldn't be right to do politics without a god.'

Basir explicitly relocated the source of virtuous politics in *dharma*. This does not imply that Basir favoured the Muslim *jāti* on the basis of his Islamic *dharma*, but that his political action was infused with the ethics of *dharma*. For example, Basir was most preoccupied with Adivasis as, in Joygram, they suffered most from structural inequality, and because other politicians failed to demonstrate solidarity with Adivasis. In Basir's perspective, the political work of an atheist politician would not display the values of equality and solidarity, as the values in themselves are *dharma*. Importantly, the communist politician Basir talked about was Muslim; he favoured a politician with *dharma* (whether Hindu, Muslim or otherwise) over a Muslim politician who had forsaken *dharma* in his greed for power and money.

The critique of the modern separation of spheres emerges from the particular political context of West Bengal, where the communist regime actively sidelined *dharma* in favour of a class ideology. For Basir, as for the majority of Joygramis, the moral bankruptcy of the communist regime in West Bengal proved that a politics devoid of *dharma* would lead to pervasive immorality in politics and in society. So *dharma* needed to be revived not only in individual belief in worship, but also to provide moral content to political practice. It is only after the hegemonic power of the communist regime dwindled, in the early 2000s, that a new freedom emerged to critique communist political practice for its lack of *dharma*. It is no surprise, therefore, that Joygrami converts tended to identify with the political party that defeated the communists, the TMC.

But whereas Basir was slowly converting to Deoband reformism, and was considering joining the TJ, so as to be able to do more ethical (and secular) politics and distinguish himself from the unethical communists, his increasingly Muslim aesthetics and performance made him increasingly illegitimate in the secular political sphere. He was thoroughly caught in the double-bind of being either a bad politician from his own perspective, or a bad politician from the perspective of the supposedly enlightened, secular (and Hindu) political elite.

Basir's complex position shows that whereas conversion to Islamic reformism was in part a manifestation of secular ethics and modern personhood, this was an illegitimate manifestation in the Indian political landscape as *dharma* is ideologically reduced to a depoliticised religion rather than a holistic ethics. This brings me to my final point, which will be addressed in the next section: vernacular theories of personhood and (vernacularised) modern categorisation together constrain the aspirations for ethical transformation to take a form that is eventually counterproductive to its aims.

CONSEQUENCES OF CONVERSION

In this final section I look at some of the consequences of modern governance for the particular Deobandi expression of Islamic reformism, and at some of the consequences of conversion to Deobandi reformism for Muslims.

The official doctrine of the TJ is apolitical (Ali 2003; Metcalf 2003; Reetz 2006) and the TJ and the Deoband focus on moral regeneration and education within the community and do not usually engage in any political rhetoric. This doctrine is reflected in scholarly analysis, which portrays the TJ as reflecting political 'quietism' (Moosa 2000: 218; cf. Kepel 1997). At first face, this seems an accurate reflection, as TJ participants in Joygram preferred staying away from involvement in politics. Wahed, Masiruddin's brother and fervent TJ proselytiser, could at times become enthusiastic about the political party of Siddiqullah Chowdhuri Saheb (the All India United Democratic Front, or AIUDF), but when I asked why he did not join the party himself, he answered, 'I do Jamaat': he attempted to create 'good people', and leave the politics to others.

102 *Fernande W. Pool*

However, such an analysis pictures TJ's apolitical practice as a free choice and fails to grasp that the TJ is constraint to exercise 'the kind of subjectivity that a secular culture authorizes' (Mahmood 2006: 328). Muslims in India do not have much choice but to limit their creative subjectivity to apolitical individual reform. Islamic organisations have public legitimacy only as 'benign', 'cultural-religious' organisations, and 'the discourse of politics must obey the tacit rhetorical rules of generality and vagueness: to encourage morality in society at large, to criticize selfishness in public life, to deplore moral decay and divisive tendencies' (Hansen 2000: 259; cf. Metcalf 1989).

But in Joygram, the TJ did not remain within the limits of quietist cultural organisation. The revived *dharma* of the community underpinned rational demands to be included in the civilised citizenry. Although Hansen argues that the TJ is ultimately inward looking (2000: 264), I suggest that the TJ was actually intended to function as a vehicle for the outward looking aspiration to cultivate modern civility and only came to reproduce the bifurcated framework of 'dirty' politics and purified Islam only because of its limited space of navigation.

There are two interrelated consequences of the constraints enacting upon conversion. First, I have argued that the moral regeneration of the individual and the community should eventually drive a more encompassing reform of the entire society. If *dharma* denotes an ethics of order and justice in all aspects of life, economic and political activities automatically would become embedded in *dharma*. But if *dharma* is limited to the space of religion, a revival of *dharma* by implication means that religion becomes an all-encompassing category. Indeed, in the reformist project, Islam is a total way of life, and comes to epistemologically occupy all that is *dharma*. Different aspects of life become associated with sacred propositions (see Rappaport 1999), and as such 'religious cosmological order expands its domains to encompass secular or mundane and social cosmologies' (el-Aswad 2012: 13). Joygrami Muslims converted to Islamic reformism to offer a challenge to an ordering of modern society into sacred and secular spaces, where secular politics and a market economy were disembedded from the religious realm. But because Muslims' ethical aspirations were confined within the religious realm, religion expanded to embed the secular within.

Second, and hermeneutically related to the first point, conversion to Islamic reformism ultimately reinforced the exclusionary mechanisms of Indian secularism. Although reformist aesthetics and moral practice were intended to drive holistic ethical renewal, it looks to the (Hindu, secular) outsider that Deobandi reformists were simply reinforcing their Muslim identity and become 'more Muslim'. So, due to the limited, depoliticised space for navigation of Muslims reified in a bounded premodern community, they reinforced the community boundaries and the suspicion of Muslims as the disloyal, religious antithesis of India's secular liberalism. This is particularly the case because, as mentioned, communities are hierarchically ordered, and the Muslim community already had a less legitimate space in the Indian democracy. Islamic reformism may further alienate Muslims from inclusion in the nation-state.

CONCLUSION

In this chapter, I have suggested an analysis that takes conversion as a diagnostic of hegemonic powers and of freedom and constraint. I have demonstrated that not only material conditions and historical processes, but also vernacular theories and modern epistemic structures offer the particular forms of freedom and constraint that together shape the mode of conversion, the Godroads, of Muslims in Joygram.

I suggested at the outset that conversion is better conceptualised as ethical transformation than as religious change. The reasons for this reconceptualisation are, first, because there are a plethora of non-religious factors, motivations and consequences involved with conversion that should be taken into account in any analysis of conversion. Ethics is better able to encapsulate all these aspects. Second, and most important, religion itself is a normative cultural category that constrains the very processes we are studying. Indeed, the ethical transitions in Joygram entail political aspirations of embedding ideologically separated spheres of life in a *dharma* of justice and order that defies any binary oppositions of religious/secular, rational/irrational, and so on.

I suggest that other modes of conversion found in other places in the world may equally be expressions of desires for holistic ethical renewal but are equally constrained within the religious framework. To call this conversion a mode of religious change, we, scholars, are equally curtailing the aspirations of modern personhood by the religious/secular binary structure of our theoretical frameworks. We are therefore not honouring the aspirations of our interlocutors and continue to deny them the holistic ethical life world they desire.

NOTES

1. All names, including place names, are pseudonyms, except for the names of well-known public figures (for example, Siddiqullah Chowdhury Saheb) and well-known places (for example, Delhi).

2. The Islamic Mission School in Howrah was founded under the name Al Ameen Mission School, which now has 32 branches across West Bengal. In Joygram, a branch of a similar institution, the Al Hilal Mission School, was opened in 2013. Al Ameen and

104 *Fernande W. Pool*

Al Hilal Mission Schools are each managed by a board of private members, usually middle-class Muslim men from Kolkata. The schools follow the curriculum of the West Bengal Board of Secondary Education complemented with a minimum of Islamic subjects (see also Gupta 2009: 126–166).

3. I conducted fieldwork in Joygram from October 2011 until September 2013.

4. This is not a randomly chosen alternative: West Bengal has been a communist state for over three decades, until 2011.

BIBLIOGRAPHY

Abu-Lughod, L. 1990. 'The Romance of Resistance: Tracing Transformations of Power through Bedouin Women.' *American Ethnologist* 17(1): 41–55.

Ahmad, I. 2009. *Islamism and Democracy in India: The Transformation of Jamaat-e-Islami.* Princeton: Princeton University Press.

Ali, J. 2003. 'Islamic Revivalism: The Case of the Tablighi Jamaat.' *Journal of Muslim Minority Affairs* 23(1): 173–181.

Asad, T. 1993. *Genealogies of Religion: Discipline and Reasons of Power in Christianity and Islam.* Baltimore: Johns Hopkins University Press.

———. 1996. 'Comments on conversion.' In *Conversion to Modernities: The Globalization of Christianity*, edited by P. van der Veer, 263–274. New York: Routledge.

———. 2003. *Formations of the Secular: Christianity, Islam, Modernity.* Stanford: Stanford University Press.

Austin-Broos, D. 2003. 'The Anthropology of Conversion: An Introduction'. In *The Anthropology of Religious Conversion*, edited by A. Buckser and S. D. Glazier, 1–13. Lanham: Rowman & Littlefield Publishers, Inc.

Bear, L. 2007. *Lines of the Nation: Indian Railway Workers, Bureaucracy, and the Intimate Historical Self.* New York: Columbia University Press.

Buckser, A. and S. D. Glazier, eds. 2003. *The Anthropology of Religious Conversion.* Lanham: Rowman & Littlefield Publishers, Inc.

Carsten, J. 2000. 'Introduction: Cultures of Relatedness.' In *Cultures of Relatedness: New Approaches to the Study of Kinship*, edited by J. Carsten, 1–36. Cambridge: Cambridge University Press.

Das, V. 2010. 'Moral and Spiritual Striving in the Everyday: To Be a Muslim in Contemporary India.' In *Ethical life in South Asia*, edited by A. Pandian and A. Daud, 232–252. Bloomington: Indiana University Press.

Deeb, L. 2006. *An Enchanted Modern: Gender and Public Piety in Shi'i Lebanon.* Princeton: Princeton University Press.

Dirks, N. B. 1986. 'From Little King to Landlord: Property, Law, and the Gift under the Madras Permanent Settlement.' *Comparative Studies in Society and History* 28(2): 307–333.

Religious Conversion as Ethical Transformation **105**

———. 1996. 'The Conversion of Caste: Location, Translation, and Appropriation.' In *Conversion to Modernities: The Globalization of Christianity*, edited by P. van der Veer, 115–136. New York: Routledge.

———. 2001. *Castes of Mind: Colonialism and the Making of Modern India.* Princeton: Princeton University Press.

Eaton, R. 1996. *The Rise of Islam and the Bengal Frontier, 1204–1760.* Berkeley: University of California Press.

Eickelman, D. F. 1992. 'Mass Higher Education and the Religious Imagination in Contemporary Arab Societies.' *American Ethnologist* 19(4): 643–655.

Eickelman, D. F. and J. W. Anderson, eds. 1999. *New Media in the Muslim World: The Emerging Public Sphere.* Bloomington: Indiana University Press.

Eickelman, D. F. and J. Piscatori. 1996. *Muslim Politics.* Princeton: Princeton University Press.

Eisenstadt, S. N. 2000. 'Multiple Modernities.' *Daedalus* 129(1): 1–29.

el-Aswad, El-Sayed. 2012. *Muslim Worldviews and Everyday Lives.* Lanham, MD: AltaMira Press.

Fischer, H. J. 1985. 'The Juggernaut's Apologia: Conversion to Islam in Black Africa.' *Africa: Journal of the International African Institute* 55(2): 153–173.

Gooren, H. 2014. 'Anthropology of Religious Conversion.' In *The Oxford Handbook of Religious Conversion*, edited by L. R. Rambo and C. E. Farhadian. Oxford: Oxford University Press.

Gupta, N. 2009. *Reading with Allah: Madrasas in West Bengal.* Delhi: Routledge.

Hansen, T. B. 1999. *The Saffron Wave: Democracy and Hindu Nationalism in Modern India.* Princeton: Princeton University Press.

———. 2000. 'Predicaments of Secularism: Muslim Identities and Politics in Mumbai.' *Journal of the Royal Anthropological Institute* 6(2): 255–272.

———. 2009. *Cool Passion: The Political Theology of Conviction.* Amsterdam: Amsterdam University Press.

Hefner, R. W., ed. 1993. *Conversion to Christianity: Historical and Anthropological Perspectives on a Great Transformation.* Berkeley: University of California Press.

———. 1993a. 'Introduction: World building and the Rationality of Conversion.' In *Conversion to Christianity: Historical and Anthropological Perspectives on a Great Transformation*, edited by R. W. Hefner, 3–45. Berkeley: University of California Press.

———. 1993b. 'Of Faith and Commitment: Christian Conversion in Modern Java.' In *Conversion to Christianity: Historical and Anthropological Perspectives on a Great Transformation*, edited by R. W. Hefner, 99–135. Berkeley: University of California Press.

———. 1998. 'Multiple Modernities: Christianity, Islam, and Hinduism in a Globalizing Age.' *Annual Review of Anthropology* 27: 83–104.

Horton, R. 1971. 'African Conversion.' *Africa: Journal of the International African Institute* 41(2): 85–108.

———. 1975a. 'On the Rationality of Conversion. Part I.' *Africa: Journal of the international African Institute* 45(3): 219–235.

———. 1975b. 'On the Rationality of Conversion. Part II.' *Africa: Journal of the international African Institute* 45(4): 373–399.

Inden, R. B. and R. W. Nicholas. 1977. *Kinship in Bengali Culture.* Chicago: University of Chicago Press.

Iqtidar, H. 2011. *Secularizing Islamists?* Chicago: University of Chicago Press.

James, W. 1929 [1902]. *The Varieties of Religious Experience: A Study in Human Nature.* New York: Penguin Books.

Janson, M. 2013. *Islam, Youth and Modernity in the Gambia: The Tablighi Jama'at.* New York: Cambridge University Press.

Kepel, G. 1997. *Allah in the West: Islamic Movements in America and Europe* Stanford: Stanford University Press.

Luhrmann, T. M. 2012. *When God Talks Back: Understanding the American Evangelical Relationship with God.* New York: Vintage Press.

Mahmood, S. 2005. *Politics of Piety: The Islamic Revival and the Feminist Subject.* Princeton: Princeton University Press.

———. 2006. 'Secularism, Hermeneutics, and Empire: The Politics of Islamic Reformation.' *Public Culture* 18(2): 323.

———. 2009. 'Religious Reason and Secular Affect: An Incommensurable Divide?' *Critical Inquiry* 35(4): 836–862.

Marriott, M. 1989. 'Constructing an Indian Ethnosociology.' *Contributions to Indian Sociology* 23(1): 1–39.

Masud, M. K., ed. 2000a. *Travellers in Faith: Studies of the Tablīghī Jamā'at as a Transnational Islamic Movement for Faith Renewal.* Leiden: Brill.

———. (2000b). 'The Growth and Development of the Tablighi Jama'at in India.' In *Travellers in Faith: Studies of the Tablīghī Jamā'at as a Transnational Islamic Movement for Faith Renewal,* edited by M. K. Masud, 3–43. Leiden: Brill

Metcalf, B. D. 1989. *Islamic Revival in British India. Deoband: 1860–1900.* Delhi: Oxford University Press.

———. 1993. 'Living Hadīth in the Tablīghī Jama'āt.' *The Journal of Asian Studies* 52(3): 584–608.

———. 2003. 'Travellers' Tales in the Tablighi Jamaat.' *The Annals of the American Academy of Political and Social Science* 588(1): 136–148.

Meyer, B. 1996. 'Modernity and Enchantment: The Image of the Devil in Popular African Christianity.' In *Conversion to Modernities: The Globalization of* Christianity, P. van der Veer, 199–230. New York: Routledge.

Religious Conversion as Ethical Transformation 107

Moosa, E. 2000. 'Worlds "Apart": Tablighi Jama'at in South Africa under Apartheid, 1963–1993.' In *Travellers in Faith: Studies of the Tablighi Jama'at as Transnational Islamic Movement for Faith Renewal*, edited by M. K. Masud, 206–221. Leiden: Brill.

Nock, A. D. 1933. *Conversion: The Old and the New in Religion from Alexander the Great to Augustine of Hippo*. Oxford: Oxford University Press.

Noor, F. A. 2014. 'The Tablighi Jamaat in West Papua, Indonesia: The Impact of a Lay Missionary Movement in a Plural Multi-religious and Multi-Ethnic Setting.' In *Proselytizing and the Limits of Religious Pluralism in Contemporary Asia*, edited by J. Finucane and R. Michael Feener, Vol. 4, 65–80. Kuala Lumpur: ARI Springer Asia Series.

Osella, F.and C. Osella. 2008a. 'Introduction: Islamic Reformism in South Asia.' *Modern Asian Studies* 42(2–3): 247–257.

———. 2008b. 'Islamism and Social Reform in Kerala, South India.' *Modern Asian Studies* 42(2–3): 317–346.

Parry, J. 2000. '"The Crisis of Corruption' and 'The Idea of India': A Worm's Eye View.' In *Morals of Legitimacy: Between Agency and System*, edited by I. Pardo, Vol. 12, 27–41. New York: Berghahn Books.

Pool, F. W. 2016. 'The Ethical life of Muslims in Secular India: Islamic Reformism in West Bengal.' PhD thesis, London School of Economics and Political Science.

Rappaport, R. A. 1999. *Ritual and Religion in the Making of Humanity*. New York: Cambridge University Press.

Reetz, D. 2006. 'Sûfî Spirituality Fires Reformist Zeal: The Tablîghî Jamâ'at in Today's India and Pakistan.' *Archives de Sciences Sociales des Religions* 135(3): 33–51.

Robinson, F. 2008. 'Islamic Reform and Modernities in South Asia.' *Modern Asian Studies* 42(2–3): 259–281.

Ruud, A. E. (2001). 'Talking Dirty about Politics: A View from a Bengali village.' In *The Everyday State and Society in Modern India*, edited by V. Bénéï and C. J. Fuller, 115–136. London: C. Hurst & Co.

Sikand, Y. 2002. *The Origins and Development of the Tablighi Jama'at, 1920–2000: A Cross Country Comparative Study*. Telangana: Orient BlackSwan.

Sachar Committee. 2006. *Sachar Committee Report: Social, Economic and Educational Status of the Muslim Community in India*. New Delhi: Government of India, Cabinet Secretariat, Report of the Prime Minister's High Level Committee. Available at: http://www.minorityaffairs.gov.in/sachar

Starrett, G. 1998. *Putting Islam to Work: Education, Politics, and Religious Transformation in Egypt*. Berkeley: University of California Press.

Taylor, C. 2007. *A Secular Age*. Cambridge: Harvard University Press.

van der Veer, P., ed. 1996a. *Conversion to Modernities: The Globalization of Christianity*. New York: Routledge.

108 *Fernande W. Pool*

————. 1996b. 'Introduction.' In *Conversion to Modernities: The Globalization of Christianity*, edited by P. Van der Veer, 1–22. New York: Routledge.

————. 2001. *Imperial Encounters: Religion and Modernity in India and Britain*. Princeton: Princeton University Press.

Viswanathan, G. 1996. 'Religious Conversion and the Politics of Dissent.' In *Conversion to Modernities: The Globalization of Christianity*, edited by P. van der Veer, 89–114. New York: Routledge.

————. 1998. *Outside the Fold: Conversion, Modernity, and Belief*. Princeton: Princeton University Press.

4

Conversion versus Unity

The Basel Mission among the Badaga on the Nilgiri Plateau, 1845–1915

Frank Heidemann

BADAGA GODROADS

Samuel Mulley grew up in the small village of Kairben, and in 1858 he became the first Badaga convert to Christianity in the Eastern Nilgiri Hills of south India. Philipp Mulley is his great-grandson and a retired pastor of the Church of South India. He recalls that one day when he walked into his forefather's village, elders showed him the tracts of lands that once belonged to his family. They told him that all this could have belonged to him if his forebear had not converted. Generally, there remains a clear memory of property and village affiliation. My Badaga friends usually add the village name of Christian Badagas when we talk about individuals in the small town of Kotagiri. The successors of the early converts explicitly call themselves 'Christian Badagas' and not 'Badaga Christians' to place the emphasis on the religious orientation (Karl 1950: 15). They live around the first mission stations in Ketti, founded in 1845, and Kotagiri, opened in 1867, in other Badaga villages such as Kalhatti, Kannerimukku, Milithen, Thandanadu, and Tuneri, and in the two British hill stations, Coonoor and Ootacamund. Today, the Christian Badagas number roughly three thousand persons. In this chapter, I confine my analysis to the spread of the gospel before Indian Independence in 1947 and focus on the first Badaga conversions of the Basel Mission (BM).

The Badaga were – and are – peasants and constituted the largest precolonial group in the Nilgiri region. Friedrich Metz (1864), one of the early missionaries of the BM, estimated that they numbered 12,000 and that each of the neighbouring Toda, Kota and Kurumba counted a few hundred. The Badaga lived in more than 300 small villages, each often inhabited by 20 or 30 people. In the twentieth century, they became successful farmers, cultivated 'European vegetables' and turned to tea production after Independence. The number of villages has hardly increased, but Badaga demographic growth is impressive. From a mere 2,207 in 1812, the population grew to 222,117 in 2001 (Hockings 2012b: 244). Irrespective of this dramatic change, today the social and religious

110   *Frank Heidemann*

systems in the villages, kinship rules and legal and political orders refer clearly to sociopolitical formations that we recognise from early ethnographic accounts (Metz 1864).

The main sources for my investigation into the first Badaga conversions of the BM are letters, memoranda and annual reports of the Basel Evangelical Mission Society (JEMB; RBEM), chapters in ethnographic descriptions (Hockings 1980: 187–193; 2013: 252–262 passim) and entries in the *Encyclopaedia of the Nilgiri Hills* (Hockings 2012a). All translations from German sources into English are my own. In Chicago, Paul Hockings offered me generous access to his private collection of books, manuscripts and field notes. The interpretations of these sources are informed by my fieldwork in the Kotagiri *taluk* of the Nilgiris district between 1988 and 2016 (Heidemann 2006), which was enriched by many years of interactions and fruitful conversations with Philipp Mulley. The present relationship of Christian Badagas to Hindus, local forms of identity conflict, and the maintenance of ethnic boundaries informed my view on the written sources on this subject. I begin with a description of the long and slow process that led to the first conversions in the nineteenth century and the Christian Badaga revolt against the transfer of the BM to the Wesleyan Church after the outbreak of the First World War, then I move into my fieldwork-based interpretations.

My examination of the early Badaga conversions focuses on two themes. First, I demonstrate that the narratives of Christian conversion were informed by a Brahmanical view on Hinduism and followed a master narrative of Brahmin conversion to Christianity, which appeared in print before the first Badaga was converted. Second, I probe the motives of the converts and then investigate the reasons for the vehement resistance exhibited by their relatives and co-villagers. The reason mission work was pursued for 13 years without a single conversion and only a very small number of baptisms in the following years seems no less relevant than the motivations of converts. Here, my broader argument is that identity politics and not opposition to a religious orientation drove Badaga resistance. The opposition to conversion was based on strong Badaga village polities and their communal policies. It is also commonplace among the Badaga that ethnic boundaries are dynamic and fluid and therefore contested (Barth 1969). The argument for a politicised reading of conversion has roots in my academic interest in political anthropology, but also in the impressive correspondence between the enraged evangelical congregations in the Nilgiri and the BM in Switzerland between 1915 and 1920.

Broadly speaking, the history of Badaga converts shows parallels to the changes in Badaga Hindu society, which transformed itself from a peasant community with a subsistence economy to a modern farming community with an

Conversion versus Unity   **111**

emphasis of diversification and a trend towards formal education. '[T]he two dimensions of conversion to modernities' (Berger and Sahoo in this volume) are part of the motivation to convert. Christian Badagas sent their children to missionary schools, introduced new agricultural technologies and adapted aspects of European public culture, including dress and mode of transport. At the same time, they opted for an individualistic lifestyle and valued ideas of enlightenment, personal freedom and brotherhood.[1] Badaga 'Godroads' headed towards modernity, right from the beginning.

CONVERSIONS IN THE BASEL EVANGELICAL MISSION REPORTS

Badaga Firstlings: The Baptism of Abraham, Joseph and Their Families, 1858–1859

'The First of the Badagas' (Der Erstling der Badagas) was the headline of the BM annual report on the development in the Nilgiri Hills of southern India in summer 1858. Based on the letter from the missionary Carl Mörike, a report with the following content was printed (JEMB 1858: 92–98): After a more than half a year of contact and talk about the gospel, a Badaga man has expressed the strong wish to be baptised. Haleya, in local standards a wealthy man of 40 years, married and the father of eight children, worked as a head supervisor at Hulikal Estate. Mörike went to the plantation owner and asked for four days of leave for Haleya to make more time for the mental and spiritual preparation required for his conversion. Haleya experienced a long period of disruption because his family and fellow Badaga objected to his decision. His wife, children and relatives were in tears and tried to stop his journey to Christianity. But he threw away his *lingam* (an amulet worn around the neck and sign of the Lingayat, the highest status group among the Badaga) and cut his long hair. On 31 January 1858, he was baptised and given the name Abraham. A few Badagas witnessed the ceremony, but many ran away for fear of evil spirits. The newly baptised Abraham then had dinner with the missionaries and, in so doing, 'thereby finally separated from [his] caste'[2] (JEMB 1958: 93).

Eight days later, Mörike accompanied Abraham to his village, but most of the villagers kept out of the way. His wife had called their children into the house and forbade them from seeing their father. Hiding in the house, she cried and shouted at the missionary. Mörike had learned Badagu, a language exclusively spoken by the Badaga, and wrote about this event (in German) to the head office in Basel. To give an impression of this scene, I have translated the German version of her words into English. She exclaimed that her husband had 'thrown away his family', was 'no longer the father of her children', that he had 'made

112 *Frank Heidemann*

them orphans' and that he 'is dead now' (JEMB 1958: 95).[3] A few days later, Mörike returned to the village and talked to Abraham's wife. She got up, and like a demon swung an axe while she spoke:

> As a young girl he [Abraham] took me from my parents' house, I gave birth to seven [*sic*] children, but he should not think that they should be his children. They should not follow him; rather I kill them and kill myself.... He is an outcaste ... [and] has no love for them or me.... He asked for the forgiveness of sins [by converting to Christianity], but he committed even larger sins [by converting]. (JEMB 1958: 96)[4]

The villagers banned him from the community and assumed that he was likely to die in solitude in the forest. Outsiders would not greet Abraham's co-villagers, and women who had married into his village were taken back to their native places. Abraham continued his work as a supervisor and found temporary accommodation on the plantation, but his fellow Badagas refused to eat with him or to stay in the same room with him. After three months, oil was poured on troubled waters: his relatives calmed and he began to visit his village (JEMB 1958: 96–98).

The second convert was Joseph, formerly Manja, who worked on the same plantation and had accompanied Abraham on his visits to the mission since 1857. He was baptised on Easter in 1858 and faced similar problems. His separation from his family lasted three months. The BM continued teaching in Badaga villages and offered special lessons to his eldest daughters. The two girls learned the gospel and the confession of faith by heart. Abraham's younger children underwent confirmation classes, and his wife gave up her resistance to Christianity. The annual reports of the BM describe in great detail the events of 25 September 1859. Abraham, his wife and eight children aged 6 months to 14 years came walking from Tschogatorre to Ketti, the father carrying the youngest in his arms, and were all baptised. One week later, Joseph's sister, age 22 and not in good health, was baptised in the same church (JEMB 1859: 108–110). In the following years, no further conversion took place near Ketti.

The Beginning of Mission Work in Local Context

Among the first missionaries were trained linguists and excellent ethnographic observers. In 1845 Gottfried Weigle came to the Hills after he had revised the Kannada version of the Bible in Mangalore. Michael Bühler collected Badaga ballads and 'One Hundred Badaga Proverbs'. The latter became the foundation of Paul Hockings' *Badaga Proverbs, Prayers, Omens and Curses* (1988). In 1849 Johann Friedrich Metz joined the mission in the Nilgiris and wrote the first comprehensive account of the Nilgiri tribes, published in German in 1857 and translated into English seven years later (1864). No doubt these missionaries were close to the Badaga people, they learned Badagu, studied their rituals and sent detailed reports to the headquarters in Basel. Tireless, they walked from one village to the next often suffering from ill health in the cold climate, slept in cowsheds or simple shelters and preached on village grounds.

In his first years, Weigle vaccinated about seven hundred children and adults, and spread the gospel in Badaga villages. 'He was in some instances listened to with attention, but more frequently has been received with great indifference, owning probably to the general inactivity of mind prevalent among the inhabitants of this secluded district, rather than to any positive aversion against the truth that he had to proclaim' (RBEM 1847: 48). In the following years, the missionaries reported on localised conflicts between the mission and Badaga villagers, which were expressed in social rejection or resulted in the closing of village schools. Often it was on the second visit to a village, when they were 'received in a less friendly way'. 'The enmity of *one* Gauda [Badaga headman] soon infects others, and we often observed the dread of losing caste, etc. spreading from one village to another' (RBEM 1849: 44–45, emphasis in original). More successful than the preaching of the gospel was the spread of literacy. In a few villages, villagers objected to the schooling, and one school had to move three times within six months, because the headmen had been 'jealous'. Catholic missions concentrated on urban areas, but the BM had a monopoly on village education. The first Badaga school, founded in 1845 in Ketti, became the first Badaga high school in 1901.

The beginning of missionary work coincided with other groundbreaking developments in the Hills. The first Englishmen entered the plateau on a hunting expedition at the beginning of the nineteenth century, the first survey was conducted and map produced in 1812, and in the following decades the first roads were built, coffee and tea plantations were established, a labour force was recruited, and in the hot summer months the British colonial government moved from Madras to Ootacamund. Before the advent of Europeans, the plateau was home to the Badaga, Toda and Kota, who paid taxes to the precolonial ruler in the plains. Badagas walked down to access market places in the surrounding area, but in the nineteenth century the wider world came to the plateau. Towns sprang up in Ootacamund, Coonoor and Kotagiri, and craftsmen, coolies, traders and administrators poured in. European men and women came to Badaga villages on horseback, and Badagas walked to European bungalows to sell milk and vegetables or worked on plantations. The transformation of this remote plateau into a well-connected hill station could not have taken place without the active participation of the dominant community. J. Bellie Gowder had his early

114 *Frank Heidemann*

contacts with the British as a coolie on a road construction project, and later became a contractor for the railway line from Kallar to Coonoor. The colonial ruler awarded him the honourable title Rao Bahadur and followed with an invitation to a grand formal reception to his village, Hubbathale. Likewise other Badagas had longstanding contacts with their European contemporaries, relationships that became crucial to the process of conversion (Hockings 2012a). In the middle of the nineteenth century, the Badaga had accepted the presence of Europeans, but the dedicated missionaries who walked into their villages and preached the gospel proved to be a different class of people.

The Second Station in Kotagiri, 1859–1887

Samuel Mulley was the first convert in the Kotagiri region. Like his contemporary J. Bellie Gowder, he grew up as a buffalo-herding boy. He was described as an intelligent person, interested in plants and animals, and he became the local scout of Catherine Cockburn. In 1859, Ms Cockburn opened a school for Badaga children in Kotagiri, which Mulley also attended. In October 1861 he was baptised and faced strong opposition in his village for doing so. He received help from a friend, a Toda near Kotagiri, obtained a piece of land, and became a respected farmer. He was the first non-European in Kotagiri to own and to ride a horse. In 1865 he married Elizabeth, a daughter of Haleya Abraham (who was significantly senior to him). Together, they had six sons and five daughters. They and their children became leading evangelists, churchmen and educators, and one became a headmaster (Mulley 2012b). Samuel Mulley died in 1929. His great-grandson is Philipp K. Mulley, a Protestant pastor and local historian who is also a well-read intellectual and author. Several entries in the *Encyclopaedia of the Nilgiri Hills* (Hockings 2012a) come from his pen.

The conversion of Daniel, formerly Jowanna, who became the forefather of another line of Christian Badagas, turned out to be much more dramatic. On 22 May 1862, he was baptised after a restless week. Jowanna was a friend and schoolmate of Samuel and had an open ear for evangelism. In a conversation with the Cockburn family, he expressed his wish to be baptised. Knowing of the difficulties ahead, the family gave him shelter. They sent a message to the Ketti mission, because there was no local pastor to do the baptism. This news spread around the villages in Kotagiri. When his father, a senior and important headman, heard of his son's intentions, he rushed to Kotagiri and reached the Cockburn home in the middle of the night. He tried to convince his son to return home, first with words and then with physical force, but without success. That same night he mobilised Badaga men from the surrounding villages to prevent the conversion. The Cockburns called for the police in Connoor. The next day Mr Hill, the police inspector, came to Kotagiri. He spoke to Jowanna, called for his father, discussed the situation with the family and decided that the boy should stay at the Cockburn house. To safeguard the property, he left nine policemen behind and returned to Coonoor. On the same day, Jowanna's sister and her husband came and spoke to him and begged him to come home. Tensions rose when the missionary from Ketti arrived and rumours spread that that the candidate for baptism had been drinking ox blood. The baptism took place in the presence of a small congregation of Tamils who were mainly in European service, and was safeguarded by the police.

The third convert in Kotagiri was Jacob Kanaka, the first Badaga pastor, who was ordained in 1887. His descendants could marry the children of Samuel Mulley and Daniel, who belonged to the Thandanadu group as an exogamous entity. Mulley and Daniel's descendants could not marry among themselves but could find marriage alliances among the Jacob Kanaka group. Therefore, most Christian Badagas could (and can right up to the present day) trace their lineage to one of the three original converts. However, in the following years there were conversions from all Badaga groups including Lingayat, Adikiri and Haruva, three vegetarian sub-groups of the Badaga community, and – to a lesser extent – from lower status groups like the Torreya. By and large, these groups follow the old Badaga marriage rules and know their clan names. They try to maintain the boundary between vegetarian and non-vegetarian clans, but as a rule girls marrying into a vegetarian group follow that diet, and those who marry into non-vegetarian clans must prepare non-vegetarian food for their affinal families. Some of the formerly 21 exogamous units have merged into 12 units among the Christian Badagas (Mulley 1971: 62). They also observe a kind of village exogamy and constitute a distinct endogamous group which Hockings (1980) and Mulley (1971) call phratrie.

The First Generation of Converts

The first generation of converts moved into towns and lived in bazaars, on plantations or on church premises. Opposition to those individuals continued and found expression in various forms. In 1890, it was reported that a newly baptised couple was affronted and cursed (BM 1891, 37). The villagers drove buffaloes onto their field and destroyed their harvest. The wife, Elizabeth, suffered from this hostility, and the husband, Zachäus, was entrapped drinking alcohol. The villagers deprived him, a brave man who had killed a tiger, of his family property. Such reports of Badaga opposition are part of the mission narrative in the nineteenth century. The missionaries explained this opposition as due to the 'force of caste': resistance was not rooted (or primarily rooted) in

116 *Frank Heidemann*

idolism and superstition, but in the social power that originated in the authority of Badaga headmen. In his *History of the Basel Mission*, Wilhelm Schlatter summarises: 'Life, work, and property were – controlled by the eldest – to such an extent collective that individualization appeared impossible' (1916: 52).[5] When Daniel was baptised, opposition arose due to his father's influence, and when schools had to be closed, the 'jealousy' of headmen was cited as the cause. In the mission reports we find many occasions that imply that a strong sense of pragmatism was at work among the Badaga. They did not – for the most part – oppose education. Missionaries wrote about the long process required for a seed to bear fruit. Their frequent use of botany analogies suggests conversion was seen as a natural process that could be endangered by calamities like droughts, and required time and care to achieve success. The result appears to be as likely as an annual harvest in a peasant village, but the cycle of growth was unknown for the first generation of converts. Reading the reports it appears that the clergymen were convinced that one day, secular pragmatism would be replaced by evangelism.

This sense of hope corresponds to the title and content of a small booklet authored by F. Büttner in 1910: *Daniel Konga – Shining Figure on the Nilagiri*. The term 'shining figure' (Lichtgestalt) refers to a respected person, often a role mode, and is used in various fields including football and politics to denote a person who illuminates and guides. Daniel Konga's life history is narrated with the components mentioned in the narratives above. The process of his conversion took a long time: Kada Konga (his Badaga name) worked for an English man in Ootacamund, and had previous contact with missionaries. He assisted Mörike in translating the Bible, and he dined with the missionaries and thereby 'broke with his caste' (Büttner 1910: 8). Later, he entrusted Lütze with his decision to convert. But he was aware 'that one coal alone does not burn' (Büttner 1910: 7) and sought company, though without success. Lütze continued his visits to Kada Konga's village, Kerehada. Christians went along with him, and they chanted church songs and prayed on his veranda. Kada Konga's father, a teacher in a BM school, did not object to his baptism but demanded his written agreement to waive his right to the parental house. Kada asked his father to touch him with his foot, a ritual act resulting in excommunication, but his father rejected his wish. Villagers destroyed Kada's field and hatched conspiracies to attack him in the night. His wife absented herself from the village, and the status of their children was unclear. Verbal attacks on Lütze increased. 'Only respect towards the whites stopped them from abuse ["Misshandlungen", which can also mean physical attack]' (Büttner 1910: 11). On 4 December 1887, Kada was baptised with the name 'Daniel Konga'. 'Heathen' (most likely Badaga) were present and an uprising, which was anticipated, did not occur. Daniel Konga did not become the founder of a new line of converts. He fell ill, and his brother Kalla, the strongest opponent of the conversion, brought him to the hospital in Calicut, where he died. 'Heathen' visited his sickbed and attended his funeral (Büttner 1910: 20).

At the beginning of the twentieth century, after 50 years of missionary work, the congregation had about five hundred members, twenty-nine schools with about seven hundred children, one high school (the first high school in the Hills), a training institute for teachers, a seminary for catechists and two orphanages. The congregation had a staff of four missionaries, one ordained pastor, nine catechists and thirty-one Christian teachers. Mission medical services had cared for thousands of patients, and a few Badaga found their way into higher education. The BM reports state that the Hindu Badagas, who strongly opposed the first conversions, had come to terms with the Christian institutions and the Christian Badagas in their midst (Karl 1950: 13 passim). Growing Christian congregations in Ootacamund, Coonoor and Kotagiri became part of the face of the towns, and churches appeared as landmarks in urban centres. English was the language of the rulers and Christianity their religion. I would argue that the Christian section of the Badaga people suffered from painful exclusion in the first generation, but that their children became part of an anglicised community that enjoyed the protection of state institutions and were able to live with less strain and fear.

The Christian Badaga Rebellion, 1920–1945

Most of the European members of the BM were Germans and had to leave India at the start of the First World War as 'enemy aliens'. In 1918 the last missionaries left Malabar, and the status of their stations remained unclear because only English missions could obtain governmental permission to continue operations. After several years of negotiation, the BM handed over their missions in Coorg and in the Nilgiris to the Wesleyan Mission. Henry Gulliford was given charge of the congregations in Ketti and Kotagiri. Soon after he first arrived in 1919, that is, even before the official transfer of BM property in 1925, he introduced new proceedings and regulations, which were not agreeable to the presbyter and other members of the congregation. The Basel Mission Archive holds a large number of letters, petitions and memoranda written by Christian Badagas. Their central complaints refer to the liturgy, the diversion of local funds to the Wesleyan Church, the neglect of schools and termination of preaching in the villages, and the use of separate cups for each group in the congregation.

118 *Frank Heidemann*

The use of separate chalices refers to the vehement discourse on untouchability in south India, the ban on entering temples, and the use of separate cups at tea stalls. Christian Tamils, usually from the lower section of the caste system, came to the Nilgiris with their European employers and were members of the same congregations. When a Tamil man wanted to marry a Badaga girl – which, I would argue, means from the Badaga point of view a clear case of hypogamy – major protest ensued, and 'even catechists, elders and teachers participated' (Schlatter 1916: 219). However, the missionaries remained firm, were able to pacify the protestors and ensured the wedding took place. The conflict between Tamil and Badaga about using the same or different chalices was taken up to the synod in Malabar in 1907. A debate about the language of the liturgy resulted in various compromises. In Kotagiri, the service was held in turns in Kannada, Tamil and Badagu. Twenty years later, the same conflict emerged when Gulliford re-introduced the system of separate cups.

To illustrate the style and the language of these documents, I quote excerpts from the letter from Kotagiri by 'the undersigned, grateful and obedient disciples of the Basel Mission, now under temporary care of the Wesleyan Missionary Society' dated 29 January 1927:

> 1. Ever since the departure of the German Missionaries our condition, spiritual, mental and moral has been precarious....
>
> 2. Briefly, we literally and in fact are like sheep without a shepherd. To mention the *spiritual* side of our condition, we have not the *Church liturgy* that we were accustomed to in the time of our German Missionaries but a new Liturgy which is dis-tasteful to us.... We refer to what is known as '*individual cups*' offered to each member ... and the whole atmosphere of priest and congregation is that we feel like '*Israel in Egypt*'....
>
> 3. As regards *education*, our children are suffering from want of encouragement ... it may be mentioned here that the strength of the Girl's Orphanage is now only above 25 where as in the time of the Basel Mission it was not less than 60.
>
> 4. To refer to an important part of our Church's Duty, the *Gospel* is not preached as of yore in the villages of our district. At present the Pastor and the Evangelist are so occupied in the business of collecting funds daily that their evangelical duties are neglected.
>
> This letter concludes by 'beseeching our *Mother Church* to come to rescue of her children' and is signed by 65 persons. (Letter 29 January 1927, italicised words in capital letters and underlined in original)

The discontent in the Kotagiri congregation about Gulliford continued to grow in the years that followed. In the 'Proceedings of a Church meeting held in the Wesleyan Church, Kotagiri at 1 p.m. on the 8th, July, 1928 ... the letters to the Revd. H. Gulliford and M. T. Martin were read and recorded and it was resolved that since the Revd. H. Gulliford [who did not attend the meeting] had refused to read the letter and said that he would burn it [rather than reading it]' (Proceedings 7 August 1928). Karl Hartenstein, Director of the BM, visited Kotagiri in December 1928 and was welcomed by 'the members of the board for the restoration of the Basel Mission on the Nilgiris and the old Basel Mission'. They printed a pamphlet with similar complaints, though in a paraphrased style (A Welcome Address 1928). After his visit, Hartenstein informed the BM that 'under the impassionate leaders, especially Mr Kanaka, approximately one third of the Kotagiri congregation, roughly 110 persons, separated and founded their own congregation' (Hartenstein 1930). Internal communications of the BM suggest that one of the complaints was Gulliford's lack of accessibility (Hartenstein 1930). His written replies to petitions made by the members of his congregation show little understanding of their views and feelings. The BM tried to pacify the situation but remained truthful with regards to the agreement with the Wesleyan Church.

Around 1930 the situation in Kotagiri worsened. In a long report dated 9 April 1930, written in German and signed by Moolky, Gulliford is called a man of finance who was only interested in the Basel property (this included: the Nilgiri Mission fund, 100,000 rupees; the Casamajor Fund, 69,500 rupees; the Ketti Badaga fund, 22,000 rupees; the Ketti Poor fund, 2,800 rupees; the Ketti Chapel fund, 10,000 rupees; and various landed property) and hated 'Basel Christians'. The pension payment to a widow was discontinued because she did not join the Wesleyan Church, and 15 families converted to 'the Romans'. Gulliford, the letter said, had ordered the chastisement of those who do not join his church ('Kirchenzucht', Moolky 1930). The congregation felt like 'human inventory' handed over from the BM to the Wesleyan Church. Forms of protest included smiling and laughing during the service. This resulted in a ban on burying their relatives on the graveyard; at a later date they could use it on payment of a fee. To bring peace to the region, William Paton of the International Mission Council wrote to W. J. Noble (29 September 1936), who used to spend his holidays in the Hills. The letter summarised these events and called the conflict 'a little group of people in the Nilgiri Hills ... [who] are more or less in revolt' (Paton 1936). Other sources speak of a 'great majority' of the former BM congregation who were by no means 'agitators' but included 'old men with grey beards' (Moolky 1930). No documents in the BM suggest that the conflict ended. After Independence in 1947, the congregations merged into the Church of South India (Hockings 2012a: 121; Mulley 2012a).

120 *Frank Heidemann*

FIELDWORK-BASED INTERPRETATIONS

Conversion as Narrative

In 1843 the first Brahmin convert of the BM, Anandrao Kaundinya, wrote a detailed report about his proselytism, and became a well-known figure in the mission. He was trained in Basel, and his autobiography was read at the occasion of his ordination as a missionary in Leonberg, southern Germany. The book was most successful and a third edition was printed in 1955 in Basel (Becker 2015: 13ff., 688). Kaundinya's religious awakening, the resistance of his family – who took away his bible and kept him in 'open captivity' – his friendship with the missionaries and the slow but steady growth of his confidence in Jesus, the promise of the forgiveness of sins and, finally, the removal of his Brahman cord, cutting of his hair and his first meal with the missionaries led to a point of no return (Becker 2015: 14–18). He became one of the 'first fruits' ('Erstlingsfrüchte'), a term used to describe the first converts of a region or community or caste. In most cases, the process of conversion was described in great detail and was associated with the hope for further conversions from their families or caste members. After the commencement of their activities in south India in 1834, missionaries sent extensive progress reports and explained in detail why Hindus were reluctant to convert to Christianity. The main reasons were: excommunication from the caste group; the loss of support from family, landed property and employment; and the irreversibility of the decision. After sharing the European missionaries' food, which might include beef and pork, the converts were polluted and could not return to their previous state (Becker 2015: 141ff.).

In the reports on the 'first fruits' among the Badaga, shared meals with a Christian were described as a crucial step in the long process of conversion. The Badaga Gowders, that is, the largest endogamous group, were and are not vegetarian, but they are not supposed to eat beef and pork, but the Lingayat minority are vegetarian. However, I found no indications that banned meats were part of the first supper of converts and missionaries. In the contemporary Badaga world, the news of meat consumption in an urban restaurant would not provoke excommunication or other kinds of severe punishment. But why was the commensal meal of missionaries and converts described as the crucial step towards a new life? The answer is twofold and lies in the missionaries' cultural knowledge and the mission narrative. The BM missionaries were the first to study the Badaga people, their language, their religion and their social system. Their Badaga knowledge prior to arrival was based on their experience in the south Indian plains, where purity and commensality were central to the social order. The narrative of the life and the baptism of Anandrao Kaundinya, whom some of the BM missionaries knew personally, became a standard narrative and established the fundamental elements of conversion stories. Doubts, scruples, hesitation, opposition from family and village, evangelical teaching and confession became the elements of his and later convert narratives. As he was a Brahmin, his shared meal with the missionaries became a major element in his story (Becker 2015: 14–15, 320). Moreover, Kaundinya could not return to his family, but Christian Badagas who recanted Christianity were reintegrated into their previous social spaces and roles.

The cultural knowledge of the Nilgiri and the resulting reports of the missionaries rested on an understanding of purity, commensality and caste barriers from a specific background developed on the Coromandel Coast, especially from a Brahmin narrative. In addition, I would argue that other symbolic systems were at work, such as proximity and directionality (Heidemann 2013). As long as the missionaries walked to the villages, they showed an important sign of respect towards their hosts. This might partly explain the resistance against Gulliford: when potential Badaga converts moved towards the missions, the directionality was reversed and Badaga opposition arose.

Unity as a Value

The first conversions took place amidst the agitation of Badaga headmen and resistance from family members. The 'firstlings' did not receive any monetary or material advantages. Instead, they lost their homes, properties, employment and – though hardly mentioned in the missionaries' reports – had an extremely difficult time trying to find a marriage partner, even for their children. The potential benefits of conversion, such as access to church education and, in later years, to jobs in European institutions or compensation for lost agricultural land, carried little weight in comparison to what was lost in the process. In sum, it appears rather unlikely that 'utilitarian' factors (Robbins 2004: 84–85) were at work as a motivation for conversion. But what were the motives? What we know is that Abraham and Samuel had voluntary contact with British people, the former with a plantation owner, the latter with the Cockburn family. Both men were described as intelligent, enterprising and open-minded. The BM documents record their religious feelings, faith in Christianity and a strong wish for the forgiveness of sins (for south India in general, see Becker 2015: 353). But the Badaga had their own system to relieve sinners of their burden. At a funeral all possible sins are named and the village community replies after each sin that it will be forgiven (Hockings 2001). I talked with recent converts in Kotagiri in 2016 about their motives for conversion, and they mentioned tensions with

122 Frank Heidemann

family, neighbours and the village elders, and that they found release in the Christian congregation. Such motives cannot be concluded or excluded from the BM records.

Hockings argues that times of stress, drought and natural disaster increased the movement towards Christian missions in the second half of the nineteenth century. Three years before the first baptism of a Badaga took place, a smallpox epidemic killed over a thousand Badagas (Hockings 2013: 212, 218–220). From a historical and sociological point of view, a further question seems to be not less important. Rather than asking why a few Badagas converted to Christianity, I prefer to focus on the continuous and vehement resistance of Badaga Hindus against conversion. Missionaries reported that this was not rooted in a rejection of a new religious orientation. After Christ appeared in a vision, a 'Christian temple' was built (Hockings 2013: 221). The Badaga did not hesitate to discuss religious matters with the missionaries. They asked about the agency of the Christian god and whether he would enable the Christians to walk on fire, as the Badaga gods did. On one occasion, they asked if the mission could effect tax relief if the entire village converted (JEMB 11852, 120). In what follows, I argue that the maintenance of social boundaries must be considered as crucial to understanding the resistance of Badaga Hindus to Christian conversion. As a point of departure, I recall moments from my own research in the villages around Kotagiri from 1988 to 2016.

In my fieldwork area, a few Badagas read the Bible and have occasional visits from a Christian priest, but they would hesitate to call themselves Christian, especially when not all members of the family share the same faith. On the days of annual temple festivals, attention is directed towards public performance. When the procession carrying an idol approaches a house, the basic question is: does the family step out and bow down in front of the god or goddess? Do they accept the blessing from the village elders and do they pay the temple tax? If they do so, there is no (or hardly any) objection towards their contact with a Christian church. If they avoid the festival days by leaving their house under the pretext of visiting a remote family member in a hospital, for example, they would be open to suspicion and rumours. If they stay inside the house and do not open the door, it is taken as a rejection of the village community. To wait in front of the house for the procession to arrive, to pay the temple tax, and to prostrate themselves in front of an idol are at the same time an acknowledgement of the headman and priest and therefore of the village-founder-turned-god, and of the jurisdiction of the village. Village rituals are understood as a celebration of unity.

The most important rite of passage is the funeral. It is not a family affair, but explicitly the privilege and duty of the village. All the men form a long row ordered according to a genealogical principle and their wives gather in a separate row, and these circle in opposite directions around the corpse, thereby making a visible and physical statement of village unity (Hockings 2001). Christians do not participate. I would argue that from the Badaga's point of view the conversion of an individual to Christianity was much more than the loss of a single person. It was a challenge to boundary maintenance and a threat to the existing order. My Badaga counterparts tell me that they reside in their own (that is, mono-caste) villages and that they object to non-Badagas living among them. If a village house is rented out to a Tamil or Keralese teacher, it is acknowledged without appreciation. The Badaga view their village as an entity in the most comprehensive way: at once social, religious, economic and political. There is a powerful belief that a village can only be strong if it is united.

A dramatic event at a funeral illustrates the clash of two views, which I like to call 'private' or 'personal' and 'public' or 'formal'. A young man died in a motorcycle accident in Chennai and his friends brought his corpse back to his village, where he had grown up and played on the cricket team. His father had married into this village long ago, but kept a house in his native place. When the preparations for the funeral were going on, a delegation from the father's native village came and demanded the body, because in patrilineal terms the corpse belongs to the father's village. The young man's friends acknowledged the formal argument, but claimed rights to the dead body because of emotional proximity and personal relationship. The delegation from the father's village did not know the young man personally, but made their claim to his body with great vigour. The claim was about the reputation of their village and – I would argue – about control of a social boundary. In the debate about the corpse incompatible arguments were exchanged. A private view stood against a public view and a personal against a formal approach. The dead man's friends resolved the conflict in their favour, at least as far as securing the body for funeral rites in the village where their friend had grown up, and went to the father's village on the next day to convey a formal excuse. The resistance to the early conversions seems to include such public views and formal arguments and to represent much more than the fear of losing a beloved individual.

Today Badaga elders and local politicians depict themselves as secular leaders and open-minded towards other religions. But a clear opposition to on-going missionary activities by evangelical movements cannot be ignored. The fear is that the unity of the Badaga people would be endangered and that the community might be split into two sections. Unity is more than a strategic dimension; it must be considered as a value. 'Ella unne' – 'all [are] one' – is a phrase I heard often, and I was told that the architecture of the village with its distinct lines of houses symbolises social proximity and brotherhood, and that processions at festivals and at funerals embody the unity felt in and by the village, evident physically

124 *Frank Heidemann*

when the men and women form rows and move together. The inextricability of religion and politics is expressed in many contexts. Priest and headman preside over the village council and represent the sacred and profane aspects of the local community (Heidemann 2010: 104ff.). The rejection of the village priest implies an abandoning of the community. Therefore, an individual and religiously motivated move towards Christianity results in a challenge to village accord and violates the central value of unity.

CONCLUSION

The process of conversion began very slowly and did not produce any baptisms for 13 years. Twenty-five years after the first conversion, a total of six Badaga men and their families became Christians (Schlatter 1916: 118). The men were described as intelligent, curious or adventurous and well integrated; they owned land, studied in mission schools or were married and had children. There is no indication that they were marginalised or in personal trouble. Hockings (2013: 215–220) rightly states that natural disaster and epidemics may have contributed to conversion, but there are no indications that individual distress influenced the first converts. Rather, I would suggest that the performances of the missionaries made an enormous impression on these few individuals. Unlike other Europeans, they learned Badagu, walked into the villages and fell on their knees when reciting the prayers. Missionaries opened schools, vaccinated children, were friendly to the natives and helpful to those in need. Metz always carried a nauseant to save those who ingested harmful substances in order to attempt suicide, a sin in Christian terms. It seems that the small number of converts had longstanding, personal relationships with missionaries and were impressed by their public prayers.

The description of the conversions follows a master narrative, which was created by Anandrao Kundinya, the first Brahmin convert in Mangalore. The missionaries considered the removal of long hair and the lingam and also the first meal in their midst as the crucial moments in the conversion process. However, from the Badaga point of view, inter-dining did not result in excommunication. The missionaries stated that the converts could not return to their community, but the opposite proved to be true. I would argue that the Brahmanical view of Hindu society became the perspective from which missionaries perceived the Badaga community. On the other hand, the missionary journals hardly mentioned the resistance of the Nilgiri congregation to their transfer to the Wesleyan Church after the BM had to leave India after 1915. But the letters and pamphlets conveyed an image of a self-conscious, organised and strong-minded congregation. They rejected the style and order of Gulliford, who stopped praying in villages and was more interested in finance. Hockings made an analysis of his diary and states in the last six months of his stay in the Nilgiris, that 'he had 346 encounters with Europeans, 6 with Tamils, one with Karanese and two with North Indians' (Hockings 1989: 355). He never had a meal with an Indian and did not mention any Badaga or Toda. No wonder, then, that Badaga resisted his preaching. The tenacity of their resistance and the courage showed in forming a new congregation against the presence and efforts of a representative of British rule is impressive.

The resistance of the Badaga headmen and of the relatives of the converts to Christian conversion is meticulously and graphically described in the missionaries' letters and printed annual reports. The villagers gathered at the mission house and voiced their protest. They excommunicated and disinherited converts, confiscated their property and imposed a ban on seeing their wives and children. In the missionaries' rationale the reason for this vehemence is 'the caste', but it remains unclear what precisely is intended by this broad term. I would argue that Badaga politics, their rituals, marriage rules, settlement pattern and jurisdiction aimed to create a clear demarcation of an ethnic boundary. They lived in mono-caste villages, worshipped their own gods, practised endogamy, spoke their own language, owned contiguous tracks of land and were the dominant group on the plateau. Participation in rituals and temple festivals was universally obligatory. Religion and politics were inextricably connected. Unity was a central value and a strategic imperative. Conversion was understood as a violation of this value and a threat to the maintenance of the ethnic boundary. On a larger scale, missionary work commenced when the Badaga lost some of their autonomy. British judges claimed the jurisdiction, administrators collected land tax and planters occupied vast tracts of land. After the Badaga lost control of their territorial boundaries, they fortified their ethnic boundaries.

Christianisation of individual Badagas was completely different from the mass conversions that took place in the Tamil plains (Manickam 1977) and as a result it also varied from the conversion of the Toda, the precolonial neighbours of the Badaga community. Walker states that Naga Christians remained Naga and Mizo Christians Mizo, but this does not hold for Toda Christians. They intermarried decades ago and more frequently with other Christian communities, have given up their language, and no longer live in their old homesteads (Walker 1986: 273). Christian Badagas consider themselves as an integral part of the Badaga community, speak Badagu and interact with other Badagas on a daily basis. Those Christian Badagas who live in the villages and practise agriculture differ little from Badaga Hindus in the way they organise life in a joint family. But those who move out of the village live in smaller family units and are engaged in white-collar jobs (cf. Mulley

126 *Frank Heidemann*

1971: 61–69; 2012b). When Hockings (2001: vii) states that they occupy the lowest status position among Badaga endogamous groups, he refers to the concept of purity and the lack of food restrictions among the Christians. But today status groups among the Badaga are exclusively effective in ritual and marriage contexts. The respect that a Badaga receives in personal interactions, however, depends on various factors, and Christian Badagas are among the well settled, educated and professionally trained members of the community. The history of Hindu Badagas and Christian Badagas show major parallels. Both were highly successful in the fields of economy, politics and education; both headed towards modernity, but maintained rooted in their own traditions. Hindu Badagas work as professionals and businesspersons in the Nilgiri district and beyond, while Christian Badagas serve in the Church of South India in various positions; among them three Badagas became bishops.

NOTES

1. Missionaries acted less hierarchical than other Europeans. They slept in villages and shared food with the Badaga.

2. 'Am Abend aßen Beide von unseres Martins Weib gekochten Reis und damit war die Kaste vollständig gebrochen' (JEMB 1958: 93).

3. 'Dieser ist nicht Euer Vater, er hat Euch ja weggeworfen, gehet nicht zu diesem Kastenlosen; Euer Vater ist gestorben und Ihr seid Waisen, habt nichts mit ihm zu schaffen' (JEMB 1958: 95).

4. 'Als junges Mädchen hat er mich von meiner Eltern Haus geholt; ich habe 7 Kinder geboren; er soll aber nicht denken, daß sie je Abrahams Kinder heißen sollen. Eher töte ich sie Alle und mich selbst, als daß ich dem Kastenlosen nachfolgen würde, oder ihm meine Kinder überlasse. Er hat keine Liebe zu mir und zu den Kindern, sonst hätte er uns nicht so weggeworfen. Er sagte, er suche Vergebung seiner Sünden und darum gehe er nach Käti und lasse sich taufen, aber die Sünden, die er jetzt auf sich geladen, sind viel größer als die deren Vergebung er jetzt gesucht' (JEMB 1958: 96).

5. 'Leben, Arbeit und Besitztum der Badaga waren unter der Aufsicht der Ältesten in solchem Grade gemeinsam, daß eine Vereinzelung undenkbar schien.'

BIBLIOGRAPHY

Basel Evangelical Mission Archive

Annual reports

JEMB 1847–1940. *Jahresbericht der evangelischen Missionsgesellschaft zu Basel.*
RBEM 1845–1914. *Report of the German Evangelical Mission on the West Coast of India.*

Letters, memoranda and petitions

A Welcome Address presented to the right Reverend Karl Stein. December 1928. United Press, Cash Bazaar, Coonoor, R.S.

Hartenstein, Karl. 1930: An das Komitee – Vorlage betr. den Nilgiris, Basel, den 8 September 1930 – Rasche Zirkulation erbeten.

Letter. 29 January 1927. To the Reverend Sengle (or Seugle). Representative of the Basel Mission Home Committee and Chairman of the Malabar Mission, Calicut, signed in Kotagiri by 65 Members of the 'Disciples of the Basel Mission'.

Moolky. 9 April 1930. Letter to the Director of the Basel Mission, Kotagiri, View Hill.

Paton, William. 29 September 1936: Letter from 'International Missionary Council', Edinburgh House, London, to Rev. W. J. Noble, Calcutta; Private and Confidential; Copy Sent to K. Hartenstein, Evang. Missions-Gesellschaft, Basel.

Literature

Barth, Fredrik. 1969. *Ethnic Groups and Boundaries: The Social Organization of Culture Difference.* Oslo: Universitetsforlaget.

Becker, Judith. 2015. *Conversio im Wandel: Basler Missionar Zwischen Europa und Südindien und die Ausbildung Einer Kontaktreligiösität, 1834–1860.* Göttingen: Vandenhoek und Ruprecht.

Büttner, F. 1910. *Daniel Konga, eine Lichtgestalt auf den Nilagiri.* Basel: Verlag der Basler Missionsgesellschaft.

Heidemann, Frank. 2006. *Akka Bakka: Religion, Politik und Duale Souveränität der Badaga in den Nilgiri Südindiens.* Münster: Lit.

———. 2010. 'The Priest and the Village Headman: Dual Sovereignty in the Nilgiri Hills.' In *The Anthropology of Value: Essays in Honour of Georg Pfeffer,* edited by Peter Berger, Roland Hardenberg, Ellen Kattner, Michael Prager, 104–119. Delhi: Pearson.

———. 2013. 'Social Aesthetics of Proximity: The Cultural Dimension of Movement and Space in South India.' *Aesthetics* 23(1): 49–67.

Hockings, Paul. 1980. *Ancient Hindu Refugees: Badaga Social History 1550–1975.* Delhi: Vikas.

———. 1988. *Counsel from the Ancients: A Study of Badaga Proverbs, Prayers, Omens and Curses.* Berlin, New York, Amsterdam: Mouton de Gruiter.

———. 1989. 'British Society in the Company, Crown and Congress Eras.' In *Blue Mountains: The Ethnography and Biogeography of a South Indian Region,* edited by Paul Hockings, 334–359. Delhi: Oxford University Press.

———. 2001. *Moratury Rituals of the Badagas of Southern India.* Chicago: Field Museum.

———, ed. 2012a. *Encyclopaedia of the Nilgiri Hills.* Delhi: Manohar.

128 *Frank Heidemann*

———. 2012b. 'Demography.' In *Encyclopaedia of the Nilgiri Hills*, edited by Paul Hockings, 252–256. Delhi: Manohar.

———. 2013. *So Long a Saga: Four Centuries of Badaga Social History*. Delhi: Manohar.

Karl, Victor. 1950. *Early Reports of the Gospel Work among Badagas of the Nilgiri Hills, South India, 1846–1946*. Ootacamund: Ootacamund and Nilgiri Press.

Manickam, Sundaraj. 1977. *The Social Setting of Christian Conversion in South India*. Wiesbaden: Steiner.

Metz, Johann Friedrich. 1864. *The Tribes Inhabiting the Neilgherry Hills: Their Social Customs and Religious Rites*. Mangalore: Basel Mission Press.

Mulley, Philipp K. 1971. 'A Study of Kinship and Marriage Patterns in the Badaga Church and Society.' Bachelor of Divinity, Serampore (College) University.

———. 2012a. 'Christianity.' In *Encyclopaedia of the Nilgiri Hills*, edited by Paul Hockings, 190–196. Delhi: Manohar.

———. 2012b. 'Mulley Family.' In *Encyclopaedia of the Nilgiri Hills*, edited by Paul Hockings, 603–605. Delhi: Manohar.

Robbins, Joel. 2004. *Becoming Sinners: Christianity and Moral Torment in a Papua New Guinea Society*. Berkeley: University of California Press.

Schlatter, Wilhelm. 1916. *Geschichte der Basler Mission*. Basel: Verlag der Basler Missionsbuchhandlung.

Walker, Anthony R. 1986. *The Toda of South India: A New Look*. Delhi: Hindustan.

5

Identity Change and the Construction of Difference

Colonial and Postcolonial Conversions among the Sumi Naga of Nagaland, Northeast India

Iliyana Angelova

'Nagaland is the most Baptist state in the world', 'The Nagas are the only Baptist nation in the world', 'Nagaland is a stronghold of Christianity in Asia' – one is almost inevitably bound to hear such statements whenever one enquires about the contemporary significance of Christianity in the state of Nagaland in northeast India. These statements are usually uttered with a great sense of pride, and while they necessarily replicate official church discourses, they also reflect individual sentiments of accomplishment. For the social scientist, however, the fact that only 100 years ago, Nagaland was certainly none of these raises a series of questions regarding the multiple sociocultural and political transformations that have affected Naga society in the span of a century or so. The issue of conversion is certainly one of the core questions in this respect.

The question as to why people convert has been a core research interest within social anthropology and other cognate disciplines, and a number of theoretical approaches have been suggested in an attempt to explicate this phenomenon. As Joel Robbins aptly points out, studies of conversion to so-called world religions usually rely either on 'utilitarian' or 'intellectualist' explanations. The former 'focuses on the worldly advantages, in terms of material goods, position, power, prestige, and so forth, that accrue to those who convert'. The latter 'emphasizes matters of meaning, and argues that converts are attracted to the new religion because it renders meaningful new situations that defy the sense-making capacities of their traditional ways of understanding the world' (Robbins 2004: 84–85). Moreover, according to Robbins, the two approaches need not be juxtaposed but rather 'can be productively used together' in a 'two-stage model of conversion': while utilitarian explanations are more useful in understanding early conversions, a focus on meaning-making is more useful in explaining why converts choose to retain their new religion (Robbins 2004: 85–87). Building on Robbins' useful model, my own ethnographic data suggests that people's

130 *Iliyana Angelova*

motivations for conversion are also heavily influenced by the wider sociocultural and political environment, and a focus on how conversion is related to the construction of collective identities will fruitfully elucidate important nuances that cannot be unequivocally described as either utilitarian or intellectualist.

Anthropological studies of conversion to Christianity have recently focused on issues of rupture, discontinuity and culture change (cf. Robbins 2004; Engelke 2004). In some ethnographic cases and in some churches, such as those described by Robbins and Engelke, it has been argued that conversion entails a radical discontinuity, a complete rupture with the past and a total culture change induced by converts' understanding of 'modernity', which is often associated with colonialism and the imposition of Western lifestyles, institutions and technologies (cf. Cannell 2006; Joshi in this volume). It is indeed often the case, and especially so in mission Christianity, that the foreign missionaries who worked among non-Christian communities such as the Naga of northeast India wittingly or unwittingly set out to effect a total change in culture among local populations by condemning and demonising many aspects of their traditional culture as contrary to the Christian understanding of morality and truth. Necessarily, such attitudes on the part of foreign missionaries often generated mistrust and outright hatred by non-Christian locals who resisted such intrusions into their ways of life in various ways.

However, as Fenella Cannell has rightly observed, despite missionary activities to the contrary, very often continuities of social and cultural custom have been maintained both in private and in public life to a far greater extent than the missionaries might have anticipated (Cannell 2006: 26–27). Therefore, in some cases, it seems analytically more useful to interpret conversion not as a rupture, but as an ongoing process in which some earlier cultural ideas and practices might be suppressed but others survive to inform the trajectory of the local form of Christianity into the future. Indeed, as Geoffrey Oddie (in this volume) suggests, the notion of *conversion*, with its implicit connotation of a sudden and dramatic spiritual experience, can be fruitfully substituted by the notion of *religious transformation*, which implies that religious change is a gradual process of movement towards Christ. This, Oddie observes, does not obfuscate the fact that some converts might indeed experience 'some kind of dramatic or sudden type of emotional conversion experience', but rather draws attention to the tacit admission that adherents often become Christian at least by stages, rather than all of a sudden. The metaphor of 'Godroads' that this volume suggests aptly captures this multi-dimensional, multi-locational and multi-relational nature of conversion as a symbolic journey, as an ongoing dynamic process with its ambivalences and ambiguities, tensions and negotiations, continuities and changes.

It is also acknowledged that while necessarily affecting individuals, religious transformations have multiple and complex implications for social organisation and identity (cf. Cannell 2006; Robinson and Clarke 2003; Young and Seitz 2013). Indeed, in my own analysis I prefer to follow Hefner and Mosse in their argument that religious change is first and foremost a matter of a changed sense of belonging in a changed socio-political environment, or, in Hefner's words, 'a new locus of self-identification' (1993: 17) and, in Mosse's words, 'the collective self-ascription as Christians – the adoption of a Christian identity' (1999: 94). Further, across South-Southeast Asia collective identities are often constructed in opposition to religiously different 'Others'. As such, religion is very often employed as a dominant marker of identity providing for group cohesion and motivating ethnic and political action (cf. Stirrat 1999; van der Veer 1994; Gellner 2009). In the Indo-Burma borderlands, in particular, religion has been crucial to the construction of group identities as it has 'both a cultural and a political dimension' (Longkumer 2009: 47). As a result, a number of ethno-nationalist movements in northeast India have been organised along religious lines (cf. Baruah 2005, 2009; Joshi 2013). In addition, the conceptualisation of conversion as an act of resistance and rebellion against the socioeconomic, religious or political status quo (Robinson and Clarke 2003: 15) is particularly useful in analysing postcolonial Naga conversions, and can be applied to other ethno-nationalist movements in northeast India as well, for example, the Mizo. As I will demonstrate later, the politicisation of Baptist Christianity among the Naga in the course of their nationalist struggle against the Indian nation-state since the mid-1950s has had an all-pervading impact on Naga identity constructions.

Based on long-term ethnographic fieldwork and archival work conducted in Nagaland, the present chapter will present some of the ways in which one of the largest Naga tribes[1] – the Sumi Naga – have engaged with Christianity throughout the twentieth century and have gradually moved towards Christ (to borrow Oddie's concept again). While acknowledging that a number of factors have played a role in Sumi conversions in the colonial and postcolonial period, in the present chapter I will suggest that they might be best explained as the result of Sumi social structure, identity construction processes and the interplay of various agents of social change among the Naga (foreign missionaries, British colonial administration, the Indian army post-1950s, and so on). I will seek to demonstrate that a combination of utilitarian and intellectual motivations has underpinned religious transformations among the Sumi and that these have occurred simultaneously rather than in stages, as Robbins suggests. The overarching framework within which these religious transformations can be best explicated is the ongoing Naga political struggle for independence from the

132 *Iliyana Angelova*

Indian nation-state, which has conditioned the ways in which the Naga have constructed and experienced their collective identity from the mid-twentieth century onwards.

THE SUMI NAGA

The Sumi (or Sema)[2] are one of the largest Naga tribes in the present-day state of Nagaland.[3] All Sumi villages were, and still are, governed by hereditary chiefs (*akukau*) who belong to the most powerful clans in the village and are descendants of the village founder. The traditional authority that hereditary chiefs continue to exercise in Sumi villages is legitimised by custom and underpinned by a series of mutually binding economic, political and kinship obligations between a chief and his fellow villagers (cf. Hutton 1921: 144–152). According to Sumi customary law, the right to succession to chieftainship passes from a chief to his younger brothers and only after that to his own sons and his younger brothers' sons. Until fairly recently, therefore, it was common practice for the chief's elder sons to break away and establish separate villages during their father's lifetime (cf. Hutton 1921: 358). Because of these succession rules, among other things, the villages of the Sumi are spread geographically not only in their traditional tribal headquarters of Zunheboto district, but also across neighbouring districts. The most significant implication of this is that the district of Dimapur, which is the commercial hub of Nagaland and a place which 'belongs to all Naga', as the popular expression goes, is dominated by Sumi villages and has become the new headquarters of the Western Sumi among whom I did most of my ethnographic fieldwork.

OVERVIEW OF EARLY (COLONIAL) SUMI CONVERSIONS, 1900S–1940S

The first foreign missionaries belonging to the erstwhile American Baptist Missionary Union[4] arrived in the frontier province of Assam in 1835, inspired by the missionary zeal of the Second Great Awakening in America and at the invitation of Captain Jenkins, then Commissioner for Assam (*BMM* June 1901: 207). From their mission stations in Assam, the American missionaries came into contact with Naga tribes inhabiting the hills surrounding the Brahmaputra valley, and established their first mission stations among the Ao Naga (1872), the Angami Naga (1883) and the Lotha Naga (1885) (cf. Downs 1992). The first two mission schools were opened at Impur (Ao area) and Kohima (Angami area) with the tacit support of the colonial administration, which had been gradually extending its control over the Naga-inhabited areas since the 1880s.[5]

However, it was only in November 1928 that the ABFMS resolved to open a dedicated mission field for work specifically among the Sumi and a separate

Sumi Baptist Association was founded in 1929 under the name of Sumi Baptist Akukuhou Kuqhakulu (Sumi Baptist Church Association, SBAK). In 1936 Revd Anderson was assigned to supervise mission work among the Sumi and was placed in charge of building a Sumi mission centre at Aizuto near Lokobomi village (Anderson 1978b). Legend has it that the land that *gaonbura*[6] Xekhepu of Lokobomi village sold to Revd Anderson was inhabited by an evil spirit that the *gaonbura* hoped would destroy the Christian mission. When this did not happen, some took it as a sign that they should convert. Be that as it may, Revd Anderson resided at the Aizuto mission centre only briefly from 1949 to 1950, and was then replaced by Revd Delano, who became the first permanently resident American missionary among the Sumi (1949–1955); his family was also the last American missionary family to leave the Naga Hills when the Indian government expelled all foreign missionaries from the then politically turbulent Naga areas.[7]

Despite the absence of resident American missionaries among the Sumi until the late 1940s, initial conversion work was conducted by itinerant Ao and Angami evangelists. Students and teachers from the mission school at Impur, for instance, are reported to have undertaken regular evangelising trips during vacations and at weekends to different Sumi villages, where they sang, preached and gave 'an example of the Christian life', which might have influenced some Sumi families to send their children to the school (Ao 2002: 36). In this way, Sumi boys started joining the mission schools in Impur and Kohima and, having completed their studies there and returned to their home villages, they became the first Sumi school teachers and evangelists. Among these boys was Ivulho Shohe of Ghokimi village, who studied in Kohima and who is held by some to be the first convert among the Sumi: he converted in 1903 and was baptised in 1906 by Revd Dickson. At the same time, the official birth-year of Christianity among the Sumi is conventionally held to be 1904: the year when the *gaonbura*s Ghopuna and Ghosuna from Ighanumi village were baptised by Revd Rivenburg in Kohima.

Although various neighbouring Naga tribes such as the Ao, Angami and Rengma have made an invaluable contribution to introducing Christianity among the Sumi, by far the greatest credit for Sumi conversions in the first three decades of the twentieth century is owed to the Sumi themselves. Pioneer Sumi evangelists such as Ashu Kushe of Chishilimi village (the first Sumi prophet or *tungkupu*),[8] Revd Yemhi of Lazami village (the first Sumi pastor ordained in 1926), Inaho Kinimi of Lumami village[9] and others have gained an almost legendary status among the Sumi because of their contribution to spreading the gospel. These individuals, together with many others who remain in the memories of the community, contributed to the mass movement of the Sumi to

134 *Iliyana Angelova*

Christianity in the 1920s and 1930s, which is recorded to have happened in a rather distinctive way – without sustained American missionary work, without mission funds, despite very poor connectivity between Sumi villages and opposition to preaching the gospel on the part of non-Christian Sumi.

While touring Sumi villages in those early years, the American Baptist missionaries witnessed this 'spontaneous movement' among the Sumi where 'many Christian groups' had their 'own meeting houses' and were holding 'regular services without visible [church] leadership' (Eaton 1997: 264). According to Revd Tanquist,

> The way this genuine Christian movement was started among the Semas with practically no direct influence from without, and the way it has progressed in spite of gross neglect on our part as a Mission, is a marvellous thing indeed…. The Sema work is conducted in true 'faith mission' style. The money has been coming, we hardly know from whence. (*Minutes* 1936: 41)

Similarly, Revd Anderson also writes of the immense promise of the underdeveloped Sumi mission field:

> The Semas are the most fruitful of our Christian Communities in the Assam Baptist Mission fields but they have not received the attention they deserved during the past year…. We must concentrate on teaching this great mass of new Christians the word of God and on establishing churches in their villages. During the last ten years the increase in membership has been on mass movement proportions. In 1925 we had 500 Sema Naga Christians; now we have 6,500 and more are coming. (*Report* 1936: 43)[10]

Revd Anderson also remarks that the building of the mission centre at Aizuto was similarly a distinctly grass-roots initiative more than anything else. He writes that, unlike any other mission centre in the Naga Hills whose construction had been fully funded by the ABFMS, the lack of funds for the Sumi forced him to ask Sumi Christians to contribute free labour to clear the land and to donate a number of construction materials, such as bamboo and thatch, for the buildings. Some non-Christians participated too, and the whole project was overseen by the local evangelists Kiyeshe and Inaho (Anderson 1978a: 62–63). In this way, the mission centre and the mission school were built with Sumi resources by the Sumi themselves. Similarly, Revd Delano remembers that upon taking office at the Aizuto mission centre in 1949, he observed the rapid changes that Sumi society was experiencing as a result of Christian conversions: 'Those were days of rapid change. The churches were growing in numbers, new believers were added daily' (Delano 1978: 27). He also explicitly acknowledges that these changes

Identity Change and the Construction of Difference · **135**

were effected by the devotional work of Sumi evangelists, some of whom became his close associates in his several years of service among the Sumi.

EXPLAINING SUMI MASS MOVEMENT TOWARDS CHRISTIANITY

Naga conversions to Christianity are conventionally attributed to missionary strategies in translating the gospel into local languages by utilising indigenous concepts, the provision of education and medical services at the mission stations, the opportunities for social mobility and government employment that English-language education made available, various economic motivations related to breaking away from the burdensome system of ritual observances, and so on (cf. Joshi 2012; Downs 1992; Eaton 1997). The American Baptist missionaries who worked among the Naga were vernacularists: they believed that salvation in Christ was most efficiently attained only if one could read the Bible oneself in one's own language and have a direct experience of God through it. Hence, they studied the Naga languages, which had hitherto existed only in oral form, and with the help of local interpreters reduced them to writing using the Roman script. Then they translated the books of the Bible and the hymnals into these languages, and implemented their literacy and proselytising programmes in the newly established mission schools.

Among the Sumi, in particular, the American missionaries and their Sumi assistants employed a number of successful linguistic strategies in their translation of the Bible,[11] which undoubtedly facilitated understanding of its message. For example, the name chosen to denote the Christian God was *Alhou*, the benevolent spirit whom the Sumi credited with creating earth and all life on it; the word selected for 'angel' was *kungumi*, which denoted a set of benevolent spirits of the sky who were believed to have a close connection with humans, and 'Satan' was translated as *tughami* – the Sumi word for a number of earth spirits who were believed to interfere actively in human affairs, usually malevolently but also benevolently when properly propitiated (for a detailed account of Sumi religion and ritual practice, see Hutton 1921). While Richard Eaton (1997) has aptly drawn attention to the differential impact of such linguistic strategies on early conversions among the Ao, Angami and Sumi, his further suggestion that this involved no religious shift at all but, rather, 'only a refinement and elaboration of a thoroughly indigenous conception' (Eaton 1997: 266) should be treated with caution. The linguistic terms used in the translation of the Bible were clearly indigenous but the ontological ideas that they came to embody differed from their original meanings. For example, in the Christian appropriation of the term *tughami*, all earth spirits were demonised, which obscured the fact that in traditional Sumi ontology many of them were actually benevolent. Further, Joshi

136 *Iliyana Angelova*

challenges the assumption that 'the Nagas had a notion of a High God, as distinct from a creative force, before missionary contact' and proposes instead a greater focus on the 'availability in churches of educational, healing and other material resources' which influenced people's conversion choices (Joshi 2007: 548).

Indeed, biomedical care and its ability to treat various ailments and afflictions has been an important factor facilitating conversion worldwide. Among the Naga, missionary and church records suggest that early Naga conversions have been influenced substantially by the provision of medical services by the Christian missionaries. Pioneer Sumi evangelists such as Ashu Kushe, for example, are remembered to have demonstrated the healing power of the new Christian God over local spirits on numerous occasions, thus gradually undermining belief in the power of the latter and their ability to intervene in human life (see Joshi in this volume for comparative data about the Angami).

With the provision of education at the mission schools came new ways of understanding the world, new opportunities to connect with other Naga tribes and the wider world and new forms of social mobility. As British administration slowly extended across the lands of the Sumi in the early and mid-twentieth century, mission-educated Sumi boys were offered the opportunity to become employed as *dobashi* (interpreters), government school teachers and petty clerks. Thus, being Christian was gradually attributed new value because of the social mobility opportunities it offered.

Another successful strategy that appears to have facilitated religious transformation among the Sumi was the decision to conduct the annual conventions of all Sumi churches in a village where the Christians were few with the implicit suggestion that in this way God's blessings would shower upon this community (cf. Chishi Swu 2004: 47–48). Although such conventions typically lasted only a few days, it seems plausible to suggest that the type of Christian fellowship that they demonstrated – interspersed with hymn singing that built on the proverbial love of music shared by Naga people[12] – must have inspired at least some newcomers to join the Christian fold. Thus, the emotive power of collective praise and worship during the annual Sumi Christian conventions must have had an impact on accelerating conversions. These initial contacts with non-Christians in partially Christian Sumi villages were later sustained through numerous repeat visits by Sumi evangelists, which helped achieve a long-term effect and lasting religious transformations.

Such repeat visits were particularly important because building up the Sumi Christian community was by no means a straightforward and unproblematic endeavour. Early missionary activity among the Sumi, as among other Naga, was necessarily slow and marked by much precarity and danger: road conditions and

Identity Change and the Construction of Difference **137**

inter-village connectivity were difficult, especially during the monsoon season; the jungles that Sumi evangelists had to cross to reach villages were dense and often impenetrable; and the threat of head-hunting[13] was ever-present, especially in Sumi villages to the east, which fell outside the scope of British administration. In addition, the co-existence of Christians and non-Christians within the same village often caused much tension and division: Sumi Christians refused to participate in village rituals related to the abundance of crops and village welfare, refused to observe some ritual prohibitions (*genna*),[14] especially if those fell on the Christian Sabbath, refused to perform any work on the Sabbath and disrupted the operation of the *aluzhi* system,[15] which was the foundation of all collective work in the village. This created new tensions, which often resulted in the persecution of Sumi converts by their own community members for allegedly having brought misfortune to the village (such as bad harvests and village fires) by violating Sumi customs; many of them were ostracised and isolated and became social outcasts or were banned from their villages. The practice of banning Christian converts from Naga villages in the early years of Christian work is documented to have been a widespread phenomenon, which caused much division within villages and the gradual formation of new, entirely Christian villages (cf. Mills 1926: 408–409; Chishi Swu 2004: 15).

At the same time, it should be noted that in the early twentieth century the membership of the young Naga Christian community was rather fluid as converts often reverted to their 'heathen' customs by propitiating spirits (especially in the event of persistent illness), consuming locally brewed rice-beer, smoking and chewing tobacco, committing adultery, and so on. This underscores the dynamic and multi-dimensional nature of Sumi journeys to Christianity with their ambiguities, uncertainties and shifting contingencies. Such instances of 'backsliding' (as described in missionary writing) also highlight potentially conflicting understandings of what constitutes Christian morality and ethics, with the necessary proviso that they too are socially constructed and historically contingent categories. For example, while 'backsliding' formed a regular source of concern for the American missionaries and resulted in excommunication, contemporary Naga Christians rarely become excommunicated on the basis of such proscriptions alone. This comes to demonstrate that the meanings and values attached to being Christian are contingent upon the particular socio-historical moment in which a Christian community seeks to redefine its boundaries.[16]

In the absence of sufficient historical data regarding early conversion motivations from the converts' perspective, the biography of the legendary Sumi evangelist Ashu Kushe (given in Chishi Swu 2004) serves as a useful point of departure in trying to analyse historical events of religious transformation among

138 Iliyana Angelova

the Sumi. Kushe's Christ-ward movement was mediated by a series of dreams in which he encountered the Christian God and was ultimately convinced of his power. Kushe thus converted not in a sudden act of revelation but through the gradual revealing of divine power in his life. He remained illiterate throughout his life and could never read the Bible, but he spent days and nights fasting and praying in the deep jungles surrounding his native village in order to receive anointment from God. His knowledge of Biblical chapters and verses derived from his contacts and conversations with other Naga evangelists and with the American missionaries whom he met at the mission centres that he visited as an itinerant evangelist. Kushe was famous among Christians and non-Christians alike for his ability to see visions, prophesy future events and exorcise evil spirits from humans and animals. Praying and signing gospel songs formed part of his daily routine, and he also composed gospel songs that are believed to have been inspired by his experience of God (Chishi Swu 2004).

Kushe is certainly remembered as a figure of 'charismatic authority' (cf. Weber 1968) who impressed those who met him with his strong personality, unfaltering confidence and perseverance in the face of adversity. His firm conviction that 'Yihovah'[17] was the only true God who saves, his visionary and healing powers and his distinctive preaching style seem to have influenced many to convert. He traversed the villages of the Sumi and neighbouring tribes, either alone or with his associates, and shared his message with 'those who listened and explained the way to lead a spirit filled life' (Chishi Swu 2004: 30). One of his strategies was to convince men of power (*dobashi* or interpreters, and village chiefs) in the truthfulness of his preaching, especially by performing miraculous healings within their families or making prophecies of future events that would eventually come true. Certainly, not all chiefs responded favourably to Kushe's visits: some did not allow the evangelist to enter their villages, others detained him and fined him for evangelising in their villages without permission, others still did not give him shelter in the village and forced him to sleep in the jungle. Many of these incidents are also narrated in the context of such chiefs (or their family members) falling sick suddenly and unexpectedly, and recovering only when Kushe comes back and prays for the afflicted who then immediately and miraculously recovers (Chishi Swu 2004: 16–17). This highlights again the importance of charismatic healing in conversion experiences.

It should also be acknowledged that Sumi evangelists, such as Ashu Kushe, visited and revisited the same village in the course of several years in order to forge personal relationships with the village chiefs (*akukau*) and their families and to support the (growing) Christian communities. Ashu Kushe himself is reported to have forged lifelong friendships with many village chiefs whom he eventually managed to convince to convert. This strategy of convincing village

Identity Change and the Construction of Difference **139**

chiefs of the truth of the Christian message was very aptly devised because it drew on the hierarchical social structure of Sumi society and its strong clan affinities that continue to form the backbone of Sumi society nowadays. As already explained above, the construction of authority among the Sumi concentrates actual and symbolic power in the hands of the village chief and the elder men from his clan. The conversion of the latter almost invariably involved the conversion of their whole families, clans and even villages in compliance with the prevalent Sumi custom of obeying traditional authority (cf. Chishi Swu 2004: 15). Even though Sumi chiefs who converted in this way violated Sumi customs and laws in the same way that ordinary converts did, unlike the latter they were not subjected to stigmatisation and public ridicule and were not banned from their villages. On the contrary, they continued to exercise their traditional authority and retained their social position; some of them, such as the *akukau* of Ighanumi village, also became church leaders in their village church. Christian conversions, therefore, had differential effects depending on one's position within Sumi social hierarchy. Hence, it can be argued that Christianity gained such popularity among the Sumi because it spread through their kinship networks and especially through the conversion of men of power and authority – village chiefs (*akukau*) and interpreters (*dobashi*).

It is clear, therefore, that as more and more Sumi chiefs adopted the 'Yihovah' religion and more mission-educated Sumi boys became upwardly mobile and started occupying various posts within the structures of the British administration in the Naga Hills, being a Christian came to be associated with prestige and authority and became a new form of social capital among the Sumi and other Naga. This is confirmed by an incident narrated by Revd Anderson in relation to the establishment of a mission school at Aizuto specifically for Sumi children:

> It was impossible for us to persuade them [the Sumi church leaders and chiefs] to make Aizuto the main educational centre for all the Semas. This caused Aizuto to lose not only financial support but also students, as these new M.E. [Middle English] Schools invited the Aizuto students to come and start schools elsewhere. Where at first the Aizuto school had pioneered there were soon several schools who competed with us in providing advanced education. (Anderson 1978b: 32)

Different village chiefs are reported to have entered into 'fierce competition' (Anderson 1978a: 63) to have schools set up in their own villages not only as a matter of prestige and a legacy they wanted to leave behind, but also because of the increasing social value of education as a result of the social mobility opportunities it provided and its association with Western modernity. Indeed, since its advent among the Naga, Christianity has been associated by its new converts with notions of modernity, and technological and moral superiority. As

140 *Iliyana Angelova*

a result, Christianity, its culture and its institutions have been consistently conceptualised as 'advanced' and 'modern', while Naga religion and culture have been rendered 'backward'. Although this shift in perceptions of value is clearly discernible in the early period of Naga religious transformations that the current section describes, it became a dominant narrative discourse in the subsequent decades of Naga history.[18] At the same time, the 'fierce competition' among Sumi chiefs to have a school established in their villages that Revd Anderson describes can also be interpreted as an attempt to continue the traditional Naga institution of *morung*[19] in which traditional knowledge and skills were imparted on boys and young men by their elders. The availability of formal education institutions in Sumi villages thus provided access to Western modernity while also serving important cultural continuity functions in relation to the production and transmission of knowledge.

As Christianity became permanently associated with Western modernity in the minds of Naga converts and as its new institutions (schools, churches, dispensaries, student hostels, and so on) became a visible feature of Naga villages, it seems plausible to suggest that lifestyles, values and worldviews also gradually changed, thus effecting an enormous transformation in Naga society within a relatively short span of time.[20] Perhaps the most important transformation of worldviews was the Christian message of love and salvation in Jesus Christ that was juxtaposed to existing traditional laws and customs that placed very strong value on warrior skills and prowess. The question of love and truth occupied a central position in the preaching of early Sumi evangelists such as Ashu Kushe. Wherever he went, he emphasised that 'Yihovah' was the only true God and through the miracles and healings that he performed he demonstrated Yihovah's power over evil spirits and affliction. His biography also informs us that 'he would urge people to be faithful and tread only on the path of truth' (Chishi Swu 2004: 30). His devout behaviour and abundant demonstrations of miracles appear to have been highly effective in transforming people's worldviews as they adopted the Christian truth he was preaching and with it, a new 'true' identity: the 'Yihovah' identity.

To return to Robbins' two-stage mode of conversion, it appears then that utilitarian and spiritual motivations have converged in early Sumi conversions, and it is difficult to argue for successive stages, especially with the lack of historical data describing the religious transformation experience from the point of view of Sumi converts. The provision of Western education at the mission schools provided new opportunities for social mobility; the availability of biomedicine helped heal afflictions widely held to be caused by malicious spiritual intervention and thus convinced many of the superiority of the Christian God over local spirits; and the conversion of Sumi chiefs entailed the conversion of their families and clans without transforming traditional ways of constructing authority.[21] In addition to such pragmatic reasons for changing one's religious affiliation as described above, the activities of divinely inspired charismatic figures such as Ashu Kushe introduced new dominant values and ideas in Naga society which transformed the ways of constructing and experiencing Naga identity. The processes of comprehensive transformation – spiritual, sociocultural, political, economic – that began among the Naga in the late nineteenth and early twentieth centuries were further accelerated in the mid-twentieth century when the expression of Naga identity began inextricably interwoven with Christianity, as the sections below will demonstrate.

THE GREAT EVANGELICAL REVIVALS OF THE 1950S AND 1970S

In a series of historical and political events which have been analysed extensively (cf. Yonuo 1974; Sema 1986) and whose detailed reiteration falls beyond the scope of this chapter, on 14 August 1947 the Naga declared their political independence from the Indian nation-state and formed their own independent national government.[22] In the ensuing decades, violence, destruction and uncertainty became common characteristics of the life of each Naga, as the Naga rebels fought an independence struggle against the inclusion of their lands within the sovereign territory of the newly formed Indian nation-state.

In 1955, when Revd Delano and his family were forced to leave the Naga lands, the Naga Baptist churches were suddenly left to take care of themselves without sufficient local church leaders (see Delano 1978: 27; Anderson 1978b: 30; *Minutes* 1959: 75). While many Naga evangelists such as Revd Longri Ao, Revd Kenneth Kerhuo and Revd Shihoto were doing their best to sustain the growing Naga Christian community, there was a general feeling of loss and of a lack of direction across Naga tribal churches as they tried to consolidate their membership and sustain their fellowship. This was amplified by the volatile political situation across the Naga-inhabited areas, which was the result of the Indo-Naga armed hostility and which saw the mass destruction of human life and property, the burning and grouping of villages, the forced dispersals of the civilian population in jungles, where they survived for two years, and so on (for a detailed account, see Maxwell 1980; Haskar and Luithui 1984; Iralu 2009).

Within this environment of fear and uncertainty, the 'wildfire' of revival spread spontaneously and quickly across all Naga areas in the late 1950s, as my elderly interlocutors narrated. This was the first Holy Spirit revival among the Naga. The first people who seem to have been influenced by it were groups of women who are said to have experienced the Holy Spirit working among them while they had gathered for a prayer meeting: they felt the need to pray long, all

142 *Iliyana Angelova*

the time, and started dancing and jumping while experiencing the power of the Holy Spirit filling their bodies. 'Whoever got that Holy Spirit, they became different from other people, so they had an experience', narrated one of my elderly interlocutors. Revival prayer meetings were first held in secret in people's houses, but as the new fellowship grew, the revivalists (*xukikithe kulumiqo*) started using the village churches for their services. Prayer services were held daily and continued for hours, often through the night, as people wept in prayer while confessing their sins and prophesying; there were also numerous examples of miracles and faith healing. Similar to earlier conversions, the performance of charismatic healings had a very strong impact on people's decisions to convert.

These forms of intense prayer, which involved explicit emotionality (where people danced, shouted, cried and, occasionally, spoke in tongues while praising God), were rather different from the strict order of the devotional services practised in Sumi Baptist churches. The initial response of the community therefore was one of bewilderment, but it was soon replaced by strong disapproval and outright condemnation, as most people 'were not convinced' and 'absolutely against'. The revivalists were considered crazy by their family members and fellow villagers, and this led to much disagreement and quarrels within families and villages, as some of my elderly interlocutors remember from their childhoods. The revivalist women, for example, were often chased out of their houses by their husbands, and many revivalists were fined by their villages, excommunicated from their Baptist churches, threatened and beaten.

Seeing the confusion and disturbance that the revival was spreading across Sumi villages, the SBAK issued a regulation which proclaimed the revival to be unbiblical, and hence a satanic form of worship, amidst fears that it would affect the unity of the Sumi Baptist church. In the regulation the SBAK instructed local churches not to support the revival and prohibited the revivalists from holding services in the village churches. Moreover, the underground Naga government (which was composed of Christian Naga) was also against the spread of the revival and became heavily involved in suppressing it by fining the revivalists (*Ghokimi Centennial Souvenir* 2006: 70–72). Despite the opposition they were facing, however, those who were in favour of the 'Spirit things', as one interlocutor called them, remained 'strong in spirit' and, in their conviction that what they were doing was dictated by God through the Holy Spirit, they broke away from the majority Baptist church in order to form their own church, the Nagaland Christian Revival Church (NCRC).[23] This was the first division within the Sumi Baptist Church based on irreconcilable contestations over 'correct' Christian orthodoxy and orthopraxy.

In the 1970s another revival wave swept across the lands of the Naga. While the First Great Revival was characterised by the repentance of sins and a (re)commitment

Identity Change and the Construction of Difference   **143**

to Christ at a time of political turmoil, the Second Great Revival brought about a renewed focus on world evangelism and missionary outreach, especially outside Nagaland. In 1970 the Nagaland Missionary Movement (renamed the Nagaland Missions Movement in 2008, or NMM) was established as a mission department of the Nagaland Baptist Church Council (NBCC)[24] with the sole vision of 'reaching out to the unreached Naga and encouraging the local Churches to send out Missionaries' (*NBCC Platinum Jubilee Souvenir* 2012: 26–27). On 1–9 March 1975 a Naga Congress on World Evangelisation was held in Dimapur under the theme 'Let the Earth Hear His Voice', during which Baptist church leaders from across Nagaland made a covenant with God 'to promote missionary activities in and outside Nagaland and to promote revival movement in the churches'. One of the resolutions of the Congress was to encourage tribal church associations and individual churches across Nagaland to dedicate themselves to a number of 'spiritual measures' intended to bring about 'the mighty outpouring of the power of the Holy Spirit upon all believers'. These measures included organising prayer cells and Bible study groups and holding evangelistic crusades in every village and town in Nagaland.[25] In a milestone Annual Convention held in 1977, it was resolved to enlist 10,000 Naga missionaries within the next six months and send them out to minister in Asia. Despite much subsequent controversy in the following years regarding the nature of this resolution (for example, was it just a resolution or a 'covenant' with God, was it binding on the present generation or a future 'prophetic voice', and so on?), this missionary vision underscored and reflected a popular idea, prevalent in Naga society, that the Naga were a chosen nation of God, much like the Israelites of the Old Testament, and that it was their duty to spread the gospel in Asia. Naga churches are reported to have taken up the evangelical zeal very seriously, and mission departments were formed in all tribal associations and individual churches.

Within this highly charged spiritual environment, the Second Great Revival began among the Sumi in 1975–1976 with an unprecedented outpouring of the Holy Spirit that saw thousands of people (re)commit their lives to Jesus amidst abundant stories of miraculous healings and prophecies and visions coming true. One of my elderly interlocutors narrated:

> In 1975, when I was in Class 8, it happened in Suruhoto; that time Revd Dr Hevukhu Achumi was the translator because missionaries from NMM had come for revival hour. So he was preaching and then something unusual happened – say, if you have pain in your stomach and they pray, you are healing; you are unable to walk but if they pray and if they tell you to walk in the name of Jesus, you are walking; all such kinds of healing that was miracle. In that way, people who already healed from their illness and from their family disturbance, they were called.[26]

144   *Iliyana Angelova*

The revival quickly spread across Sumi villages, and prayer groups were formed. 'In the heydays of the Revival it was a real moment, impressive, people don't want to sleep at night, want to pray together, to sing, they shout, dance, clap, jump. Many people confessed their sins and received real joy, rejoiced in the Lord', remembered one pastor the spirit of those days.[27]

The fact that this time many Sumi Baptists believed that the revival was a true manifestation of God's power through the Holy Spirit can be attributed to the influence of several factors. To begin with, the NBCC, in its capacity as the apex church body of Naga Baptists, played an active role in spreading the revival in the understanding that it was necessary for fulfilling the Great Commission of Jesus Christ. Moreover, in November 1972 a number of American pastors, who were family members of the American Baptist missionaries who had worked among the Naga, were allowed to enter Nagaland[28] in order to attend the Centennial Jubilee of Christianity in Nagaland. Later the same month the influential American evangelical preacher Billy Graham also visited Nagaland and organised a revival crusade in Kohima, which drew a mammoth crowd of tens of thousands of people, many of whom had walked for days from their remote villages in order to attend. This revival crusade and the presence and preaching of other American pastors in Nagaland during the Centennial celebrations must have played a major role in triggering the second revival wave among the Naga and in shaping its form. Indeed, as Simon Coleman has observed in his work with a church in Sweden, 'visits from important foreign preachers can be seen as catalysing revival' (Coleman 2000: 102). At the same time, unlike the First Revival of the 1950s, this one was not suppressed by the Naga underground leaders; rather, it was promoted by them as part of their political agenda to resist the Indian nation-state by turning all Naga into Baptist Christians.

THE POLITICISATION OF CHRISTIANITY: 'NAGALAND FOR CHRIST'

From the inception of the Naga nationalist movement in the early twentieth century, concerted efforts have been made by Naga political leaders to help forge a collective Naga national identity based on the tropes of 'difference' and 'uniqueness' in comparison to the rest of India, and therefore right to self-determination. The perception of difference, while not entirely the product of colonialism, was certainly accentuated by a number of isolationist and protectionist policies introduced by the British in the administered Naga areas.[29] At the same time, the classificatory projects of the colonial administrators (as seen in area maps, census reports and ethnographic publications) expanded the locus of people's identifications from their villages to larger social groups. And by bringing children from different Naga tribes into their mission schools, the American Baptist missionaries also helped to create a 'powerful pan-Naga sense of solidarity' (Jacobs 1990: 156) and a notion of nationhood, which was constructed in addition to prevailing traditional tribal sentiments, affiliations and loyalties. In the context of the antagonistic Indo-Naga relations, especially since the 1950s, these perceptions of distinctiveness and a shared Naga nationhood were strengthened further. In their attempts to distinguish themselves as far as possible from their Indian counterparts in whose nation-state they found themselves upon the retreat of the British, the Naga drew on symbols and identities that were deemed to be as distant from the Indian ones as possible, and re-created their own distinctiveness by accentuating what they perceived to be the most un-Indian thing: Christianity.

In a series of official Naga political documents from the 1950s to the 1980s, it becomes clear that conversion to Christianity was increasingly being intertwined with the political project of constructing a collective Naga identity. These documents demonstrate that Naga political leaders had gradually come to the understanding that Nagaland should be created as a Christian state. For example, in the first Constitution (or *Yehzabo*) of Nagaland in 1956, God's name is invoked several times, but the *Yehzabo* only states that 'Religion will be free' without specifying explicitly what that religion is (cited in Keyho 2008: 26). At the same time, it was obvious that the Naga nationalist struggle was originally conceptualised as a Christian struggle although to a lesser extent in the 1950s than in the 1970s. Elwin writes:

> In 1956, an order was circulated by the Chief of the 'Country Guard Government of Nagaland' that 'God ought to be included in every practical field in Nagas and, therefore, as many pastors as possible should be appointed to prepare the war affairs'. Services were regularly held in the various hide-outs and there was a great deal of propaganda that since Nagaland was to be the first completely Christian State in Asia ... it was the duty of Christians to fight the 'Hindu Government' in order to preserve their religion. (Elwin 1961: 63)

It was during this early period of the Naga nationalist struggle that the slogan 'Nagaland for Christ' started to appear more pronouncedly in the public space. According to missionary records that I consulted, the first reference to this slogan was made in the context of Naga missionary activity: in 1958 the Ao Naga started a mission and outreach campaign among the border Naga tribes under the theme 'Naga Land for Christ' (*Minutes* 1959: 76). This missionary campaign was directly inspired by earlier American missionary efforts to encourage the Naga themselves to be active evangelists for Christ. The 'Naga Land for Christ'

146 *Iliyana Angelova*

evangelistic campaign seems to have gained some momentum among Naga Baptist churches in the early 1960s, as Elwin observed that Naga churches were decorated with posters reading 'Nagaland for Christ' (Elwin 1961: 63).

By the mid-1960s, the practice of daily prayer at noon had been firmly established among Naga national workers and their officers (Iralu 2009: 250), and all top political leaders had already converted to Christianity. Nevertheless, in the 1970s there were still some Naga, especially among the older generations, in the eastern regions and in remoter villages, who were practising the traditional Naga religion. Although no animosity was explicitly demonstrated against non-Christian Naga, belonging to the traditional Naga religion was increasingly being associated with 'backwardness'. The final amendment of the *Yehzabo* from 1971 (Part X: Religion, Art. 136) reflects this complex religious situation by stipulating that 'Protestant Christianity and Naga Religion are recognised religions in Nagaland'.

In the late 1970s the slogan 'Nagaland for Christ' reappeared again in the context of the renewed Naga commitment to missionary outreach as part of the Second Great Evangelical Revival, but it was soon appropriated by the Naga underground leaders as an ideological unifier of the national struggle. This was particularly true for the political agenda of the NSCN-IM,[30] the most influential splinter faction of the Naga nationalist movement. As top NSCN-IM leaders (some of whom came from chiefly lineages while others did not) became influenced by the revival, so did the lower functionaries, and conversion was made a prerequisite for joining the national struggle. More importantly, however, the NSCN-IM not only used the slogan to legitimise their struggle and grant it divine sanction, but also took it upon themselves to convert all Naga.[31] The slogan 'Nagaland for Christ' was immediately promoted in official NSCN-IM documents, including its manifesto, which states in the section on religion that 'we stand for the faith in God and the salvation of mankind in Jesus, the Christ, alone, that is "Nagaland for Christ"' (cited in Haskar and Luithui 1984: 137). No mention is made of the religious dualism that was present in the *Yehzabo*. Henceforth, all official NSCN-IM publications start with an explicit invocation to God in the triple formula 'Praise the Lord! Praise the Lord! Praise the Lord!' This demonstrates that in the political agenda of the NSCN-IM at least, Christianity has become an inseparable, if not a crucial, part of a political agenda, which identifies 'true' Naga by their faith: Christianity. This consistent politicisation of Christianity in Naga nationalist discourses since the inception of the Naga independence movement, but more pronouncedly since the 1970s–1980s, has irreversibly shifted public attention away from the initial evangelistic meaning of the slogan 'Nagaland for Christ' to an explicitly political agenda. At the same time, it has also played a decisive role in effecting conversions among all

Naga in this later period when being Naga became permanently associated with being Christian.

CONCLUSION

Nagaland is currently one of the states with the highest percentage of Christian population in India. Although there is no available census data on the exact number of Christians among the Sumi or any other Naga tribe, it is still possible to estimate numbers based on village church records. This makes it possible to claim that Baptist Christianity is currently the most popular denomination among the Sumi, followed by the indigenous NCRC. Using Joel Robbins' two-stage model of conversion as a point of departure, the present chapter has argued that this religious transformation among the Sumi is the product of historical processes underpinned by the simultaneous and complex interplay between utilitarian and intellectualist motivations in the first several decades of the twentieth century. These varied from availing of the social mobility opportunities that mission education provided, to escaping burdensome economic obligations in elaborate village rituals, to healing afflictions, to partaking in what was perceived as Western modernity and its technological advances, to various spiritual encounters with God and so on. Moreover, as Joshi (in this volume) rightly observes, it is sometimes difficult to distinguish analytically between the two categories as what appear utilitarian or pragmatic reasons for conversion might be experienced as 'genuinely felt emotional responses' by the converts themselves. By providing glimpses into the life-history of Ashu Kushe – the first Sumi prophet (*tungkupu*) – the chapter has also suggested that Sumi conversions might be best understood in the context of Sumi social structure and its hierarchical organisation, where the conversion of Sumi chiefs (*akukau*) entailed the conversion of their families and clans without affecting the customary ways of constructing political and symbolic authority among the Sumi. This does not invalidate the power of individual choice but rather pinpoints that conversion is often also a collective decision as individuals are embedded in networks of social relations and obligations. In addition, despite its apparent radical discontinuity with the 'heathen' past, conversion among the Sumi and other Naga is actually underpinned by continuities of socio-cultural custom and social organisation (see Angelova 2017).

At the same time, although reported to have been of mass movement proportions among the Sumi compared to other Naga tribes such as the Angami, for example, early Sumi conversions were not unequivocally welcomed and created multiple conflicts and fissures within the community: both between Christian and non-Christian Sumi as well as among the Christians themselves

148 *Iliyana Angelova*

in relation to what it meant to be a 'true' Christian. In the early decades of Naga conversions this usually entailed adopting a Western/American lifestyle, a new worldview based on God's commandments and ultimately a new identity – a 'Yihovah' (Christian) identity. In the postcolonial period of Naga history this focus on religious transformation as identity change translated into a political project of conversion as a form of resistance to the Indian nation-state (cf. Joshi in this volume). From the beginning of the Naga nationalist struggle, the tropes of difference and right to self-determination have been central to the construction and articulation of the Naga national identity. In these articulations 'difference' was created and reinforced as a value, as a positive assertion of perceived cultural and ethnic uniqueness within the paradigm of antagonistic majority (Hindu) – minority (Christian) relations. As a result of the specific unfolding of geo-politics in the Indo-Burma borderlands in the latter part of the twentieth century, therefore, Naga conversions to Christianity have become an ideological tool for constructing ethnic distinctiveness and advancing claims for political autonomy. As Nagaland was thus gradually being transformed into a Christian nation and a 'stronghold of Christianity in Asia', as my interlocutors declared, being Christian has become one of the most important identity markers of the people and a resource they could draw upon in the construction of their individual personhood and their collective nationhood.

NOTES

1. Throughout the chapter, the terms 'tribe' and 'tribal' will be used normatively and without further qualification in recognition of their special status in India where many communities, including the Naga, have been recognised as 'scheduled tribes' and granted constitutional privileges in terms of political representation and access to government jobs and education quotas. However, it is acknowledged that the usage of these terms is ethnographically contingent anywhere, including in India, where they continue to carry strong pejorative connotations of backwardness and lack of development.

2. The ethnonym 'Sema', by which the Angami Naga referred to their neighbours to the northeast, was codified in colonial writing and was in widespread use until recently, when it was replaced by the ethnonym 'Sumi' as an indigenous term by which the 'Sema' denoted themselves. This change in nomenclature was initiated by the Sumi Hoho, the apex tribal association of the Sumi, and promulgated via a government administrative order of 24 September 1992 (Assumi 2009: 6). In reality, both ethnonyms are used interchangeably by those to whom they refer, but since 'Sumi' is the indigenous term (and is hence more appropriate), I will retain it throughout my discussion.

3. The Naga tribes (more than 30 in number, of which 14 have been recognised as 'indigenous' to the state of Nagaland) speak a variety of Tibeto-Burman languages and

reside in the highland borderland regions between India and Myanmar in the present-day Indian states of Nagaland, Manipur, Arunachal Pradesh and Assam and the Sagaing Administrative Division of Myanmar. Prior to converting to Christianity, the Naga were animists.

4. The American Baptist Missionary Union was later renamed the American Baptist Foreign Mission Society (ABFMS) and is currently operating under the name of American Baptist International Ministries.

5. For a history of British colonial administration among the Naga, see Elwin (1961), Joshi (2012) and Yonuo (1974).

6. *Gaonbura* – a village headman.

7. This expulsion was the result of security concerns shared by the new Indian government that the American missionaries in northeast India could be connected with the nationalist struggles of the hill tribes in the changed geo-political environment of the 1950s.

8. Ashu Kushe is remembered as one of the most active Sumi evangelists who contributed to mass conversions not only among the Sumi but also among neighbouring tribes (Sangtam, Yimchungru, Chakhesang, Angami and Rengma). He was the son of the village soothsayer.

9. Inaho was a *dobashi* (that is, an Assamese-speaking Naga, who acted as an interpreter and intermediary between the British Government and Naga villages) who was notorious for persecuting Sumi Baptists and American missionaries until he had a Pauline experience and converted in 1927 (*NBCC Platinum Jubilee Souvenir* 2012: 188–189).

10. The number of Sumi converts continued to grow steadily in the next couple of decades as is obvious from missionary records: in 1950, there were 16,422 registered Sumi Christians (*Minutes* 1951: 41), and in 1958, there were 18,226 (*Minutes* 1959: 79). Even though one might question the exact reliability of these figures, the fact remains that in terms of conversion rates the Sumi were the second most numerous Naga converts after the Ao (*Minutes* 1959: 76–80).

11. The first Reader and a short hymnal were translated into Sutsa (the Sumi language) in 1908 by Ivulho Shohe and Revd Dickson. The full version of the New Testament was translated by Revd Anderson in 1944 (Anderson 1978b: 31), and the full translation of the whole Bible was completed by Revd Nitoyi Achumi of Yezami village between 1969 and 1983 (Aye 2005: 92).

12. For a discussion of Naga love of music and the instrumentality of music for Naga conversions, see Hutton (1921) and Ao (2002), respectively. For a similar observation of the role of Christian music in conversions, see Hrangkhuma (1998), James (1988) and Jones (in this volume).

13. Head-hunting was widely practised by all Naga tribes as an institutionalised way of achieving social status and prestige based on one's ability to kill 'enemies'. The latter category was loosely defined and shifted on a regular basis as villages formed and broke alliances.

14. *Genna* – a term of Assamese origin (*achini* and *apini* in Sutsa) used to describe a taboo of various sorts, which might affect individuals, village wards (*khel*) or the whole village. The term is also used to denote the particular ceremony which marks the beginning and the end of the above periods of prohibition.

15. *Aluzhi* (from Sutsa) – a mixed working group of people belonging to the same age group who (used to) work in the fields together and perform other manual work in the village as required.

16. For a discussion of what constitutes contemporary Sumi notions of being a 'good' Christian, see Angelova (2015).

17. It should be noted that for many early Sumi Christians the term 'Christianity' was unfamiliar, and they identified their new faith and identity as 'Yihovah' (cf. Chishi Swu 2004).

18. For a discussion of contemporary processes of reinvention and reconceptualization of Naga cultural heritage (described as a 'cultural revival'), see Angelova (2015).

19. *Morung* – a bachelor's dormitory, which was an important social and ritual institution among the Naga.

20. For a detailed discussion of Sumi worldviews and Christian conversion, see Chophy (2019).

21. However, even though the formal authority of Sumi chiefs did not diminish as a result of their adoption of Christianity, a new figure of non-traditional authority emerged in Naga society since the end of the nineteenth century: the pastor. Both in the past and at present, Sumi pastors may or may not belong to a chiefly lineage but they embody a form of authority parallel to those of village chiefs, which is not customary but divinely sanctioned.

22. With the intensification of the Indo-Naga military conflict, in 1953 the Naga national government was forced to go underground.

23. The NCRC is an indigenous church which was established in Nagaland in 1964. It is currently the second largest denomination among the Sumi, with 66 churches in 2012 (*NCRC Souvenir* 2012: 38).

24. The NBCC is the apex church body for all Naga Baptist tribal church associations.

25. http://www.nbcc.in/missions.html#2.

26. Formal interview conducted on 3 August 2012.

27. Formal interview conducted on 16 December 2011.

28. For security reasons, the Indian government had restricted foreigners' access to Nagaland from the late 1950s to the early 2000s. The foreign nationals who attended the Centennial celebrations, therefore, were granted special exemption from this rule – for the few days of their visit.

29. These were especially the 1873 Bengal Eastern Frontier Regulation (otherwise known as the Inner Line Regulation) and the 1880 Frontier Tracts Regulation II. The former delimited the territorial bounds of British jurisdiction, prohibited the access of

non-locals to Naga territories without a special licence and ensured the preservation of Naga land ownership and customary practices; the latter classified the Naga areas as 'backward tracts' and further guaranteed that the Naga Hills would be administered in a different way to the rest of British India.

30. NSCN-IM (National Socialist Council of Nagaland, Isak-Muivah).

31. The conversion of the Eastern Naga of Nagaland state and Myanmar, for example, is attributed not only to the activity of Naga evangelists, but also to NSCN-IM cadres (see Jacobs 1990: 177).

BIBLIOGRAPHY

Anderson, Bengt Ivan. 1978a. *We Lived in Nagaland: The Experiences of a Missionary Family*. No publisher information.

———. 1978b. 'A Brief Historical Sketch of the American Baptist Mission Work in the Sema Naga Tribe, Nagaland.' *Sema Baptist Diamond Jubilee Souvenir 1904–1978*, 29–33. Aizuto, Nagaland: No publisher information.

Angelova, Iliyana. 2015. *Baptist Christianity and the Politics of Identity among the Sumi Naga of Nagaland, Northeast India*. University of Oxford, unpublished DPhil thesis.

———. 2017. 'Colonial Rule, Christianity and Sociocultural (Dis)continuities among the Sumi Naga.' *The South Asianist* 5(1), special issue '*The Nagas in the 21st Century*': 20–45.

Ao, Bendangyabang A. 2002. *History of Christianity in Nagaland: The Ao Naga Tribal Christian Mission Enterprise 1872–1972*. Mokokchung, Nagaland: Shalom Ministry Publication.

Assumi, Zhekugha. 2009. *The Sumi Ahuna*. Dimapur: Heritage Publishing House.

Aye, Khashito. 2005. *The Impact of Christian Education (100 Years of Christianity in Sumi Baptist Churches, 1903–2003)*. Dimapur, Nagaland: Christian Education Ministry.

Baruah, Sanjib. 2005. *Durable Disorder: Understanding the Politics of Northeast India*. New Delhi: Oxford University Press.

———, ed. 2009. *Beyond Counter-Insurgency: Breaking the Impasse in Northeast India*. New Delhi: Oxford University Press.

Cannell, Fenella. 2006. 'Introduction: The Anthropology of Christianity.' In *The Anthropology of Christianity*, edited by Fenella Cannell, 1–50. Durham: Duke University Press.

Chishi Swu, Isak. 2004. *Ashu Kushe (2004 Sumi Christian Centenary, in Memory of Kushe Chishilimi)*. Dimapur: Kushe Humanity Foundation.

Chophy, Kanato. 2019. *Constructing the Divine: Religion and Worldview of a Naga Tribe in North-East India*. London: Routledge.

Coleman, Simon. 2000. *The Globalisation of Charismatic Christianity: Spreading the Gospel of Prosperity*. Cambridge: Cambridge University Press.

152 *Iliyana Angelova*

Delano, Robert Fletcher. 1978. 'Remembering God's Goodness and Grace.' In *Sema Baptist Diamond Jubilee Souvenir 1904–1978*, 26–28. Aizuto, Nagaland: No publisher information.

Downs, Frederick. 1992. *History of Christianity in India*, Volume 5: *North-East India in the Nineteenth and Twentieth Centuries*, Part 5. Bangalore: The Church History Association of India.

Eaton, Richard. 1997. 'Comparative History as World History: Religious Conversion in Modern India.' *Journal of World History* 8(2): 243–271.

Elwin, Verrier. 1961. *Nagaland*. Shillong: Research Department, Adviser's Secretariat.

Engelke, Matthew. 2004. 'Discontinuity and the Discourse of Conversion.' *Journal of Religion in Africa* 34 (1–2): 82–109.

Gellner, David. ed. 2009. *Ethnic Activism and Civil Society in South Asia*. London: Sage.

Haskar, Nandita and Luingam Luithui. 1984. *Nagaland File: A Question of Human Rights*. New Delhi: Lancer International.

Hefner, Robert. 1993. 'Introduction: World Building and the Rationality of Conversion.' In *Conversion to Christianity: Historical and Anthropological Perspectives on a Great Transformation*, edited by Robert Hefner, 3–44. Berkeley: University of California Press.

Hrangkhuma, F. 1998. 'Christianity among the Mizo in Mizoram.' In *Christianity in India: Search for Liberation and Identity*, edited by F. Hrangkhuma, 265–311. Delhi: ISPCK.

Hutton, John Henry. 1921. *The Sema Nagas*. London: Macmillan & Co.

Iralu, Kaka. 2009. *The Naga Saga: A Historical Account of the 62 Years of Indo-Naga War and the Story of Those Who Were Never Allowed to Tell It*. Kohima: Published by the author.

Jacobs, Julian. 1990. *The Nagas: Hill Peoples of Northeast India*. Stuttgart: Mayer.

James, Wendy. 1988. 'Uduk Faith in a Five-note Scale: Mission Music and the Spread of the Gospel.' In *Vernacular Christianity: Essays in the Social Anthropology of Religion (Presented to Godfrey Lienhardt)*, edited by Wendy James and Douglas Johnson, 131–145. New York: Lilian Barber Press.

Joshi, Vibha. 2007. 'The Birth of Christian Enthusiasm among the Angami of Nagaland.' *Journal of South Asian Studies* 30(3): 541–557. DOI: 10.1080/0085640 0701714120.

———. 2012. *A Matter of Belief: Christian Conversion and Healing in Northeast India*. Oxford: Berghahn Books.

———. 2013. 'The Micropolitics of Borders: The Issue of Greater Nagaland or Nagalim.' In *Borderland Lives in Northern South Asia*, edited by David Gellner, 163–193. Durham, North Carolina: Duke University Press.

Keyho, Biseto Medom. 2008. *My Journey in the Nagaland Freedom Movement*. Kohima: published by the author.

Longkumer, Arkotong. 2009. 'Exploring the Diversity of Religion: The Geo-Political Dimensions of Fieldwork and Identity in the North East of India.' *Fieldwork in Religion* 4(1): 46–66. DOI 10.1558/fiel.v4i1.46.

Maxwell, Neville. 1980. *India, the Nagas and the Northeast.* Minority Rights Group Report No 17. London: Minority Rights Group.

Mills, James Philip. 1926. *The Ao Nagas.* London: Macmillan & Co.

Mosse, David. 1999. 'Responding to Subordination: Identity and Change among South Indian Untouchable Castes.' In *Identity and Affect: Experiences of Identity in a Globalising World*, edited by John Campbell and Alan Rew, 64–104. London: Pluto Press.

Robbins, Joel. 2004. *Becoming Sinners: Christianity and Moral Torment in a Papua New Guinea Society.* Berkeley: University of California Press.

Robinson, Rowena and Sathianathan Clarke. 2003. 'Introduction: The Many Meanings of Religious Conversion on the Indian Subcontinent.' In *Religious Conversion in India: Modes, Motivations, and Meanings*, edited by Rowena Robinson and Sathianathan Clarke, 1–21. New Delhi: Oxford University Press.

Sema, Hokishe. 1986. *Emergence of Nagaland: Socio-Economic and Political Transformation and the Future.* New Delhi: Vikas Publishing House.

Stirrat, R. L. 1999. 'Constructing Identities in Nineteenth-Century Colombo.' In *Identity and Affect: Experiences of Identity in a Globalising World*, edited by John Campbell and Alan Rew, 39–63. London: Pluto Press.

van der Veer, Peter. 1994. *Religious Nationalism: Hindus and Muslims in India.* Berkeley: University of California Press.

Yonuo, Asoso. 1974. *The Rising Nagas: A Historical and Political Study.* Delhi: Vivek Publishing House.

Young, Richard Fox and Jonathan A. Seitz. 2013. 'Introduction.' In *Asia in the Making of Christianity: Conversion, Agency, and Indigeneity, 1600s to the Present*, edited by Richard Fox Young and Jonathan A. Seitz, 1–26. Leiden: Brill.

Periodicals – Baptist Missionary Magazine (BMM)

Baptist Missionary Magazine (1873–1909). June 1901, 81(6). American Periodicals Series Online.

Archival Documentation Accessed at the Library and Archive of the Council of Baptist Churches of Northeast India (CBCNEI) in Guwahati, Assam

Minutes. 1936. Assam Baptist Missionary Conference. 3–6 February 1936. Jorhat.

Minutes. 1951. First Annual Meeting, Council of Baptist Churches in Assam. 30 December 1950–5 January 1951. Gauhati.

154 *Iliyana Angelova*

Minutes. 1959. Ninth Annual Session, Council of Baptist Churches of Assam and Manipur. 7–11 January 1959. Tura.

Report. 1936. Assam Baptist Missionary Conference, 1–6 December 1936. Gauhati.

Christian Souvenirs

Ghokimi Centennial Souvenir. 2006. *Ghokimi Baptist Church, Christian Centenary Celebration Souvenir 1906–2006.* Pughoboto: SABAK.

NBCC Platinum Jubilee Souvenir. 2012. *One New Humanity in Christ: Nagaland Baptist Church Council Celebrates Platinum Jubilee 1937–2012.* Kohima: NBCC.

NCRC Souvenir. 2012. *Nagaland Christian Revival Church Souvenir Revival: Golden Jubilee (1962–2012).* No publication details.

6

Conversion to Christianity and Healing

The Naga of Northeast India

Vibha Joshi

The Naga people of Nagaland in northeastern India have over two or three generations converted almost entirely to Christianity from their indigenous animistic religion. Situating the phenomenon of conversion in its socio-political and historical context, I begin by exploring how the concept of Christian 'rupture' with the past advocated by Joel Robbins (2004) can be applied to conversion among the Naga. Taking into account the history of Christianity among the Naga, I suggest that the role of healing in early evangelising, and its continued relevance in the current attempts at reconciliation among Naga themselves, modifies significantly the notion of rupture to the extent that it may have opposite consequences to those originally envisaged by missionaries. I further argue that among the Naga the theme of healing is the connecting thread which runs through the historical and contemporary role of Christianity and its continued importance in the shift from individual to collective healing.

It is true that early missionaries to Nagaland wanted to create a 'rupture' with what they regarded as the heathen beliefs and practices of the past, including the local religion of animism. Animism, however, comprised important traditional healing practices, which were not easily banned. At the same time, missionaries brought in Western biomedicine, which was eagerly accepted by the local Naga.

From the missionaries' viewpoint, and that of the earliest Naga Christian converts, traditional healing and biomedicine were incompatible. However, this potential conflict in healing methods and accompanying beliefs did not result in a straightforward and unambiguous clash. For, although many animistic practices were successfully banished or marginalised by the missionaries, many traditional healers acknowledged the evident success of modern biomedical healing and so, rather than opposing this new mode of healing, grafted themselves and a selection of their traditional practices onto Christianity, by becoming Christians themselves. They therefore in effect created a bridge between traditional and modern healing in the idiom of Christianity. The missionaries had not intended this bridging of tradition and modernity through such conversion. It was therefore an unintended consequence of their teachings in the power and faith of healing, from both spiritual and biomedical perspectives.

However, the result was that 'healing' as a general idiom grew enormously as an inextricable part of Naga Christianity alongside an increasingly rapid rate of conversion. The idiom came in due course to extend its concern with the treatment of bodily ailments and to embrace also the idea of wartime reconciliation, that is, 'healing the wounds of war'. As internal factional struggles among the Naga and wars with first the British and then the Indian state grew ever more ferocious over the years, traditional healing and its merged identity with modern healing thus became the basis of the idea of political reconciliation among the factions, all under the rubric of Christianity. The 'rupture' with the past that early Christianity had sought therefore paradoxically allowed for an unexpected accommodation of otherwise opposed religious approaches and actually encouraged Christian conversion to flourish.

This development seems at first sight counter-intuitive in the light of conventional views to the effect that traditional religious and healing practices are normally superseded by those of modernity. After all, the boundaries between religions tend to harden once each claims that it alone can offer access to spiritual truth and proper modes of behaviour and worship, as has often been the case in the opposition between Christianity and pre-existing and traditional religions. Such claims are made by such religious guardians as clerics, influential lay members or elders and become the basis of their authority and of the particular religion's alleged conservatism and purity. Under such stringent conditions religious followers find it difficult to abandon their existing creed and practices in favour of others. Such 'apostasy' is in some cases dealt with severely but, in a lesser form, characterises all forms of authoritarian religious membership, ranging from physical violence to social exclusion. Yet, the so-called market element produced by religions co-existing and competing, either explicitly or tacitly, means that people may well be attracted by a creed or cult different from their own and may forsake their original one, either as a requirement of the new membership or out of a wish to pursue a single belief. While less authoritarian religions may not prohibit multiple membership and so allow adherents the possibility of following beliefs and practices taken from more than one, the trend in recent decades has been in the opposite direction. Thus, since the Second World War, increasingly rapid modes of global communication and interaction and the postcolonial opening up of world areas to new forms of capitalist trade and consumerism have been accompanied by a kind of regional, ethnic and nationalist backlash or resistance, often expressed religiously. This has frequently had the consequence of exacerbating conflicts along these lines in the idiom of religious exclusivity, even if the underlying sources of conflict are of a politico-economic or social nature.

Alongside the competitive religious search for spiritual comfort and reassurance, there are often more tangible benefits sought, such as new methods of healing and new forms of education, which become subsumed in the general acceptance of the new religion to which a follower has converted. The large-scale conversion of the Naga over the last three generations from their indigenous animistic religion to different Christian sects has been accompanied by such new ideas of personal as well as spiritual well-being.

A distinctive wider feature of Naga conversion is that, unlike converts in such other areas of mainland India as Orissa who have sometimes become Christian to escape persecution, the Naga have not been subject to attacks and predations from neighbours and have remained the sole owners of their lands. They have however struggled with first the British colonialists and later the Indian government to retain and enhance their sovereignty. Their adoption of Christianity rather than Hinduism, Islam, Buddhism, Sikhism or Jainism may be interpreted as an expression of their collective wish to assert their socio-cultural and ethno-linguistic distinctiveness and separateness from the rest of India.[1] While nowadays the Naga are more and more united in their adoption of Christianity, notwithstanding differences among the various sects, tensions between converts and animists were historically strong and even today permeate social relationships, including the area of healing and medicine, for which adjustments and reconciliations are constantly attempted. Healing, in other words, has throughout the colonial and postcolonial periods been the basis of a continuity of tradition into modernity, including collective and individual expectations and aspirations. It is in the increasing use of Christianity to articulate nationalist sentiment and political organisation that healing has become an idiom to reconcile internal divisions arising from competing factions of the struggle for autonomy, statehood and nationhood.

CONVERSION AND CHRISTIANITY

The use by the Naga of Christianity for expressing their autonomy of or independence from mainland India raises the question of how far, if at all, we can identify special features of Christianity which lend themselves to this task. For instance, does the hierarchical organisation of Catholicism have a different influence than the more egalitarian but sometimes factional mode of operation among Baptists in Nagaland? Or, more generally, does Christianity as a whole, its texts and its association with missions teaching Western education and medicine, foster a kind of modernity which fits Western forms of capitalist consumerism, technological dominance and nation-based political organisation, and so stands apart from other global narratives offered by other religions? If so,

158 *Vibha Joshi*

then it is a modernity which juggles Naga demands for nationalist autonomy with the Christian call for universal tolerance of others, a call which takes the form of attempts at reconciling the competing factions making up the nationalist struggle.

The turn by many anthropologists to the study of Christianity as a field separate from, say, Islam or Buddhism probably reinforces the view that it does indeed have a distinctive influence as an organisational form on the peoples who adopt it. However, it is perhaps best, as has been suggested by other scholars, to see apparently disparate religions as overlapping with each other in certain respects. Thus, Christianity is not always 'tolerant' of others and includes sects which celebrate spiritual charisma and miracles in their organisational beliefs and practices not unlike some Sufi orders, just as Islam itself preaches peace alongside Christianity in some of its texts. In this chapter, the attempt is to portray Christianity and Christian conversion as the Naga themselves understand it, for all their differences of interpretation. No attempt is made to generalise to world Christianity in general.

My understanding of Christianity in Nagaland from Naga viewpoints was arrived at through a prior interest, not in religion, but in traditional healers. This was the focus of the initial fieldwork among Angami Naga in 1985 and 1990s. A key pre-Christian festival of the Angami called Sekrenyi addressed questions of both bodily and spiritual health. Some of the participants in the festival were Christian converts and evidently had to adjust and reconcile their originally animistic practices with those demanded of them by their new faith. It was necessary therefore to acknowledge the inextricable and mutual involvement of traditional healing and Christianity including its modernist trappings such as biomedicine and, initially, missionary dismissal of indigenous beliefs as superstition. At no point, then, was it a study of Christianity as a system but rather of the Naga as a people, many of whom are Christian and most of whom have at some point encountered the challenges and sometimes conflicts in the relationship of healing to Christianity and animism. Overall, then, it became clear that the study of Naga healers necessitated following the path of Christianity among them, understanding why some joined the religion while others did not.

Religious conversion is here a process involving a play of motivations, incentives, inducements, encouragements, directives and constraints operating among various actors in a history of precolonial, colonial and postcolonial contexts. Conversion can refer to a change from one absolute belief to another, or it may be fragmentary and full of stops, starts, reverses, advances, contraction and outreach. While many Christian communities emphasise, perhaps increasingly, the indigenous and independent nature of their churches, conversions are nevertheless set ultimately within a global network of connections

Conversion to Christianity and Healing   **159**

through the work of missions and proselytisation, as historically we see in Nagaland.

Noting the changes undergone by religions in their global transfer Csordas draws attention to their transportability as the 'means by which they traverse geographic and cultural space' (Csordas 2009: xxx) through networks and global connections. What is not fully explained is the agency of both the 'transporter' and 'recipient', and the criteria by which converts choose one religion, or part of a religion, rather than another. In other words, what can a new religion offer, and what is appropriated by converts?

Early missionary strategy among the Naga was to prioritise 'civilising' and 'educating the pagans'. This was the precursor of what we have later called the expression of modernity through new lifestyles and techniques. These included the introduction of biomedical hygiene practices, biomedicine itself, different (though not always better) skills of vegetable gardening and animal husbandry. Moreover, as part of educational instruction, it involved imparting the ability to argue and debate with colonial and postcolonial authority, even if initially on the latter's terms. Modernity, as the (at least partial) rejection of tradition and greater emphasis on individualism and increasing faith in education and new technologies, was thus broadly an intended consequence of Christian missionising attempts to convert. What was not really intended or envisaged was the later development of the modernist idea of ethnic-national self-determination. This accelerated in the decades following the end of the Second World War, following Naga conscription into British forces during the war itself, and was sustained by the increasing numbers of educated and articulate Naga campaigners. Modernity, as an increasingly pervasive and nominally coherent worldview, thus became intertwined with Christian conversion (see van der Veer 1996).

Within this general drive towards Christian conversion, individuals had and continue to have specific and often varying reasons to convert: recovery from sickness or injury as a result of biomedical treatment after unsuccessfully trying traditional therapy; a wish to escape traditional constraints on behaviour by adopting Christian prohibitions on them and adopting alternative behaviour; following the example and recommendations of already converted relatives and friends; accepting the missionary view that Christian beliefs were more rational than those of traditional animism, dubbed 'superstition'; and, in the case of re-conversion, switching from one form of Christianity to another, as in the rejection of hierarchical communication with God through a priest rather than more directly through personal prayer and spiritual embrace. Also, the perceived pragmatic benefits of conversion or changing one's Christian denomination cannot be underestimated. Smilde (2007: 7) was told by one acquaintance that her reason for leaving the Catholic Church was due to a 'better deal' being offered

160 *Vibha Joshi*

by the evangelical church when the family moved from a small town to the bigger city of Bogota. The Naga make similar claims. Of course, there may be no such material benefits of conversion, or conversion may not be viewed as such and may instead be expressed emotionally during, say, a crisis, as the pull of spiritual intensity and performativity of prayer. Obtaining practical advantages through conversion or by changing denominations or sects does not, after all, by itself devalue piety, provided that the sanctity and sincerity of worship are shared by the Christian community as a whole: one's commitment to God moves with the person, ostensibly regardless of improved circumstances, though in practice sometimes influenced by them. Conversion is thus to some extent part of an implicit bargain between church and potential church-goer.

These individual motivations for Christian conversion are common among the Naga, but, returning to Robbins's characterisation of Christian conversion as involving a 'Paulin' rupture (2004), to what extent can the Naga conversion experience also be explained as a break from the past? Working among the small community of Urapmin in Papua New Guinea, Robbins shows a stark contrast between their beliefs and practices before and after conversion. The change is commonly recorded in many parts of the world as a re-birth, or adopting a 'new life' and discarding a previous one. Following Eisenstadt's theory of the Eurasian axial age of the eighth to third centuries BCE (Eisenstadt 1982: 294–296; Robbins 2012: 8–10; see also Csordas 2009), Christianity is seen as creating a transcendent world of God sharply separated from the mundane world of everyday humanity, whereas the pre-Christian cosmos of animism is made up of ancestral and other spiritual entities which interact and engage with humanity on a practical level within the same world. Thus, although animists make a clear distinction between themselves and non-human beings, they do not regard the latter as inhabiting humanly inaccessible transcendence. Anthropologists making this distinction are aware that the 'radical discontinuity' between past and present allegedly created by Christianity (Cannell 2006: 14) and understood through the 'trope of rupture' (Bialecki, Haynes and Robbins 2008: 1144–1145) is always in tension with continuing pre-Christian spiritual practices and theories of self, cosmos and society. But they insist that there is ineluctable movement through Christianity to this cosmic division between divine transcendence and the mundane human order. They claim that to stay with the counter-argument that people can accommodate both pre-Christian and Christian beliefs in indefinite syncretistic continuity is to deny that people can enlarge their orbit of understanding and learn anything new.

At first sight, the idea of rupture does generally seem to characterise Naga conversion, especially since the Second World War. It was only three generations ago when few Naga were Christian and indigenous animistic beliefs dominated.

Conversion to Christianity and Healing **161**

But the process has not been smooth. While Christianity gained a foothold through education and biomedicine, it also experienced setbacks, including diffidence and what was called 'backsliding' on the part of converts, and the subsequent disbanding of some churches and schools due to missionaries' differing opinions as to what being a Christian should mean and involve. The uneven process of Christian conversion among the Naga is most evident in its early stages but persists at present time in its interpretation and use of healing as an important Christian idiom of reconciliation, with some Christians rejecting those aspects allegedly rooted in pre-Christian animism and others accepting the amalgamation. Healing has then become a trope of significant ambivalence and contestation under the influence of modernity, including ideas of nationhood, educational aspiration and global inclusiveness.

CASE STUDY OF THE NAGA

The two million Naga of Nagaland in northeastern India regard themselves as made up of a number of tribes, with distinctive Tibeto-Burman languages and customs and history, a demarcation which was reaffirmed and perpetuated under British colonial rule. Some Naga groups share their migration histories, myths of origin and material culture. The British administrators writing about the Naga have mentioned coming across 'mixed' villages containing clans from different Naga groups (Hutton 1929; Ham and Saul 2008; Wouters 2017). While some high-level generalisations can be made about the Naga as a whole, I studied intensively one such group, the Angami, and my discussion is largely confined to them.

In the following sections I will first discuss the history of Christianity and Christian denominations among the Naga, the role of healing in evangelising, the attitude of missionaries towards traditional healers, and their practices based on traditional disease etiology. I will then discuss the impact of Christianity on traditional healing followed by the present role of Christianity in the processes of healing both individual and collective.

Before continuing, it is worth outlining a history of the denominations among the Naga. The American Baptists gained a firm foothold among the Naga in the early twentieth century. The Baptist strategy was to make the church self-sufficient and train local evangelists who would proselytise in interior villages, practised to this very day. This became relevant when, at India's independence in 1947, all the American and other foreign missionaries were expelled from the Naga area due to their alleged involvement with the Naga independence movement. Christianity has moreover also been spread through the various underground organisations. Of general note, however, is the considerable increase

162 *Vibha Joshi*

in conversion to Christianity of all kinds since the Second World War, resulting in nearly 90 per cent of the population today being Christian. A turning point may well have been the battle of Kohima in the Angami area of Nagaland in 1944 when Allied forces defeated a Japanese incursion. But the nationalist struggle had an important role in the rapid conversion and Christian revival that swept through the Naga region in the 1950s, 1960s and 1970s.

At present among the Angami several denominations are followed, the most dominant being Baptist, followed by Catholic and Pentecostal, Jehovah's Witness, Seventh Day Adventists and several revival churches. This multiple development of denominations has not always been harmonious. Villages have been divided by them, churches have been resisted or have themselves resisted and broken away from each other and there has been violence and the burning of churches, with some suffering fines or finding it difficult to find land on which to build. And yet, despite such differences, conversion to Christianity overall is a marker of what the Naga see as their totally separate identity from mainland India, which is largely non-Christian. The Naga are linguistically and culturally Tibeto-Burman, unlike most of the rest of India which speaks Indo-Aryan, Austro-Asiatic and Dravidian languages.

The root of such differentiations is evident when we consider the history of Christianity among the Naga. The first contact with some Naga villages were made by the American Baptist missionary Reverend Charles Bronson during the period 1838–1841, at the time when the British were exploring the region for tea plantation (Clark 1978 [1907]; Barpujari 1986; Joshi 2012). Captain Jenkins, a British officer interested in both perpetuating Christianity among the Naga and using them as labour in the plantation, supported the American Baptist missionary. Reverend Bronson had to close the mission in hill villages due to illness and death in his family and non-cooperation of the Naga villagers in the plantation work (ibid.). After a gap of nearly four decades, in 1872, Reverend E. W. Clark and his Assamese assistant, Godhula Brown, opened the first mission station in the Ao Naga area which remained outside the British administration until 1889. Missionaries were, however, sent to the Angami and Lotha Naga areas in the south which were already under the British (see also Angelova in this volume for Christianity among another group, the Sumi Naga).

The story told of the second, and more successful, contact with American Baptist missionary has gained a legendary status over the years. As recollected by Mary Clark, the missionary wife of Reverend Clark in her memoirs, it is said that the Clarks, who were based in Sibsagar at the Mission press, made their first contact with the members of the Ao Naga community who would come down to the market in the Assam plains to barter their hill produce in exchange for iron and other items (Clark 1978 [1907]). According to Mary Clark, the Naga

Conversion to Christianity and Healing **163**

observed the activities in the missionary press and the Clarks seized the opportunity to ask them whether they would like the Naga children to be taught reading and writing and got an answer in the affirmative. Encouraged by this the Clarks sent their assistant Godhula Brown, an Assamese convert, to an Ao Naga village. Mary Clark writes that Godhula was able to learn a little of the local language, and in 1871, persuade the Ao men to take him to their village. In the village he was kept under observation inside a temporary shelter built for him outside the village, as they doubted his motive and thought him to be a British colonial spy. But Godhula remained nonplussed and carried on reading the Bible and singing 'sweet' hymns in Assamese language (ibid.: 11). Eventually he was able to interest the Naga villagers in the new religion and about 40 men escorted him to Sibsagar in the Assam plains when he returned to report to the Clarks. In 1872 he went back to the Naga village with his wife to establish a Christian community and returned after seven months with nine Naga men ready to be baptised (ibid.: 13; Alem 1997: 41). Mary Clark writes that 60 warriors came down to take Reverend Clark up to the mountain village on a particular day which was 'fixed upon a certain phase of the next moon' (1978 [1907]: 13). It took Reverend Clark three days and two nights to reach and after spending a few days with the Naga he returned to Sibsagar and declared that he had found his life-work, which was to be spent in the Naga hills evangelising among the Naga.

The information on the initial missionary period of contact is gleaned from the memoirs that Mary Mead Clark wrote and the letters of the missionaries to the Home Board and to their families in the United States. While the writing is typical of the missionary speak/vocabulary (Beidelman 1982), with references to 'lost sheep and a field ripe for harvest', it also provides an idea of the struggles of the missionaries and that of the people they had undertaken to convert. It was also a move from orality to literacy as Ranger has noted in the case of African communities and along with it an imposition of a certain way of living which required people to imbibe new ideas (Ranger 1981; also Comaroff and Comaroff 1991). The overarching missionary aim was to demonstrate the efficacy of prayer and the supremacy of the Christian God over Naga animism.

Of indispensable support to the missionaries in this aim was the introduction and teaching of rudimentary medicine which went alongside that of literacy and education generally. While medicine, the printed word and printing press was what attracted the Naga to invite the missionaries, the missionaries themselves saw merit in teaching the Naga to read and write, principally so that they could read and comment on the Bible as well as help in the translation of the gospel into the local language. E. W. Clark was the first to write a primer in the Ao language and, as happened elsewhere, the language learned by the missionaries became the translated language of the gospel. Among the Ao, the gospel was

164 *Vibha Joshi*

thus translated into the Mongsen dialect rather than the numerically dominant Chongli. But since educating the Naga was not their primary goal, the Home Board of American Baptist Mission initially discouraged it. While Reverend Clark could see the merit in imparting primary education to the Naga, for, as he wrote in his letters, Ao Naga villages welcomed the evangelists who doubled as primary school teachers (Joshi 2012: 165–174).

Reverend Clark also established the first Christian village, Molungyimsing, made of converts expelled by their parent village for not participating in communal rituals and for not contributing to the village funds (Smith 1925: 190; Mills 1935). In Angami area such separate units were named 'basa' or new. And one still comes across territorial divisions named Basa Khel in some villages in which converts were asked to move out to from their parent village.[2]

As I have discussed elsewhere (Joshi 2012), the missionaries could make inroads into the Angami area by opening primary schools and then later secondary schools with the help of sympathetic British officers. In the American Baptist Mission Society's archives, I came across several letters written by missionaries (especially by Reverend Clark and Reverend Supplee) to the Home Board in which they emphasised the important role education had played in evagelisation. The educated Christian Naga students were sent as teacher-evangelists to the villages which had expressed interest in education, and these villages hosted the teacher and bore all expenses. Later, when the British government also opened schools, educated Christian Nagas joined those as teachers (Joshi 2012: 170; see also Angelova in this volume for similar process amongst the Sumi Naga).

While literacy provided the tools for reading and writing the gospel, it was not sufficient to deal with the etiology of disease and illnesses in the indigenous belief system which supported personalistic theories of illness and supernatural causes. Reverend Clark noted that providing some kind of relief from illness would help the missionaries in stopping backsliding to animal sacrifices and consultation with Naga divinational, shamanistic healers. In the beginning the missionaries used rudimentary medical knowledge to gain the confidence of the villagers. To show the compassionate side of the Christian God, Western medicine was administered along with reading verses from scriptures.

Recollecting an incident during the early days of their missionary stay among the Ao Naga in Naga Hills, Mary Clark wrote that to intimidate the missionaries, the non-Christians from the village had planned ambushing for human heads, only to return from the plains 'without booty, but racked with fever, thus affording the missionary an opportunity of exercising some medical skill and taming their savagery' (1997 [1907]: 18). Succinctly summing up the role of medicine, she wrote: 'Some knowledge of medicine also is of great advantage; it

Conversion to Christianity and Healing **165**

is an open door into many homes, and puts an end to consulting soothsayers and sacrificing to demons' (ibid.: 68).

Acknowledging the importance of medicine in the spreading of the gospel, Reverend E. W. Clark requested the American Baptist Association for an extra supply of medicines for common ailments like fever, stomach and body aches. In fact, in 1881 Reverend Clark wrote to the secretary of the Missionary Union that knowledge of basic medicine should be included as one of the qualifications a future missionary to the Naga Hills should have and that he himself found a basic medicine book called *Household Practice of Medicine* by W. M. Carpenter very useful in the mission work (cf. Puthenpurakal 1984: 218). He even suggested that a theology student planning to join the mission could 'take some medical lectures', and furthermore that if the person did not have enough time to combine his theology course with that on basic medicine, he should 'substitute medical lectures for some of the less important to him of the theology lectures' (Clark 1881; cf. Puthenpurakal 1984: 83–84).

However, Clark was cautious to note that the Naga should not suppose that missionaries were there to give them medicine rather than preach the gospel, that is, their main aim was the 'preaching of the Gospel and not the doctoring of the body' and that 'what healing Jesus did was instantaneously. No expense for medicine or instruments, no time lost in diagnosing and studying cases, no time lost in nursing. His healing did not interfere with his preaching' (cf. Puthenpurakal 1984: 84).

In later years medical missionaries were appointed and in fact one of the missionaries to the Angami Naga, Reverend Sidney Rivenburg, who served at missions to both the Ao and Angami Naga, went back to America to complete a course in medicine before returning to Naga Hills in the capacity of medical missionary.

The use of traditional medicine (even herbs) and healing by the Naga and consultation of healers who were divinely inspired were seen as intertwined with the indigenous religion and an etiology of disease causation (based on the belief in spirits contrary to that of the Christian Holy Spirit).

Writing in a letter to her parents in the United States, about their Christian mailman[3] who had been attacked by a tiger, Hattie Rivenberg, wife of Reverend Sydney Riverburg, mentioned the man's desire to sacrifice animals to appease the spirits when his wounds did not heal:

> One of the worst experiences we have had occurred soon after we came, when our mailman was attacked by what he called a tiger.... Sidney and I stitched up the mailman's wounds, which were deep and many ... we had no idea he could recover, but he did. Maggots got into his wounds and we supposed they would finish what

166 *Vibha Joshi*

the tiger had left. He was discouraged, and wanted to sacrifice. Sydney told him that if he did, he would not continue dressing his wounds. (September 1885; cf. Rivenburg 1941: 49–50)

Notably, comments by Reverend S. Rivenburg exemplify this schism in a letter to the Home Board when he was stationed in the Ao Naga village of Molung:

> Being alone in this heathen village our time has not all been spent in learning Naga roots and stems. Before the missionaries came the Nagas knew no medicine [*sic* but meaning biomedicine] for their ills save the hair of flying squirrels and similar powerful potions, but now they know the value of [bio] medicine many think they cannot do without it. In some cases we go to their houses but when practicable they come to the house or send. How many have been helped in this way, it is impossible to say. I remember one afternoon 12 such persons came for medicine. (Rivenburg 8 January 1886)

Evident in the insistence of the missionaries to suppress use of traditional practices is the tension between biomedical and spiritual healing provided by the missionaries and the spiritual and non-spiritual healing by the traditional practitioners. It is a running theme in medical/healing discourse of the missionaries. What could be envisaged as an insistence on a break from traditionally held concepts, a rupture of sorts. As we will see in the following text, the tension that was evident during the introductory period of Christianity continues but also certain syncretic forms have emerged over the years.

Recognising the need for combining medical treatment with evangelising, Reverend Rivenburg went back to America in 1892 to study medicine, returning as a medical missionary in 1895 to Kohima, which was by then the headquarters of the British administration in the Naga Hills. Rivenburg's wife Hattie's letter to her family is revealing of the changed attitude of the villagers to Reverend Dr Rivenburg and his success in evangelising as a result of his medical practice:

> Since our return to Assam, the attitude of the Kohima village folk has completely changed toward us. Before, they were coldly curious. Now they are definitely more friendly and respectful, not only as we pass, but as Sidney and the Christians try to tell them of our religion. We feel that one reason is because Sidney is a full-fledged doctor. He seems to have an uncanny accuracy in diagnosing these oriental diseases. He has had some amazing recoveries among his patients. Now as he goes into those smoky, dirty huts to sit for hours beside some sufferer, seeking to find a remedy that will allay the suffering, and praying for that person's salvation, his actions speak to them louder than any mere words of the love of god who *gave* his Son to prove that love. (Hattie Rivenburg, letter, in 1941: 91; cf. Joshi 2012: 179)

Conversion to Christianity and Healing **167**

The first missionaries also opened dispensaries or sold medicines. In one of his letters, Rivenburg remarked that he had employed one of the evangelists, who had been successful in contacting people, to sell medicine to the villagers at a nominal cost as it would be 'well for the Nagas to get the notion of buying medicines' (Sydney Rivenburg, n.d., in Rivenburg 1944: 112). Rivenburg as well as another medically qualified missionary, Reverend Pettigrew, also helped vaccinate the villagers against small pox during campaigns by the British administration. Of course, the new diseases and illnesses that came along with annexation were tackled by means of biomedicine (see also Thomas 2016: 42). Rivenburg and Pettigrew both were also rewarded with the top civilian medal of Kaiser-I-Hind by the British administration for their medical services (Joshi 2012: 180, 191; Downs 1971: 165).

MEDICINE, MISSIONARY AND COMMUNITY HEALTH

While the reaction of early missionaries to traditional healing is interesting in the light of their own practice of using Western medicine along with reading verses from scriptures, medical work was a method also used by the Catholic missionaries, who gained entry to the Naga Hills through their work in the Kohima Civil Hospital in the 1950s. The Catholic missionaries were until then kept at bay because of the vehement opposition by the American Baptist missionaries and the practice of the British administration to divide the northeastern Indian region amongst different missions. As I have written elsewhere (Joshi 2012), a symbiotic relationship developed between the British administration and the American Baptist missionaries in the education and health fields.

Catholics gained entry by sending medical sisters to the Kohima Civil Hospital, which was built by the British after the Second World War battle of Kohima as a gesture of gratitude for the help the Naga people had provided in winning the battle. India gained independence in August 1947, and it is alleged that the district commissioner for the Naga Hills, who was a Catholic from Goa, allowed the medical sisters from a Spanish order to help in the hospital (George 1990). Surreptitiously, the medical sisters formed a small Catholic community which later grew into a church. It is claimed that independently of this, Catholicism was also introduced by the local Naga among the Kyong or Lotha Nagas. Baptists continued to oppose this. Reverend Longri Ao, being most vociferous, even wrote a pamphlet against Roman Catholicism (Rao 1986: 57).[4] Any attempt at establishing a separate Catholic Church was met with opposition which has continued in some villages up to now.[5] Interestingly, during the revival movements in in the 1950s, 1960s and the 1970s, formation of breakaway

168 *Vibha Joshi*

churches was suppressed among the Ao Naga by threat of excommunication from the village, whereas among the Angami Naga, in some villages new churches were established by the breakaway community. For example, in Kohima village there are nearly seven churches belonging to different denominations. In Naga townships of Kohima and Dimapur there are a number of churches reflecting the tribal, linguistic and denominational divide. Some new age churches cater to the English-speaking laity/congregation, especially college students and mixed-marriage families where parents are from different linguistic backgrounds. The spatial distribution of the churches in the village is indicative of the difficulty in finding a place to build a new church. In the beginning of Christianity, the Baptist missionary E. W. Clark was given a plot of land which was considered haunted on which to build his church and this was the first church in Impur (the name literally means nobody's land, as it was considered haunted, therefore unsuitable, Downs 1971: 116). In many villages the later entry of the Catholic Church is visible in the form of the Catholic Church building being at the outskirts of the village, for example, in the Angami village of Khonoma. But church buildings are the most dominant structures in Naga villages and towns and have contributed to the religious landscape, which in pre-Christianity times was dominated by outstanding natural features such as large boulders/rocks, lakes and rivers.[6]

CONTEMPORARY CHRISTIANITY AND HEALING

Interestingly, in present times, in some primary health clinics or PHCs, one finds Biblical verses that relate to the healing miracles of Jesus, written above the entrance to the consulting rooms. An example is the PHC near Kigwema village where on the doors to the nurses' and compounder's room, I had seen posters with Biblical verses that had been presented to the PHC by the Christian endeavour force and the Christian community of Kigwema.

In recent years the theological colleges, such as Oriental Theological Seminary, have reintroduced basic knowledge of community medicine in their syllabus. Community health work has become part of the initiative of tenting as an aspect of mission work, that is, as a means to make inroads and be accepted by local non-Christian community.[7] The missionary work is part of the initial call for sending out a 100,000 missionaries to different parts of India and neighbouring countries, which was envisaged in the 1970s by the Naga Baptist Church Council.

How did traditional healers adjust to the new ways of healing and the new religion? In my extensive research on the topic (Joshi 2012; 2008; 2007), I interviewed both divinational and non-divinational Angami traditional healers (also Ao and Konyak divinational healers during my travels in the 1990s, Joshi

2004; 1994). While some divinational healers had retained their belief in traditional spirits and had resisted conversion to Christianity, some others had converted on the insistence of family members and peers. The ones who had converted initially thought that they would lose their power to help others, but that did not happen. The healers ordinarily do not charge any fee for their treatment but accept gifts in kind if offered, as they see their healing powers as a gift from God which they ought to share freely, in the sense of doing good, called *zevi* in Angami. I also met healers who claimed that they were inspired by the Holy Spirit and some of whom, though had known about their 'talent' themselves, had kept it secret. They were eventually coaxed into sharing their gift to heal when their special powers were said to have been revealed as prophecy to local women's prayer groups. The attitude of the Christian Naga is mixed towards healers who are divinely inspired. Some have claimed that such healers and that those who prophesised are nominally Christian (Zeliang 2014; Ao 1994). However, the healers, especially masseurs, herbalists and those who use Christian charismatic healing through prayer are sought after by the Naga, who seek different kinds of medicines for a variety of ailments in an atmosphere of medical pluralism. One of the well-known herbalists among the Angami is a Catholic priest, who has his own herbal farm and training centre. It is said that healing powers/gifts may be passed down the family lineage, and I have found, using the biographical /genealogical method, that the some of the healers reportedly have indeed had gifted individuals in their lineage.

Besides individual healing by Christian and non-Christian healers, the Naga have Baptist and revival prayer groups that pray for a family or an individual as needed and also Baptist and Catholic prayer centre retreats, where those needing help with alcoholism, addiction or wanting to pray for a family member can spend some days. Many prayer centres have been established in the past decade, and their increasing popularity is said to have to have contributed to diminishing attendance in the churches.[8]

One feature of Baptist Christianity since the revival movements that began in the 1950s has been the large-scale prayer sessions during which it is claimed that a miraculous healing would take place. As I have written elsewhere (Joshi 2012), Christian revivalism coincided with an increase in the suppression of the Naga nationalist movement by the Indian state (see also Linyü 2004). In 1972 Reverend Billy Graham was invited to Nagaland to mark the centenary of Baptist Christianity. Although entry into Nagaland was earlier banned for foreigners, Christian leaders were given permission by the Indian government for him to enter the state.[9] It was during the 1970s that large-scale Christian gatherings appeared to have increased in number and intensity, appearing even more today among Pentecostals. Large gatherings by Baptists are given over to reviving

170 *Vibha Joshi*

Christian spirits. For these, preachers from outside Nagaland are invited, from India and from abroad, mainly the United States. In 2011 I attended a large prayer event that was organised by the south Indian charismatic preacher Paul Dhinakaran. At the expansive venue, besides the mass preaching and praying conducted in the evenings over three consecutive days, several smaller healing and prayer sessions were conducted by evangelists and prayer group leaders throughout the day. Throughout the year, the youth groups of various Naga churches of different denominations also conduct collective praying and healing meetings.

FORUM FOR POLITICAL RECONCILIATION

Prayers meetings may be called by and for any nationalist group, of which there are about seven, who have often been in conflict with each other. This results from the fact that the Naga have for years sought formal separation from India. This nationalist struggle has involved violence between Indian and Naga forces but also among the Naga themselves. Despite a stated Christian commitment to heal such divisions and seek tolerance and peace among nationalists and others, many attempts by Christian leaders to reconcile warring factions have failed, and it is a moot question as to why this is so, given that other variably successful attempts at political reconciliation through Christianity have been made in other parts of the world (for example, South Africa and Chile). Recurrent traditional rivalries permeating the nationalist movement and creating the enduring factions may have been at least partly responsible.

The 1950s were an important turning point for the factions of the Naga nationalist movement. They became more militant when their passive requests to the Indian government for independence failed. In a state of emergency, the Indian government responded with the heavy deployment of armed forces. There were heavy casualties on both sides. The intense Indian security operations and increasing violence in fact coincided with the emergence of the revival churches from the 1950s to 1970s.

The emergency resulted in the expulsion of all foreigners, including the American Baptist missionaries, who had to leave by the mid-1950s. International links with them continued, however. Local Naga pastors and travelling evangelists took over the task of converting all Naga communities to Christianity. Their aim was to create a Naga Christian nation in the idiom of a brotherhood. Despite being persecuted by the Indian security forces because of their different religion, they embarked on a remarkable course of Christian conversion among the Naga. In fact, the more they were persecuted, the more the Naga sought refuge in the religion. Within a few decades, Nagaland became almost entirely

Christian. What are the implications of this for the way in which Christianity thereafter became a vehicle of political protest?

There was Baptist hegemony, with Catholics also participating in the movement and holding senior positions in it. Those Naga who did not follow Christianity, including many Zeme Naga, preferred to follow their charismatic leader Rani Gaidinliu and her reformed Papaua religion called Heraka (see Longkumer 2007; 2010 for a detailed study). Zeme were therefore persecuted by nationalists and, gradually, Baptists, while at the same time Christianity came to be seen as a vehicle of modernity and made inroads into the region (Longkumer 2010).

CONVERSION AS PROTEST

While Christianity became a key distinguishing mark of Naga identity at the height of the Naga nationalist movement (in contrast with their Hindu, Muslim and Buddhist neighbours), this clearly took time to develop. In the 1960s, the British journalist Young noted that many non-Christians in fact converted only after joining the 'underground' Naga military force. He describes the regimental routine amongst the underground Naga beginning with a morning prayer and with grace before meals (Young 1961). It was then that some Naga pastors joined the underground insurgents as travelling evangelists – converting the cadres and villagers and presenting the Naga as a Christian people.[10] But there were also church leaders and theologians such as Reverends Longri Ao and Ben Wati, who resisted the invitation by the leader of the Naga Angami Zapu Phizo to join the movement[11] as they did not support the violence. Naga nationalists adopted the slogan 'Nagaland for Christ' in the 1950s, and in recent years the leaders of the prominent nationalists faction have increasingly portrayed the Naga struggle for sovereignty as that of a 'chosen people' who are being denied their 'promised land'.

The 'Christianisation' of nationalism continued even after the ceasefire and negotiations between the Indian government and Naga nationalists in 1997. For instance, the leaders of one of the three Naga factions claimed to represent all Naga. They wished to evangelise neighbouring groups, including those Naga who live outside Nagaland state itself but whom they regard as part of a greater Nagaland (or Nagalim as they call it). They have their own agenda for the Nagaland Mission Movement, set up by the Naga Baptist Church Council. Their aim is to send 10,000 missionaries worldwide, but especially to neighbouring Myanmar where other Naga live. They say they wish to complete the 'unfinished' task of the original American Baptist Mission.

The rate of conversion created sufficient numbers of Christians among the Naga such that the religion in effect became a political resource. In this role, it

172 *Vibha Joshi*

created and drew on an international network of Christian contacts. It grew into the Naga Mission Movement. Let me now turn to this suggestion of Christianity as a resource. It reinforced nationalism, changed customary practices and attitudes, and was increasingly seen as a possible route to peace through the Christian idea of healing.

RELIGION AS A RESOURCE

The Naga missionaries sent outside Nagaland went to different parts of India and other international locations, including Southeast Asia. They included teachers, doctors, engineers and development aid workers. Coming into Nagaland have been South Korean missionaries, especially the Withee Mission who opened a Bible college in Nagaland and trained Naga youths to be missionaries. There are fellowships for students and families living outside their village/town/state.

The study of theology has been popular among the Naga. There are now more than 30 colleges for theology and Bible study. Becoming a pastor has become a sought-after career choice in the region. Many Naga study theology outside Nagaland and in international seminaries in the United States, United Kingdom, Singapore and South Korea. Naga mission members also go as volunteers to teach at Bible colleges on the Burma–Thailand border.

The most important general way in which Christianity is seen as a possible healing resource is as a means of settling conflict among the Naga themselves. But Naga Christianity is not a homogeneous resource. On one hand, it spreads internationally, with Naga missionaries going out to the world, and other foreign missionaries coming into Nagaland. On the other hand, many Naga in Nagaland place emphasis on their Christianity as being largely indigenous and an emblem of Naga distinctiveness.

Do the two tendencies, one outgoing and the other inward-looking, pull against each other, or is the external world network in fact part of the Christian resource for political reconciliation in Nagaland? In other words, does global Christianity offer the Naga career paths that enable them to escape the internal problems and violence of Nagaland? Or do these external relationships offer a conduit for external ideas and assistance to come into Nagaland and to help reconciliation?

The key idiom of Christian healing is not only seen as potentially able to bring together these internally disparate tendencies, it can also be appealed to as part of an external, worldwide Christian concept often invoked in conflict situations. The provision of large-scale collective healing alongside that for individual worshippers mirrors these micro- and macro-dimensions. In other words, the idea of healing is held by members of the Naga global Christian diaspora as well as in the villages, thus bridging wide-flung and local communities.

It may be debated how much the idiom of healing through reconciliation is more salient in Christianity than in other world religions. Its use does seem widespread, with Naga Christian leaders often drawing on Biblical parables and pronouncements (for example, *Matthew 5: 9: Blessed are the peacemakers: for they shall be called the children of God*, King James Bible), and rhetorically urging the resolution of conflict within and between communities through ideas of tolerance and the healing of souls.

NAGA CHRISTIANITY AND POLITICAL RECONCILIATION

A Forum for Naga Reconciliation was set up by members of civil society (who are mainly Christian) and by leaders of the Nagaland Baptist Church Council and the Catholic Church. We may distinguish two dimensions of reconciliation among the Naga. One is conceptual and perhaps philosophical. The other is organisational.

The conceptual basis includes notions such as 'healing', 'forgiveness', 'confession', 'apology', 'truth', 'interior self-reflection' and 'counselling' in the vocabulary of attempts at reconciliation in different parts of the world. Among the Naga these English language terms are also widely used, sometimes alongside translated equivalents in the indigenous Naga languages, often chosen through Bible translation. These other languages include Nagamese, derived from Hindi and Assamese, and the different Naga Tibeto-Burman languages.

'Forgiveness' is the most widely used Christian-derived concept in reconciliation attempts. The Nagamese word for 'forgiveness' is *mafi*, as used in Bible translation. Its meaning shades into that of tolerance and presupposes confession of culpabililty. Let me give a Naga gloss on this and other terms used in reconciliation attempts.

We can ask the question of whether forgiveness is a kind of sacrifice. That is to say, the victim gives a pardon to the perpetrator and, as a Christian, should expect no return. But it may be that forgiveness among Naga has to be part of an exchange: the victim pardons but the perpetrator should admit guilt and apologise, accepting the truth of the victim's claim.

In fact, although the Naga nationalists do talk of the possibilities of forgiveness, they also insist that their killings were a necessary part of the Naga nationalism. That there is nothing to apologise for or be guilty about. The repeated reconciliation attempts become exercises in unreciprocated expressions of forgiveness, despite the rhetoric expressing a wish for reconciliation.

174 *Vibha Joshi*

The notion of healing especially applies to a community that has suffered a loss of sons, daughters, husbands and fathers as a result of fighting between the nationalist factions. It is healing directed at the wounds of internal conflict, not those resulting from the strife with the government of India. Christianity is increasingly turned to as the only likely source of healing for the violence resulting from the warring factions of the Naga nationalist movement.

The trend in much of world Christianity has been for counselling to be offered to people suffering the stress of so-called modernity, that is, urbanisation, family breakdown and joblessness. But among the Naga, the counselling is for victims of violence, for instance, the organisation Initiatives of Change (the former Moral Re-armament) counsels orphans of inter-factional killings.

And what is the place of Christian meditation in this saga of Naga violence? Christianity has often been regarded as encouraging self-reflection. In fact, there is a stated and apparent turn among Naga Christians towards self-correction rather than blaming external factors. It is especially evident in reconciliation attempts at village level, where Christian introspection combines with traditional dispute settlement methods of negotiation and commensality. It is important, in other words, to understand the play of concepts and terms in use in reconciliation attempts, their place in Christian discourse, and their role in failure and success.

The second dimension of reconciliation that I consider important is that of organisation. How do the various parties to conflict, whether Christian or non-Christian, actually set up the conditions for reconciliation to be attempted? There are three levels of organisation: village dispute settlement; large scale healing sessions; and international assemblies. Let me give examples of each in turn.

Taking a case of village reconciliation first, two nationalist leaders came into dispute and in 1956 one was killed by the followers of the other. They belonged to different clans from the same village, which then had fifty years of conflict over the assassination. The village committee eventually negotiated for peace over eight years, with the help of the Initiatives of Change organisation. They finally agreed in 2006 to hold a day of prayer, silence, self-retrospection and village confinement. This combined Christian elements with the Naga traditional practice of village cloistering. Some fasted while others shared food. The elder of the clan held responsible for the killing duly asked for forgiveness. A large gathering of members of both clans then congregated in the village, shared a communal feast and set up a commemorative monolith for the slain leader.

Second, as mentioned above, large-scale healing assemblies have become a regular occurrence in Nagaland. They are organised by Baptist as well as Pentecostal churches. The Forum for Naga Reconciliation held an assembly in February of each year until 2015 in which the Naga general public could hear

Conversion to Christianity and Healing **175**

and question representatives of the Naga nationalist factions. These well-attended sessions begin with Christian prayer and choir singing by Naga nationalists and civilians. The Naga church has also helped organise friendly football matches between teams made up of Naga nationalist factions and Naga church leaders and members. These matches have been described as challenging by the church leaders in view of the fact that they had to ask the Naga nationalists to come to the matches unarmed.

Third, there are gatherings of members of international churches. These include UK Quakers (Friends of Peace), who have been involved in the peace process since the 1960s, and the American Baptist International Ministries who made a public appeal during the celebration in 1997 of 125 years of Baptist Christianity in Nagaland, which also coincided with a ceasefire between Indian security forces and a prominent Naga faction. These Baptists have trained Naga Christian leaders in the art of negotiation. Meetings regularly held with them in Chiangmai, Thailand, by the Forum for Naga Reconciliation include representatives of the Naga factions.

Thus, attempts at reconciliation have been going on for at least two decades. They have involved people at different levels of organisation, from villages to international assemblies. The rhetoric of the search for peace sits uneasily with the various attempts to secure it.

To conclude, in this chapter, I have approached Christian conversion among the Naga by exploring how far the concept of rupture, as proposed by Robbins (2004), can be applied. Situating religious change and conversion in sociopolitical and historical context, I have shown that the role of healing and its continued relevance in the current attempts at bringing peace and reconciliation among the Naga modifies the notion of rupture. I have further shown that among the Naga the theme of healing is the connecting thread which runs through the historical and contemporary role of Christianity, its layers of interaction with indigenous concept of healing (and peacemaking) and its continued importance in the shift from individual to collective healing.

NOTES

1. See also Joshi (2013) and Angelova in this volume. Eaton (1984; 1997) in a historical analysis has used Horton's concept of macrocosm and adjustment of cosmological beliefs to explain Naga conversion, but I do not agree with his correlation between modes of cultivation, types of cosmological beliefs and rate of conversion among different Naga communities which is based only on secondary data.

2. In a recent article, Mepfhü-o writes that some of the converts from Rüsoma village told her that they were not asked to leave but had left on their own accord to separate

themselves from the heathens (2016: 377). The author confirms later in the text (ibid.: 378) what I had been told when I visited the same village in the early 1990s that converts were asked to leave due to non-conformance (Joshi 2012: 181).

3. Mailmen were employed to take the mail on foot to Assam and carry back mail from there to the Naga Hills.

4. In the biography of Reverend Longro Ao, Rao writes that Reverend Ao's opposition was not only to the tenets of Catholocism, that is, the infallibility of the Pope, but also to the Roman Catholic educational institutions as he claimed they were being used for proselytisation and were being funded by the Indian government (1986: 55–58).

5. Latest reporting of the burning down of Catholic churches and fining of villagers for creating schism in the community which is majority Baptist occurred in July 2010 in Pouchuri Naga village of Anatangre. The action was directed by the village council made up of Baptist Christian members who had passed a resolution in 1991 that no other denominations were allowed to have a church in the village (*Morung Express* 27 July 2010; see also *American Baptist News*, baptistnews.com 27 July2010).

6. In April 2017, the nine-storey-high largest church in Nagaland, the Sumi Baptist Church Zuneboto, also claimed to be one of the largest in Asia, was inaugurated in the Sumi Naga town of Zunheboto (*Indian Express* 22 April 2017, accessed 23 April 2017).

7. In 2011, I attended (and observed) the introductory session on the first day of a workshop on community health at the Oriental Theological Seminary on the outskirts of Dimapur.

8. Personal conversation with Dr Panger of Oriental Theological Seminary in September 2015 in Berlin, Germany. See also a news report, 'The Important Role of Prayer Centres in Nagaland', in the Nagaland broadsheet *Morung Express*, 18 January 2015, accessed 20 January 2015).

9. Currently, Indians require an Inner Line Permit and foreigners require a Restricted Area Permit since 2000. The Restricted Area Permit for foreigners was lifted in 2010 to promote tourism and continues to be so for 2019.

10. Personal conversation in March 2011, in Dimapur, with Reverend V. K. Nuh, who was himself a chaplain in the Naga National Council, the first nationalist group.

11. Personal conversation with late Reverend Ben Wati in Oxford, September 2010.

BIBLIOGRAPHY

Alem, O. 1997. 'From Darkness to Light.' In *Collection of Essays*. Kohima: Nagaland Baptist Church Council.

Ao, O. A. 1994. *Tsungremology: Ao Naga Christian Theology*. Mokokchung: Clark Theological College.

Barpujari, H. K. 1986. *The American Missionaries and Northeast India (1836–1900 AD): A Documentary Study*. Delhi: Spectrum Publications.

Bialecki, Jon, Naomi Haynes and Joel Robbins 2008. 'The Anthropology of Christianity.' *Religion Compass* 2(6): 1139–1158.

Beidelman, T. O. 1982. *Colonial Evangelism: A Socio-historical Study of an East African Mission at the Grassroots*. Bloomington: Indiana University Press.

Cannell, F., ed. 2006. *The Anthropology of Christianity*. Durham and London: Duke University Press.

Clark, M. M. 1978 [1907]. *A Corner in India*. Philadelphia: American Baptist Publication Society.

Comaroff, J. and J. Comaroff. 1991. *Of Revelation and Revolution: Christianity, Colonialism, and Consciousness in South Africa*. Chicago: University of Chicago Press.

Csordas, Thomas, ed. 2009. *Transnational Transcendence: Essays on Religion and Globalizatin*. Berkeley: University of California Press.

Eaton, Richard M. 1984. 'Conversion to Christianity among the Nagas, 1876–1971.' *Indian Economic and Social History Review* 11(1): 1–43.

———. 1997. 'Comparative History as World History: Religious Conversion in Modern India.' *Journal of World History* 8(2): 243–271

Eisenstadt, S. N. 1982. 'The Axial Age: The Emergence of Transcendental Visions and the Rise of the Clerics.' *Archives Europeennes de Sociologie* 23(2): 294–314.

Ham, P. Van, and J. Saul. 2008. *Expedition Naga: Diaries from the Hills in Northeast India 1921–1937 and 2002–2003*. Woodbridge, UK: Antique Collectors' Club.

Hutton, John Henry. 1929. 'Diaries of Two Tours in the Unadministered Area East of the Naga Hills.' *Memoirs of the Asiatic Society of Bengal* 11(1): 1–72.

Joshi, Vibha (as V. J. Patel). 1994. 'Shamans of Nagaland.' *The India Magazine* (May issue): 18–27.

Joshi, Vibha. 2004. 'Human and Spiritual Agency in Angami Healing Part I & Part II.' *Anthropology and Medicine* 11(3): 269–291.

———. 2007. 'The Birth of Christian Enthusiasm among the Angami in Nagaland.' *South Asia: Journal of South Asian Studies* 30(3), special issue: 541–557.

———. 2008. 'Pluralistic Beliefs: Christianity and Healing among the Angami Naga', in *Naga Identities*, edited by Michael Oppitiz et al., 393–402. Gent: Snoeck Publishers.

———. 2012. *A Matter of Belief: Christian Conversion and Healing in North-East India*. Oxford and New York: Berghahn.

———. 2013. 'Micro Politics of Borders: The Issue of Greater Nagaland (or Nagalim).' In *Borderlands of Northern South Asia: Non-State Perspectives*, edited by Gellner, David N., 163–193. Durham, NC: Duke University Press.

Linyü, K. 2004. *Christian Movements in Nagaland*. Kohima: N.V. Press.

Longkumer, Arkotong. 2007. 'Religious and Economic Reform: The Gaidinliu Movement and the Heraka in the North Cachar Hills.' *South Asia: Journal of South Asian Studies* 30(3): 499–515.

178 *Vibha Joshi*

——. 2010. *Reform, Identity and Narratives of Belonging: The Heraka Movement in Northeast India*. London: Continuum.

Mepfhü-o, Ketholenuo. 2016. 'Conversion: Perception of the Christian 'Self' and the 'Other'.' *Asian Ethnicity* 17(3): 370–383.

Mills, James Philip. 1935. 'The Effect on the Tribes of Naga Hills District of Contacts with Civilization.' *Census of India 1931* 1 (Part III, ethnographical, B. ethnographical notes): 147–149.

Puthenpurakal, Joseph. 1984. *Baptists Mission in Nagaland: Historical and Ecumenical Perspective*. Shillong: Vendrame Missiological Institute.

Ranger, Terence. 1981. 'Godly Medicine: The Ambiguities of Medical Mission in Southeastern Tanzania 1900–45.' *Social Science and Medicine* 15(3): 261–277.

Rao, O. M. 1986. *Longri Ao: A Biography*. Guwahati: Christian Literature Centre.

Rivenburg, Narola, ed. 1941. *The Star of the Naga Hills: Letters from Rev. Sidney & H. Rivenburg, Pioneer Missionaries in Assam, 1883–1923*. Philadelphia: American Baptist Press.

Robbins, Joel. 2012. 'Transcendence and the Anthropology of Christianity: Language, Change and Individualism.' *Suomen Antropologi: Journal of the Finnish Anthropological Society* 37(2): 5–23.

Smilde, D. 2007. *Reason to Believe: Cultural Agency in Latin American Evangelism*. Berkeley: University of California Press.

Smith, W. C. 1925. *The Ao Naga Tribe of Assam: A Study in Ethnology and Sociology*. London: Macmillan and Co. Limited.

Thomas, John. 2016. *Evangelising the Nation: Religion and the Formation of Naga Political Identity*. New Delhi, London, New York: Routledge.

van der Veer, Peter, ed. 1996. *Conversion to Modernities: The Globalization of Christianity*. New York and London: Routledge.

Wouters, Jelle J. P. 2017. 'The Making of Tribes: The Chang and Chakhesang Nagas in Indias northeast.' *Contributions to Indian Sociology* 51(1): 79–104.

Zeliang, Elungkiebe. 2014. *Charismatic Movements in the Baptist Churches in North East India; A Zeliangrong Perspective*. Delhi: ISPCK.

Archives

Letters (and Reports) of the American Baptist Historical Society Archives. American Baptist Church Centre, Valley Forge, Pennsylvania (now in Atlanta, GA): Clark, E. W. 1872–1911 and Rivenburg, S. 1885–1923.

7
Reshaping the American Evangelical Conversion Narrative in Nineteenth-Century North India

Arun W. Jones

In the year 1884, a north Indian Christian by the name of Zahur-al-Haqq, from what is now the state of Uttar Pradesh, penned a religious autobiography in Urdu, which was translated the following year into English as a 31-page pamphlet simply entitled *Autobiography of Rev. Zahur-Al-Haqq*.[1] This work is in fact an extended conversion narrative that recounts Haqq's religious commitments and changes from his childhood to the time of writing, and also summarises his career as a worker in the mission of the Methodist Episcopal Church, an American Protestant evangelical denomination that had been active in India since 1856.[2] Haqq was 50 years old when he wrote his work in Urdu and had been a Christian for 25 years; he would go on to live for 12 more years, dying in 1896 (Barclay 1949: 456). Two years before writing his autobiography, he had been named to the position of Presiding Elder in the Methodist mission in India, the first Indian so appointed. The Presiding Elder was the second highest official, after bishop, in the American Methodist ecclesiastical hierarchy, and since at that time there were no Methodist bishops residing in India, Haqq was part of the cadre of the most senior Methodist leaders in his country, the rest of whom were American missionaries.[3]

This chapter engages in a close reading of Haqq's narrative in order to explore some personal, religious and social dimensions of conversion to evangelical Christianity in nineteenth-century British north India, and to delineate differences between Indian and American Methodist understandings of religious conversion. The fundamental argument is that Haqq adapted an American Methodist template of spiritual autobiography in order to elaborate a distinctly Indian Methodist model for religious movement and change.

Two preliminary observations need to be made about this examination of Haqq's writing. First, the essay does not by any means assume that the autobiography is a completely reliable or unquestionably authentic historical account of the events described. In terms of its reliability, an autobiography may contain unintentional or even intentional factual errors. For example, Haqq's

180 *Arun W. Jones*

Autobiography definitively states on the cover page that he was the first convert of the Methodist mission in India. That claim, however, is questionable in light of the evidence from a number of sources (Barclay 1949: 456–457).[4] On the other hand, the claim seems to have been important at least for the translator and her husband, American missionaries who worked closely with Haqq, and perhaps was important for him as well.[5] As far as the historicity of an autobiography is concerned, it is an act of recollection that serves one or more purposes at the time of its writing. It also can borrow both form and content from extant conventions regarding autobiographical writing (Marshall 2009: 88; Bauman 2008: ch. 3; Hindmarsh 2014: 353–358). While Haqq never explicitly states his intent in writing this work, its content indicates that he wanted to propose a particularly Indian understanding of Methodist conversion. However, he did so by adopting and adapting the American Methodist spiritual autobiography to craft his own story. Such shaping and reshaping do not render the narrative useless as a historical document. In truth, 'reality' is usually communicated through some narrative (Hindmarsh 2014: 359). The main contours of Haqq's life can be ascertained from his work, even when details can be called into question. One reason to trust the general outline of Haqq's autobiography is that people who had known him well since his youth were alive at the time of his writing, and thus were witnesses to many of the events he describes. For example, Haqq's observation that Mrs Humphrey was 'alarmed' when he, as a Muslim, first came to attend a Methodist worship service is corroborated in a letter she wrote to her mother soon after that occasion (al-Haqq 1885: 16; E. J. Humphrey 1866: 134).[6]

The second preliminary observation is that Indians converted to, and deconverted from, Christianity for a whole host of personal and social reasons. Moreover, their social and religious locations in Indian society strongly influenced how they experienced conversion and what they expected from it. For example, one of the several attractions of Christianity for persons from low-caste and untouchable groups in nineteenth-century north India was that it provided them with opportunities for improving their social status (see Bauman 1949). However, as such persons became aware after baptism of the social norms and expectations that accompanied the new faith, a number of them were not willing to sacrifice certain hereditary customs (such as those pertaining to marriage or diet) for this way of life, and took up their previous religious and social identities.[7] Given that a large number of the converts in the Methodist mission came from such low status groups means that Haqq's conversion experience is in some ways unique, since he came from a socially respectable Muslim family of teachers. In the nineteenth century, very few converts in the American Methodist mission came from this class and religious background.[8]

Again, this does not mean that Haqq's autobiography is valueless for shedding light on Indian conversions to evangelical Christianity more generally. For one thing, Haqq had worked for over 20 years with the poor and low-status groups who made up the bulk of the Methodist converts in the 1880s, and his success in relating to them was one reason he was picked to be a Presiding Elder.[9] He had learned that several issues concerning conversion to Christianity confronted the great majority of converts regardless of their social background. For example, the navigation of continuity and change in the process of conversion, an issue he interestingly elucidates in his *Autobiography*, was just as pertinent to low-caste and untouchable groups as to his own life. Second, Haqq was the most senior Indian leader of his day in the Methodist hierarchy in India, and so he was in many ways an exemplary convert to Christianity. This chapter contends that he used this position to articulate a broadly Indian understanding of conversion in his Methodist tradition.[10] It is telling that he draws from Hindu more than Islamic traditions in his understanding of Indian religiosity. The fact that he wrote his *Autobiography* for public consumption indicates that he wanted to communicate publicly what Christian conversion generally in the Indian context could entail.

HAQQ'S *AUTOBIOGRAPHY* AND THE STUDY OF CONVERSION

In the introduction to this volume of essays, the authors helpfully use the image of a road – a 'godroad' in fact – to describe the process of conversion, and 'the complex, conflict-ridden and at times contradictory processes of engaging with religious traditions' that conversion entails (Berger and Sahoo, introduction to this volume). However, this chapter argues that Zahur-al-Haqq's *Autobiography* does not simply describe a journey – however convoluted it may be – on a road from Sunni Islam to Protestant Christianity. Rather, Haqq's conversion narrative also provides a map for all those who are interested in, or find themselves travelling along, the rather unknown landscape of conversion to Christianity in the context of nineteenth-century north India. Using his life experiences as a guide and marker, he charts out a 'godroad' which shows how Indians can make sense of, and negotiate, the confusing and sometimes treacherous topography of religious transitions.

Zahur-al-Haqq's conversion narrative touches on three fundamental questions that have occupied scholars studying religious conversion, especially conversion to Christianity.[11] The first question is to what degree conversion creates a rupture in the life of the convert, and to what extent conversion actually entails deep continuities in that life. The idea that conversion represents a radical break from the past and an embrace of a completely new way of life is the typical Protestant

182 *Arun W. Jones*

evangelical view of conversion. This view emerged in the eighteenth century, was forcefully propagated by evangelical missions (such as the Methodists) in the nineteenth century, and still is regnant within several Christian groups and movements. Certain scholars are taking seriously the claims of rupture made by converts, and are trying to understand the role such ruptures play in their identities.[12] Other scholars focus on the continuities in the pre- and post-conversion lives of converts. Carried to extremes, such views 'produce accounts in which Christianity is represented as syncretized to such an extent that it is in reality nothing more than traditional religion tricked up in new clothes' (Robbins 2004: 30). Haqq tells of both continuities and ruptures in his conversion experiences, although he relates the two in an interesting way: he sees changes in his religious life as being possible only because of underlying continuities in it.

The second scholarly question that Haqq's narrative touches is whether conversion is a gradual process or a singular event. Marc Baer, for example, argues that 'conversion is a decision or experience followed by a gradually unfolding, dynamic process through which an individual embarks on a religious transformation' (Baer 2008: 13). Others have viewed conversion as a decisive moment of radical change in one's life (Rambo and Farhadian 2014: 5; Hindmarsh 2014: 343–344.). Haqq again incorporates both these themes in his conversion narrative. In fact, he writes about several conversions in his life, with accompanying changes of religious and social perspective. Yet running through these changes is a 'gradually unfolding, dynamic process', to use the words of Marc Baer, of seeking truth and arriving at joy and bliss.

A final scholarly issue that is pertinent to a study of Haqq's *Autobiography* is the question of whether Christian conversion is fundamentally a process of keeping but reorienting one's culture to new goals, or whether it is a process of constructing a new 'Christian' culture. Andrew Walls views Christian conversion as a long process where a given culture is turned towards the purposes of Christ, as he puts it. Describing the gradual penetration of Christian beliefs into the Hellenistic world, he claims:

> Greek and Roman thought ... was a total system, undergirding the law, reflection, education, literature, intellectual life of a substantial section of contemporary humanity.... The whole system of thought, apparently so assured and final, had to go to school again with Christ.... It was impossible either to ignore the previous system of ideas, or to abandon it, or to leave it as it was. It had to be penetrated, invaded, brought into relation with the word about Christ and the Scriptures which contained it. (Walls 1996: 53)

Robert Hefner, on the other hand, sees conversion as the process of accepting a new identity in a new social and intellectual structure. '[C]onversion implies the acceptance of a new locus of self-definition, a new, though not necessarily exclusive, reference point for one's identity.... [Conversion] always involves commitment to a new kind of moral authority and a new or reconceptualized social identity' (Hefner 1993: 17). Here again, Haqq's story refuses to conform to the dichotomies of scholarship and blends different perspectives into the author's understanding of Christian conversion. On the one hand, Christianity answers some of the deepest needs and questions of Indian religions, at least as he experienced them. Thus, the purpose of Christian mission in India was to understand and enter into the religious cultures of India, in order to 'translate' the faith for new thought forms and patterns. On the other hand, Haqq adopted Christianity as it was understood and promulgated by Western missionaries, accepting 'a new locus of self-definition' and a new 'reference point' for his identity, to use the words of Hefner. He was so successful in this process that he became promoted to the highest position of leadership possible among Methodists in India at the time. Yet part of the reason for his elevation to this position was his ability to understand Indian religious traditions, and 'translate' Christianity into Indian idioms (see Thoburn 1887: 207–208).

AMERICAN METHODIST SPIRITUAL NARRATIVES

Haqq did not compose his *Autobiography* in a narrative void. The spiritual autobiography was a well-known and often-used genre of British and American Methodist writing, and the oral retelling of one's spiritual journey and moment(s) of conversion was a common Methodist practice. So, Haqq would have known the spiritual biographies of his missionary mentors and colleagues.[13] However, 'conversion' for Methodists in America meant something very different than changing one's religious affiliation. In America, Methodists viewed conversion as a movement from what they considered nominal Christianity – which could in fact include regular participation in church activities – to a highly dedicated Christianity that was only possible when the individual was especially possessed by God's spirit. This moment of conversion was a singular highly emotional experience, often accompanied by dramatic physical manifestations. Needless to say, the American Methodist understanding of conversion was confounded by Indian realities, where conversion normally meant changing one's religious identity. To adapt to this situation, American Methodists in India often spoke of conversion in two ways: the first being a shift from one religious tradition to another, and the second being a deep, spiritual commitment by Christians to the Christian faith. So, Mrs Humphrey could speak of the baptism of Zahur-al-Haqq as 'the deliberate turning' from erroneous Islam to truthful Christianity, and she could also speak of an Indian Methodist as 'a converted Methodist in its

184 *Arun W. Jones*

true signification, that is, an earnest Christian. He sometimes frightens the people in the bazars, by preaching to them in terrific strains of the sure wrath of God' (E. J. Humphrey 1866: 137, 262.). Haqq's *Autobiography* tells of both these kinds of religious conversions.

Generally speaking, there are five stages in a nineteenth-century American Methodist spiritual autobiography. It begins by recounting the pre-conversion life of the author, who lives without the true knowledge of God (even though often she or he is a practising Christian). Knowledge here is not cognitive, but an affective state where one personally 'feels' God's spirit in one's life. In the first stage of the spiritual journey, the author experiences a conviction of sin and spiritual struggles. Second, there follows the narrator's conversion, typically a single dramatic event marked by a sensation of the assurance of the forgiveness of sins. The third stage follows the conversion, and is characterised by more struggles of the soul. Then fourth comes an experience of 'entire sanctification' or a sense of complete cleansing from all sin, as the spirit of God (Holy Spirit) enters into the life of the believer. This sanctification is capped by the last stage that is a call to Christian vocation, for example, to become a preacher or a missionary (Campbell 2013: 249).

Haqq adopts the form of the Methodist spiritual autobiography; he also has five religious periods in his life. Growing up a Muslim, he experiences the first stage at 'about twenty years of age' when he experiences a spiritual restlessness, as he searches for truth and peace for his soul (al-Haqq 1885: 8–9). In the second stage, he converts to the Methodist form of Christianity and is baptised. This is followed by a third stage of turmoil, when his family members employ various means to try and get him to return to his natal religion and community. They are unsuccessful, and Haqq starts to work with the Methodists as a teacher and then preacher. After several years, he experiences a special baptism of the Holy Spirit – the fourth stage of the American spiritual autobiography. Finally, he recounts how he is ordained a Methodist minister, the fifth and last stage of the Methodist spiritual journey.

While Haqq's *Autobiography* receives its initial template from American Methodists, it is also quite radically adapted to his north Indian experience and context. First, the content of each of these stages, and the ways they are linked, are strikingly different for him than for his missionary coreligionists. Second, while the American spiritual autobiography relates a journey (not simply cognitive or behavioural but also necessarily affective) from godlessness to godliness, Haqq relates a journey where he is searching for truth, for rest for his soul, and where he gains full knowledge of God, and joy or bliss. There was no period in his life, in Haqq's view, that God was not actively present and working in him and with him.

Reshaping the American Evangelical Conversion Narrative **185**

Finally, while the American narrative is composed of a series of decisive changes in a spiritual development where the author moves from one stage to another, Haqq also stresses continuities through all the stages in his religious journey.

Haqq is drawing on several different understandings of religious change, albeit not systematically, in his autobiography. First is the Methodist missionary understanding, in which there are several stages involving one or more conversions, as a person from a different religious tradition successively becomes a 'true' Christian. A second is an Indic understanding where salvation – which is liberation (*moksha*) from the cycles of birth and rebirth – is reached by realising truth (*satya*), as opposed to ignorance, and this liberation/salvation is experienced as bliss (*ananda*) (Flood 1996: 85; Johnson 2010: 17). While Haqq does not refer at all to *moksha*, he does speak of truth and bliss. A third is another Indic understanding drawn from *bhakti*, which posits that devotion to (or participation in) a divine saviour is the true path to salvation (Carman 2005: 856). In Book Nine of the *Bhagavad Gita*, Krishna tells Arjuna, 'For whoever depends on me, Partha, however low their origins – whether they are women, farmers and merchants, or even labourers and serfs – they go by the highest path' (Johnson 1994: 43). Krishna here claims to be the true divine saviour of all, and the one who should be worshiped and adored in order to attain salvation, which is bliss (Hopkins 1971: 122–123). While salvation as liberation from rebirth and experience of bliss is the theoretical and sometimes very real goal of *bhakti*, in practice the protection (often conceived as refuge) and grace (*prasada*) of the divine can be more important for the devotee. Or the devotee may wish ultimately to surrender to the Lord, 'satisfied to adore him' (Francis and Schmid 2014: 8–9). A fourth understanding of religious change for Haqq comes out of his personal experience, both in his own life and the lives of other converts. For one, he sees religious change as possible only due to certain religious continuities in the converts' lives. In other words, change is predicated on continuity between different stages of a convert's life. Second, he observes that religious change is possible only when experienced in a new religious community.

It would not be very illuminating simply to describe Haqq's view of religious change and conversion as hybrid, which it no doubt is. Haqq combines these understandings in a particular way. The American Methodist religious autobiography provides the template for religious change. The goal of religious change, however, is truth and bliss, and the means for religious change is provided by *bhakti*. Finally, the necessary condition for religious conversion to Christianity is to connect new religious understandings with old ones, to base important changes on deep continuities. And these changes are fully realised only in Christian community.

186 *Arun W. Jones*

HAQQ'S AUTOBIOGRAPHY

So how did Haqq's life unfold? Haqq relates that he was born a Sunni Muslim in 1834 in a village in the district of Shahjahanpur, and that when he turned 12, he began his education under the direction of his 'honored father', a schoolmaster, learning languages, astronomy, astrology 'and a kind of sorcery' (al-Haqq 1885: 7). He was also well instructed in the Islamic faith, and writes that he was considered a 'faithful and zealous' Muslim. There is no condemnation in the *Autobiography* of Haqq's parents for the religious training they gave him. At the age of 20, Haqq says, he became religiously restless, desiring to 'ascertain the one true religion' among the many options available to him in the north Indian context.[14]

In response to this spiritual agitation, Haqq eventually joined a *bhakti* group called the 'Parnami' or Pranami sect, which had been established in the beginning of the seventeenth century by a Gujarati named Mahamati Prannath (Toffin 2012: 234; Khan 2002: 8–9).[15] Although Haqq calls the Pranamis Hindus, the founder had fused together Islamic and Hindu teachings in his theology (Khan 2002: 10, 12).[16] It may be that by categorising Pranamis as Hindus, Haqq is averring that his religious knowledge and experience include Hindu traditions. According to the nineteenth-century Orientalist H. H. Wilson, Pranamis (he terms them 'Pran Nathis') had to assent to the belief that the essence of Islam and Hinduism were one and the same, and the group members shared together in communal meals. Hindu and Muslim members of the sect continued to live with and even identify with their religious community of origin, which would explain why Haqq wrote that he continued to practise Islam while still a Pranami (Wilson 1846: 226–227; al-Haqq 1885: 9).

Already Haqq is delineating a difference between Indian and American conceptions of religious turmoil which leads to conversion. Whereas in American narratives it is conviction of sin and a deep sense of guilt that pushes the individual towards conversion, for Haqq it is a search for 'truth' and 'rest of soul' that drives him to investigate different religious claims. He does not mention sin or guilt – so crucial to the Western Christian paradigm of conversion – at this point in his narrative (al-Haqq 1885: 9–10).

Moreover, even in the first stage of the spiritual journey, Haqq has a conversion, albeit an unfruitful one according to him, as he joins the Pranamis. Yet this conversion did not entail any great break from his family. While Haqq moved beyond the Sunni orthodoxy of his family of origin by joining a *bhakti* sect, this movement from Islam did not require him to cease practising his former faith; rather, it required that he emphasise the commonalities between certain Islamic and Hindu thought. Haqq here signals a second way that he – and by extension other Indians – experienced religious conversion quite differently in the Indian context, in contrast to the American one. In the former, one moved to apprehensions of new and different truths by relying on one's previous religious understandings and attachments. *Change required continuity.* In the Western Protestant paradigm, however, conversion from one faith to another typically meant renouncing one's previous religious convictions and connections for new ones.[17] In the words of one missionary, it was 'the deliberate turning from error to truth, from darkness to light, from Satan to God' (E. J. Humphrey 1866: 137).

Haqq writes that he found 'some satisfaction' in the worship of the Pranami group. This worship was focused on singing and on devotion (both aural and visual) to religious texts, especially the *Qulzam Swarup*, the Pranamis' sacred book (Grierson 1919: 150–151). Yet Haqq still could not find the 'rest of the soul' that he greatly desired; 'of [the Pranamis'] religious experience I had not a particle', he writes (al-Haqq 1885: 9).[18] So, adapting the template of American spiritual autobiography, Haqq describes the first stage of his religious journey as a period not of sinfulness but of spiritual restlessness both as a Muslim and Pranami, and this stage already included in it one religious conversion.

It was through the public preaching of the American Methodist missionary J. L. Humphrey and the Eurasian Methodist evangelist Joseph Fieldbrave, in the city of Bareilly, that Haqq was brought into contact with Christianity in 1859. His turn to the Methodists was his second – and more important – religious conversion, and the second stage of his Methodist spiritual journey. The evangelical preachers' message, as he remembers it, was that Jesus is the saviour of the world.[19] The claim that a particular divinity (such as Krishna) alone provides salvation is at the core of the theology of *bhakti*. Haqq admits that most often after hearing such messages, people lose interest in them over time. It was not so with him: 'my desire to learn more of these important matters constantly increased, and a determination to receive the *truth* took root in my heart' (al-Haqq 1885: 10, italics in original).

Haqq states that he was led to take seriously the Christian preachers' claims about Jesus by examining what the Qur'an said about him. He writes: 'I received much light from the teaching of the Koran; that is to say, the account of the visit of the angel Gabriel to the Virgin Mary, and the birth of the holy child without an earthly father, his power, etc., was very helpful to me' (ibid.: 9–10). Haqq, in his characteristically laconic style, makes a startling assertion here: that it was his upbringing in Islam that allowed him to take seriously the Christian claims about Jesus. Once again Haqq changes the content of the American spiritual narrative. Not only is Haqq claiming that continuities are important; he is averring that the discontinuities – the rupture, in his case, caused by Christian allegiance – are possible *because of* previous allegiances. These provide the

188 *Arun W. Jones*

foundation, the material and the warrant for change. The foundation was the Islam taught by his parents; the material and the warrant for change came from the Qur'an. So, elements of the previous stage in life continue into the present one, providing necessary continuity. In fact, he did not change his name at baptism, which was a relatively common practice for converts (ibid.: 30–31).[20]

Haqq also writes that two factors not related to theological truth were pivotal in his conversion to Christianity in its Methodist form. The first was the kindness he witnessed and experienced from the preachers. He saw them being verbally and physically harassed as they preached in the bazaar, but they responded with 'words of kindness and love' to the harassment. As they walked home, Haqq began conversing with the preachers, and asked for a Persian or Urdu translation of the gospels, which he received. Fieldbrave invited the inquisitive young man to his home, introduced him to his family, and after a long conversation asked him to stay the night. Because of Haqq's dietary restrictions, the host had to order special food from the market for his guest, who was then provided a bed in the house. 'But I could not sleep much,' writes Haqq, 'it seemed so strange to me that these people should show so much love to me, a stranger, and have so much confidence in me. The kind of treatment I then received greatly increased my desire to understand the doctrines of the Christian religion' (al-Haqq 1885: 15). Again, Haqq stakes out new ground, in contradistinction to the Western evangelical expectations of his missionary colleagues, of the process of conversion. He claims that a loving community is integral to religious conversion. In American evangelicalism, in contrast, conversion occurred when one had a personal and powerful experience of God's spirit. This experience usually took place in the context of a Christian community, but the vital element in American Methodist understandings of conversion was the individual's personal experience of God. Haqq's search for true religion led him to seek new communities: first the Pranamis and then the Methodists. Truth is not merely intellectually or affectively discerned for Haqq; it is made real in community. Here he shows how his life exemplified the experience of Indians more generally who converted to Christianity from various social and religious backgrounds: the positive experience of Christian community was crucial in their apprehension of the faith. In fact, one Indian Presbyterian minister could argue that the provision of positive community was a duty for missionaries:

> When a Hindu or a Mohammedan embraces the Christian religion, the missionary has in most cases to provide him with a house to live in, and get him some means of subsistence. He has to educate his converts and their children. He has to teach them good manners, self-reliance, energy and industry. When they are in difficulty or distress, the missionary has to come forward and help them out of it. In fact he

Reshaping the American Evangelical Conversion Narrative   **189**

has to seek and promote their temporal welfare as much as their spiritual good, and be to them as a father to his children. (Chatterjee 1873: 337)

A second crucial factor, according to Haqq, in his pivot to evangelical Christianity was a Methodist worship service. In fact, Haqq juxtaposes the two events in his memoir: 'Soon after this [that is, the night at the Fieldbrave home] the thought came into my heart it would be well for me to see the manner of Christian worship' (al-Haqq 1885: 16). Christian community led him to Christian worship. He returned during the week for religious instruction and then on Sunday for worship. He attended Sunday school afterwards, following which he immediately asked for baptism, which Humphrey administered some time later.

Why was Methodist worship so crucial to him? We do know that Methodist worship manifested some important resemblances to Pranami worship, which Haqq says he found satisfying. Both traditions stressed an aniconic devotion to a divinity, a focus on scripture, and religious singing. This last feature was important to Haqq: he was known to be a good singer and musically gifted (E. J. Humphrey 1866: 262). The *Autobiography* relates an incident when Haqq took a cousin, who had come to try and convince him to return to the family faith, to a Methodist worship service. The cousin purportedly said: 'You have committed no fault in becoming a Christian, for this worship is so excellent that from witnessing it my heart is exceedingly joyful, and the music of that instrument, with the melody of the Christians' voices, has stirred me deeply' (al-Haqq 1885: 20–21). Whatever the cousin's actual reactions to a Methodist worship service, this incident probably tells us more about Haqq's reasons for joining the Methodists, namely the musical element in worship – something he enjoyed among the Pranamis. Once again, continuities provided the foundations and material which made possible the discontinuities and ruptures accompanying conversion. And once again Haqq's life exemplified more general dynamics of Indian conversion to evangelical Christianity, for singing in worship was important to both evangelicals and to Indians from various communities at the bottom of the socio-religious hierarchy (Jones 2017: xv–xxi).

Along with the experiences of Methodist community and worship, the message of Jesus as divine saviour was crucial in Haqq's decision to be baptised and join the Christian group he had come to know. He writes that this decision was made when he heard Rev. Humphrey expounding on the scripture verse: 'For what shall it profit a man, if he shall gain the whole world, and lose his own soul? Or what shall a man give in exchange for his soul?' (al-Haqq 1885: 17). According to his wife, Humphrey interpreted 'gain the whole world' as acquisition of the world's wealth, as opposed to belief in the Lord Jesus Christ and living a good life as manifestation of that belief (E. J. Humphrey 1866: 135). The promise

190 *Arun W. Jones*

of an end to restlessness of the soul was an important reason that Haqq joined the Methodist community.

Once Haqq had been baptised, he entered into the third stage of his spiritual journey. However, again this stage differed from the American pattern. Instead of experiencing the post-conversion torment of the soul, Haqq describes his experience of torment from his family who tried to persuade him to return to his Muslim community. This experience was well known to many (though certainly not all) Indians who joined a Christian community, no matter what their background. As one Indian minister from Allahabad put it,

> We are all aware that a Hindoo or a Mahomedan may believe what he likes, he may be a Christian in heart; but let him pass the Rubicon, let him only go through the waters of baptism, let his relatives and neighbours only know that he has been with the missionary and joined the faith of the Feringies openly, from that very moment his trials and sufferings begin; from that very time he is cursed, maltreated and shunned; henceforth he is considered a degraded outcast. (Mohun 1873: 359)

Haqq writes that some of his friends shunned him, and people in general distrusted him so much that he had to give up his teaching job and be employed as a teacher by the Methodist mission. His family and friends made several and continued efforts to bring him back to the fold. His 'honorable father' visited him and tried to induce him to return home and to his faith. A cousin also visited him. He was asked to go home to Tilhar, where his family members tried to convince him, using many different tactics, to renounce his new religious identity. All these overtures were to no avail; Haqq remained a Methodist. However, instead of cutting off his family, he continued to talk to them, argue with them and communicate with them to the best of his ability. It is surprising, in fact, that after his baptism he risked going back to his village and home. Moreover, the *Autobiography* never betrays any sense of anger or reproach against his family; and in fact Haqq claims that his father faced disapproval from his community for his compassionate treatment of his wayward son (al-Haqq 1885: 19). Such a benign portrayal of his father and family members is called into question by other source material, which relates that Haqq's life was threatened by them (Alter and Alter 1986: 174–175; J. L. Humphrey 1905: 120). As in his description of his 'conversion' to the Pranami group, Haqq here wishes to modulate the abrupt shift from Muslim to Christian communities by showing continued engagement with his family of origin.

Haqq's immersion into and dedication to the Methodist system in India shaped and formed his work and perspectives.[21] In his *Autobiography* he describes the places he worked and the kind of work that he did, which was teaching, assisting missionaries, preaching and then supervising various mission activities.

Reshaping the American Evangelical Conversion Narrative 191

About a decade after his baptism, Haqq was deemed ready to be ordained as a Methodist minister. On his way to Bareilly to seek ordination, he stopped at Moradabad where he was urged by his missionary mentors to experience a 'baptism of the Holy Spirit'. As he recalls it, 'efforts were put forth in order that any who had not experienced this inward work might become aware of the fact and seek and obtain a full knowledge of the blessings promised in the Gospel to those who seek in faith' (al-Haqq 1885: 27). The idea that Christians should seek a distinguishable baptism of the Holy Spirit in which they would completely dedicate their life to holiness had emerged in American evangelical, especially Methodist, circles in the 1850s, and after that gained more and more popularity (Dayton 1993). The Methodist missionary James Thoburn was instrumental in promoting the idea and practice of a second spiritual baptism in India beginning in the late 1860s (Thoburn 1887: 195–196, 211). The consternation that this teaching could cause in India (not to mention the United States) is reflected in Haqq's reaction to this new teaching.

> I became much disturbed in my mind, and began to say in my heart: What strange words are these? What, am I not even now fully a Christian? I received baptism a long time ago. I have been preaching the Gospel for years, and have kept the ordinances of the Church. What lack I yet that is needful for me to obtain? (al-Haqq 1885: 27)

Nonetheless, and perhaps not surprisingly given that he was seeking ordination as a Methodist minister, Haqq went through the process of receiving this second baptism – the fourth stage in his spiritual journey according to the Methodist template. He 'put away all worldly thoughts' and began to consider his spiritual state. He 'fled for refuge to God' – words that are very familiar in *bhakti* devotionalism – with the knowledge that if he did not receive this second baptism his profession of Christianity was worthless. He realised his 'entire weakness and sin', Haqq writes, 'wept much' at his condition, but then was comforted by God and experienced a great change within himself. It is at this point in his *Autobiography* that sin is mentioned as a factor in his spiritual life. 'My sorrow and distress were removed, and perfect joy came into my heart instead!' The changed heart resulted in a changed person, he claims: he acquired a new motive for his work, and his 'disposition and temper were all made new.' It was '*as if Christ were more closely connected with me*', writes Haqq. Right after this baptism of the Holy Spirit, Haqq continued on his journey to Bareilly and was ordained a Methodist minister: the last and final stage in the Methodist spiritual journey. After another decade of success in pastoral work, administration and evangelism, Haqq was appointed Presiding Elder in 1882, the first Indian elevated to that position. He ends his narrative with an avowal that he wishes to

192 *Arun W. Jones*

'remain faithful in the service of God' so that at death he may 'enter into everlasting bliss' (ibid.: 32).

CONVERSION AND POLITICS

There is one feature of Haqq's autobiography that is noticeable because of what he does not say. Haqq barely makes any mention of the north Indian political situation, which was full of strife and conflict at the time of his (first) baptism, and was highly pertinent to Christian mission work. Haqq converted to Christianity in Bareilly in 1858. Just one year earlier, Bareilly – along with numerous other cities in north India – had been a crucial site for the Uprising of 1857, also known as the Indian Mutiny, against the rule of the British East India Company. In the Uprising, Christian missions had been closely identified with the British regime, and several Indian, Eurasian and European Christian civilians had been targeted and killed. Moreover, in the post-Uprising British imaginary, Muslims were especially responsible for violence and bloodshed in the conflict. Haqq mentions this larger political context only briefly. After hearing the Christian preaching for the first time, he writes, 'I had not at this time conversed with any English person, and as the mutiny had only recently been put down, I ... [feared that] if I sought the society of Christians, I might fall into some difficulty and danger from the prejudice and anger of my own people' (ibid.: 10). Later on, he writes, he was nervous when he first conversed with Humphrey and Fieldbrave, thinking they would hold his religion against him. A third time he mentions Muslim–Christian tensions is when he describes his first visit to a Methodist worship, and Mrs Humphrey was nervous that a Muslim was in attendance. Besides these three instances, Haqq does not mention the tense political situation of the time.

It is dangerous to make arguments from relative silence, but two observations can be made about the role of politics in Haqq's narrative. The first is that Haqq repeats a number of times in his work that his life quest is to find religious truth, which he eventually did find in Christianity. In this quest the political affairs of the world, which he briefly mentions three times, always present themselves as impediments to his goal. Politics (like family) was a distraction, for Haqq, from the true purpose of the religious life. This conflict between worldly and religious goals is a leitmotif in Indian thought. For example, ascetics such as *sannyasi*s or *faqir*s extract themselves from worldly concerns in order to pursue their religious journeys. Just as importantly, several well-known north Indian *bhakti* poets found that their social and political ties to the world were impediments to their religious goals. So, according to their hagiographies, the sixteenth-century Rajput poet-princess Mirabai famously renounced her marriage and family ties in order to devote her life to Krishna, while the fifteenth- and sixteenth-century untouchable poet-saint Ravidas of Benares endured Brahmin contumely in his worship of God (Hawley 2005; Burchett 2009: 120–121). Like Indian religious virtuosi, Haqq experienced worldly connections and affairs as problematic.

Second and finally, Haqq presents himself as a Christian who has understood and even appreciated different religious communities: his Sunni Muslim family, the 'Hindu' Pranami brotherhood and the Methodist sect. The hostility and suspicion engendered by the 1857 Uprising are antithetical to his religious temperament, which tends to the irenic and ecumenical, and so he contrasts the religious life to the politics around him. For him, it may be argued, Indian Christians are not to be involved in the communal and sectarian strife of society – whether that is religious, political or social – but rather are to form communities of love, hospitality and worship, such as he first experienced in the family of the Eurasian preacher Joseph Fieldbrave 25 years previously in Bareilly, India, one year after the bloody Uprising in that city.

CONCLUSION

In his straightforward yet thoughtfully challenging *Autobiography*, Zahur-al-Haqq presents a distinctly Indian pattern and model for conversion to Methodist Christianity. From a distance, and to a certain extent, this model resembles an American Methodist spiritual autobiography of the nineteenth century. Like such American narratives, Haqq's work has five stages leading the individual with a troubled soul to peace and joy in Jesus Christ and a new life filled with the Holy Spirit. A closer examination of Haqq's narrative, however, reveals significant departures from Western Methodist understandings of the spiritual journey.

For one, although Haqq narrates decisive moments of religious change in his life, the overall trajectory of that life is a movement towards the truth of knowing the divine saviour, Jesus Christ, and experiencing joy in this world and bliss for eternity. In other words, abrupt disruptions in religious life are incorporated into a continuous if convoluted movement towards complete consonance with the life of God. Yet God has always been present in his life, in one way or another. Second, while Haqq does not hesitate to describe discontinuities in his religious life, he insists that those are only possible because of underlying continuities. Religious diversions and innovations are possible only because previous religious beliefs, practices and experiences have provided the foundation, the warrant and some of the material for change.

Finally, Haqq demonstrates, by posing his life as a counterpoint to American spiritual autobiographies, that Indian Methodism needs to be Indian. Methodism needs to be translated, in the sense articulated by Andrew Walls, into the Indian

194 *Arun W. Jones*

religious context, so that it makes sense for religious seekers of truth and joy, so that it responds to the songs and convictions of *bhakti*. Yet Haqq's life is also authentically Methodist, complete with a second 'baptism of the Holy Spirit' and a call to faithful ministry in the Methodist Church. Haqq depicts a new religious world for the Indian context, with adherents occupying new places and spaces relative to each other and to Indian society at large. Presenting his life as a 'godroad' from Islam and *bhakti* religiosity to evangelical Christianity, Haqq describes the destination as a new Indian religious community, with its own internal beliefs, ethics and organisation, yet still responding to ancient and ongoing Indian religious impulses and desires.

NOTES

1. al-Haqq (1885). His name is spelt a number of different ways in extant sources.

2. Throughout the nineteenth century, by far the most dominant form of Protestantism in terms of numbers and influence in the United States was evangelicalism, a form of 'heart religion' begun in the eighteenth century in Great Britain and British North America.

3. While it is true that in theory his appointment meant that 'American Methodist preachers who had come to India as missionaries received their appointments in Annual Conference at the hands of an ex-Mohammedan', in fact when the Amroha District was formed in 1882 with Zahur-al-Haqq as its Presiding Elder, all of the preachers were Indians (Messmore 1903: 189; Barclay 1949: 626).

4. The date that Haqq gives for his baptism is also wrong, as it was not a Sunday. See al-Haqq (1885: 17) and J. L. Humphrey (1905: 112).

5. Not only does Humphrey claim in the title of the translated *Autobiography* that Haqq was the first convert of the Methodist mission in India, she also makes that claim in her collection of letters to her mother: Mrs E. J. (Emily Jane) Humphrey (1866: 137). This particular letter is dated 10 June 1859. See also J. L. Humphrey (1905: 112–115).

6. His summary of Rev. Humphrey's message that caught his attention is also reported in Mrs Humphrey's book (al-Haqq 1885: 17; E. J. Humphrey 1866: 135–136).

7. See *Second Annual Report of the India Mission Conference of the Methodist Episcopal Church, U.S.A. for the Year 1866* (Lucknow, India: American Methodist Mission Press, 1867), 49; Messmore (1903: 159–160).

8. For the Muslim community in north India in the nineteenth century, see Metcalf (1982).

9. See Thoburn (1887: 207–108) for an example of Haqq's ability to relate to low status Indians.

10. For such a use of autobiography, see Hindmarsh (2014: 354–355).

11. For a fuller account of scholarly issues in conversion studies, see Rambo and Farhadian (2014: 8).

12. For example, see Bauman (2015: 83–91) and Meyer (1998: 318).

13. Here I am indebted to the work of Campbell (2013: 243–260). See also Hempton (2005: 60–68), Hindmarsh (2005), and Rivers (1978: 189–203).

14. Haqq gives no clue as to why he became dissatisfied with Islam.

15. Haqq's autobiography uses 'Parnami', while current scholarship uses 'Pranami'. See also Mukharya (1989: 113–126); Das Gupta (1989: 127–135); Ali (1989); Grierson (1919); Wilson (1846: 226–227).

16. He even incorporated Jewish and Christian elements into the religion: Mukharya (1989: 116–117).

17. Rambo (1993: 12–18) lays out three different taxonomies of conversion, some of which may be helpful in locating Haqq's turn to the Pranamis in a larger framework. For an interesting discussion of *bhakti* and Christianity, see Carman (1968).

18. The emphasis on the importance of religious experience is very typical of Methodism.

19. It is interesting to read Humphrey's account of this encounter between Haqq and the evangelist. In the missionary's version, it was he who approached Haqq after the preaching, and not Haqq who approached the evangelists. The two men portray themselves as taking the initiative in their respective accounts (J. L. Humphrey 1905: 110–112). Fieldbrave was a lay preacher at the time – he was received into Conference in 1867. See 'Memoir of Rev. Joseph Fieldbrave' (1869: 60). That he is Eurasian is reported by J. E. Scott (1906: 48).

20. See the importance he places on his name for calculating his date of birth. Changing one's name did not necessarily mean adopting a Western or biblical name: one could adopt a new Indian name such as 'Abdul Masih', or 'Servant of Christ'.

21. For the annual reports of Haqq's mission work, see al-Haqq (1869: 38; 1870: 37–38).

BIBLIOGRAPHY

al-Haqq, Zahur. 1869. 'Report of the Amroha and Babukhera Station.' In *Fourth Annual Report of the Mission Stations of the Methodist Episcopal Church, U.S.A., in India. For the Year 1868*, 38. Lucknow, India: American Methodist Mission Press.

———. 1870. 'Report of the Amroha and Babukhera Station.' In *Fifth Annual Report of the Mission Stations of the Methodist Episcopal Church, U.S.A., in India. For the Year 1869*, 37–38. Lucknow, India: American Methodist Mission Press.

———. 1885. *Autobiography of Rev. Zahur-Al-Haqq: First Convert in the Mission of the Methodist Episcopal Church in India*. Translated by E. J. Humphrey. New York: The Missionary Society.

Ali, Hafiz Md. Tahir. 1989. 'Influence of Islam and Sufism on Prannath's Religious Movement.' In *Medieval Bhakti Movements in India*, edited by Narendra Nath Bhattacharyya, 136–148. New Delhi: Munshiram Manoharlal.

196 Arun W. Jones

Alter, James P. and John Alter. 1986. *In the Doab and Rohilkhand: North Indian Christianity, 1815–1915*. Delhi: ISPCK.

Baer, Marc David. 2008. *Honored by the Glory of Islam: Conversion and Conquest in Ottoman Europe*. New York: Oxford University Press.

Barclay, Wade Crawford. 1949. *History of Methodist Missions*, 6 vols. Vol. 3. New York: Board of Missions and Church Extension of the Methodist Church.

Bauman, Chad M. 2008. *Christian Identity and Dalit Religion in Hindu India, 1868–1947*. Grand Rapids, MI: Eerdmans.

———. 2015. *Pentecostals, Proselytization, and Anti-Christian Violence in Contemporary India*. New York, NY: Oxford University Press.

Berger, Peter and Sarbeswar Sahoo. 2020. 'Introduction.' *Godroads: Modalities of Conversion in India*. Delhi: Cambridge University Press.

Burchett, Patton. 2009. 'Bhakti Rhetoric in the Hagiography of "Untouchable" Saints: Discerning Bhakti's Ambivalence on Caste and Brahminhood.' *International Journal of Hindu Studies* 13(2) August: 115–141.

Campbell, Ted A. 2013. 'Spiritual Biography and Autobiography.' In *The Cambridge Companion to American Methodism*, edited by Jason E Vickers, 243–260. New York: Cambridge University Press.

Carman, John B. 1968 'Is Christian Faith a Form of Bhakti?' *The Visva Bharati Journal of Philosophy* (3–4): 24–37.

———. 2005. 'Bhakti.' In *The Encyclopedia of Religion*, 15 vols, edited by Lindsay Jones, Vol. 2, 856–860. Detroit: Macmillan Reference USA, 2nd ed.

Chatterjee, K. C. 1873. 'The Relations of Missionaries to Converts in Secular Matters.' In *Report of the General Missionary Conference held at Allahabad, 1872–73*, 337–349. London: Seeley, Jackson and Halliday.

Das Gupta, Bhagwan. 1989. 'Pranami Sampradaya of Bundelkhand.' In *Medieval Bhakti Movements in India*, edited by Narendra Nath Bhattacharyya, 127–135. New Delhi: Munshiram Manoharlal.

Dayton, Donald W. 1993. 'From "Christian Perfection" to the "Baptism of the Holy Ghost."' In *Perspectives on American Methodism: Interpretive Essays*, edited by Russell E. Richey, Kenneth E. Rowe, and Jean Miller Schmidt, 289–297. Nashville, Tenn: Kingswood Books.

Flood, Gavin D. 1996. *An Introduction to Hinduism*. New York: Cambridge University Press.

Francis, Emmanuel and Charlotte Schmid. 2014. 'Introduction: Towards an Archaeology of Bhakti.' In *The Archaeology of Bhakti I: Mathura and Maturai, Back and Forth*, edited by Emmanuel Francis and Charlotte Schmid. Pondicherry, India: Institut Français de Pondichery.

Grierson, G. A. 1919. 'Prannathis.' In *Encyclopedia of Religion and Ethics*, 13 vols, edited by James Hastings, Vol. 10. 150–151. Edinburgh: T. & T. Clark.

Hawley, John Stratton. 2005. 'Mirabai as Wife and Yogi', In *Three Bhakti Voices*, edited by John Stratton Hawley, 117–130. New Delhi: Oxford University Press.

Hefner, Robert W. 1993. 'Introduction: World Building and the Rationality of Conversion.' In *Conversion to Christianity: Historical and Anthropological Perspectives on a Great Transformation*, edited by Robert W. Hefner, 3–44. Berkeley, CA: University of California Press.

Hempton, David. 2005. *Methodism: Empire of the Spirit*. New Haven: Yale University Press.

Hindmarsh, Bruce. 2005. *The Evangelical Conversion Narrative: Spiritual Autobiography in Early Modern England*. New York: Oxford University Press.

———. 2014. 'Religious Conversion as Narrative and Autobiography.' In *The Oxford Handbook of Religious Conversion*, edited by Lewis R. Rambo and Charles E. Farhadian, 343–368. New York: Oxford University Press.

Hopkins, Thomas J. 1971. *The Hindu Religious Tradition*. Encino, CA: Dickenson Publishing Company.

Humphrey, Emily Jane. 1866. *Six Years in India: Or, Sketches of India and Its People*. New York: Hunt & Eaton.

Humphrey, James Lorenzo. 1905. *Twenty-One Years in India*. Cincinnati: Jennings and Graham.

Johnson, W. J. 2010. *Oxford Dictionary of Hinduism*. Oxford, New York: Oxford University Press.

———, trans. 1994. *The Bhagavad Gita*. New York: Oxford University Press.

Jones, Arun W. 2017. *Missionary Christianity and Local Religion: American Evangelicalism in North India, 1836–1870*. Waco, TX: Baylor University Press.

Khan, Dominique-Sila. 2002. *The Pranami Faith, Beyond 'Hindu' and 'Muslim.'* Bangalore: Yoginder Sikand.

Marshall, Ruth. 2009. *Political Spiritualities: The Pentecostal Revolution in Nigeria*. Chicago: University of Chicago Press.

'Memoir of Rev. Joseph Fieldbrave.' 1869. *Fourth Annual Report of the Mission Stations of the Methodist Episcopal Church, U.S.A., in India. For the Year 1868*, 60. Lucknow, India: American Methodist Mission Press.

Messmore, J. H. 1903. *The Life of Edwin Wallace Parker, D. D.: Missionary Bishop of Southern Asia, Forty-One Years a Missionary in India*. New York: Cincinnati: Eaton & Mains, Jennings & Pye.

Metcalf, Barbara Daly. 1982. *Islamic Revival in British India: Deoband, 1860–1900*. Princeton, NJ: Princeton University Press.

Meyer, Birgit. 1998. '"Make a Complete Break with the Past." Memory and Post-Colonial Modernity in Ghanaian Pentecostalist Discourse.' *Journal of Religion in Africa* 28(3): 316–349.

Mohun, David. 1873. 'The Christian Village System.' In *Report of the General Missionary Conference, Held at Allahabad, 1872–73: With a Missionary Map of India*, 356–364. London: Seeley, Jackson, and Halliday.

Mukharya, P. S. 1989. 'Sant Prannath and the Pranami Sect.' In *Medieval Bhakti Movements in India*, edited by Narendra Nath Bhattacharyya, 113–126. New Delhi: Munshiram Manoharlal.

Rambo, Lewis. 1993. *Understanding Religious Conversion*, 12–18. New Haven: Yale University Press.

Rambo, Lewis R. and Charles E. Farhadian. 2014. 'Introduction: Conversion and Global Transformation.' In *The Oxford Handbook of Religious Conversion*, edited by Lewis R. Rambo and Charles E. Farhadian, 1–22. New York: Oxford University Press.

Rivers, Isabel. 1978. '"Strangers and Pilgrims": Sources and Patterns of Methodist Narrative.' In *Augustan Worlds: Essays in Honor of A. R. Humphreys*, edited by J. C. Hilson, M. M. B. Jones, and J. R. Watson, 189–203. Leicester: Leicester University Press.

Robbins, Joel. 2004. *Becoming Sinners: Christianity and Moral Torment in a Papua New Guinea Society*. Berkeley: University of California Press.

Scott, J. E. 1906. *History of Fifty Years*. Madras: Methodist Episcopal Press.

Second Annual Report of the India Mission Conference of the Methodist Episcopal Church, U.S.A. for the Year 1866. 1867. Lucknow, India: American Methodist Mission Press.

Thoburn, James M. 1887. *My Missionary Apprenticeship*. New York: Phillips & Hunt.

Toffin, Gerard. 2012. 'The Power of Boundaries: Transnational Links Among Krishna Pranamis of India and Nepal.' In *Public Hinduisms*, edited by John Zavos, 232–247. New Delhi: Sage.

Walls, Andrew F. 1996. *The Missionary Movement in Christian History*. Maryknoll, NY: Orbis Books.

Wilson, Horace Hayman. 1846. *Sketch of the Religious Sects of the Hindus*. Calcutta: Bishop's College Press.

8

Cultural Transformations through Performance Arts in Early Twentieth-Century South India*

Rajalakshmi Nadadur Kannan

The anti-colonial movements and nationalist discourses of the early twentieth century India are much researched topics. Within the context of nationalism, scholars have shown how the construction of Hinduism as a unifying identity marker functioned as an ideology which contributed to a religion-based identity politics that intertwined with nationalism during these movements (King 1999; 2010; Oddie 2006; 2010; Sugirtharajah 2010). These discourses, as Chatterjee (1993) and others have shown, involved appropriation of colonial (including the missionary) discourses on gender, religion and linguistics. In this chapter, I focus on the historical developments in south India and its nationalistic politics during the early twentieth century. Here, performance arts (mainly music and dance) served as tools to construct newer understandings of national identity as Hindu identity, Indian culture as Hindu culture and Indian subject-hood as Hindu subject-hood as part of a cultural transformation to change the nation into a sacralised land. The colonial city of Madras (now Chennai) served as the centre for these developments. The rhetoric surrounding these developments was that of a nostalgia for a historical (mythical, utopic) Hindu nation, and the efforts to reclaim what was seen as a past/lost glory through sacralisation of performance arts and aesthetic preferences. What the south Indian nationalists hailed as the 'renaissance' in colonial Madras (Iyer 1931), performance arts and aesthetic preferences became intertwined with religious identity, specifically Hindu identity, and Indian culture.

That contemporary south Indian classical performance arts are a gendered historical construction of south Indian nationalists has been explored by scholars (Meduri 1996; Allen 1997; 1998; Subramanian 1999; 2006; Weidman 2006; Soneji 2012). Also, it is now well known that the nationalistic discourses, in the Indian National Congress (INC), which was dominant in north India, and in south India were gendered too (Chatterjee 1993; Meduri 1996; Ray 2000; Weidman 2006; Chakrabarty 2007). However, my interest lies in understanding how sacralising performance arts was used as a tool to sacralise the nation, and sacralising aesthetic preferences was used as a tool to sacralise the pan-Indian identity that was also gendered. A question that arises here is: can this be considered as a process of conversion? In line with the other contributions to this volume, this chapter uses a broader definition of the term 'conversion'. Whilst a normative definition would point to shifting from one tradition or belief or faith to another, this chapter illustrates a conversion to an ideology – from a mere audience of performance arts to connoisseurs; from a context where the secular, politics and religion were not distinguished to a hegemonic discourse where the distinction was made clear, in other words, a conversion to a religious, Hindu ideology. Thus, the identity of an Indian subject was conflated with a Hindu identity, music was transformed to Carnatic Music, and dance into Bharatnatyam.[1] These hegemonic identity markers were arrived at by ostracising many communities and groups, and these communities had to either conform to these newly emerging religious identities or be marginalised further. Nationalism in this context was a shift to an ideological position wherein sacralised arts were seen as Indian/Hindu identity, and the others were not. Much like the larger/ hegemonic nationalist movements, this was gendered (Chakrabarty 1999) and class-based, as the nationalists involved in this project were colonial elites, a group consisting of Brahmins and upper-class non-Brahmins.

Reification of this ideological position was undertaken in various ways, which this chapter will discuss in detail. The historical development of revival arts was a large-scale organised effort of the nationalists, consisting of educated Brahmins and upper-class non-Brahmins, that was given much importance by the INC. This analysis is crucial not the least because this historically constructed understanding of Indian identity/subjecthood is still persistent in popular discourses on India. Even today, within the so-called classical music and dance community, there exists a certain rigid understanding of what these arts represent; they are always seen as religious, and there is a general rejection of other forms of performance arts that do not conform to the traditions of these communities. Moreover, these classical arts continue to be deified and mysticised by patrons and audiences. However, there are attempts by musicians to challenge the hegemony through various ways including making these arts widely available through forums such as YouTube (Nadadur Kannan 2014). What has been embedded in these narratives is the ubiquitous presence of faith – primarily Hinduism; here, nationalism was/is Hinduism.

Using Bourdieu's theorisation of cultural capital and identity politics, it is this shift – from arts to religious/classical arts, from performance arts to religious/ cultural capital – that I will focus on in this chapter. However, these historical developments were not a seamless process of shifting affiliations from a non- nationalistic to a nationalistic, religious position; rather, these were complex,

Cultural Transformations through Performance Arts 201

involving a multitude of players with overlapping discourses. Such complexity provides a good example for the main theme of this book, which is 'godroads'. Using primary sources – of speeches, writings and essays by nationalists between 1920 and 1947 – I will show how this rhetoric took shape and became an ideological position during a period of much political volatility. Fundamental to these developments was the appropriation of colonial discourses and methodologies to construct nationalistic discourses. This included narratives on religion (specifically, Christianity), culture (Western versus Eastern) and national identity. Works such as *Ornamentalism* (2002) have shown that under the metanarratives of colonisation, there were the day-to-day, meticulous administrative, mundane work that managed the actual workings of the British Empire. Similarly, beneath the grand gestures of marches and protests, the mundane and painstaking efforts of the nationalists to shape the nationalistic narratives, and the language they used must be considered. This chapter analyses such efforts as recorded in the archives.

This chapter focuses primarily on south India because the nationalist movements in south India were tinged with the regional political and ideological upheavals that marked them as different from the Gandhian nationalistic discourses of the rest of the nation. Many nationalists were former members of the INC but broke away from the party to form regional-level nationalistic groups based on linguistic identities to protest against what they argued as the dominance of Brahmanism and of Sanskrit. Within this nation-building process, many aspects of the societies were utilised such as gender, language, religion, performance arts, and so on. A term often used in this essay is 'colonial elites'; this refers to the south Indian nationalists who, as mentioned earlier, were Brahmins and upper-class non-Brahmins. They represented the cream of the society due to their access to some form of Western education, upper economic class, and so on. This is important because much of their rhetoric surrounding performance arts and aesthetic preferences involved a Bourdieusian understanding of cultural capital, which this chapter will explore. An additional note on the primary sources needs to be provided: much of the archival materials containing speeches, essays and other writings come from the *Journal of Madras Music Academy*, a publication by a premier cultural institution in south India called the Madras Music Academy. There is a crucial reason for this: this institution was founded as a part of the art revival and cultural transformation in order to reify the nationalist discourses on cultural capital. This chapter analyses the journal issues from 1927 to 1947, from the year of the first issue published to the year of Indian independence. Of course, these nationalistic activities did not cease the moment India became an independent nation. But, for the sake of practicality and relevance, 1947 has been chosen as the final year of analysis of the journal issues for this essay.

202 *Rajalakshmi Nadadur Kannan*

This chapter is divided in the following way. The next section begins by looking at the changing colonial politics and administrative policies in India that provided a context for the emerging nationalistic narratives on performance arts. The chapter then gives a detailed analysis of the various measures undertaken by the south Indian nationalists to initiate the cultural transformations. The chapter then looks at one of the most important communities who were marginalised by these developments. The chapter ends by drawing broader themes and conclusions from these developments.

SHIFTING PERFORMANCE SPACES AND CONTEXTS IN EARLY TWENTIETH-CENTURY SOUTH INDIA

Leading up to the nineteenth century, performance arts were patronised by the kings in South India (and elsewhere in India too). Patronage offered to performance arts and temples were interconnected and deeply embedded in the legitimacy of kingship (Dirks 1993; Nadadur Kannan 2014). For instance, bestowing honours and titles on the performers in turn encouraged the performers to extoll the legacies of the kings, which both popularised and solidified the kings' sovereignty in relation to the neighbouring kingdoms. In the latter part of the nineteenth century, the British colonial government began annexing many small kingdoms, reducing the kingships to mere landholdings called the *zamindari* system (Breckenridge 1977: 76). This change in the policies of the colonial government restricted the powers of the kings severely with regard to patronage to performance arts and temples (Breckenridge 1977; Dirks 1993; Nadadur Kannan 2014). For instance, wherein it was common for the kings to donate lands and other gifts to those whom they patronised, the reduction of sovereignty meant reduced ability to provide patronage. Traditional performers were greatly affected by these developments; many lost their access to royal patronage resulting in their migration to urban centres such as colonial Madras, which began to serve as a capital for the Madras Presidency encompassing the whole of south India, for newer opportunities. Colonial Madras provided ample space for the migrating performance artists amongst the colonial elites who were the primary audience for these arts (Subramanian 2006: 24). One of the aspects of the growing nationalist movements was a need for an identity to represent, unite the colonised people, and reflect their traditions amongst what the nationalists called an increasingly Westernised environment. To these nationalists, true traditions lay in the pre-British kingdoms from where the artists were migrating. Thus, the performance arts brought to the urban colonial Madras by these artists became embedded in this social context, that is, nationalistic politics (Subramanian 1999; Ries 1969; Higgins 1976) that

Cultural Transformations through Performance Arts **203**

represented a pre-colonial past. These arts thus came under intense scrutiny. From the second decade of the twentieth century, the reshaping and reconstruction of performance arts, and their role as a pan Indian identity began as deliberate efforts by the nationalists in colonial Madras. What Chatterjee (1993) defines as 'classicization' pertaining to similar developments in colonial Bengal, they did this partially by borrowing the colonial narratives on religion, gender and culture, and partially by constructing newer ideological positions through their own newer understandings of indigenous traditions and practices. The 'renaissance', as one nationalist called the process (Iyer 1929: 31), in colonial Madras, and the reconstruction of arts, was a collective movement to which performers and former patrons of art, *zamindar*s and middle-class nationalists from urban Madras contributed through both patronage and advocacy.

Much of their ideological positioning came from the notion that the then current state of arts was of defilement and profanity; that arts must be purified in order to be restored to its original forms of sacrality. This understanding of sacrality was conflated with Hinduism, which they understood as quintessentially representing the authentic Indian culture. The history of performance arts as reconstructed by the colonial elites in the early twentieth century was, in many ways, a task of essentially choosing specific strands of history to put together a cogent, selective and favourable memory of the past. This was a mysticised and sacralised view of the Indian cultural history. Beginning from 1927, with the support of the INC, the nationalists began organising a series of music conferences during which their discourses became reified as ideological positions through speeches and essays. The All India Music Conference, which began in 1927 as a forum to address the status and the role of performance arts in the society, also was deliberately begun as a nationalistic endeavour. Although the first few conferences specifically addressed music, these efforts were aimed collectively at music, dance and, as an extension, drama. The first conference passed a resolution emphasising the need for institutionalising performance arts in order to prune practices that defiled the arts and to purify the arts to restore its sacrality. The Madras Music Academy (or the Academy in short), which later published these speeches and essays in their journal, was founded in 1928 for these purposes. The Academy continues to serve as a principal cultural institution for performance arts education (primarily south Indian classical music, also known as Carnatic Music) and performance; it also continues to set the rubric for pedagogy and performance. The speakers and writers at the early music conferences and the journal were nationalists consisting of Brahmins and upper-class non-Brahmins who were able to, rather successfully, appropriate colonial discourses on religion, gender and culture; their familiarity with the West enabled them to juxtapose Indian and Western cultures to argue for the superiority of the former. Often

204 *Rajalakshmi Nadadur Kannan*

times, they used the language of modernity drawing on science and secularity for this purpose. As the journal documents, every speaker and writer meticulously drove home this point and emphasised the need for practising a standardised pure form of performance arts.

CONSTRUCTION OF SOCIAL AND CULTURAL CAPITAL

Pierre Bourdieu's now much-quoted works on cultural capital and identity politics serve a helpful theoretical framework to understand the historical developments surrounding performance arts. He discusses the role of aesthetic preferences that mark the characteristics of a class or classes that perform the function of stratifying a society based on such tastes and preferences (1984: 1). Much of what the south Indian colonial elites did as part of nationalist movements can be conceivably understood using Bourdieu's theorisation. A closer analysis of the speeches and writings of the colonial elites reveals a meticulous process of constructing various categories for their nation-building process. These efforts must be seen as what Derrida and later Butler theorised as moments of performativity. Butler posits that performativity as a 'reiteration of norms which precede, constrain, and exceed the performer and in that sense cannot be taken as the fabrication of the performer's "will" or "choice" ....' (1993: 24, emphasis original). In every speech, article and essay, nationalists forcefully argued for restoring the lost sacrality of performance arts by pruning practices that were seen as modern and Western. But intrinsic to performativity was an ideological position from which they argued that revival of performance arts, and hence the classificatory system of aesthetic preferences, was essential. Bourdieu argues that social contexts give rise to a certain system of tastes and preferences that are then used to legitimise social differences (1984: 7). Thus, 'a work of art has meaning and interest only for someone who possesses the cultural competence, that is, the code, into which it is encoded' (ibid.: 2). What the archives reveal is not only the construction of social differences, but also the code itself. In other words, Bourdieu argues that the cultural capital precedes the classification of the society; that the cultural capital that conforms to the hegemonic aesthetic preferences become part of a code that enables those who possess it to be part of that dominant social group. As colonial elites, south Indian nationalists assumed to have possessed this code, and assumed the role of custodians of performance arts. However, as these self-appointed custodians, they constructed a code and the cultural capital to enable their nation-building process. Thus, whilst they argued that they alone knew and understood performance arts, its history, traditions and sacrality better, they also constructed a specific kind of educational capital, institutionalised cultural capital, and embodied/ritualistic cultural capital, and

Cultural Transformations through Performance Arts **205**

made these capital accessible to only certain groups of people, thereby trying to solidify a newly constructed cultural capital that the future performers must conform to if they wished to belong to this exclusive social group. This way, they ensured that performance arts, and by extension pan Indian identity, will remain in the hands of a specific group. In the following sections, I describe the construction of various forms of cultural capital these nationalists embarked upon.

Sacralising Culture by Sacralising Performance Arts

Sacralising performance arts was a key component of constructing a specific cultural identity. Mysticisation of these arts then meant an uncritical glorified past that could be easily constructed. Essentially, this revival of arts was a nostalgia for that glorified past and an effort to return to them. The nationalists never questioned the notion that performance arts were divine. This position was a predisposition from which all arguments defining Indian culture were made. Thus, to these nationalists, the issue at hand was not how to convince their intended audiences that performance arts were indeed divine; rather it was how to convince an entire community of performers and audiences to discard their own aesthetic preferences, and shift to the newer position – in other words, from audiences to connoisseurs. Arts were often deified, and spoken of as mysticised entities that had the ability to transform the performers and listeners, transcending the mundane and transporting them to a higher, spiritual realm. In this narrative, arts were no longer spiritual tools, but divine themselves because deities have performed them in the historical stories and poetries (such as the Ramayana and the Mahabharata). These arts had the ability to deify the performers and the audience because they embodied the divine by merely performing and listening to them. For instance, in an article called 'The Ideal Gayaka' (*gayaka* lit. male performer), Narayandas argued:

> He [a good musician] is born and not made … it is said that unless one is endowed with the musical nerve, he [*sic*] can neither sing nor appreciate music … a gayaka (lit. male musician) [*sic*] is like a celestial being amongst men…. [T]he expression of a Gayaka is itself a true poem … he is to discharge a sacred duty'. (1930: 117–119)

We must pay attention to the gendered language and the idealisation of a performer. Both became crucial when marginalising communities that were adhering to older forms of arts, which I discuss in the forthcoming sections. Similarly, during the Ninth Madras Music Conference, Sir P. S. Sivasvami Iyer said: '… music unalloyed by words is capable of transporting you to the realm of the spiritual, to communion with the Infinite and filling you in a deep and undefinable sense of the mystery of the universe' (1935–1937: 172). By making deliberate connections to the Vedas and Puranic texts, the Madras elites established the notion that these classical forms of performance arts were religious, and Hindu. In every issue of the journal that consisted of articles, transcripts of speeches and reports on music conferences from the corresponding years, authors reiterated the connection arts had with ancient texts such as the Vedas and Upanishads (Krishnacharya 1929: 7). Moreover, the music was argued to have been present in epic poems such as the Ramayana and the Mahabharata in which the protagonists Rama and Krishna are believed to be the reincarnations of Hindu deity Vishnu. By tracing these genealogical and historical connections to specific Hindu texts, the implicit and, sometimes, explicit notion was that performance arts – music and dance – were Hindu (Tatti 1929: 2–6). Thus, those aspects of performance arts that could be directly connected to Hindu deities were considered sacred; everything else was considered profane.

Bourdieu argues that in emphasising the need for 'pure gaze', and in setting one aesthetic preference apart from the others, the 'human' element is often rejected – a dichotomy is constructed in which human is considered mundane and pedestrian '… that reduces the aesthetic animal to pure and simple animality, to palpable sexual desire' (1984: 31–32). Pure aesthetics here must then transcend the human from the mundane to the supernatural realm. Construction of performance arts as sacred involved using this idea, as the quote from Narayandas earlier illustrates. In 1929, the Zamindar of Seithur argued in a speech given during the conference:

> It [music] is a soul food for the higher man.… In the emotional, mental and higher planes, music soothes a man's soul, transforms his being and makes him realize his divinity. The Shastras say that through knowledge of music you can reach God. It is therefore our bounden duty to revive the art of music.… We must give this divine art its place in the national life.… (1929: 25–26)

Such references to the transcendental power of performance arts were a common refrain during the conference. Part of what enabled the nationalists to reify these ideas came from mysticisation of certain eighteenth-century composers. The biographies of these composers, which were popularised in the nineteenth and twentieth centuries, were utilised extensively by the colonial elites to argue for the arts' transcendental nature; that these arts, when practised and performed correctly, take humans closer to the divine realm. Whilst the nationalists wrote about several eighteenth-century composers, three eighteenth century male composers (now called the Trinity) were specifically popularised as mystic composers: Tyāgarājā (1767–1847), Mutthuswāmy Dikshitar (1776–1835) and Shyama Sastri (1762–1827). Perhaps because these composers were patronised by kings who were historically known for their contributions to the arts – for instance, King Serfoji II – and that their students wrote their biographies, therefore permanently fixing their lives in text rather than in oral tradition, the nationalists chose these composers. However, it must be acknowledged that their compositions are rich in poetry, melody, and so on. Of the three, however, Tyāgarājā – owing to the colloquial form of language of his compositions – became more accessible, and hence more popular. In fact, the 1947 issue of the journal was entirely devoted to commemorating the composer's life and works. Indeed, the nationalists specifically talked about Tyāgarājā's devotion and the 'mysterious power' that connected him to God and gave him the peace that he could not find in this material world (Bhagavatar 1931: 19). His compositions were hailed as 'gospels', and he was credited with having 'harmonized art with religion' and having 'infused a spiritual vitality into music' (ibid.: 19, 22). Often, biographies of these saint-composers, as they were called, were infused with their encounters with the divine. The purpose of such stories and drawing explicit divine connections was to provide a genealogical justification for claiming that arts were sacred. In other words, like common mythological stories, these stories emphasised that these performance arts directly descended from the divine. Thus, part of the nationalistic project was to rewrite the history of performance arts as divine; however, sacralising the society by sacralising art involved identifying practices and traditions that were unsuitable for these newer narratives.

Constructing the 'Other'

As Bourdieu argued, part of defining 'pure gaze' was to differentiate between human and divine practices. South Indian nationalists deliberately drew distinctions between human versus divine realms in which the performance arts occupied the latter. In this narrative, the nationalists argued that the then musicians had fallen into the human realm by succumbing to profane practices of materialism, and by improperly following the traditions of performance arts (Row 1933: 1). This being targeted towards the then performers and the audience who supported such performances, they also criticised the modern society. Thus, they constructed multiple others to construct the dichotomy between sacred and profane. While I discuss this dichotomy in this section, I discuss another marginalised community in the forthcoming section. The dichotomy of sacred/ profane was constructed using several different discourses. The first was by drawing distinctions between the indigenous traditions and that of the West, positing the former as superior to the latter. Direct comparisons, in addition to references to colonisation, were drawn between Indian culture and Western culture. Here, culture was seen by the nationalists as a static sphere that was historically pure. Any changes to the culture brought in by colonisation and social transformations were considered as the causes of impurity. For instance, Dr U. Rama Rao, the then president of the Academy, at the Second Music Conference in 1929 said the following in his speech:

> Then came a series of foreign invasions [in India], the Mohmedans, the Moghuls, the Greeks, the Portuguese, the Dutch, the Danes, the French and the English and India thereafter became the scene of battles and bloodshed. All progress in art and science was thus given a set-back and Music also suffered along with the rest.... (1929: 26)

With these kinds of rhetoric, the nationalists drove home the following point: that historically performance arts were pure and sacred; in the intervening centuries, due to colonialisation and the profanity it induced, performance arts became defiled. It was now their responsibility to re-establish its superiority and purity in order to show the true representation of Hindu/Indian culture.

Whilst emphasising the arts' connection to the Hindu past, the nationalists also defined what art was not, and the importance of making that distinction. As the quote from Dr Rao shows, the nationalists argued that the current state of arts was defiled and profane because the performers had strayed from their classical past. Colonialism was identified as the cause, but the colonial elites tended to criticise the performers for not adhering to the traditions. Thus, in order to establish the classical nature of arts, the nationalists distinguished these classical arts from that of the Western arts. During a talk in Edinburgh, the text of which was published in the *Journal of Madras Music Academy* 1935–1937 issue, Mr V. K. Narayana Menon said the following: 'The Eastern mind is transcendental, speculative; the Western, critical. The East has always insisted on emotional sincerity; the West on intellectual sincerity.... The Western singer is mainly a vehicle.... The Eastern voice is free from harmonics' (134–135). In fact, Narayanaswami Aiyar, a member of the Expert Committee at *The Madras Music Academy*, wrote, 'Englishmen are as much acquainted with our music as a frog with politics' (1933: 156). This deliberate drawing of distinction between East and West was directly aimed at nationalistic purposes. In fact, over the years, speakers directly addressed the nationalistic purposes of this project. To them, the revival of performance arts was the path forward or, in other words, a guide for a new country to establish itself as culturally superior to the West (Radhakrishnan 1931: 143). However, the emphasis was laid on the notion that Indian culture was superior to the West, and that was because of its religiosity. Often, this was done by making deliberate connections to mystic composers and poets as discussed in the previous section. Between 1929 and 1947, the journal was replete with such rhetoric emphasising the superiority of Indian arts (Nadadur Kannan 2014). Part of reviving the arts involved transforming the audiences into connoisseurs. The Indian colonial elites believed that this responsibility rested principally on the performers. Accordingly, they attempted to control the type of arts available to the audiences. For instance, in an opening address in 1945, the philanthropist Dr Alagappa Chettiar argued that the availability of more opportunities for performance and increased access to these performances – in short, performances being open to the general public as opposed to a chosen few during kingly patronage – has not been beneficial to the arts itself. 'Democracy therefore has been a mixed blessing for music and the proportion of evil is greater than the proportion of good' (1945: 3). Often, they emphasised that it was the responsibility of the performers to provide the audiences with good quality performance (which in this context meant performance with devotion and authenticity approved by the Indian colonial elites) to elevate the aesthetic preference of the audiences that would then become their cultural capital portraying their 'stylization of life' (Bourdieu 1984: 174). Allen (1998) and Schofield (2010) have argued that these distinctions between traditional and modern arts were based on classical/non-classical categories. The East versus West and religiosity versus materialism dichotomies pointed to their understanding of a strong inner spiritual domain versus a materialistic outer domain, Indian culture representing the former and the West representing the latter. To emphasise the strength and uniqueness of the inner domain, other domains had to be made less so. Moreover, to reify an ideological position on these classical arts, a claim to prune the current practices of defilement had to be made. To shift performance arts from entertainment to religious, the non-conforming aspects needed to be identified. As Bourdieu (1984: 5) has argued, this is a part of stratifying a society based on aesthetic tastes and preference in which 'popular taste' refers to those that '... performs a systematic reduction of the things of art to the things of life'. In his opening address at the 1943 music conference, Sir M. V. Rao argued that due to Western influence 'we became insensible of our heritage, forgot our traditions and gloried in imitating whatever happened to be the fashion in the West' but encouraged the 'renaissance of the Indian spirit' that makes a 'future worthy of that past' (1943: 2).

Another way the nationalists emphasised the superiority of Indian performance arts was by arguing that these arts were worthy of scientific study. Chatterjee (1993: 121) argues that nationalist discourses in colonial Bengal involved attempts at 'match[ing] their [coloniser's] strength' to 'ultimately overthrow' them. This was how the nationalists appropriated colonial discourses to show that their culture was superior to that of the West. The nationalists did not necessarily distinguish between religion and secular as the colonial discourses (based on Enlightenment) did; rather, they provided a newer understanding of secular. Speaking in 1931, Dr U. Rama Rao, the then president of the Academy, argued that due to the divine origins of music, it has the 'qualities of healing, soothing and softening the distressed minds and bodies.... For the musician, it is a form of breathing or Pranayama [a type of yoga] exercise' (1931: 69). To them, these arts were dynamic – they were sacred, but also scientifically sound, traditional and yet modern. That these were traditional and religious, but not archaic; and that these were invincible in that they are traditionally and scientifically sound. Science too indicated the idea that the arts were worthy of empirical and objective evaluation much like science in the West, thus indicating that the colonial elites' acknowledgement of superiority awarded to science. For instance, some speakers at the Music Conferences emphasised on the therapeutic nature of these arts (especially music) in connection to its compatibility with science (Raman 1934: 97–100). To them, Carnatic Music is, therefore, modern in this sense. Thus, if Western classical music could be systematised through notation and theories and institutionalised through instruction in educational institutions and research (as in the field of musicology), then so could Indian music be (Sastri 1931: 192). What they distinguished between was profane art and sacred art, which they did by arguing that some performances lack devotion. How they measured that is not entirely clear, neither is the answer to the question what constitutes 'proper' devotion.

Speeches and articles also referred to the golden era of royal patronage to performance arts, which were then abolished by the colonial government. It is noteworthy, again, that many of these speakers were those former royal patrons who lost their kingship to the colonial government after annexation of their kingdoms as mentioned in the introduction to this chapter. Why was patronage so important to the nationalists, one might ask. Patronage to arts was an essential part of kingship – within this economy, the king represented the divine, thereby maintaining the divine connection to these arts (Dirks 1993; Nadadur Kannan 2014). One must read between the lines here: patronage ensured that performance arts remained within the hands of certain trustworthy patrons, but in urban centres where there were European influences in addition to access to materialistic life, these arts have been corrupted. The fundamental argument here was that tradition was good; modern, not so. The one clear way of establishing that was to dichotomise between good and bad arts, sacred and profane arts. Even in the quote cited earlier, Sir Rao argues that due to various reasons, people of India forgot their culture and traditions, and got waylaid. For instance, the nationalists deliberately made distinction between *margi* and *desi* styles of musical performances – *margi* being the indigenous styles of performance, while *desi* being those that had a mix of foreign culture. Between the two styles, *margi* was pure, *desi* was not; even if *desi* encompasses certain aspects of *margi*, it would never attain the status of *margi* style. It is this distinction that the nationalists used against music in the fledgling film industry in south India in the early twenieth century (Nadadur Kannan 2014). Moreover, the nationalists bemoaned the lack of *bhakti* (lit. devotion) in the performances of those days. Any kind of deviation from their prescribed rules was deemed impure (Iyer 1931: 15–16). We must place these narratives within the context of the then colonial Madras. As mentioned above, the urban space encompassed a wider audience, including Europeans. This meant that the nature and types of performances transformed to fit the needs of the audience. Thus, for instance, dance performances often encompassed acrobatics, and sensuality, to cater to the audience. Moreover, the early twentieth century also saw the emergence of gramophone records and introduction of microphones in performances. The changing nature of performance arts unnerved the nationalists deeply even if eventually they adapted to the technologies (Srinivasan 1945: 21). To them, the empirical establishment of what constituted pure arts was to refer to historical texts and treatises such *Sangita Sastra* and *Natyasastra*, which lay down various rules of performances. In doing so, they established these as canonical texts on performance arts, and on authentic Indian culture much like how the *Manusmriti* reified caste classification, and the Vedas and the Bhagawad Gita reified Hinduism in colonial discourses. Thus, profane here was unsuitable performance practices; and profane was also materialism, which they accused *devadāsi*s of for providing newer forms of performances to cater to European audiences (as described earlier), for being some of the first gramophone record artists and film artistes. I discuss more on this in the section on marginalised communities.

INSTITUTIONALISING AND STANDARDISING PERFORMANCE ARTS

Emphasis was placed to institutionalise and standardise performance of arts. With the establishment of the Academy, a foundation for future work had been set up. Beginning from 1929, the nationalists argued for the need for oversight of performances and teaching. As Dr U. Rama Rao argued in 1929, the Academy was established '... as a stable organization, to promote among other things, the study and practice of music and restore it to its blissful state of yore in India....' (23). The nationalists also requested for a need for individual committees to supervise the standardisation of each of the technical aspects of performance such as *raga* (lit. tunes) and *tala* (lit. rhythmic cycles). During every music conference (held annually since 1930) conducted by the Academy, the members delved into the minute technicalities of music (and later, dance) to establish a standardised, hegemonic system. Each music conference, and the resulting journal issues, contained careful analysis and constructions of notes of each *raga* and *tala*. One must understand the magnitude of this project: every *raga* has seven notes; there are 72 *raga*s that act as 'mother' *raga*. In addition, offshoots for these 72 *raga*s were created using different combinations of the seven notes of each 'mother' *raga*; thus, the members looked at hundreds of *raga*s, one at a time. As mentioned in the previous section, often the speakers and writers referred to the ancient texts that they now claimed to be canonical for these arts. The aim was to standardise both orthodoxy and orthopraxy; but such standardisation was possible through a uniform notating system. It is noteworthy that performance arts until then were mostly an oral tradition; to notate then marks a shift in the approach towards these arts – an emphasis on orthodoxy, and reification of orthopraxy within such orthodoxy (Sastri 1931: 192). The Madras Music Academy encouraged the projects of notating Carnatic Music and emphasised the importance of 'proper' music education in colleges and universities. Setting up colleges and universities were seen as institutionalising performance arts; by 1931, the Academy had established Teachers' College of Music and by 1932 the University of Madras had introduced courses and examinations in music. In the next section I discuss the importance laid upon arts pedagogy.

The institutions themselves were often praised for enabling this process. Speeches and articles extolled the Divine Providence of the Academy to be able to rescue the arts from decay. Such mysticisation of the institutions further reified their place in this ideological process. They set the standard to which all other institutions had to subscribe. However, because the institutions were themselves divine, their words were canonical. By the extension of this rationale, these institutions, especially the Academy, became a sacred space for performers. Thus, the Academy argued for creating 'respectable' spaces for performances to take place, and that this would lead to the redemption of the arts themselves (Bhagavatar 1933: 144). One must pay attention to this rhetoric: by creating performance spaces for arts, the nationalists were essentially bringing back the arts to what they saw as the legitimate religious space. In the name of reclaiming, thus, the arts were taken from the public spaces of the urban/colonial Madras to private spaces created by the nationalists, which ensured a nearly complete control of the cultural capital. To this day, being able to perform at the Academy during the 'music season' that is celebrated in the month of December every year is a landmark in an artist's career. These developments achieved what the nationalists had attempted – performance arts were reified as divine and Hindu, they were standardised and systematised according to the rubric laid out by the nationalists, and those practices that were deemed defiling to these arts were removed. It is those practices that the concluding section focuses on because

Education as a Tool for Sacralising Performance Arts

South Indian nationalists meticulously emphasised an importance of a standardised pedagogy. They believed that this was the only way to not only shift the performance arts to religious arts, but also retain the authenticity of the arts. With the founding of the Academy, this became possible. The Academy played (and continues to play) a major role in reifying performance arts into an ideological category. The nationalists sought support from patrons, musicians and the educated elites in the society – both financial and in kind – for the Academy during the conferences. Often, these were framed as a moral obligation to support and revive performance arts. In addition, patrons and members argued for the need to found regional branches, but that these must fall under the management of the Academy to ensure uniformity and standard of performance arts.

By 1930, the University of Madras had introduced exams and conferred diplomas in music. The Academy also began the Teachers' College of Music and conducted music competitions. Other prominent institutions established included a music department at the University of Madras in 1932, and music classes for women in Queen Mary's College in 1933 and Kalakshetra in 1935 (Weidman 2006: 82). While many nationalists lamented the lack of devotion among current performers due to improper learning techniques, patrons like Dr Raja Sir Annamalai Chettiar (1933: 84) emphasised the importance of good teacher–student relationship and setting up good standards of music. Thus, the Academy set standards for music pedagogy by analysing and debating what rudimentary exercises should be taught and at what point the teacher ought to permit the creativity of the student to flourish.

Thus, the principal idea behind establishing an education system for these arts was to standardise pedagogy. But the underlying argument that the nationalists made was that these arts, especially music, can be studied scientifically. I briefly discussed this in the previous sections whilst illustrating how they saw these arts as being dynamic with the ability to be traditional and modern simultaneously. Nationalists argued that educational institutions reified this argument (Iyer 1935–1937: 151). Nationalists called for establishment of scholarships and more institutions for these purposes (Zamindar of Seithur 1929: 25–26). More importantly, education on arts was also about refining the tastes of the audiences. As discussed in the earlier sections, some of the nationalists saw the democratisation of music – availability of music performance spaces for performers and audiences – as a banality because this meant there was no quality

214 *Rajalakshmi Nadadur Kannan*

control for music. The onus was, of course, laid on the performers to maintain the standard of the performances and to maintain the sacrality. Of course, it was arbitrary whether or not a performer maintained the sacrality. But the nationalists also argued that if standardising pedagogy of arts was available to the general audience, they would learn to appreciate only pure arts. These nationalists were already unnerved by the technological advancements such as gramophone and microphone introduced in the performances. In 1945, Dr Alagappa Chettiar argued for the need for 'intelligent appreciation' of music made possible by educating the audiences (1945: 6). This was the transformation of audiences to connoisseurs. Other nationalists chided the audiences for appreciating embellishments and other tricks in performances that lacked devotion (Iyer 1931: 15–16). Sir Menon suggested that education of performance arts be incorporated at the elementary schooling level to raise children with the critical ability to appreciate good music (K. R. Menon 1945: 24). Indeed, during the 1934 music conference, the committee at the Madras Music Academy passed a resolution requesting the government to appoint a Board of Censors to regulate gramophone records being released to prevent quality of music from deteriorating (T. V. S. Rao 1934: 119), and recommendations were made to send representatives to the Board of Censors for Films to preserve the authenticity of Carnatic Music in the films. A common criticism was laid on audience who were drawn to music transmitted on loud speakers and radio because learning music through these mediums did not ensure quality (Sambamoorthy 1939: 89). If anything, the mechanical reproduction of music through gramophone records and radio further democratised these arts, especially music. Thus, the nationalists sought to control every aspect of performance arts – education, performance and experience.

REVIVING PERFORMANCE ARTS BY MARGINALISING COMMUNITIES

In addition to highlighting the greatness of Indian arts, nationalists often lamented the defilement these arts had to go through owing to various reasons, one being the lack of religiosity and discipline among the then performers. As the journal archives reveal, during every music conference, organisers and patrons addressed performers directly asking them to adhere to the traditions – here meaning sacrality. How that was measured was not often clear, but it was apparent that these nationalists detested certain practices whilst encouraging others. For instance, music education and music competitions were strongly encouraged (which is discussed in the following section) whilst any developments that were deemed as modern were thoroughly discouraged. Moreover, traditional communities such as *devadāsis* were thoroughly detested. In fact, *devadāsi* history is intertwined with this arts-revival episode of south Indian national history.

Cultural Transformations through Performance Arts **215**

Needless to say, it reveals a complex, contradictory development that marginalised *devadāsi*s whilst reviving the very arts (music and dance) that was taken from their community (Srinivasan 1985; Whitehead 1998; Kerserboom 1998; Soneji 2012; Nadadur Kannan 2014, 2019).

The most important aspect of this revival process was the gendering of performance arts by gendering the nation. Historically, music and dance were performed by traditional communities consisting of *devadāsi*s (usually referred to as the dancing girls). As traditional performers, *devadāsi*s were patronised by the kings and were exponents of dance and music. They performed as part of a band called *chinna melam* (lit. small band) comprising *devadāsi*s, male musicians and other instrumentalists. *Devadāsi*s and their bands performed in various settings such as festivals, temples and royal courts. Early Orientalist accounts of *devadāsi*s often described their presence in the temples, which reified their position as temple dancers – they came to be associated with temples especially in the early twentieth century. It is crucial to note that Hindu women, in general, did not take up music or dance not because it was degrading to be public performers but because their rights were severely restricted up until the early twentieth century when arts revival deliberately removed performances arts from *devadāsi*s and placed them in the hands of middle-class Brahmin/Hindu women. As unique traditional communities, *devadāsi*s did not come under the purview of the Hindu laws. Wherein women had several restrictions placed upon them by the Hindu laws, *devadāsi*s had rights to education, adoption and inheritance; they also did not follow the Hindu laws of conjugality – *devadāsi*s had multiple sexual partners who were often their patrons. All these components of the *devadāsi* communities were seen as a tradition until the early twentieth century, when gendered nationalism increased in vigour and *devadāsi*s were directly targeted. With the abolishment of patronage, *devadāsi*s, much like other traditional performers, moved to colonial Madras where their performances and their sexuality came under severe scrutiny (Srinivasan 1985; Whitehead 1998; Kerserboom 1998; Soneji 2012; Nadadur Kannan 2014, 2018). Within the context of hyper-nationalism that involved appropriated Victorian sense of morality, and a construction of hyper-feminine Indian/Hindu woman who was the guardian of the inner domain of spirituality through monogamous conjugality and religiosity (Chatterjee 1993), *devadāsi*s were made to stand in contrast as a representation of immorality. This aligned well with the nationalists' discourse on the degeneration of performance arts.

Often, their references to defilement of music and dance referred to the performances of *devadāsi*s in the public sphere. To them, performance arts transcended the bodily materialism, and those arts to be performed by *devadāsi*s pointed to the deterioration. Hence, they often referred to reclaiming the glorious past, which I have discussed in the previous sections. Much has been written about the legal and judicial treatment of *devadāsi*s (Srinivasan 1985; Whitehead 1998; Kerserboom 1998; Parker 1998; Soneji 2012), whilst elsewhere I have written about how developments leading up to the abolition of *devadāsi* traditions amount to state violence against a marginalised group (Nadadur Kannan 2017). Nationalists, especially Dr Mutthulakshmi Reddy, actively worked to petition the colonial government to abolish *devadāsi* traditions. They claimed that *devadāsi*s were a blot on Indian culture and pan Indian identity because they did not conform to monogamous conjugality (Soneji 2012). This particular aspect of their tradition was wilfully misrepresented to mean that *devadāsi*s were prostitutes. That *devadāsi*s followed a lifestyle that amounted to what was defined as prostitution was an issue for nationalists because they were actively involved in constructing a sacralised nation in which women were the custodians of the inner spiritual sphere whilst men were responsible for the outer political sphere (Chatterjee 1993: 130). Within this dichotomy, women were idealised as having qualities to transcend the materiality of life. This 'new woman' as the nationalists called her was different from the common woman defined as being 'coarse, vulgar ... sexually promiscuous ... maidservants, washer women, barbers, peddlers ... prostitutes' (ibid.: 127). This new woman was also the ideal representation of the now feminised Mother India. In the newly emerging patriarchy, *devadāsi*s were the polar opposite of the ideal Indian (Hindu) woman. In fact, Dr Reddy and theosophists such as Anne Besant, who gave unequivocal support to Dr Reddy's efforts, directly argued that *devadāsi*s were polluting the sacrality of temples (Whitehead 1998: 98–99). *Devadāsi* traditions represented a subversive nature, and the patriarchy, with the help of nationalists both men and women, came down heavily on them.

In *devadāsi*s, the gendered nationalism and performance arts intertwined; in fact, it is fair to say that *devadāsi*s were the perfect embodied signifier of the nationalism in early twentieth-century south India. For the colonial elites, who were self-appointed custodians of performance arts, revival of arts meant active sacralisation of arts, as discussed in the previous sections. By making deliberate connections to historical Sanskrit texts, they hinted at an exclusivity in that performance arts were accessible to only those who understood and adhered to the practices described in these texts. The nationalists, deliberately, encouraged middle-class women to take up these performance arts as a way to rescue and revive them (Bhagavatar 1933: 114). It is worth noting that all the historical texts that the nationalists claimed to be canonical for performance arts were written by men. The narrative then went this way: These canonical texts had laid down the ideal, pure cultural practices, *devadāsi*s (women) defiled arts with their lifestyles; now, it was in the hands of middle-class 'new women' to be guardians of this cultural/spiritual realm.

Cultural Transformations through Performance Arts **217**

More importantly, within the newly designated space, women could express their creativity through religious performance arts now that these arts have been purified and sanitised. Sure enough, theosophist Rukmini Devi Arundale, who had an influential social standing, became the first Brahmin woman to learn the dance, thereby removing dance from traditional communities and (with the help of the Madras Music Academy) giving it a profile in the eyes of Brahmins who became the patrons of the newly constructed cultural capital by encouraging Indian middle-class women to learn and perform these arts (Meduri 2008: 136). Arundale can be credited with single-handedly transforming the face of performance arts, specifically dance. She deliberately interpreted compositions to refer to sacrality and incorporated Hindu iconography in performance spaces. She argued that dance was an expression of one's soul and spirituality, going as far as to say: 'In India, religion and classical dance are combined because both express the idea of creation, of rhythmic movement, of the influence of spirit upon matter.... Religion, is Divinity expressed inwardly; Art is Divinity expressed outwardly' (Meduri 2008: 136). It is important to note that the *devadāsi* repertoire contained references to the divine in many forms. But by signifying sacrality on the performance stage, by incorporating prayers and Hindu iconography, she etched religion and performance arts in the minds of the audience, with much support from the Academy and the nationalists. In contemporary classical dance performances, these scenes are ubiquitous. Even those nationalists and former patrons who were seemingly in support of *devadāsi* communities argued that newer performance spaces such as the Academy would reform the *devadāsi*s from their immoral life – the deified space – and the new middle-class female performers will have a reforming effect on them (Meduri 2008: 137). Thus, systematically, *devadāsi*s were removed from their traditional, performance spaces, their roles in the society diminished, and pushed into complete oblivion when their tradition was abolished in 1947. Soneji's ethnographic work (2012) traces the history of *devadāsi* communities, some of whom live on the fringes of society having lost their livelihood, and in contemporary times, having to live with the stigma of prostitution, for if one thing this revival movement established, it was to solidify in the minds of the people that *devadāsi*s were prostitutes, leaving them with no other option but to live a marginalised life in the newer form of patriarchy the nationalists constructed.

CONCLUSION

This chapter has given a summary of how cultural, religious and national identities were formed in south India in the early twentieth century through

218 *Rajalakshmi Nadadur Kannan*

hegemonic narratives. I have illustrated how these were complex movements with many simultaneous developments that overlapped, contradicted and supported each other. The nationalists did not expect a prepossessed cultural capital from the audience. Rather, they determined what constituted cultural capital that was needed to conform to the aesthetic preferences laid out by them, and provided the means to acquire such capital through institutionalisation and pedagogy of arts. This was what I referred to in the previous sections whilst discussing the construction of cultural capital. Yet this must not be seen as an opportunity that they provided to make arts available to everyone. First, the cultural transformation from performance arts to religious arts resulted in reification of a hegemonic identity at the cost of marginalising communities and peoples. Second, in this nation-building process, performance arts became almost exclusive to Brahmins and upper-class non-Brahmin communities because the nationalists rejected what was seen as popular music; the institutions for both performance and pedagogy did not necessarily include other communities. Lastly, the effects of such developments can be seen in the way the right-wing groups such as the Rashtriya Swayamsevak Sangh (RSS) have infused Hindu identity into music compositions that is taught in schools that are sympathetic to the goals of the RSS, and at their training sessions called Shakhas. It is common to hear RSS compositions repeatedly claiming that India is for Hindus only. This is not to say that the construction of Hinduism as a unifying religious identity would not have taken place in south India. After all, the larger Gandhian nationalist movements adopted some of those rhetoric in the rest of India. Despite its unique nationalism tinged with ethno-linguistic politics, south Indian nationalist movements, through performance arts, solidified the class–caste distinctions, severely marginalising communities whilst defining a sphere almost exclusively to certain communities. These arts continue to be practised (mostly uncritically) the way they were reconstructed in the early twentieth century. These identities formed during the early twentieth century continue to be embodied by the performers and the audience.

NOTES

*Thanks to Rebekah Johnson for helping with the access to a key text for this article. A note about the writing style: This article analyses and deconstructs, and therefore uses, many contentious terms such as authentic art, true Indian culture, religion and sacrality. For the sake of not impending the flow of the article, these terms have not been enclosed with single quotation marks.

1. Throughout this article, I refer to Carnatic Music and Bharatnatyam collectively as performance arts because the revival movement targeted both arts.

BIBLIOGRAPHY

Books, Articles and Essays

Allen, Matthew Harp. 1997. 'Rewriting the Script for South Indian Dance. *The Drama Review* 41(3): 63–100.

———. 1998. 'Tales Tunes Tell: Deepening the Dialogue Between "Classical" and "Nonclassical" in the Music of India.' *Yearbook for Traditional Music* 30: 22–52.

Bourdieu, Pierre. 1984. *Distinctions: A Social Critique of the Judgment of Taste*, trans. R. Nice. Massachusetts: Harvard University Press.

Breckenridge, Carol Appadurai. 1977. 'From Protector to Litigant – Changing Relations between Hindu Temples and the Raja of Ramnad.' *Indian Economic Social History Review* 14(75): 75–106.

Butler, Judith. 1993. 'Critically Queer.' *A Journal of Lesbian and Gay Studies* 1(1): 17–32.

Chakrabarty, Dipesh. 2007. *Provincializing Europe: Postcolonial Thought and Historical Difference.* 2nd ed. Princeton: Princeton University Press.

Chatterjee, Partha. 1993. *The Nation and Its Fragments: Colonial and Postcolonial Histories.* Princeton, New Jersey: Princeton University Press.

Dirks, Nicholas. 1993. *The Hollow Crown: Ethnohistory of an Indian Kingdom.* Michigan: University of Michigan Press.

Fitzgerald, Timothy. 2007. 'Encompassing Religion, Privatized Religions and the Invention of Modern Politics.' In *Religion and the Secular: Historical and Colonial Formations*, edited by Timothy Fitzgerald, 211–240. London: Equinox Publishing Ltd.

———. 2011. *Religion and Politics in International Relations: The Modern Myth.* London: Continuum International Publishing Group.

Higgins, Jon B. 1976. 'From Prince to Populace: Patronage as a Determinant of Change in South Indian (Karnatak) Music.' *Asian Music* 7(2): 20–26.

Kerserboom, Saskia C. 1998. *Nityasumangalī: Devadāsi Tradition in South India.* New Delhi: Motilal Banarsidass Publications.

King, Richard. 1999. *Orientalism and Religion: Postcolonial Theory, India and the 'Mystic East'.* New York: Routledge.

———. 2010. 'Colonialism, Hinduism and the Discourse of Religion.' In *Rethinking Religion in India: The Colonial Construction of Hinduism*, edited by Esther Block, Marianne Keppens and Rajaram Hegde, 95–113. Oxon: Routledge.

Meduri, Avanthi. 1996. *Nation, Woman, Representation: The Sutured History of the Devadāsis and Her Dance.* New York: New York University Press.

———. 2008. 'Temple Stage as Historical Allegory in Bharatnatyam: Rukmini Devi as Dancer-Historian.' *Performing Pasts: Reinventing the Arts in Modern South India*, edited by Indira Viswanathan Peterson and Davesh Soneji, 133–164. Oxford: Oxford University Press.

220 *Rajalakshmi Nadadur Kannan*

Nadadur Kannan, Rajalakshmi. 2014. 'Performing 'Religious' Music: Interrogating Karnatic Music in a Postcolonial Setting.' PhD diss., University of Stirling.

———. 2017. 'Gendered Violence and Displacement of Devadāsis in the Early 20th Century South India.' *Sikh Formations: Religion, Culture, Theory* 13(1).

———. 2019. 'Redefinition and Representations of Sex and Body in the Early 20th Century Public Sphere in South India.' In *Colonialism and Material Cultures*, edited by Michael Marten/Rajalakshmi Nadadur Kannan, *Anthropos* 114(2).

Oddie, Geoffrey A. 2006. *Imagined Hinduism: British Protestant Missionary Constructions of Hinduism, 1793–1900*. New Delhi: Sage Publications.

———. 2010. 'Hindu Religious Identity with a Special Reference to the Origin and Significance of the Term 'Hinduism', c. 1787–1947.' In *Rethinking Religion in India: The Colonial Construction of Hinduism*, edited by Esther Block, Marianne Keppens and Rajaram Hegde, 41–55. Oxon: Routledge.

Ray, Sangeetha. 2000. *En-gendering India: Woman and Nation in Colonial and Postcolonial Narratives*. Durham, NC: Duke University Press.

Ries, Raymond. 1969. 'The Cultural Setting of South Indian Music.' *Asian Music* 1(2): 22–31.

Schofield, Katherine Butler. 2010. 'Reviving the Golden Age Again.' *Ethnomusicology* 54(3): 484–517.

Srinivasan, Amrit. 1985. 'Reform and Revival: The Devadāsi and Her Dance.' *Economic and Political Weekly* 20(44): 1869–1876.

Subramanian, Lakshmi. 1999. 'The Reinvention of a Tradition: Carnatic Music and the Madras Music Academy 1900–1947.' *The Indian Economic and Social History Review* 36(2): 131–163.

———. 2006. *From the Tanjore Court to the Madras Music Academy: A Social History of Music in South India*. New Delhi: Oxford University Press.

Sugirtharajah, Sharadha. 2010. 'Colonialism and Religion.' In *Rethinking Religion in India: The Colonial Construction of Hinduism*, edited by Esther Bloch, Marianne Keppens and Rajaram Hegde, 69–78. London and New York: Routledge.

Weidman, Amanda. 2006. *Singing the Classical, Voicing the Modern: The Postcolonial Politics of Music in South India*. Durham, NC: Duke University Press.

Whitehead, Judith. 1998. 'Community Honour/Sexual Boundaries: A Discursive Analysis of the Criminalization of Devadāsi in Madras, India, 1920–1947.' In *Prostitution: On Whores, Hustlers and Johns*, edited by James Elias, Vern L. Bullough, Veronica Elias, Gwen Brewer and Joycelyn Elders, 91–101. New York: Prometheus.

Archival Materials

Aiyar, Narayanaswami. 1933. 'The Mechanization of South Indian Music.' *Journal of Madras Music Academy* 4(1–4): 156–157.

Bhagavatar, Muthiah. 1933. 'Proceedings of the Sixth Music Conference.' *Journal of Madras Music Academy* 4(1–4): 113–114.

Bhagavatar, Nemam Natarāja. 1931. 'The Art of Sri Tyagaraja Swami.' *Journal of the Madras Music Academy* 2(1): 18–22.

Chettiar, Dr Alagappa. 1945. 'Opening Address.' *Journal of Madras Music Academy* 16(1–4): 2–6.

Chettiar, Raja Sir Annamalai. 1933. 'Opening Address.' *Journal of Madras Music Academy* 4(1–4): 88–91.

Iyer, Narayanaswamy. 1931. 'The Soul of South Indian Music – Rāga Bhava.' *The Journal of Madras Music Academy* 2(1): 15–17.

Iyer, M. S. Ramaswami. 1929. 'Music Performances, Teaching of Music etc.' *Journal of Madras Music Academy*: 31–34.

Iyer, Sir Sivasvami. 1935–1937. 'The Opening Address.' *Journal of Madras Music Academy* 6–8: 170–174.

Krishnacharya, Hulugur. 1929. 'Introduction to the Study of Bharatiya Sangita Sastra.' *Journal of Madras Music Academy*: 7–14.

Menon, Narayana. 1935–1937. 'Talk on Indian Music in Edinburgh.' *Journal of Madras Music Academy* 6–8: 134–135.

Menon, Sir K. Ramunni. 1945. 'Address.' *Journal of Madras Music Academy* 16(1–4): 34–35.

Narayandas, A. 1930. 'The Idea Gayaka.' *Journal of Madras Music Academy* 1(1): 116–119.

Radhakrishnan, Sir S. 1931. 'Man and His Music.' *Journal of Madras Music Academy* 2(3): 142–144.

Raman, Sir C. V. 1934. 'Opening Address.' *Journal of Madras Music Academy* 5(1–4): 97–100.

Rao, Dr U. Rama. 1929. 'Welcome Speech.' *Journal of Madras Music Academy* 1: 23–25.

———. 1931. 'Welcome Address.' *Journal of Madras Music Academy* 2(1): 67–69.

Rao, Subba, T. V., ed. 1934. 'Official Report.' *Journal of Madras Music Academy* 5(1–4): 119–121.

Rao, Sir Venkatasubba M. 1943. 'The Opening Address.' *Journal of Madras Music Academy* 14 (1–4): 2–7.

Row, Subba. 1993. 'The Decline of Taste.' *Journal of Madras Music Academic* 4 (1–4): 1.

Sambamoorthy, P. 1939. 'The Teaching of Music.' *Journal of Madras Music Academy* 10(1–4): 76–98.

Sastri, Pandit S. Subramanya. 1931. 'A Plea for a Rational System of Simplified Musical Notation.' *Journal of Madras Music Academy* 2(4): 192–197.

Srinivasan, R. 1945. 'Guarding Classical Music from Unhealthy Influences.' *Journal of Madras Music Academy* 16 (1–4): 21.

Tatti, Somarao. 1929. 'History of Karnatak Music.' *Journal of Madras Music Academy* 16: 2–6.

Zamindar of Seithur. 1929. 'Opening Address.' *Journal of Madras Music Academy* 16: 25–26.

9

Reservation and Religious Freedom

Understanding Conversion and Hindu–Christian Conflict in Odisha and Rajasthan

Sarbeswar Sahoo

This chapter seeks to analyse the increasing incidents of Hindu–Christian conflict in India. 'While Hindu–Muslim violence has been extensively analysed, Hindu–Christian violence was until recently so rare that scholars have seldom investigated the phenomenon' (Bauman and Leech 2012: 2195). In *Ethnic Conflict and Civic Life*, Ashutosh Varshney (2002) argues that Hindu–Muslim conflict has been the 'master narrative' of postcolonial Indian political history. Besides the Partition violence, which killed 6,00,000 to 1 million people (Frankel 2000: 6), data shows that more than 1,100 cases of Hindu–Muslim conflict have occurred in India between 1950 and 1995, resulting in around 7,000 deaths (Chaudhuri 2015: 2). Though there are disagreements among historians on the causes and origins of Hindu–Muslim antagonism, scholars of secular, modern historiography of India have particularly held the British colonial state and its 'divide and rule' policy responsible for conflict between Hindus and Muslims.

Compared to Hindu–Muslim conflicts, Hindu–Christian conflict in colonial India was very small scale. Some possible reasons are: First, the percentage of Christian population was extremely small. According to data, Christians constituted a mere 0.71 per cent in 1881. Although their number increased, they still remained below 1 per cent (0.98 per cent) by 1901 (Joshi, Srinivas and Bajaj 2005: 9). Second, the Christian population was mostly confined to certain regions of the country. So, when some conflicts occurred between Hindus and Christians, they were small scale and largely confined to a particular locality. Finally, Christian missionaries did not receive open support of the colonial state.

The relationship between the colonial state and the missionaries was ambiguous. Colonial administrators like Lord William Bentinck, as Governor of Madras, actively encouraged missionaries to carry out their work of converting Hindus. Similarly, Lord Macaulay supported Christian missionaries as he believed that they could play an important role in imparting English education to Indians, which would not only produce loyal colonial subjects but would strengthen the roots of British Empire in India. He famously noted: '[W]e must do our best to form a class who may be interpreters between us and the millions whom we govern; a class of persons, Indians in blood and colour, but English in taste, in opinions, in morals and in intellect' (cited in Tharoor 2017). In contrast to Bentinck and Macaulay, a large number of colonial administrators feared that interfering in indigenous religious and faith systems may antagonise 'local sensibilities' and destabilise trade and business relations of the British East India Company (Dirks 1996: 116). The missionaries were therefore very cautious in the preaching of the gospel, and the colonial state officially refrained from providing open support to missionary activities in India.

However, church pressure in England,[1] the growing legitimation crisis of Empire and the passing of the Charter Act of 1813 conspired to open India up to Christian proselytisation on a significant basis (Dirks 1996). Although Christian missionaries recognised caste as the core of Indian tradition and religiosity, they disdained it heavily and described it as 'the single greatest impediment to conversion' (Dirks 1996: 116). They viewed caste as an irrational institution that not only promoted Brahmanic hegemony but also evil customs and practices such as sati and child marriage. Missionaries 'frequently wrote detailed accounts of Hindu morality (or rather, lack of it) and ritual practice, documenting everything from the mistreatment of women among the highest castes to the performance of human sacrifice among the jungle-dwelling tribal groups of central India' (Dirks 1996: 116–117).

In order to end the evil practices of caste and to bring 'civilisation' to India, the missionaries often pressurised the colonial state to intervene actively in Indian society. In addition, the missionaries started their social and moral reform activities with the caste Hindus. However, the caste Hindus heavily opposed the missionary activities and as a result the colonial missionary success in converting caste Hindus was little (Seth 2007: 29). Given this, the missionaries, instead of appealing to the caste Hindus, concentrated themselves at the 'margins', particularly among the low caste Hindus or Dalits[2] and tribals. The reasons for this are that the missionaries considered (*a*) the low-caste Hindus as people with no religion – they are exterior to and oppressed under Hinduism (Sinha 1991: 65) – and (*b*) the tribals as aboriginals and backward and that it is their moral duty to 'civilise' these backward people (Hardiman 2006). As a consequence of this, today, Dalit and tribal converts constitute 50 per cent and 20 per cent, respectively, of all Christians in India (Robinson 2003: 29).

Missionary activities among Dalits and tribal population in different regions of India have received strong resistance from conservative caste Hindus, particularly Hindu nationalists, often resulting in Hindu–Christian conflicts. The United States Commission on International Religious Freedom (USCIRF 2016: 159) in its annual report pointed out that religious tolerance has declined

224 *Sarbeswar Sahoo*

and religious freedom violations have increased in India over the last few years. Minority communities, especially Christians, Muslims and Sikhs, have experienced threats, intimidation, harassment and violence, largely at the hands of Hindu nationalist groups. The report also pointed out that there were at least 365 major attacks on Christians and their institutions during 2015, compared to 120 in 2014; these incidents affected more than 8,000 Christians (USCIRF 2016: 161). Added to this, the Evangelical Fellowship of India (EFI) reported 134 incidents of violence in the first half-year of 2016 (EFI 2016: 4).

Violence against Christians in India has taken many forms. In particular, such violence has included 'any form of physical assault or coercion (e.g., murder, kidnapping, rape, beatings), and/or any act that could intentionally or inadvertently harm an individual or group (e.g., throwing rocks through windows, arson, etc.)' (Bauman 2015: 17). The EFI has recoded anti-Christian violence in the form of arrest, church attack, church burning, hate campaign, kidnapping, murder, physical violence, threat, desecration, false allegation, vandalising and disruption of worship services. As per their report, of the 134 incidents that occurred in the first half-year of 2016, the highest number of incidents (60) was physical violence against Christians (EFI 2016: 6). Such attacks against Christians have increased over the years. Data shows that between 1964 and 1996, only 38 incidents of violence against Christians were registered in the country. However, in 1997 alone, 24 incidents were noted, and by 1998, the number had gone up to 90, though some Christian spokespersons claimed that the true figure is several times higher (Lal 2006: 767–774). In the last decade, especially, conflict between Hindus and Christians has increased substantially. Bauman and Leech (2012: 2195) note that on average, Christians are now attacked 200 times a year, although the scope and severity of those attacks vary widely.

Given this, the fundamental question is: why are Christians being increasingly targeted in recent years? In other words, what could explain the phenomenon of rising Hindu–Christian conflict in India? Emphasising the specificity of sociocultural and historical context, this chapter discusses the complex politics between Christianity and Hindu nationalism in India. It is observed that conversion is believed to be one of the major factors leading to such conflicts. Specifically, Hindu nationalist organisations such as the Rashtriya Swayamsevak Sangh (RSS), the Vishwa Hindu Parishad (VHP) and the Vanvasi Kalyan Parishad (VKP) have argued that violence against Christians is a result of the 'anger of patriotic youth against anti-national forces ... the direct result of *conversion* of Hindus to Christianity by Christian priests' (Melanchthon 2002: 104, emphasis added). Considering this, the chapter examines the complex political dynamics of conversion in India and discusses this through the case studies of Odisha and Rajasthan.

HISTORY OF HINDU–CHRISTIAN CONFLICT

How can we understand the increasing Hindu–Christian conflict in India? As the data above suggests, Hindu–Christian conflict became a major problem in India during the 1990s. During this time, the Sangh Parivar[3] felt increasingly threatened by the intensification of Christian missionary activity and considered Christian proselytisation a threat to the unity and integrity of the (Hindu) nation. In particular, the AD2000 and Beyond Movement[4] and the Joshua Project,[5] which claimed that India is 'the number one target' and 'on top of God's Agenda', provided evidence of the intensification of missionary activity (Zavos 2001: 75). Additionally, the Pope, during a visit to India in November 1999, declared during the Papal High Mass that 'the first millennium saw the Cross planted in the soil of Europe and the second in America and Africa. May the third millennium witness a great harvest of faith on this vast and vital continent' (Melanchthon 2002: 106). Hindu nationalists viewed this declaration as a deliberate attempt by the Christian leadership to actively convert Hindus to Christianity in order to 'revive Christendom for re-establishing Western supremacy' (Shortt 2012: 156).

In such contexts of rising animosity and antagonism, two incidents of anti-Christian violence occurred that could be described as central to understanding Hindu–Christian conflict in contemporary India. The first major incident took place in Dang district in southern Gujarat. In 1998, the Bharatiya Janata Party (BJP) had returned to power in Gujarat, which emboldened the Hindu nationalists to carry out unprecedented hate campaigns against religious minorities. Some handbills were found carrying messages such as: Hindus wake up, Christians run away. Other handbills noted:

> Conversion activity by Christian Priests is the most dangerous burning problem at present in Dang district. Innocent and illiterate tribals are converted through cheating, alluring by offering temptations and other deceiving activities, under the pretext of services, these devils are taking advantage of tribal society and exploit them. In the world, wherever these Christian priests have looted its people and have made them helpless. Lie and deceit are their religion.... Hindus, awake and struggle, continuous with these robbers who snatch away your rights by telling lies and teach these people a lesson.... (Human Rights Watch 1999)

Following such hate campaigns, the Human Rights Watch recorded several instances of violence. In February 1998, a prayer hall in Divan Tembrum village was attacked and worshippers were physically assaulted; in April, a crowd of 400 attacked St Antony's Catholic Church; and in June, several prayer halls were burned in Dang district. The major incident of anti-Christian violence, however,

226 *Sarbeswar Sahoo*

occurred in December–January 1998–1999 which began on the Christmas day and lasted for more than ten days, leading to the destruction of 36 churches, assault of many individuals and looting of their properties.

The second critical incident occurred in January 1999. The Australian pastor Graham Staines and his wife, Gladys Staines, had been working for leprosy patients in tribal-dominated Mayurbhanj and Keonjhar districts of Odisha. Staines first came to Mayurbhanj in 1965 and worked with the Leprosy Home run by the Leprosy Mission of Australia. He devoted himself to the service of tribals and preached Bible to people, which was severely opposed by the local Hindu nationalist organisation, the Bajrang Dal. It accused Staines of converting tribals to Christianity. For years Staines regularly visited the nearby Manoharpur village to teach people a range of topics from health and hygiene to the Bible. But on 20 January 1999, when he arrived in the village with his two sons, Phillip, 10, and Timothy, 7, they were brutally murdered by the activists of Bajarang Dal. One Hindu nationalist activist emphasised that 'he was killed because he was proselytizing' but his widow, Gladys Staines, insists that 'Graham was never into conversions. All he did was to spread the message of the Lord' (Banerjee 1999).

DEBATES ON CONVERSION

These two dreadful instances of conflict breached the level of tolerance of people and generated strong protests against the Hindu nationalist BJP-led coalition government of the time at the national level. Following pressures from the coalition partners, Prime Minister A. B. Vajpayee criticised the anti-Christian violence and directed the state governments to take action. However, when Vajpayee visited the Dang district on 10 January 1999, he downplayed the gravity of the attacks (Venkatesan 1999). This invited criticisms even from the international community. The Catholic and Protestant churches severely criticised the 'organised attacks' and also referred to the 'reconversion' programmes carried out by the Sangh Parivar. Considering all this, Prime Minister Vajpayee called for a 'national debate on conversion' in January 1999. Christians maintained that the problem of violence is not religious, but political. They argued that the Sangh Parivar is using intolerance and exclusivism not only to deny people of their fundamental right to religious freedom but also to undermine the secular, pluralist principles of the Indian constitution.

In contrast, Hindu nationalists levelled a series of accusations against Christian missionaries and petitioned the government to issue a 'total ban on conversion'. In particular, they accused Christian missionaries of being provocative and deliberately using material and monetary means to convert people to Christianity. Moreover, the activists of the RSS, the VHP and the

Reservation and Religious Freedom **227**

VKP argued that missionaries were playing the politics of minoritism and were actively involved in demonising the Hindu gods and goddesses. As a consequence, increasing numbers of Dalits and tribals had converted out of Hinduism, posing a significant threat to Hindu religion. These claims of Hindu nationalists received a positive boost with the publication of the Justice D. P. Wadhwa Commission report, which was set up by the national government to look into the Graham Staines murder case. Although the report praised the hard work and dedication of Graham Staines, it pointed out his involvement in religious conversion. The report concluded that Staines used social work as a medium to actively propagate his religion and convert tribals to Christianity.

Given this, two sets of issues emerged in the debates on conversion. The first one was related to the question of caste oppression, social inequalities within Hinduism and the prospect of equality and dignity that Christianity promised to offer to Dalits and tribals through conversion. The second issue dealt with the question of freedom of religion and the use of force/inducement in conversion.

Caste, Conversion and Equality

As mentioned earlier, although Christian missionaries recognised caste as the core of Indian tradition and religiosity, they disdained it heavily. For them, caste was the repository of all evil customs and practices, which denied people (of lower castes) dignity, freedom and choice. In order to end the evil practices of caste and to bring dignity and equality, the missionaries began their civilising mission. The first attempt was to *rationalise* caste by separating the 'civil' from the 'superstitious' (Mosse 2012: 6). In this regard, Jesuit missionaries played a significant role. They described Christianity as a rationalising religion and the local traditions as superstitious, and thus, attempted to rationalise local culture by reforming indigenous customs and secularising caste. With this caste was denied its religious significance and practised only as a civil institution (Mosse 2012). Broadly, the missionaries advocated Christianity as caste-less and believed that caste consciousness and identity will be completely eradicated with conversion. Conversion was presented as emancipatory – as a 'social revolt' against Hindu caste hierarchy and a moment marking 'a complete break with the past' identities (cf. Meyer 1998).

Hindu nationalists questioned this missionary claim and showed how caste and caste-based discrimination exist among Christians of India (Fuller 1976). They pointed out that past low-caste identities and belief systems continue to define and restructure Dalit Christians' life world. Even long after conversion, they remained socially and economically marginalised and are discriminated against by high-caste Christians (Sahoo 2017). As Fuller (1976) has, in his study

228 *Sarbeswar Sahoo*

on caste among Kerala Christians, argued, 'the various Protestant churches in Kerala are regarded as low in status because almost all their members are converted Harijans [ex-untouchables]'. Hindu nationalists thus allege that Christian missionaries are converting (low caste) Hindus by making false promises of equality and freedom. They also allege that in the postcolonial period, instead of eradicating caste, Christianity has not just accommodated caste, but has actively used it to claim special benefits from the state through the reservation system. For Hindu nationalists, the Christian claim to reservation benefits is illegitimate because these benefits are meant for only those castes which suffered discrimination under Hinduism. The Christian claim to reservation benefits has thus generated discontent among low-caste Hindus, often resulting in violence against Christians to whom they are losing a portion of their reservation benefits. The politics of reservation was a major reason behind violence against Christians in Odisha in 2008, which will be discussed later.

Freedom of Religion versus Force and Inducements

Christians of India have strongly criticised anti-Christian violence and maintained that the right to convert is part of one's fundamental right to freedom of religion. According to them, the Constitution of India, in its article 25, grants the right to freedom of religion, which entails that 'all persons are equally entitled to freedom of conscience and the right to freely profess, practice, and propagate religion subject to public order, morality and health'.[6] Although, theoretically, Hindu nationalists do not have anything against conversion *per se*, they, however, strongly oppose it because they find that missionaries are taking advantage of the poverty and marginalisation of poor Dalits and tribals of Indian society and converting them to Christianity by providing incentives and inducements. This is supported by the fact that in India the number of missionaries had increased from 1,744 in 1947 to 15,000 in 1999 (Kim 2005: 235).

Alluding to the same constitutional principles, the Hindu nationalists argue that conversion to Christianity violates the fundamental right to freedom of religion. According to them, although the Constitution allows conversion on the basis of individual free will and internal spiritual transformation, it bans the same through force, fraud and other unfair and unethical means. They view all conversions in India today as motivated by force, fraudulent means or inducements and, hence, described all conversions as 'acts of violence' against humanity (Bauman 2015: 175; Kim 2005: 229), thus, demanding stricter laws and punishments against conversion.

In this context, the Hindu nationalists demanded the enactment and strict implementation of anti-conversion laws, ironically known as the Freedom of

Religions Act. The history of this Act goes back to the early 1950s when the visit of the conservative Congress Party chief minister of Madhya Pradesh, Ravi Shankar Shukla, was severely resisted by the tribals. Chief Minister Shukla had learnt that a majority of the tribals had been converted to Christianity and it was the missionaries who were inciting the tribals to demand a separate state. In order to understand the nature of mission activities among the tribals, Chief Minister Shukla appointed a commission under the chairmanship of Justice B. S. Niyogi in 1954. The Niyogi commission submitted its report in 1956, which concluded that

> [e]vangelization in India appears to be a part of uniform world policy to revive Christendom for re-establishing western supremacy and is not by spiritual motives. The objective is apparently to create Christian majority pockets promoted with a view to disrupt the solidarity of the non-Christian societies, and the mass conversion of a considerable section of Adivasis with this ulterior motive is fraught with danger to the security of the State. (Cited in Jaffrelot 2011: 201)

The conclusions of the Niyogi report created fear among the Hindus. This fear became stronger with the creation of Nagaland as a separate state in 1963 where four-fifths of the Naga tribes were Christians (Jaffrelot 2011: 202). In order, therefore, to stop religious conversion, the state of Odisha enacted the first Freedom of Religions Act in 1967 that prohibited conversion from one religion to another by the use of force or inducement or by fraudulent means. Other states such as Madhya Pradesh (1968) and Arunachal Pradesh (1978) also enacted similar laws. The Christians of India argued that these laws have been used to restrict, as opposed to protect or promote, religious freedom of individuals (Sahoo 2018: 70). These laws were appealed in the court. In 1977, 'the Supreme Court, in the case of *Rev Stanislaus vs. the State of Madhya Pradesh* delivered a verdict that essentially undermined religious freedom and strengthened the above legislations' (Sahoo 2018: 70). In particular, Justice A. N. Ray, who delivered the judgment, interpreted the word 'propagate' in article 25 to mean to 'transmit or to spread one's religion by an exposition of its tenets', but to not include the right to convert another person to one's own religion (Parthasarathy 2014). Parthasarathy (2014) argues that

> in confusing a person's liberty to exercise free conscience for another person's right to propagate religion, Justice Ray's verdict produced damaging results. A conclusion that propagation ought to be restricted only to the edification of religious tenets is a reasoning that gratifies the interests of the majority, and the majority alone.

According to Sen (2010: 121), in the *Stanislaus* case, 'the Supreme Court came up with an impoverished version of the right to propagate religion which

230 *Sarbeswar Sahoo*

interpreted conversion as impinging on "'freedom of conscience'". The Hindu nationalists have, however, followed the Supreme Court's line of argument and advocated for enactment of stricter laws to ban conversion. According to them, states like Odisha experienced intense missionary activity because the existing anti-conversion laws are not properly implemented. They have thus demanded strict implementation of these Acts as well as enactment of similar laws in other states where conversion was becoming a problem. Following the rising indigenous Christian missionary activities and anti-Christian violence in the late 1990s and early 2000s, other states such as Chhattisgarh (2000), Tamil Nadu (enacted in 2002, but repealed in 2004), Gujarat (2003) and Himachal Pradesh (2006) enacted similar laws, which banned conversion. The BJP government of Rajasthan also tried to enact a similar law in 2007, but the governor did not approve it. Later on, in 2008, the government passed the Rajasthan Religious Freedom Bill, which will be discussed later.

HINDU–CHRISTIAN CONFLICT IN ODISHA, 2007–2008

In December 2007, the tribal-dominated Kandhamal district of the eastern Indian state of Odisha experienced the worst conflict between Hindus and Christians. On 24 December 2007, while Dalit Christians of Brahmanigaon in Kandhamal district were preparing for Christmas celebration, the Kui Samaj, a Kandha tribal organisation who had strained relations with the Dalit Christian Pana community, had called for a strike to press a variety of political demands (Bauman 2010: 265). The Kandhas warned Dalit Christians not to construct the Christmas *pandal* in the village; they also closed the local market. However, the Christian community requested the police to open the local market for last minute shopping for Christmas celebration. Although the police opened the market, a large group of Hindu religious activists tried to forcefully close the market, but was unsuccessful. A few hours later, the group returned and began to physically abuse the Christians in the market (Bauman 2014: 192). It was during the same time that a Hindu *sadhu*, Swami Lakshmanananda Saraswati, was visiting the locality to conduct sacred Hindu rituals. According to Saraswati, his vehicle was stopped and a group of Christians attacked him. This incident aggravated communal tension in the region, leading to riots between Hindus and Christians over the next few days. According to some reports, 'mobs destroyed 95 churches, several convents, mission schools and parish houses, and 730 homes, around 120 of which were Hindu homes destroyed by Christians' (Bauman 2014: 193).

As a result of the riot, 'around 3,000 Christians entered refugee camps established by the government' (Bauman 2014: 193). And just when the situation was beginning to become normal, a second round of violence occurred between

Hindus and Christians in August 2008, following the assassination of Swami Lakshmananda. According to Kanungo (2008: 16), the Christians of Odisha experienced 'the fury of worst-ever communal rage'. Several churches were set on fire, Christian institutions were destroyed, and pastors and nuns were attacked. Several reports mentioned that some 50 Christians were killed, 5,000 dwellings razed by radical Hindu mobs, more than 13,000 displaced mobs found temporary home in refugee camps, and it was feared that as many as 50,000 others went into hiding in the nearby forests and hills (Kumar and Kumara 2008). Some other reports pointed out that the violence claimed more than a hundred deaths and more than 25,000 victims resided in refugee camps. According to the official reports, a total of 232 churches were destroyed and 2,202,912 persons were residents of refugee camps during the entire period (Rehman 2016: 221). While some referred to it as 'Hindu–Christian conflict', 'riot', 'anti-Christian violence' or 'communal conflict', others called it a 'pogrom' – a deliberately orchestrated mass violence against Christian religious minorities. Biswamoy Pati (2008) declared that Odisha is 'in a crucified state'.

Most newspapers and investigative agencies pointed out that the killing of the popular Hindu saint Swami Lakshmanananda Saraswati and his four disciples, including a woman, acted as the triggering event leading to violence between Hindus and Christians. Swami Lakshmanananda, who had been affiliated to the VHP, was very controversial for his anti-conversion activities and constant criticism of the Maoists. He had come to Kandhamal (then Phulbani) in 1969 with two major objectives: (*a*) bringing the Adivasis closer to the 'mainstream' Hindu religious system through a planned process of Sanskritisation and Hinduisation, which Hardiman (2003: 255) refers to as 'internal conversion', and (*b*) resisting Christian missionary activities and their proselytisation agenda among the marginalised population. Although the Maoists/Naxalites assumed responsibility for the killing of Lakshmanananda for he had been 'mixing religion with politics' and pursuing a 'fascist' and divisive communal agenda (Kanungo 2008: 16), supporters of Lakshmanananda and the Hindu nationalist organisations suspected the involvement of local Christians in the crime.[7] They vowed to teach the perpetrators a lesson. The Odisha State Secretary of the VHP, Gouri Prasad Rath, said: 'Christians have killed Swamiji. We will give a befitting reply' (*Times of India* 2008).

The Socio-historical Context and Kandha–Pana Relations

Kandhamal is one of the poorest and economically most backward districts of Odisha, which was carved out of Phulbani district in 1994. The name of the district is derived from the name of the Kandha tribe who constitute a majority

232 *Sarbeswar Sahoo*

(around 52 per cent) of the district's population. The Kandha are 'cultivators' and practise shifting agriculture. As per the Constitution, the Kandha are categorised as Scheduled Tribe (ST); their cosmologies and religious belief structures are different from that of the 'mainstream' religions such as Hinduism, Christianity or Islam. The Kandha speak the ethnic Kui language and believe in animism. Pfeffer (2014: 180) argues that what distinguishes the Kandha from 'Hindus' is their buffalo and cow sacrifice rituals and widespread habit of beef consumption as integral to their religious belief system.

The second-most dominant ethnic group in the region are the Pana, the majority of whom also speak the Kui language. Occupationally, the Pana are involved in 'weaving'; they also act as petty commercial agents for dominant cultivators of the village (Pfeffer 2014: 174). As per the Constitution, the Pana are designated as Scheduled Castes (SCs). The Hindu social structure has placed SCs outside the four-fold division of the caste system and treated them as untouchables. Extreme exploitation and denial of human dignity have often forced SCs to convert *out of* Hinduism and find equality and self-respect in Buddhism, Islam or Christianity. Recognising their marginalisation under the Hindu caste system, the Constitution of India has provided them special benefits by reserving 15 per cent of seats in government education and jobs. In Kandhamal, the Pana constitute around 17 per cent of the population.

Land is a major source of livelihood in Kandhamal. Only 12 per cent of the total land is cultivable; about 71 per cent of the land comprises forest and the remaining area is barren (Grover and Uma 2017: 28). The scarcity of cultivable land has brought different communities, especially the Kandha and the Pana, into conflict. While the Kandha own about 77 per cent of the cultivable land, the Pana own a mere 9 per cent (Grover and Uma 2017: 28). The Odisha Scheduled Areas Transfer of Immovable Property (by Scheduled Tribe) Regulation Act, 1956, which was amended in 2002, protects the land owned by the STs and restricts land transfers from STs to non-STs. It is, however, observed that due to poverty and indebtedness, Kandha land is often mortgaged to Panas on a long-term basis. The Kandha are also made to work on their own land for the Pana and other upper caste Hindus to cover regular interest instalment due on permanent debts (Pfeffer 2014: 177). Because of this, the Kandha have eventually become alienated from their land.

Given this, the Kandha have accused the Pana of land grabbing. They argue that the Pana have often used fraudulent means to claim the Kandha ST status, so that they can have access to the cultivable land of the Kandha and reservation benefits under the ST category of the government welfare schemes. Moreover, the Pana of Kandhamal demanded ST status and supported a petition of the Phulbani Kui Jankalyan Sangh (PKJS) that advocated classifying the SC Pana community as an ST community. The PKJS argued in a petition to the Odisha High Court that the Pana community deserved ST status because a 2002 Presidential Order had said that the Kui community should be considered an ST, and therefore the Pana, a Kui-speaking community, were historically undifferentiated from the Kandha (Bauman 2010: 272). The Kandha perceived PKJS's petition as a threat to their collective interest and thus vehemently opposed the demand of the Pana.

The Politics of Conversion and Reservation

The demand for ST status by the Pana and the opposition to it by the Kandha has been complicated by the politics of conversion and reservation. Both the Kandha and the Pana of the region have, irrespective of access to land or lack of it, suffered from extreme poverty and economic and social marginalisation. Data suggests that more than 70 per cent of the people of the district lived below the poverty line. The Government of Odisha also failed to provide basic social welfare facilities such as education and primary healthcare. Considering the prevalence of high rates of poverty and lack of basic education and healthcare, Christian missionaries have come forward to run schools and hospitals as 'alternatives' (Pati 2008). According to Pfeffer (2014: 177), the Spanish Benedictine and Scottish Methodist missionaries were the first Christian missionaries to enter the present-day Kandhamal district in the 1930s to open schools and hospitals, which were later taken over by Oriya Christians. Because of the missionary work, although some Kandhas have converted to Christianity, their percentage is very small. In fact, over the last few decades, with the work of Hindu nationalists, the Kandha have increasingly become Hinduised. They follow Hindu rites and rituals and celebrate Hindu functions and festivities; they have over the years come closer to the 'mainstream' Hindu social and religious life.

Hindu nationalists have had a long presence in Odisha, starting with the work of the RSS in the 1940s.[8] The unique features of Hinduism manifested in the Jagannath cult have provided a congenial climate for the growth of Hindu nationalism in Odisha (Kanungo 2003: 3293). In particular, Lord Jagannath who is considered the supreme deity of Odisha has acted as a major symbol of Brahmanical Hinduism. He also acted as a symbol of reinforcing Odiya ethnic identity and nationalism, developed through Odiya, Hindu and Indian identity. As Odisha was a predominantly Hindu province and since Jagannath was a powerful symbol of Odiya identity, there was no such distinction between Odiya nationalism and Hindu nationalism (Kanungo 2003: 3294). This provided the RSS a conducive atmosphere to spread its ideology in Odisha.

234 *Sarbeswar Sahoo*

In addition to being the prime symbol of Brahmanical Hinduism, what is interesting about the Jagannath cult is that it also shares a close connection with the Adivasi culture and history. It is widely believed that Jagannath was initially worshipped as Nilamadhaba by the *savara* tribes. Because of this connection with Lord Jagannath, the tribes of Odisha in general and the Kandha in particular have enthusiastically followed Hinduism and come closer to the caste Hindu social and religious order. In fact, this process has been actively facilitated by the RSS and other Hindu nationalist organisations.

In contrast to the Kandha, the Pana have moved away from Hinduism. Data shows that more than 70 per cent of the SC Pana of Kandhamal have converted to Christianity. According to the government's reservation policy, while STs are allowed to have reservation, SCs are denied of the same after they have gone through religious conversion. The Pana have, with their conversion, received good education from the missionary schools and have noticeably become wealthier. However, because of conversion, the Pana are denied reservation benefits. Only those Panas who have not converted to Christianity are legally entitled to receive SC status and can have access to the government's reservation benefits. The Kandha and the upper caste Hindus of the locality argue that the success of the Pana is largely because of their Christianisation (Bauman 2010: 272). According to them, the Pana are very 'cunning' who have used fraudulent means (forged certificates) to take benefits of reservation which are not meant for them. For example, (*a*) while some Christian Panas hide their Christian identity, others convert superficially back to Hinduism to claim the SC status and (*b*) the Pana, who speak Kui language like the Kandha, are fraudulently claiming Kandha ST status and taking the benefits of reservation (Bauman 2010: 272). This has antagonised the Kandha who fear that they are losing out to the Pana of the region.

The upper caste Hindus of the locality also found it difficult to accept the economic and educational rise of the Pana in the region. For them, it has become hard to believe that the Pana who used to be untouchables are now asserting themselves and posing a threat to upper caste hegemony. As Kanungo (2008: 17) argues, the upper caste Hindus would prefer a 'docile' Kandha to a 'defiant' Pana any day; it is not really the latter's religion so much as his informed consciousness. However, religion here becomes an additional stick to beat the Dalit Pana.

Hindu nationalists considered conversion to Christianity as 'denationalising' and heavily opposed it. Specifically in Kandhmal, they argued that conversion of the Pana and the Kandha to Christianity is achieved through inducements and incentives and anti-Christian violence is a mere reaction against it. Infuriated by the growth of Christians, especially the large-scale conversion of the Pana and the Kandha, Lakshmanananda and various Hindu nationalist groups had actively

Reservation and Religious Freedom **235**

pursued the anti-conversion agenda and organised purification rituals (*suddhi*) to bring the converts back to Hinduism – a process referred to as reconversion.[9]

In addition, the Hindu nationalists portrayed the Pana as land grabbers and exploiters of the Kandha. By taking advantage of the Hinduisation of the Kandha and their closeness to upper caste Hindus of the region, the RSS and other Hindu nationalist organisations mobilised the Kandha against the Pana. One objective was to create fear among the Pana and chase them away from the locality, so that their land and property could be grabbed. Eventually, mobilisation of the Kandha against the Pana widened the ethnic cleavage, leading to the 2008 Kandhamal violence. The RSS' spokesperson Ram Madhav, discussing the Kandhamal violence, said: '[T]here is absolute freedom for Christians to propagate their religion. But when you indulge in fraudulent conversions, there is a localised reaction.' He further noted that 'Christian missionaries' conversion zeal is responsible for all the violence against Christians in India' (cited in Bauman 2010: 280). This shows how caste–tribe relations and the politics of conversion and reservation played a major role in fomenting Hindu–Christian conflict in the Kandhamal district of Odisha in 2008.

VIOLENCE AND 'FREEDOM OF RELIGION' IN RAJASTHAN

Rajasthan is geographically the largest state of India. According to the 2011 Census, around 88.5 per cent of its population is Hindu, 9 per cent is Muslim, 1.27 per cent is Sikh and a mere 0.14 per cent is Christian. However, it is observed that Christianity has a strong presence in south Rajasthan where it is rapidly growing among the tribal groups. Although tribals constitute 13.5 per cent of Rajasthan's total population, they are heavily concentrated in the southern part of the state. The 2011 Census points out that in Banswara 76.4 per cent, in Dungarpur 70.6 per cent, in Pratapgarh 63.4 per cent, in Udaipur 49.7 per cent and in Sirohi 28.2 per cent people are tribal, the majority of them belonging to the Bhil, Garasia and Mina tribes. Although anthropological literature has pointed out the differences between these tribal groups and caste Hindus, these tribes identify themselves as Hindus. They believe in Hindu gods and goddesses, follow Hindu beliefs and customs, and celebrate Hindu rituals and functions. Weisgrau (2013: 247) notes that 'their religion, ritual cycles, and social patterns combine Hindu norms with localised practices, systems of worship, and ritual cycles'.

According to Mann and Mann (1989), such self-identification of tribals as Hindus is a consequence of the long process of acculturation or Hinduisation that occurred among the west-Indian tribes when they first came in contact with the dominant caste Hindus who entered the tribal belt not only as rulers but also

236 *Sarbeswar Sahoo*

as trading, priestly and service castes. The tribes Sanskritised themselves and acquired the cultural and behavioural traits of upper caste Hindus to elevate their position and status in society. Although such interaction between tribals and upper caste Hindus existed for a long time, it became intensified in the medieval period during the time of Maharana Pratap. The Hinduisation process gained further ground in the early twentieth century with the work of Govind Giri, a social and religious reformer, who started the Bhagat movement, which aimed to reform the social practices of tribals and improve their moral character (Hardiman 2003). Most recently, this work has been carried out by Hindu nationalist organisations, especially the Rajasthan Vanvasi Kalyan Parishad (RVKP), which was established in the tribal-dominated Kotra regions in 1978. The major objective of the RVKP has been to bring tribals closer to Hindu society and stop Christian missionary activities in the region.

However, it is observed that over the last few decades, an increasing number of tribals, especially Bhil, have converted to Christianity. According to Sridhar (1999), the tribal-dominated Udaipur district alone witnessed an increase of Christian population by 80 per cent between 1981 and 1991. A pastor in Baghpura village informed me in 2006–2007 that there are more than 15 church groups that are actively working with tribals of Jhadol block in Udaipur district (interview 26 November 2006). Udaipur district in south Rajasthan has emerged as the epicentre of missionary activity in Rajasthan. While the major growth of Christianity has occurred during the postcolonial period, Christianity has had a long history in the region. Christian missionaries first came to tribal areas with the establishment of the Mewar Bhil Corps by the British in Kherwada and Kotra blocks of Udaipur district in 1841 (Chaudhary 1986: 130). As part of their 'civilising mission', the missionaries provided educational and medical services to the tribals. Colonial medicine, in particular, played a major role in bringing tribals closer to Christian missionaries.

In the process of providing social services and welfare benefits, Christian missionaries preached the gospel, which eventually resulted in the conversion of many tribals to Christianity. In 1991, there were 0.10 per cent (47,989) Christians in Rajasthan which grew to 0.12 per cent (72,660) in 2001 and 0.14 per cent in 2011. The Hindu nationalists have accused Christian missionaries of taking advantage of the poverty and marginalisation of tribals and converting them to Christianity by providing them material and monetary benefits. In response, a Catholic priest in Udaipur noted that they have been present in the tribal regions for more than one hundred years, and if they had actively pursued the religious conversion project, the whole tribal belt would now be Christian. Moreover, the Christian population is not increasing. In the Census, Christians constitute only 0.1 per cent of Rajasthan's population; it has remained unchanged over the last few decades (interview 27 January 2012). The Hindu nationalists have rejected such claims of Christian missionaries and have argued that many of these tribals who have converted to Christianity have not followed the formal legal procedures of conversion because this might affect them negatively. They further argue that this has consequently created a large number of secret or 'crypto Christians' (Kent 2011: 676) who remain undocumented in the Census records. In order thus to stop conversion, the Hindu nationalists have resisted Christian missionary activity in the region, which has often resulted in conflict between the two communities.

A Chronicle of Conflict and the Problem of Freedom of Religion

Although Rajasthan has not witnessed large-scale Hindu–Christian conflicts like Odisha or Gujarat, it has experienced a large number of small clashes between the two communities for which it has been referred to as a 'communally sensitive' state. This phenomenon is quite recent, as Rajasthan does not have a notable history of religious conflict. Except for the flare-up in Jaipur in November 1989 (Mayaram 1993), the state has been comparatively riot-free since the 1950s (Copland 1998: 208–209). However, recent National Crime Record Bureau data shows that Rajasthan witnessed the highest number of riots on a regular basis between 1990 and 2001. While riots are usually characterised as forms of civil disorder, in India they are very often the result of religious conflict. Although there is a no clear data available, newspaper reports point out that attacks against Christian missionaries and converted tribals have increased significantly in Rajasthan in recent years (Ahmad 2016; Carvalho 2005; 2013).

These newspaper reports noted that most of the attacks and atrocities were carried out by Hindu nationalist organisations, which suggest an alarming pattern of violence. Intimidation and physical attacks on priests, the burning of the Bible, bans on missionary schools, false allegations of forced conversion, destruction of Christian institutions such as schools, hospitals and orphanages, and attacks on Christian meetings and congregations have become regular events in Rajasthan. As Carvalho chronicles:

> In Rajasthan on June 9, 2005 mobs of extremists attacked two Catholic convents; on June 11, a mob attacked a third convent and held the nuns captive overnight; on June 12, extremists broke into the Holy Trinity Church in Jaipur, capital of Rajasthan, and threw rotten eggs and blue-colored water at a shrine dedicated to the infant Jesus. On October 16 in Rajasthan state, members of the Hindu extremist group RSS accused Catholics holding a procession of planning forced conversions among tribal people in Udaipur district. Bishop Joseph Pathalil's car

238 *Sarbeswar Sahoo*

was pelted with stones as he left the procession, but he escaped unharmed. Also in Udaipur district, on October 25 five nuns waiting at a bus stop were beaten with sticks. (Carvalho 2005)

Most recently, on 10 January 2016, newspapers reported that Hindu radicals beat up a group of eight to ten Christians on their way to a church service in Palan village. On the same day, a mob in Tonk city of Rajasthan stormed into a church premises while local Christians were preparing for the Sunday service. They beat up the pastor, destroyed the Bible and damaged church property. Instead of arresting the attackers, the police arrested the pastor of the local church and his wife on accusations of converting people to Christianity.[10] Similar attacks were also recorded in several other districts in December 2016, raising fears and apprehensions among Christians about how safe the Christmas will be (Ahmad 2016).

Christian communities in Rajasthan severely criticised the attacks by Hindu nationalists and presented themselves as innocent victims of violence. They argued that such violence is perpetrated by 'fundamentalists with an ideology of intolerance, cultural exclusivism and dominion, who deny the pluralistic cultural heritage and the rights of the poor' (Kim 2005: 226). Furthermore, they have argued that the Constitution of India provides every citizen the right to freely profess, practise and propagate religion, and such violence against religious minorities violates the freedom of religion. The Hindu nationalists have, however, used the same constitutional principles and argued that although the Constitution guarantees everyone's freedom of religion, it bans religious conversion carried out by using force or fraudulent means. According to them, Christian missionaries in Rajasthan are taking advantage of the poverty and marginality of the tribals and using development activities such as provision of free education, healthcare and other development activities as inducements to attract tribals to the church and eventually convert them to Christianity. As a consequence, they argue, Christianity has been growing rapidly among the tribals. Hindu nationalists have, thus, argued that conversion of tribals through material inducements and through force is a violation of the fundamental right to freedom of religion.

In Rajasthan, data suggests that there is a strong sense of resentment among ordinary people towards conversion. According to Lodha (2004: 5461), 67 per cent of people in Rajasthan heavily oppose religious conversion carried out by missionaries. Banking on such sentiments, the Hindu nationalists vowed to (*a*) implement a ban on religious conversion and (*b*) bring back those Christian tribals who, through conversion, have left Hinduism. However, the absence of an anti-conversion law in Rajasthan prevented Hindu nationalists from achieving

Reservation and Religious Freedom **239**

their objective. As discussed earlier, in the early 2000s, several Indian states had enacted state-level anti-conversion laws, known as the Freedom of Religions Act. The BJP government of Rajasthan during 2003–2008 under the chief ministership of Ms Vasundhara Raje also wanted to pass a similar law. On 7 April 2006, the Rajasthan government introduced the Rajasthan Dharma Swatantraya (Religious Freedom) Bill in the state assembly, which aimed to stop conversion from one religion to another by the use of force or allurement or by fraudulent means and to promote freedom of conscience. The bill stated:

> It has been observed by the state government that some religious and other institutions, bodies and individuals are found to be involved in unlawful conversion from one religion to another by allurement or by fraudulent means or forcibly which at times has caused annoyance in the community belonging to other religions. The inter-religion fabric is weakened by such illegal activities and causes law and order problem for the law enforcing machinery of the State. In order to curb such illegal activities and to maintain harmony amongst persons of various religions, it has been considered expedient to enact a special law for the purpose.[11]

The bill was sent to Governor Pratibha Patil for approval, but she returned it in May 2006 on the ground that it violated the fundamental right to religion of the individual and asked the state government to get it cleared by the then president, A. P. J. Abdul Kalam. BJP members of the legislative assembly (MLA) Jogeshwar Garg and Subhash Bahedia argued that 'a law restricting forcible religious conversions was the need of the hour as such activities had adversely affected communal harmony' (*The Hindu* 2008b). Garg also emphasised that 'problems of fanaticism, terrorism and secessionism have always arisen in the areas where Hindus were reduced to minority by large-scale conversions' (*The Hindu* 2008b). Madan Dilawar, the Social Welfare Minister in the BJP government in Rajasthan, also pointed out that 'in tribal areas and localities of poor Dalits, all kinds of efforts were being made to tempt or force people to change their religion and we will not tolerate these designs' (*Compass Direct News* 2008).

The Rajasthan state government had forwarded the bill to President A. P. J. Abdul Kalam. However, it remained pending with him. In the meantime, former governor of Rajasthan, Pratibha Patil became the President of India. Knowing that she will keep the bill pending, the BJP government in Rajasthan reintroduced the Religious Freedom Bill in 2008 with certain changes. The Opposition Congress members such as C. P. Joshi, B. D. Kalla and Zubair Khan declared the bill 'unconstitutional' (*The Hindu* 2008b). Congress MLA Harimohan Sharma argued that 'introducing a second Bill on the same subject while the first is pending the assent of the President of India is not valid. The State has not withdrawn the previous Act' (*The Hindu* 2008a).

240 *Sarbeswar Sahoo*

Despite criticisms and oppositions, the bill was passed in the assembly on 20 March 2008. It makes the provision of stricter punishment. In the case of the offence committed in respect of a minor, a woman or a person belonging to an SC or ST, the minimum punishment would be two years, which could be extended to five years and a fine up to 50,000 rupees (*The Hindu* 2008a). It also makes it mandatory for anyone intending to convert to send a notice to the district magistrate at least 30 days in advance who will get the matter enquired into. However, it adds that the same requirement will not be applied to a person who is wishing to 'reconvert' people to their 'original religion' or to the 'religion of one's forefathers'. Hindu nationalists do not consider reconversion or *shuddhikaran* to be conversion because they are just bringing those who have 'strayed' from the Hindu fold back to their native religion. Thus, by providing legal protection, the BJP government has actively encouraged Hindu nationalists not just to reconvert Christian tribals to the Hindu fold but also take stringent action against conversion, which has often resulted in violence against minorities.

CONCLUSION

The above discussion shows that the politics of conversion is complex and contextually dependent. In the case of Odisha, it is observed that conversion politics is rooted in the changing relationship between different caste and tribal communities as well as in the politics of reservation. The upper caste Hindus found the assertion of the (Christian) Pana community intolerable and feared that it would challenge their hegemony in the region. The tribal Kandha similarly disliked the Pana. For them, the Pana were cunning who used fraudulent means to take benefits of reservation, which were originally meant for tribals and Hindus. In such context, the upper caste Hindus, in collaboration with the Hindu nationalists, mobilised the Kandha against the Pana, which resulted in the Kandhamal violence of 2008.

Although religion was important, it is specifically the caste domination/subordination and politics of reservation that played important roles in politicising as well as polarising communities. It all happened in the political context when the Hindu nationalists were a part of the BJP–BJD coalition government in Odisha led by Chief Minister Naveen Patnaik. Though Patnaik was strongly committed to the spirit of secularism, he became weak when his party entered into an alliance with the BJP. The government was unable to control recurring violence, and by the 2009 elections, the coalition between the BJP and the Biju Janata Dal (BJD) had fallen apart. The BJD admitted that it was the Kandhamal violence that forced them to sever their ties with the BJP. This shows that

Reservation and Religious Freedom **241**

although the state was not an active partner, it was nonetheless implicitly involved in the Kandhmal violence.

Compared to Odisha, the major issue concerning conversion in Rajasthan has been related to freedom of religion. Christian missionaries have argued that Hindu nationalists have used violence to create fear among religious minorities, which violates individual's right to religious freedom. In contrast, Hindu nationalists have argued that missionaries have been using force and fraudulent means and allurements to convert tribals to Christianity, which is a violation of constitutional rights to freedom of religion. They demanded a stringent anti-conversion law to ban conversion. In this regard, the BJP-led state of Rajasthan played a proactive role in passing a new anti-conversion law in the state assembly that restricts religious conversion activities carried out by Christian missionaries. It has added a provision in the law which argues that bringing people back to their 'original religion' (here Hinduism) cannot be considered conversion. This particularly shows how the meanings of conversion differ in context and how the BJP government provided legal protection for one kind of conversion (that is, 'internal conversion') but vilified another kind.

Moreover, the two case examples show that violence is *not* simply a conflict between Christian missionaries and Hindu nationalists. A variety of agents and institutions such as Christian missionaries, Hindu nationalists, upper caste Hindus, low caste Pana, Kandha and Bhil tribals, political parties, legal institutions and the state have played vital roles in politicising and polarising the issue, often leading to conflict and violence. In particular, this chapter shows sensitivity to contextual factors and urges scholars to understand the complex nature of conflict between Hindus and Christians in India.

NOTES

1. Mission ethnographies, which provided detailed accounts of the difficulties faced by missionaries in India, became openly circulated around local church societies in England. This generated support for missionaries in India (Dirks 1996: 117).

2. The word 'Dalit' means broken/ground down. It refers to people who were traditionally regarded as untouchables in India and are historically involved in ritually impure occupations such as leatherwork, butchering and removal of rubbish. The Constitution of India calls them Scheduled Castes (SCs) and today they constitute around 15 per cent of the Indian population.

3. Sangh Parivar refers to the family of Hindu nationalist organisations affiliated to the RSS. It includes organisations such as the BJP, the VHP, the VKA, the Bajrang Dal and several others.

4. The AD2000 and Beyond Movement was established in 1990 with the aim of encouraging cooperation (amongst different Christian organisations) in establishing a church within every unreached people group and making the gospel available to every person by the year 2020. The movement is focused on the so-called 10/40 Window, an area of North Africa and Asia between 10 degrees north and 40 degrees north latitude, where 95 per cent of the world's least evangelised poor are found (Zavos 2001: 75).

5. The Joshua Project emerged as an elaboration of the ideas of AD2000 in 1995. This project specifically emphasises north India as an area of strategic importance for missionary efforts (Zavos 2001: 75–76).

6. In article 16, the Constitution has also granted 'equality of opportunity to all citizens without discrimination on various grounds, inter alia, religion' (Bielefeldt, Ghanea and Wiener 2016: 349).

7. Rehman (2016) notes that there were eight attempts on Swami Lakshmanananda's life between 1969 and 2007.

8. The RSS has 6,000 *shakha*s in Odisha with 150,000 cadres. It has 391 Saraswati Shishu Mandir schools, with 111,000 students preparing for future leadership. Vanvasi Kalyan Ashram runs 1,534 projects and schools in 21 Adivasi concentrated districts. The Sangh has initiated 1,200 Ekal Vidyalayas in Odisha (Rehman 2016: 222).

9. The first well-organised reconversion to Hinduism was made between 1880 and 1930 by the Arya Samaj, founded by Swami Dayanand Saraswati in 1875. Reconversion was legitimised in the context of increasing Christian and Islamic proselytisation, which were thought to be the main causes of the demographic decline of the Hindus in India. Despite this, 'conversion' received opposition from within Hinduism and it is in this context that the Arya Samaj discovered the Indian tradition of *shuddhi* (purification) – initially meant to purify caste members who had become polluted – to legitimise '(re) conversion' in Hinduism (Vandevelde 2011: 35–36). Since the 1950s, the Hindu nationalists have reintroduced the concept of reconversion/purification. For them, conversion of Hindus to other religions is nothing but 'luring away of people through material inducements'. It is therefore important to bring back those Hindus who had drifted to Islam or Christianity because of 'inducements' (Katju 2015: 23). Considering this, the Hindu nationalists have in recent years actively promoted (re)conversions to Hinduism through ritual purification. For more on *shuddhi*, see Vandevelde (2011) and for politics of reconversion, see (Katju 2015).

10. See https://www.barnabasfund.org/news/One-incident-of-violence-against-Indias-Christians-every-day-in-2015-and-the-trend-continues-in-2016, accessed on 17 April 2017.

11. Rajasthan Freedom of Religion Bill, 2006, http://www.kandhamal.net/DownloadMat/Rajasthan_Freedom_of_Religion_Bill.pdf, accessed on 14 August 2017.

BIBLIOGRAPHY

Ahmad, S. 2016. 'Rajasthan: Attacks on Christian Community Stoke Fears ahead of Christmas.' *Hindustan Times*, 20 December.

Banerjee, R. 1999. 'Burning Shame.' *India Today*, 8 February.

Bauman, C. M. 2010. 'Identity, Conversion, and Violence: Dalits, Adivasis and the 2007–08 Riots in Orissa.' In *Margins of Faith: Dalit and Tribal Christianity in India*, edited by R. Robinson and J. M. Kujur, 263–290. New Delhi: Sage.

———. 2014. 'The Interreligious Riot as a Cultural System.' In *Constructing Indian Christianities*, edited by C. M. Bauman and R. F. Young, 188–214. New Delhi: Routledge.

———. 2015. *Pentecostals, Proselytization, and Anti-Christian Violence in Contemporary India*. New York: Oxford University Press.

Bauman, C. M. and T. Leech. 2012. 'Political Competition, Relative Deprivation, and Perceived Threat: A Research Note on Anti-Christian Violence in India.' *Ethnic and Racial Studies* 35(12): 2195–2216.

Bielefeldt, H., N. Ghanea, and M. Wiener. 2016. *Freedom of Religion or Belief*. Oxford: Oxford University Press.

Carvalho, N. 2005. 'A Year of Violence against India's Catholics.' *Compass Direct*, 19 December.

———. 2013. 'Rajasthan: Hindu Extremists attack Christian Family, Tell Them to Convert or Be Killed.' *AsiaNews.it*, 19 August.

Chaudhary, N. D. 1986. 'Tribal Development in Rajasthan.' In *Tribal Development*, edited by J. P. Singh and N. N. Vyas, 129–144. Udaipur: Tribal Research Institute.

Chaudhuri, A. R. 2015. 'Colonisation and Religious Violence: Evidence from India.' http://www.isid.ac.in/~epu/acegd2015/papers/ArkaRoyChaudhuri.pdf, accessed on 1 March 2017.

Compass Direct News. 2008. 'India: Rajasthan Passes New 'Anti-Conversion' Bill.' 26 March.

Copland, I. 1998. 'The Further Shores of Partition: Ethnic Cleansing in Rajasthan 1947.' *Past and Present* 160(1): 203–239.

Dirks, N. B. 1996. 'The Conversion of Caste.' In *Conversion to Modernities*, edited by P. van der Veer, 115–136. New York: Routledge.

Evangelical Fellowship of India (EFI). 2016. *Hate and Targeted Violence against Christians in India*. New Delhi: Evangelical Fellowship of India.

Frankel, F. R. 2000. 'Introduction: Contextual Democracy.' In *Transforming India*, edited by F. R. Frankel et al., 1–25. New Delhi: Oxford University Press.

Fuller, C. J. 1976. 'Kerala Christians and the Caste System.' *Man* 11(1): 53–70.

Grover, V. and S. Uma. 2017. *Kandhamal: Introspection of Initiative for Justice 2007–2015*. New Delhi: Media House and United Christian Forum.

244 *Sarbeswar Sahoo*

Hardiman, D. 2003. 'Assertion, Conversion, and Indian Nationalism: Govind's Movement amongst the Bhils.' In *Religious Conversion in India: Modes, Motivations and Meaning*, edited by R. Robinson and S. Clarke, 255–283. New Delhi: Oxford University Press.

———. 2006. *Healing Bodies, Saving Souls: Medical Missions in Asia and Africa.* Amsterdam: Rodopi.

Human Rights Watch. 1999. *India: Politics by Other Means – Attacks against Christians in India* 11(6[C]), October.

Jaffrelot, C. 2011. 'India: The Politics of (Re)Conversion to Hinduism of Christian Aboriginals.' In *Annual Review of the Sociology of Religion – Vol. 2: Religion and Politics*, edited by P. Michel and E. Pace, 197–215. Leiden: Brill Publications.

Joshi, A. P., M. D. Srinivas and J. K. Bajaj 2005. *An Illustrated Presentation on Religious Demography of India*. Chennai: Centre for Policy Studies.

Kanungo, P. 2003. 'Hindutva's Entry into a 'Hindu Province': Early Years of RSS in Orissa.' *Economic and Political Weekly* 38(31): 3293–3303.

———. 2008. 'Hindutva's Fury against Christians in Orissa.' *Economic and Political Weekly* 43(37): 16–19.

Katju, M. 2015. 'The Politics of *Ghar Wapsi*.' *Economic and Political Weekly* 50(1): 21–24.

Kent, E. 2011. 'Secret Christians of Sivakashi: Gender, Syncretism, and Crypto-Religion in Early Twentieth Century South India.' *Journal of the American Academy of Religion* 79(3): 676–705.

Kim, S. C. H. 2005. 'The Debate on Conversion Initiated by the Sangh Parivar, 1998–1999.' *Transformation* 24(1): 224–237.

Kumar, A. and K. Kumara. 2008. 'India: Hindu Communalists Target Christian Minority in Orissa and Other States.' World Socialist Website, 7 October.

Lal, V. 2006. 'Anti-Christian Violence in India.' In *The Politics behind Anti-Christian Violence*, edited by R. Puniyani, 767–774. Delhi: Media House.

Lodha, S. 2004. 'Rajasthan: India Shines as BJP Trounces Congress.' *Economic and Political Weekly* 39(51): 5456–5462.

Mayaram, S. 1993. 'Communal Violence in Jaipur.' *Economic and Political Weekly* 28(46–47): 2524–2541.

Melanchthon, M. 2002. 'Persecution of Indian Christians.' *Dialog: A Journal of Theology* 41(2): 103–113.

Meyer, B. 1998. '"Make a Complete Break with the Past': Memory and Post-colonial Modernity in Ghanaian Pentecostalist Discourse.' *Journal of Religion in Africa* 28(3): 316–349.

Mosse, D. 2012. *The Saint in the Banyan Tree: Christianity and Caste Society in India.* Berkeley: University of California Press.

Parthasarathy, S. 2014. 'Conversion and Freedom of Religion.' *The Hindu*, 23 December.

Pati, B. 2008. 'In a Crucified State.' *Hindustan Times*, 25 September.

Rehman, M. 2016. 'Politics of Anti-Christian Violence in Kandhamal, 2008.' In *Communalism in Postcolonial India: Changing Contours*, edited by M. Rehman, 216–233. New Delhi: Routledge.

Robinson, R. 2003. *Christians of India*. New Delhi: Sage Publications.

Sahoo, S. 2017. 'Caste.' In *Wiley Blackwell Encyclopedia of Social Theory*, edited by B. S. Turner, 1–7. New York: Blackwell.

———. 2018. *Pentecostalism and Politics of Conversion in India*. New Delhi: Cambridge University Press.

Sen, R. 2010. *Articles of Faith: Religion, Secularism and the Indian Supreme Court*. New Delhi: Oxford University Press.

Seth, S. 2007. 'Secular Enlightenment and Christian Conversion: Missionaries and Education in Colonial India.' In *Education and Social Change in South Asia*, Krishna Kumar and Joachim Oesterheld, 29–32. Hyderabad: Orient Longman.

Shortt, R. 2012. *Christianophobia: A Faith under Attack*. London: Rider Books.

Sinha, A. 1991. *Against the Few: Struggles of India's Rural Poor*. London: Zed.

Sridhar, V. 1999. 'A Numbers Game.' *Frontline* 16(25), 27 November–10 December.

Tharoor, S. 2017. 'But What about the Railways…? The Myth of Britain's Gift to India.' *The Guardian*, 8 March.

The Hindu. 2008a. 'Rajasthan Reintroduces Religious Freedom Bill.' 14 March.

———. 2008b. 'Religious Freedom Bill Passed in Rajasthan.' 21 March.

Times of India. 2008. 'Leader's Death: VHP Calls for Odisha Bandh.' 25 August.

USCIRF. 2016. *Annual Report of the United States Commission on International Religious Freedom*. Washington, DC: USCIRF.

Vandevelde, I. 2011. 'Reconversion to Hinduism: A Hindu Nationalist Reaction against Conversion to Christianity and Islam.' *South Asia: Journal of South Asian Studies* 34(1): 31–50.

Varshney, A. 2002. *Ethnic Conflict and Civic Life*. New Haven: Yale University Press.

Venkatesan, V. 1999. 'A Hate Campaign in Gujarat.' *Frontline* 16(2), 16–29 January.

Zavos, J. 2001. 'Conversion and the Assertive Margins: An Analysis of Hindu Nationalist Discourse and Recent Attacks on Indian Christians.' *South Asia: Journal of South Asian Studies* 24(2): 73–89.

10

Rupture and Resilience

Dynamics between a Hindu Reform Movement and an Indigenous Religion in Highland Odisha*

Peter Berger

It is April 1999, two old men are the first to reach the shrine of Gumang or Pat Kanda, outside the Gadaba village of Gudapada.[2] They are the sacrificer (*pujari*) and the ritual cook (*randari*), the most senior men in the village in terms of ritual status. They have followed the narrow paths out of the village and through the dry fields on the hard laterite soil that has not seen a drop of rain since the end of the monsoon in October. They climb down to wet rice fields that are constructed in the bed of the river. After balancing on the narrow earthen division separating two paddies, they climb up again on the other side and reach the most important shrine of the village, consisting merely of a small roofed structure without walls, but with thick beams supporting the roof only about a metre above the ground. Below the roof, a single stone protrudes about 30 cm out of the earth, the local representation of *dorom* or the sun-moon deity. Shortly afterwards, other men assemble and clear the area of dry leaves and branches. Then they take the tiles off the roof of the small shrine and repair the wooden structure before covering it again. A few of the older men only wear loincloth, but most wear a *lungi* or *dhoti* and a shirt. One young man stands out, not only because he is tall, but because he is dressed in a bright red garment (Hindi: *kurta*). Once the sacrificial site has been prepared, the *pujari* 'sacrifices' a coconut before two animals – a cock and a goat – are ritually killed. The man in red is given some pieces of the coconut and leaves before the animals are killed. Later, he is not to be seen among the groups eating different parts of the sacrificial animals at different places. Did the man participate in the ritual or not?

Krusna Sisa, the man dressed in red, is a member of a religious movement known locally as Olek Dormo, and called Mahima Dharma in Dhenkanal, its region of origin. Ascetics (*babas*) probably came to Koraput in the early 1970s to seek new adherents to their movement. At the time of my first stay in the region, in 1996, most villages had a few Oleks. Since then, in some villages their numbers have increased considerably, although in Gudapada this has not been the case. In

Rupture and Resilience **247**

addition to their dress, usually not in red, as in the above-mentioned instance, but in ochre, the most conspicuous difference from the other Gadaba, and indeed most indigenous communities (Desia) of the highlands, is their diet. Olek Dormo asks them to refrain from eating meat and drinking alcohol, both practices that are crucial for Gadaba ritual and social life. Surprisingly, one hears both Olek and Gadaba[2] state that there is no difference in terms of religion, only that the former do not eat meat and they abstain from alcohol. This chapter, then, is an attempt to understand such statements and to investigate the relationship between Olek Dormo and Gadaba religion. More specifically, this relationship is examined from three different perspectives: first, from the point of view of the Olek themselves; second, from the perspective of the other Gadaba; and third, from my angle as an anthropologist and outsider. With reference to these perspectives, I will look more closely at the processes and narratives of conversion and reconversion, as well as at the kinds of interaction between the Olek and the Gadaba and the participation of the former in Gadaba social and ritual life.

The question of whether 'conversion' is an appropriate analytical concept is perhaps not the most pertinent to the discussion in this chapter. However, the scholarly debates have been quite concerned with this term and as such it will be useful to relate the case under discussion to some of the theoretical issues that have arisen. To begin with, the definitions of 'conversion' offered by anthropologists differ considerably. Robert Baum (1990: 370)[3] defines conversion as the acceptance of a 'new source of religious authority', whereas Hefner (1993: 17), in his well-known contribution, focuses on the question of identity: 'conversion implies the acceptance of a new locus of self-definition, a new, though not necessarily exclusive, reference point for one's identity'. While both Baum and Hefner thus focus on the perspective of the converts with regard to religious authorities and a new understanding of the self, Joel Robbins (2004; 2009) focuses more on the transformation of ideas in the process of conversion, irrespective of the actors explicitly 'accepting' it or not. While the perspective of the actors will also be important in the present contribution – with regard to the first two points of view mentioned above – the analytical perspective adopted by Robbins offers a significant complementary view. As will be seen, I draw quite different conclusions than my Gadaba interlocutors. Robbins (2009), in particular, discusses 'radical change', which he argues can be said to have occurred when a new paramount value (in Louis Dumont's terms) has been adopted, which then determines the relationships between and the elaboration of other ideas in the culture.

Although Robbins also discusses how elements of the old religion may continue to be articulated in subordinate contexts, the kind of conversion he

248 *Peter Berger*

describes with reference to the Urapmin of Papua New Guinea was both sudden and relatively complete. As other scholars point out (for example, Fox Young and Seitz 2013), however, conversion has to be neither abrupt nor radical. Baum, for example, emphasises that the old traditions usually continue to be relevant, at least in certain 'areas' (ibid.: 371). He even argues that such cases of 'sudden and far-reaching conversion' (ibid.: 375) are rather the exception, and indeed it may be that such revolutionary changes are most often found with regard to charismatic forms of Protestantism. Consequently, in the five models of conversion he distinguishes (also potentially regarded as different phases of a process), Baum focuses on the often tense dialogue between the two religious systems involved. The first model is that of radical conversion mentioned above, while the final one is that of reconversion due to insurmountable tensions between the old and the new religions. In between, as it were, Baum presents three further patterns: first, the 'mission Christian stance' (1990: 376) where, often in an initial phase, a new faith represented by an external religious authority (such as missionaries) is completely accepted, while aspects of the ideas pertaining to the old religion are rejected.[4] This is still close to the model of radical change. Second is a model Baum calls 'indigenization', where a real dialogue between the old and new systems takes place. Thus, on the one hand, old moral questions are posed to the new religion and, on the other, new ideas are applied to 'traditional concerns' (1990: 376). Finally, there is a 'syncretic mode', involving 'dual allegiance by recognizing two sources of religious authority' (1990: 376).

What is not explicitly discussed by Baum but is important in the present case is the question of acknowledgement. With reference to the work of Hans Reithofer (2005), Strathern and Steward (2009: 23) point out that 'a rhetoric of rupture and change is accompanied by a more concealed and unemphasized, but strongly present, practice of continuity'. As will be shown, in the case of the Olek Dormo among the Gadaba, the reverse is rather the case; there is a discourse of continuity that – in the eyes of the anthropologist, at least in certain respects – is counterpointed by an unacknowledged rupture.

Before I turn to the discussion of the questions outlined above, the case of the Olek Dormo has to be located in a general landscape of religious and cultural change among the Gadaba. In the 1970s, about the time Mahima Dharma was introduced to Koraput, some Gadaba became Christian Seventh Day Adventists. However, it appears that the conversion rates remained low, as by the end of the last century, I could only identify a few villages in which Christians lived, while most Gadaba I know had no contact with Christians at all, except in extreme emergencies, for which several Gadaba consulted a nearby hospital that had been established in the early 1990s by Christians who were mostly from south India. Furthermore, I could discern other developments during the past 20 years.

Among the young people who were born around the time I first visited the region, two trends can be distinguished. Some have chosen the path of education and have even become teachers themselves, thus clearly striving for upward social mobility in society at large. Others now engage in prolonged wage-labour trips and invest much of their money in a new lifestyle, examples of which they see in movies (Gudapada was added to the power grid in 2006). What both share is that they are oriented towards a particular form of mainstream Hindu modernity, and although the way they are associated with this mainstream culture differs, an initial element of 'humiliation' (Sahlins 2005; cf. Berger 2014) can be identified in both. Another response to the dominant lowland Hindu culture is an activist stance that emphasises the difference of their 'Adivasi culture'. I recognised the beginnings of this in 2010, and in 2016 I found that a 'Gadaba Society' (Gadaba Samaj) had been recently established, although most of my local friends had not yet even heard of it.

I do not yet know enough about the Gadaba Christians, and more research is needed on their history and contemporary practices, but with respect to the other trends I briefly described, the Olek seem to be different, as the experience of humiliation as the trigger to renounce old ways and to strive towards a new identity seems to be absent. In the following section, I will briefly outline some of the main aspects of Gadaba religion and Olek Dormo, and subsequently I will discuss the three different views mentioned above: the Olek view, the Gadaba view and my assessment of the situation.

GADABA RELIGION

As I came to know it in the course of my fieldwork, Gadaba religion pivots on sacrifice and the related alimentary process of feeding, sharing and devouring.[5] In the context of life-cycle rituals, sacrificial food is fed by different agnatic and affinal groups in order to bring about a ritual transformation of the person, either further *into* or *out of* the society of the living. The vignette with which I started this chapter is one example of the rituals performed in an annual cycle that is closely related to the cultivation cycles of rice and millet in particular (Berger 2018). In such contexts, the Gadaba of a certain locality – called earth people – share sacrificial food with local deities. The exchange of food, as well as living buffaloes and cattle, between different groups at different levels of the social structure is vital for the maintenance of a social order that is at the same time a moral order. Through these regular processes of sharing and exchange, *niam* is upheld, *niam* – poorly defined – being 'tradition' or the way things should be done. Mostly ritual actions are related to *niam*, including intermarriage. When *niam* is followed, things are considered *bol soman*, 'good and even'.[6] Opposed to

250 *Peter Berger*

this harmonious ritual equilibrium is the domain of 'devouring', that is, the activities of actors who do not subscribe to reciprocity but consume violently and unilaterally. Among them are humans who commit acts of sorcery (*onkar*, 'envy' or *nosto*, 'destruction'), enraged spirits of the dead and, most of all, the demons *soni* and *rau*. No commensality is possible with the latter, and Gadaba try either to pacify them through offering substitute lives (that is, sacrifices) or turning the hunter into prey, as one line of the spell against angry spirits of the deceased makes clear: 'You are the goat, I am the tiger.'

Among the Gadaba, morality is clearly embedded in ritual actions that constitute order in the socio-cosmological sense. Their religion is thus an example of a 'social or communal religion' (Gellner 1999: 142) which focuses on relationships that the living engage in among themselves and with non-human agents. Soteriological ideas are absent in Gadaba religion, as are related ideas about merit, sin or the retribution of deeds that are so common in India. Among the Gadaba, reincarnation is considered to be a completely automatic process, whereby the life force moves between alternate generations. Humans can only be reborn as humans, and nothing a person does in life matters for his or her ritual status after death. Killing someone is not a bad action in religious terms, but dying a 'wrong' death – obviously not always a matter of preference – is considered a transgression (*umrang*[*7] or *dos*) of *niam* that requires specific ritual attention. Thus, transgression and the automatic response it triggers are important. There is no idea of 'sin', understood as 'belief in an innate tendency of human nature to evil' (Fürer-Haimendorf 1974: 547). Animals can also commit transgressions, for example, a dog that walks on top of a house has his ears cut off by the Gadaba. Thus, a dog on the top of a house is 'wrong' in relation to the socio-cosmic order, but not a 'sin'.

How the Hill Reddy, who live to the south of the Gadaba, think about this describes the situation quite well:

> The moral behaviour of men is not the concern of any of the deities.... Sacrifices and offerings are necessary to stave off the anger of gods annoyed by the breach of a taboo or the neglect of their cult, but they are not intended as expiation of a sinful act believed to have brought about a change in the offender's spiritual and ritual status. (Fürer-Haimendorf 1974: 545)

Fürer-Haimendorf (1974: 553) concludes more generally: 'Even though such [tribal] societies may judge human conduct as meritorious or reprehensible in social terms, they do not link offences against the social order with a change in the relations between men and gods.'

This orientation towards a social religion also affects the kind of specialists the Gadaba recognise. Sacrificers and healers are all 'normal Gadaba', who cultivate their fields and do not have higher status or necessarily know more about religious matters than anyone else. As appointed village dignitaries (such as the *pujari*) or by personal calling (healers and ritual media), they are specialists in the communication and interaction with spirits, gods and demons. However, they are not spiritual leaders and are not considered holy men and women themselves (cf. Bailey 1981). Accordingly, the interaction with them has no consequence for one's ritual status, certainly not a spiritual one in the sense of gaining merit or removing sin. Asceticism is also unconnected to salvation, as it is only a necessary temporary step in the preparation of a ritual (thus, according to *niam*), such as a person abstaining from food (not necessarily liquor) before a sacrifice.

The Gadaba have an idea of moral perfection that is complementary to the reciprocity of exchanging food, humans (women in marriage, the dead in death rituals) and animals according to *niam*, and the opposite of the greedy 'negative reciprocity' (Sahlins 1965: 147f.) of the demons. However, this moral ideal which neither social nor ritual practices usually live up to is not located in a divine sphere but realised in a particular and most highly valued kind of social relationship between two groups whose interactions are choreographed by reciprocal 'prescriptive altruism'[8] (Berger 2015: 179f.; 2017).

With its communal orientation and absence of ideas or practices related to liberation, Gadaba religion thus clearly stands in contrast to the soteriological focus of a Hindu reform movement such as Mahima Dharma and Brahmanical forms of Hinduism (Berger 2016). At the same time, it is important to realise that Gadaba religion, like many indigenous religions all over the world, is non-literate and focused on practice. There is no dogma, and while there clearly is a cosmology, I would not speak of 'belief'. Gadaba simply assume the existence of spirits; they do not believe in them. While I was asked to perform sacrifices for the house I lived in, no one ever investigated whether I believed in the earth deity to whom the sacrifice was addressed. *Niam* is a kind of floating signifier for 'tradition' but clearly not exclusive and is likely to have accommodated changes throughout history without them being acknowledged as such.

OLEK DORMO

Mahima Dharma is a Hindu reform movement that originated in the first half of the nineteenth century in Odisha.[9] Its founder, Mahima Gosvami, is worshipped by adherents of Mahima Dharma as the incarnation of the god Alekh, the one true god, beyond description and 'unwritten' (*alekh*). God Alekh cannot be represented, and 'idol worship' is opposed by Mahima Dharmis. In 1881, they attempted to enter the Jagannath temple in Puri by force to remove

252 *Peter Berger*

and burn the *murti* of Jagannath (Eschmann 1978: 394). Various scholars have worked on the movement since the 1970s and the details do not concern us here. Suffice it to say that a very strict monastic order has been set up, with a centre in Joranda (where the founder is buried) and satellite monasteries in other places. Meditation is a key practice for monks or *baba*s to attain the goal of liberation, something its founder is said to have achieved at death. As mentioned earlier, Mahima Dharma attempted to establish itself in the highlands of the Koraput region of southern Odisha in the 1970s, where the movement is referred to as Olek Dormo. The village of Lamda, close to Nandapur – formerly the location of the king – serves as the regional centre of the Olek and it is here that new converts receive their initiation (*dikhya*) and the Olek of the region assemble for annual meetings, when *baba*s from Joranda also visit.

While most work on the movement focuses on the monastic tradition in Dhenkanal, Lidia Guzy (2002) studied both the movement in Joranda and the Olek Dormo in Koraput in a comparative ethnography. Her work in Koraput did not focus on the Gadaba, however, but on the Rona, one of several other indigenous communities – all indigenous people being referred to by the term Desia, 'of the land' – populating the Koraput plateau (see Berger 2002; on the Rona, see Otten 2006). The Rona were the former militia of the king and regionally have a higher status than the tribal communities such as the Gadaba or Bonda, which is signified by their sacred thread. Ideally, Rona do not drink liquor or consume beef or pork, all of which the Gadaba enjoy – beef until very recently (Berger 2014) – and this may be a significant difference with respect to the acceptance of Olek Dormo as well as the motives for conversion.

Although Guzy does not refer to Baum's patterns of conversion, her ethnography clearly shows how the Rona have indigenised Mahima Dharma and how the latter is in close and reciprocal dialogue with the traditional religion. As the Rona also had no soteriological orientation, the monastic dimension was of little importance to them. However, as a lifestyle, asceticism has a strong influence on the new Oleks, with its strict abstinence from all kinds of meat as well as bloody sacrifices. What the old tradition brought to the new form of Olek Dormo was the institution of ritual medium or *gurumai*, to which Guzy pays considerable attention in her monograph. Known among all indigenous communities, *gurumai* are ritual specialists (often women) who become possessed by deities and thus enable humans to talk directly to and interact with gods. Among the Rona Olek, a new kind of Olek *gurumai* developed, with a strong focus on music and divine speech in the séances, clearly quite different from the ascetic focus of the *baba*s from Dhenkanal. However, while *gurumai* are also important specialists among the Gadaba, I have not encountered the specific Olek *gurumai* among Gadaba converts. Another example of indigenisation of

Mahima Dharma by the Olek of Koraput is presented by their clothes, the most conspicuous aspect of the Olek. The ochre clothes that the initiates receive during their *dikhya* in Lamda, Guzy says (2002: 312), not only signify asceticism but, for the local Olek, also clearly refer to the earth goddess, who is among the most important deities for all Desia.

In her assessment of the Olek Dormo of the Rona, Guzy thus clearly recognises both continuity and change, a dynamic she depicts with the idea of bricolage. In addition to the continuities mentioned above, she sees the new 'permanent religious ethic of restriction' (2007: 116) as a transformation of the short-term ritual fasting that preceded ritual communication with deities in traditional Rona religion (as among the Gadaba). Moreover, the séances of the Olek *gurumai* would indicate the perpetuation of 'the traditional value of ecstasy' (ibid.: 125). At the same time, the new ethic of abstinence would constitute an 'inverted set of traditional ideas and values' (ibid.: 116) – that is, no alcohol, no meat, no bloody sacrifice – and the Olek would, as 'new indigenous moralists', thus reject 'the common ritual values' (ibid.: 125) of the Desia. However, what these values consist of is not so clear.

GADABA OLEK

Since my first stay in the area in 1996 until my most recent one in 2019, I have been in contact with the Gadaba Olek in different villages, although they were previously not the focus of my research. I noticed their interactions with other Gadaba, had conversations with them, heard people talk about them and witnessed some of their rituals. In the following, I will mainly focus on three men and their families, all of which live in Gudapada, the village that I know best. They represent complementary cases, as one of them is an early convert or second-generation Olek, one of them is a recent convert, and the third was a convert but gave up Olek Dormo for very specific reasons. The case of recent conversion is particularly interesting and relevant as it concerns the son of the village sacrificer (*pujari*). With regard to these three families, I will discuss their narratives of and motives for conversion, their relationships with the Olek and other Gadaba, as well as their ideas about sameness and differences between Olek Dormo and Gadaba religion.

Podu Sisa, and along with him his wife Samli, and later his children, became Olek about 10 years ago.[10] At the time of my stay in the village at the beginning of 1999, he was a young man who had just 'brought' his wife to the village. However, the marriage was not ritually consummated for a long time. Although this is not uncommon, the village was not happy with this situation. As the likely successor of his father as village sacrificer (*pujari*), he had to be married in order

254 *Peter Berger*

to fully join the sacrificial community, even representing it as a totality. I will return to this in a later section.

The motives for conversion are usually of two types: either illness or alcohol addiction. In Podu's case both causes were combined. Illness is generally related to relationships of devouring. Harmful agents, human or non-human, violently 'eat' one's body or harvest. Alcohol consumption is part of social and ritual life, and a large majority of Gadaba (men, women and sometimes children) drink regularly, many heavily, beer, liquor (both self-made) or the fermented juice of the sago palm (*Caryota urens*). There is no clear-cut indigenous definition of 'alcoholism' but it is generally assumed that when people 'eat' their land – that is, start selling it to have means for further consumption – then something is seriously wrong. Moreover, although domestic life is not necessarily peaceful, heavy drinking increases conflicts between siblings, spouses, parents and children. This was also the situation faced by Podu, who ended up working on other people's land and had conflicts within the family and with other villagers. To make matters worse, nearly all of the members of the house became seriously ill. In March 2000, Podu came to my house after nightfall to borrow a torch. He had injured one hand – he said he cut himself with a knife – and seemed agitated and distressed. The ritual medium and diviner of the village had diagnosed harmful objects sent by sorcery to his house as the cause of their illness, and that night a ritual was scheduled to find and destroy these objects (cf. Berger 2015: 475ff.). But the trouble lingered on. When he went on a wage-labour trip, he was attacked by sorcery and temporarily lost his eyesight. Later, he told me how he had been advised by another Olek to join the movement and to quit alcohol and meat consumption. He did so, with the result being that he now lived in a condition of *suk santi*, happiness and peace, as he and his wife, Samli, say:

> [Podu] We don't face any trouble ... [being Olek], it is good (*bol*). [Samli] With affection (*kusi*). [Podu] we have to live in happiness-peace (*suko santi*) with people, we don't ... [Samli] argue with others. [Podu] We don't attach [black magic] to anyone, we don't have to get angry (*ragi*), [we] have to [live in] peace [and] beauty (*santi sundoro*).

I often heard such statements emphasising peace or happiness-peace (*suk santi*) from other converts.

The experience of another way of conversing with others that Podu and Samli narrate conveys the impression of quite a radical shift. Samli now has long matted hair and she told me that it became like this in a single night. That night she involuntarily entered a state of *baya* (divine trance) and could not recognise anyone; she said that she 'lost herself' (*hoji goli*), that her body and mind (*deho mon*) changed, and that she had no feeling (*chetna*). Podu thought she would die

Rupture and Resilience **255**

but it was only the advent of god, as Samli says: 'Bagwan (god) came ... that is how we came to wear this [that is, the ochre clothes as sign of Olek Dormo], wife and husband'. Although less dramatic, Podu mentioned another event in the context of his conversion: his *karandi* stones disappeared. Such stones can be found in the villages of the area as collective shrines but also in individual houses. Associated with the hunt and also, according to some, with powers of divination, this deity reveals itself in the form of stones, whose number may change over time. The deity may also announce its first appearance through dreams. When such a deity reveals itself in a house and its inhabitants do not recognise the divine presence, the deity makes a crying sound, and if still not attended to, the people of the house may become ill. If the deity is acknowledged, then it will receive regular bloody sacrifices. When he became Olek Dormo, Podu says, the stones in his house disappeared. For him it may signify the power of his new religious adherence, but it also has a practical component, as he would not have been able to provide animal sacrifices for *karandi* anymore.

The persistence of a bloodthirsty domestic deity after their conversion to Olek Dormo had been precisely the problem for Nondo Kirsani and his family, which finally led them to abandon Olek Dormo again. About the same age as Podu, Nondo converted to Olek Dormo for the common reasons outlined above. However, sometime afterwards, all his children became seriously ill and his wife was close to death. The cause identified was the anger of a deity that had been installed in his house by one of his ancestors. Like the *karandi* stones, only a few Gadaba have these *boti dandi* in their homes. These deities are made of iron by the blacksmith and are also referred to as Durga. The one I saw in another house – the home of the *gurumai* of the village – was a vertical construction of iron bars (*dandi*, generally referring to a staff) less than a metre high, which also consisted of places to put a small oil lamp (*boti*). These deities demand bloody sacrifices and are considered very powerful. It is most likely that people who install such deities are healers, ritual media or diviners, who depend on powerful support for their work against sorcerers and demons.[11] Nondo was not a healer, and when he became an Olek, he only offered 'white' (*sukol*) gifts (coconuts, flowers, and so on) to the deity, no longer 'bloody' (*rudi*) ones, which obviously enraged the deity, who subsequently made Nondo's family ill. However, the iron deity belonged to the whole sub-group (*kutum*) and thus this was not a private affair. As abandoning such a deity is a risky business, Nondo decided that the more viable solution would be to give up being Olek, which he did.

Rumours have it that the father of Krusna Sisa actually abandoned such an iron deity when converting to Olek Dormo, probably in the early 1970s. Krusna was about one year old, he says, when he became very ill and no healer or doctor could help him. The *baba*s from Dhenkanal had only just arrived in Koraput and

256 *Peter Berger*

established themselves in Lamda, where Krusna's father went and converted. His son survived. Through his father's conversion, Krusna became Olek and later his wife, Moti, also converted. Like Podu, Krusna explained that husband and wife should both be Olek because this is *suk santi*, but also because commensality within the household would be impossible otherwise. When Krusna's father died, he was buried with a stone monument on top, right next to the cremation ground of the Gadaba. Burial is one aspect that clearly distinguishes the Olek from the Gadaba, who cremate their dead. I have been told that the Olek are buried in a sitting posture, with an earthen pot with two holes for the eyes over their head. The ritual is called *samadhi kara* – which clearly refers to the ascetic dimension of Mahima Dharma – and it is performed, Krusna says, 'to give the soul peace' (*atma santi pai*). While the death rituals thus clearly differ from the Gadaba practice, the place of burial indicates his identification with the Gadaba of the village.

Except for these death rituals, the Olek Gadaba say that their ritual activities do not differ much from those of the rest of the village. One deity that is present in every Gadaba house is *doron deli*, the central pillar of the house, which is considered a representation of the earth deity (*bosmoti*). Gadaba do not worship this deity on a daily basis, but only during certain life-cycle rituals and annual festivals in which the deity receives bloody offerings. Olek Gadaba, by contrast, worship this deity more often. Podu worships every Monday and Thursday in the inner room of the house where *doron deli* is located. When I asked him which deity he would perform the *puja* for, he answered, '*bosmoti*, of course'. Other than *doron deli* there is no *murti* that is worshipped, but Podu brings earth from a termite mound (*birom*) into the sacred room for the *puja*. As Guzy (2002) also points out, termite mounds are especially venerated by the Olek as representations of the earth. In another Gadaba village, the Olek worship – as *isvor* or Shiva – a termite mound that grew out of the veranda of a house. Krusna worships on a daily basis in his house, 'calling god' (*prabunko dakibo*) in the morning after taking a bath and in the evening after dinner. On occasions such as the name-giving ceremony for children, called *sutok sorani*, which is common among all Gadaba, when Oleks from other villages visit the host, or when Krusna invites other Oleks at greater intervals, a kind of juice (*pana*) is prepared and offered to the deity (*prabhu*). This worship is also a means of protection. Krusna explained this to me in the general conceptual framework of sorcery (*nosto*, 'destruction'). 'This is nothing to talk about', he said echoing the general secrecy that surrounds such practices, and then continued:

> When someone does *nosto* against us, we don't know, how can we know? ... Thus, when we face trouble in our house because they do *nosto*, we also prepare this [that is, preparing this juice, *pana*] and call god ..., if he helps us, those people who did *nosto* will face trouble.

The juice is a new means that other Gadaba do not employ; however, the pattern of interaction is the same. When attacked by sorcery, Gadaba seek the help of healers and diviners, who first identify the causes of the illness and then act against them, also asking for divine support in their fight against their attackers. Another form of religious practice is visits to Lamda, the regional Olek centre which has an Olek temple. In particular, in the months of January and February, the Olek of the region meet there for collective worship.

Podu and Samli, as well as Krusna and Moti, all think of themselves as participating fully in the social and ritual life of the village. Moreover, they emphasise that Olek Dorma and Gadaba religion are one and the same (*soman*). I have heard different variations of the following statement by Podu:

> Other people do not say 'you're Olek', people say nothing like this.... For our own well-being we joined Olek Dormo.... We don't do sorcery; we do not try to kill people even if people do sorcery against us. As many people as there are in the village, we mix with all of them and live together with them with pleasure.... We don't think we are different people, that Olek Dormo is different. There is no [separate] Olek Dormo, it is one *dormo*, isn't it? We mix, it is the same worship, only that we do not sacrifice chicken and don't eat meat, that's different.

Accordingly, they emphasise that they provide money (*chanda*) for the village sacrifices like everybody else. They participate in death rituals and feasts, the only difference being that they receive different food and cook for themselves, and do not drink beer or liquor. Moreover, even if they do not drink themselves, they do provide beer for non-Olek guests during ceremonies they host. In such cases, the beer is consumed in another house close to their own. As such, they do not condemn the consumption of beer and liquor in general. Also, they are involved in the general life of the village. Krusna, for example, is very active in this regard, and participates in dances and the annual ritual hunt. At the beginning of the chapter, I described the way he participated in the worship of Gumang or Pat Kanda. In that context, though a year later, Krusna's mother severely criticised the performance of the sacrifice. That year, no drums were beaten and no music played during the worship. Together with the wife of the village headman, Krusna's mother awaited the men returning from the sacrifice at the village border. The two old women had crossed their hands behind their heads and were wailing as if a person had died, in this way articulating their criticism publicly. Later she told me that there would be no joy (*sarda*) without music, and she feared that the practice might decline further in the future. Clearly, she identified with the rituals of the village.

The Olek do not, however, participate in the ritual that the Gadaba are most known for, the secondary funeral for the dead called *go'ter* (cf. Berger 2015; Pfeffer 2001). In this last of four ritual steps that transform the liminal spirits

258 *Peter Berger*

into permanent ancestors, the deceased of a whole local group are temporarily brought back to life in the bodies of water buffaloes, which are then given away to external agnates and slaughtered. Krusna did give money for a buffalo for his paternal uncle when the Sisa group of the village performed the ritual in the 1990s; however, his own father's spirit could no longer be involved in the ritual. After initiation, Krusna says, to give a buffalo 'in his name' was not possible. As pointed out earlier, the death rituals are an instance when ritual practices differ considerably.

Restrictions on commensality limit the range of interaction between the Olek and the Gadaba, and, generally, the Olek do not accept food cooked by the Gadaba. Gadaba life-cycle rituals, however, require being fed by different relatives, and this holds true in particular for marriage. Due to a lack of resources, as both Krusna and Podu told me, they have not performed an 'Olek wedding' (Olek *biba*). Both their cases represent an adaptation of the usual Gadaba wedding ritual and alimentary practice. As Moti told me, in the case of Krusna and herself, they were only fed with flat rice (*chura*) mixed with cold water by their ritual relations.[12] The wedding of Podu and Samli followed the regular pattern more closely. As is common, a cow[13] and a goat were sacrificed and bride and groom were fed by different relatives. However, they were fed neither flat rice nor actual sacrificial food (*tsoru*) that contains cooked rice and the meat of the sacrificial animals, but were fed *kordi bat*. This is another type of ritual food containing bamboo sprouts (*kordi*), fish and rice, all cooked. While sacrificial food actually transforms the ritual status of a person – thus having severe consequences if people not eligible to consume this food do so by accident, and definitely a case of *umrang** or transgression – *kordi* rice marks moments of auspicious transition, without bringing that transition about. In both cases, the significance of being fed in the context of wedding rituals was thus acknowledged, but only in one case did this involve cooked rice, and in none of them sacrificial meat, as is usual.

However, even among themselves, the Olek do not inter-dine freely. Some Oleks will not eat at Krusna's house because they have not conducted an Olek wedding. Krusna, in his turn, considers his own practice of being Olek as more refined, more in line with Olek tradition (*niti niam*) in comparison with Podu. He sponsored a ritual (called *jal katiba*, 'cutting the net') performed by Olek gurus, something Podu has not done. Accordingly, he does not eat at Podu's house and is also careful about eating at other Olek houses as he cannot be sure if the ritual has been performed. As Krusna says: 'Where [people] call the soul (*atma dakibo*) for eating, in these houses we like to eat. In those houses who do not call the soul for eating we don't want to eat, also if they are Olek.' Such multiple distinctions with reference to spiritual status contrasts markedly with commensality among Gadaba. All Gadaba eat at each other's houses, and exchanging cooked food between households (known as 'walking rice') is a very prominent feature during village festivals. The only restriction concerns sacrificial food (*tsoru*), for which more rules apply, depending on the context; however, everyday consumption among Gadaba is free of restrictions on inter-dining.

GADABA PERSPECTIVE ON OLEK DORMO

Gadaba often stated that Olek Dormo and their own religion are the same, except for the feature of blood sacrifice. Indeed, there are several indicators that support such a perspective. For example, I encountered a situation in which the Gadaba engaged an Olek healer (*dissari*) for a name-giving ritual for a child, as well as the inverse situation, in which a Gadaba *dissari* conducted a ritual for Olek clients. The strongest evidence, however, is provided by the fact that the Gadaba of Gudapada selected Podu as their village sacrificer (*pujari*) after he had become an Olek Dormo adherent.

In order to adequately assess this decision, more background needs to be provided. Ghasi Sisa, Podu's father, had been a *pujari* for a very long time, probably several decades. A *pujari* is the most senior person in the village in terms of ritual status, and stands in a *pars pro toto* relationship with the village. Thus, the *pujari* represents the village as a whole. This can be inferred from various statements and practices. His house (and his house deity), for example, is homologous to the central shrine of the earth deity of the village. At a shrine, it is the *pujari* who starts eating the sacrificial food first, and he also ritually initiates many agricultural activities of the annual cycle, such as the first ploughing, and is then followed by every household. In addition, it is also said that deities make the *pujari* ill in the case of other people's transgressions or ritual negligence. The *pujari* and the village thus have a very close and reciprocal relationship, and the condition of one is reflected in and has an impact on the other. His most important task, which he always conducts with his counterpart, the ritual cook (*randari*), is the performance of sacrifices at the shrines of the village, such as for Pat Kanda, sketched at the beginning of this contribution.

Throughout most of my initial fieldwork period of 22 months between 1999 and 2003, criticisms of the *pujari* were articulated. Villagers wanted Podu to take over the job but he was reluctant, repeatedly saying he would have no money for his marriage. During March 2000, the situation became more urgent. As mentioned above, during that period, the whole family of the *pujari* became ill, including Ghasi Sisa. At that time, the village headman informed the other villagers that the Pat Kanda deity had approached him in a dream requesting

260 *Peter Berger*

that the *pujari* should be replaced. This situation was confirmed by the *gurumai* (ritual medium) of the village, who had communicated with the deities in a séance. A public meeting was held and the situation discussed. During that meeting the different 'faults' of the *pujari* were not openly discussed; however, people told me, as they had done before, that he would drink too much, even before a sacrifice, that he would eat leftovers randomly, that his illness would also be a sign of his weakness as a *pujari* and that would be inauspicious (*osub*) for the village. All in all, the 'gods would no longer listen to him' (*maphru tar kota suni nai*).

Immediately after that meeting a delegation of men went to the village of the *boro dissari*, the 'senior astrologer', who advises the village on important matters, such as the starting dates for festivals. Significantly, these senior astrologers are regularly 'outsiders'. They not only come from a different village but from a different ethnic group as well. In the case of Gudapada, the senior astrologer was a Rona. He consulted his almanac (*panji*) and suggested that Podu should be the new *pujari*. However, first Podu had to marry ritually. A few weeks later, shortly before the important sacrifice for Pat Kanda, another village dignitary – the *barik* or village herald – was visited in his dreams by the deity, who asked why the *pujari* had not been replaced. The *barik* is responsible for buying the sacrificial animals for collective rituals at the weekly market and in his dream the goat, shortly before being sacrificed, turned its head away from the sacrificer. Thus alerted, the *barik* even wanted to organise an ad hoc wedding ceremony for Podu, but this initiative did not work out in the end and the old *pujari* once more had to conduct the ritual, although people did not have good feelings about it.

This background story demonstrates two things: first, the concern of the people indicated the significance of the *pujari* for the general well-being of the village; and, second, that the lifestyle of the *pujari* does matter to some extent. There were other men who drank as much as the *pujari* but no one was concerned about that. Moreover, his lifestyle was not considered a transgression, certainly not a 'sin'. However, the intimate correspondence between the *pujari* and the village makes such a lifestyle problematic, and it did affect his ability to communicate properly with deities and conduct the rituals carefully.

When I returned to Gudapada in 2010 after six years of absence from the village, I found that Podu had become the new *pujari*, before which he and Samli had finally been ritually married after having both converted to Olek Dormo. Thus, the situation was not that the village accepted the conversion of their *pujari* who was already in office, but they selected someone to become the *pujari* although he was already an adherent of Olek Dormo. The fact that, unlike Krusna and Moti, the *pujari*-to-be and his wife were actually fed with cooked rice during their wedding and that animals were sacrificed according to *niam*,

Rupture and Resilience **261**

but no meat was consumed by the bride and groom themselves, clearly shows how demands on both sides – being Olek and having a proper *pujari* with a proper ritual status – were carefully considered and the ritual performance adapted accordingly. As Baum would say (1990: 376), in a process of indigenisation, the actors involved negotiated the concerns of both religions in a specific situation.

In 2019, Podu was still fulfilling his role as *pujari* for the village and not a single person I spoke to then or during earlier visits voiced any doubts or criticism about his performance, quite in contrast to the earlier situation when Podu's father held the position. At the various shrines in the village, Podu invokes the deities and 'sacrifices' the coconut, but leaves the killing to other Gadaba of the Sisa group, from which the sacrificers are always recruited. As I could not personally witness Podu in his role as *pujari* during village sacrifices, I cannot say to what extent he actually participates, for example, whether he shares some of the rice cooked at the shrine with the other Gadaba, or if he only shares in the 'meat' of the coconut, as Krusna did. What is clear, however, is that all of the villagers I talked to consider his participation sufficient and appreciate his performance as the *pujari*.

THE OUTSIDE PERSPECTIVE

That the Olek and the Gadaba emphasise similarity and continuity in their religions is certainly not mere rhetoric. Not only do I think that they hold this view sincerely, but the case of Podu becoming the *pujari*, a ritual role so vital for the village as a whole, is particularly clear evidence that no fundamental differences are recognised, or, stated differently, the similarities are conceived to be elementary. In this section, I will outline why, from my perspective, the situation looks quite different and is more complex, but an initial important question is what makes this assessment – the similarity assumption – possible at all.

There may be further aspects that make this view feasible, but I want to mention three here: the notion of *niam*, the lack of dogmatism and the postcolonial administrative situation. It is quite possible that Gadaba religion has remained rather constant for a long time, perhaps even 'for scores of generations', as Fürer-Haimendorf (1984: 71) claims. However, it is also conceivable that changes have been accommodated quite often. The notion of *niam* – which is nowhere written in stone but is a ritual practice that is constantly re-enacted and also re-negotiated according to circumstances – can encompass change without acknowledging it. There has also been no need thus far to rationalise Gadaba religion in Weber's sense, for example, to make it more systematic, in competition with other

262 *Peter Berger*

religions; to define a key religious symbol, a book or a place of worship; and no Gadaba-ism in the way there has been Bali-ism, as described by Geertz (1973a). Not being overly self-conscious or concerned about what the essence or the boundaries of their religion are, and also not having experts presiding over these issues, means that adaptions can be made without creating strife. Finally, the administrative classification in postcolonial Odisha may also play a role. Gadaba are aware that they are classified as 'Hindu' by the administration in the 10-year census, but also their children are classified as such in public primary schools. Administratively, their religious identity is thus defined in explicit opposition to Christians and Muslims, and I regularly encountered statements emphasising the fundamental alterity of Christians in particular and their religious practices and the relational logic of Gadaba being thus Hindu (as they are not Christians). As Olek Dormo is recognizably 'Hindu', it suggests a closeness to Gadaba religion in administrative terms that is actually lacking from an anthropological perspective.

One of the major shifts that adherence to Olek Dormo effects, and which in my view also partly explains the attractiveness for converts, is the elaboration of a new domain hitherto relatively unmarked in moral terms. Baum has suggested that certain ideas from the old religion remain important in the context of conversion in certain 'areas' (1990: 371). I think it is very useful conceptually to distinguish such areas or domains, 'locations' as we called them in the introduction to this volume. In this case, I argue, it is the domain of lifestyle, basically left fallow in Gadaba religion, that receives particular attention and new meaning through the Olek Dormo perspective. As outlined above, Gadaba religion embeds morality in sacrificial and alimentary ritual processes, leaving the 'area' of lifestyle mainly blank. While the distribution and consumption of food is highly regulated in the context of ritual, everyday dietary practices are not restricted or explicitly regulated in religious terms. Excessive drinking or violence may not be approved socially, but it is not divinely sanctioned either.

However, while such behaviour may lead to severe domestic problems and conflicts from which people actually suffer, traditional religion provided no means to deal with the situation, or even acknowledging it as a 'problem'. I am reminded of another context in which I observed such a lack of meaningful patterns, then with regard to the management of suffering. In the context of death, it is the Gadaba women who conventionally have the role of expressing grief. At a very young age, girls learn to cross their hands behind their heads – like Krusna's mother in her critique of the sacrificial practice – and to mourn and wail ad hoc when required to by the situation. In contrast, there are no behavioural

Rupture and Resilience **263**

patterns that enable men to express grief, although it is not regarded as inappropriate when they do show emotions. This led to a situation in which a desperate father, whose adolescent son had died, did a summersault on the cremation ground to give physical expression to his distress, and other men had to rush to him to hold him tight. My argument with regard to Olek Dormo is that as far as illness is concerned, Olek Dormo is just one of several options that the Gadaba have to seek divine support, but it actually offers unique avenues for action in cases of social and economic crisis that are frequently the result of excessive alcohol consumption. Olek Dormo offers a new framework within which to articulate these concerns, to make them visible and approachable. It does so by 'ethicizing' (cf. Obeyesekere 1980: 146) the domain of lifestyle and providing a new 'model for' the world (Geertz 1973b), dealing with such a situation in the long term.

The question, then, is whether the adoption of Olek Dormo also results in a new 'model of' the world, a new kind of cosmology. The examples provided here show that adherents of Olek Dormo assume the existence and significance of non-human agents as do all Gadaba, and maintain active relationships with them, although the forms of interaction are restricted by the demands of the new lifestyle. Thus, Krusna sponsored the buffalo for the death ritual for his uncle, although he was not able to provide one for his own father. He participates in village rituals but does not share the sacrificial food, only the coconut 'meat'. Nondo recognised the continuing power of his blood thirsty iron deity, which forced him to reconvert. The Olek and the Gadaba, therefore, continue to share the same basic conceptualisations of the world.

At the same time, there are also discernible shifts on the level of ideas and values. In the eyes of the Gadaba, the Olek abstinence from alcohol in particular leads towards a more harmonious domestic and village life. 'Peacefulness' (*santi*) or 'happiness-peacefulness' (*suk santi*) – perhaps to be understood as happiness through peacefulness – is generally emphasised as the main motive, aim and achievement, and in my view represents a new value, one that significantly informs the social practice of adherents to Olek Dormo. The traditional moral value of 'good and even' (*bol soman*) is considerably different from the value of 'peacefulness', as the former refers to the ritual equilibrium of processes of sharing and exchange involving humans, gods and the dead, a system of reciprocities completely unconnected to everyday interaction. In contrast, Gadaba social life is not particularly peaceful, and a certain 'anger' (*risa, ragi*) is expected and generally appreciated, even if also lamented, and frequently displayed publicly, especially by young men (Berger 2010). For the Olek, *santi* or *suk santi* may have the quality of a new paramount value in Robbins' terms (2009), as it seems to function as the

264 *Peter Berger*

main guiding principle in their lives and the yardstick with which to evaluate everything else.

Thus, I would agree with Guzy's assessment of the Rona Olek as also applying to the Gadaba Olek Dormo that a 'permanent religious ethic of restriction' is implied (Guzy 2007: 116). One could perhaps also argue that 'the restrictive code of behavior represents an inverted set of traditional ideas and values' (ibid.), in the sense that *suk santi* as a value contrasts markedly with the positive value of aggressiveness that is especially associated with young men. However, I would not call this an inversion of values, as the Gadaba Olek continue to recognise the values associated with *niam* as articulated in their sacrificial alimentary processes, including the idea of 'good and even' (*bol soman*) relationships. Rather than an inversion, *suk santi* as a value provides a new frame of reference for the Olek without discarding traditional values. I would also not describe the Olek Gadaba in Gudapada as 'new indigenous moralists' (Guzy 2007: 125), as they do not denigrate or look down on alcohol, meat consumption or blood sacrifice. They have made a choice for themselves and their families, but they accept that others do not follow their lifestyle. This is evident, for instance, when Olek hosts offer beer to their guests or participate financially in the village sacrifices. Given that they still presume the power of local deities, the Olek even depend on the continued performance of the animal sacrifices.

In addition, as far as ritual practice is concerned, I would assess the change effected through the adoption of Olek Dormo as considerable. Obviously, new rituals are conducted (such as fire sacrifice) and old ones abandoned, especially in the context of death (*samadhi kara* rather than *go'ter*). Also, there is a greater emphasis on 'prayer' and perhaps on the spirituality of food, connected to a different discourse about 'soul' (*atma*), as can be inferred from Krusna's statement about the (im)possibility of commensality even among the Olek. More fundamental, perhaps, is the change in patterns of exchange. Gadaba ritual practice consists of constant flows of food, drink and animals between different local groups in the context of the life cycle. Although more empirical evidence is needed, my hunch is that the Olek Gadaba participate to a lesser extent in this web of exchanges than other Gadaba due to their restrictions on inter-dining and feasting. Moreover, Olek Dormo introduced the idea of a sacred centre, such as the village of Lamda, with sacred personae from whose presence the adherents benefit spiritually. As pointed out earlier, in Gadaba ritual life there are no ritual centres and no sacred men or women. The only comparable aspect that comes to mind is the function of the divine king, whose capital in Nandapur constitutes the 'navel' of the world, an idea the Gadaba entertain although the king has long gone. Absent from traditional Gadaba religion, this 'centrism' among the Olek Gadaba aligns with a new emphasis on the individual refinement of the self.

CONCLUSION

Traditional Gadaba religion and Olek Dormo both value blood sacrifice, meat and alcohol, but in inverse ways. In Gadaba religion, sacrificial food epitomises society, and the alimentary processes of sharing and exchange maintain the socio-cosmic order. Olek Dormo, conversely, values these practices by making them the main point of restriction and the focus of an ascetic lifestyle. How, then, is it possible that both the Gadaba Olek and the non-Olek Gadaba claim that their religion is one and the same and regard what both of them value most, though in different ways – either as part of a sacrificial ideology or as an expression of an ascetic lifestyle – thereby as an epiphenomenon?

I have argued that the Olek and the Gadaba both regard their religions as fundamentally similar. This emphasis on sameness is not mere rhetoric but is also reflected in ritual practice, most importantly by the selection of an adherent of Olek Dormo as the new village sacrificer. Moreover, there are a number of features that help maintain the similarity assumption and that camouflage differences, such as the flexible notion of 'tradition' (*niam*), the nature of Gadaba religion, with its lack of dogmatic formulations, and the postcolonial administrative classification that equates Gadaba with Hindus, while constructing Muslims and Christians as fundamentally different.

In contrast to the local views, the perspective from outside provides a more multidimensional picture and in my view Olek Dormo transforms Gadaba religion in significant ways. In particular, Olek Dormo shapes an unmarked area in Gadaba religion, namely the domain of lifestyle, which was previously unelaborated in moral and religious terms. In other words, Olek Dormo offers a new *Godroad* that leads through hitherto morally uncharted territory. Seen from this new road, the landscape looks different; it offers a new perspective. Whereas traditional Gadaba religion embeds morality in processes of sacrifice, sharing and exchange, Olek Dormo 'ethicizes' (Obeyesekere 1980) everyday practices, especially with regard to food and drink. This is attractive to some Gadaba, I argue, because economic and social difficulties arising out of excessive alcohol consumption can be articulated, approached and dealt with in a new way. In contrast to Olek Dormo as an avenue to fight illness – the other main motive for conversion – this new quotidian lifestyle morality provides a language with which to address issues of domestic conflict arising out of alcohol consumption and also provides behavioural patterns, offering a long-term solution to the newly defined 'problem'. While this problem had previously been socially perceived, it is now newly framed with reference to the new religious value of *suk santi* (happiness-peacefulness).

Olek Dormo thus not only provides a new 'model for' (Geertz 1973b) the world with its ascetic lifestyle but also has an impact at the level of values. Clearly,

266 *Peter Berger*

the Olek still share the basic worldview of the Gadaba, which includes ideas about the cause of illness, and how to act against attacks of sorcery, as well as the ontology of deities and their agency. However, the ethnographic evidence suggests that the idea of *suk santi* has developed into a new crucial value for the Olek, which is the measuring rod for evaluating social relationships and, as a moral standard, informs the behaviour of the Olek. Against this value, excessive alcohol consumption and violence stand out as transgressions, now in a religious sense. This contrasts markedly with the indigenous idea of 'anger' that is considered a standard behaviour of young men in particular and is generally approved, although it is also lamented about in some contexts.

The theology of liberation as a defining feature of Mahima Dharma in Dhenkanal is not found among the Olek discussed here. However, the idea of the individual progress of a newly discovered spiritual self, though not very elaborated, seems to inform Olek religious practices and interactions among them. Gadaba religion knows only the ritual development of a person through his or her lifetime and beyond. Alimentary actions ritually transform people to enable them to participate fully in ritual life. Through being fed sacrificial food at their wedding, for instance, men are eligible to participate in sacrificial commensality at the village level. However, besides these ritual transformations, there are no further refinements of the self and hence no gradations of spiritual development recognised. Among the Olek, this seems to be different, at least in some cases, as can be inferred from Krusna's statement about the relevance of 'calling the soul' to eat and its consequences for commensality.

This spiritual and individualistic element, in the sense of a refinement of the self – that can be achieved partly through a realisation of *suk santi* – corresponds to an element of centrality that was lacking in Gadaba religion. There are no sacred centres or sacred personae among the Gadaba. Ritual specialists communicate with non-human agents or may provide their bodies as ritual media, but they are not themselves sacred. Similarly, deities are present in the landscape of particular localities, but religious centres that are recognised by all Gadaba are absent.

All this – the religious appropriation of lifestyle, the elaboration of a new value and the concomitant development of a spiritual rather than a ritual status, the orientation towards a centre and gurus as 'centre-persons' – indicates quite substantial differences between Olek Dormo and Gadaba religion. These changes not only affect the adherents of Olek Dormo, probably a diverse group in itself as the differences in ritual practice between Podu and Krusna indicate, but have a more general influence on Gadaba religion as a whole. This is so, in particular, I think, because the practices and restrictions Olek Dormo propagates with regard to alcohol and meat consumption are reinforced by other strands in the contemporary socio-religious landscape oriented towards the 'Hindu-mainstream', which discourage 'superstition', cow sacrifices, 'wasteful practices' and consumption of liquor.

Considering the concept of 'conversion', all three perspectives mentioned in the introduction seem to work. With Hefner, one can say that the Olek have a new locus of identity, without letting go of other dimensions of identification, such as being Gadaba of the village of Gudapada. Along with Baum, it can also be said that the Olek generally accept the new religious authority of gurus who visit the regional centre of Lamda. However, this acceptance may not be very pervasive and it is certainly not exclusive. The Oleks that this contribution has been concerned with are clearly in a process of indigenisation, as described by Baum, re-embedding and negotiating different elements of the indigenous religion and Olek Dormo. The relevance of being fed by certain relatives and affines during marriage, on the one hand, shows the process of mutual adaptation: although the Olek in general do not accept food from the Gadaba, they are fed during the wedding ritual. On the other hand, the example of the wedding rituals also highlights differences: while Krusna and Moti only accepted uncooked food, Podu and Samli were fed with cooked rice. Both couples did not consume any sacrificial meat, but the latter case even involved the killing of a cow, an act that is no longer performed at most wedding rituals. Finally, the adoption of the new value of *suk santi* and its concomitant implications with regard to lifestyle, sacrificial practice, more spiritual notions of the self and the devaluation of other ideas related to violence or youthful aggressiveness ('anger') may indicate a significant shift in the system of values. Given the resilience of indigenous ideas about gods, demons or illness, and also the continued assumption of the relevance of blood sacrifice, I would not speak of a radical change yet. To do justice to the complexity of these issues, more ethnographic research has to be conducted.

Although the concept of 'conversion', as formulated by the scholars mentioned, seems to work in the case discussed here, I do not think the term is appropriate in describing the dynamics between Olek Dormo and Gadaba religion. While I do not consider the concept particularly problematic, it does not add much analytically either. More importantly, to speak about conversion there must, in my view, be a clear acknowledgement of the transformation by the actors themselves. As I have shown, however, the considerable changes that 'conversion' to Olek Dormo entails are not perceived as such by my interlocutors, Olek or not. Therefore, I would prefer to understand the adoption of Olek Dormo as one aspect in a wider and complex dynamic of cultural and religious change.

268 *Peter Berger*

NOTES

*This contribution is dedicated to Ben den Ouden, a student of mine who tragically died in an accident at the time this chapter was written. Ben wrote his MA thesis on a comparison of the process of conversion among the Khasi, Naga and Sora of India and he also brought to my attention the article by Robert Baum that is also referred to in this contribution and the introduction to this volume.

1. Names of places and personal names have been changed.

2. Of course, the Olek are also Gadaba and – as will become clear – consider themselves as such. Often, I only refer here to 'Olek' and 'Gadaba' in order to avoid the frequent use of formulations such as 'non-Olek Gadaba' or 'traditional Gadaba'.

3. This innovative article is generally overlooked in the discussions of conversion, at least as far as some of the major contributors to this debate is concerned (for example, Cannell 2006; Hefner 1993; Engelke 2004; Meyer 1998 or Robbins 2004). Moreover, also in Gooren's (2014) recent overview, Baum is not mentioned.

4. He describes a similar situation that Sahlins calls 'humiliation' (Baum 1990: 374; Sahlins 2005 [1992]: 37f.).

5. After an initial research period in 1996, ethnographic fieldwork was conducted for 22 months between 1999 and 2003. I revisited the region in 2004, 2010, 2016 and 2019. For an elaborate description and analysis of Gadaba society and religion, see my monograph (Berger 2015; for a short overview, see Berger 2017).

6. As well as meaning 'even', the word *soman* also means 'same', 'equal', 'correct' and 'good' (cf. Gustafsson 1987; Mahapatra 1985; Malten no date).

7. Words marked by an asterisk are Gutob, the Austro-Asiatic language of the southern Munda branch that is only spoken by the senior or Boro Gadaba, on whom my research is focused; all other indigenous terms are from Desia, the Indo-European *lingua franca* of the Koraput plateau.

8. I here adapt a term from Meyer Fortes (1969: 251).

9. See Eschmann (1978), Guzy (2002, 2007a, 2007b), Beltz (2007) and Banerjee-Dube (2001).

10. Most Gadaba have no habit of calculating in years and thus do not care much whether any event occurred three or four years ago or took place in 2008 or 2010.

11. Also, the most common portable weapon of a healer is an iron instrument (*jupan*) made by the local blacksmith.

12. Usually the couple is fed by the following people/groups: both mothers' brothers, wife's father (if different from the groom's mother's brother), the 'four brothers' (village agnates) and the 'twelve brothers' (Gadaba as totality). Each of the people/groups sacrifice, cook and feed the couple on their own (cf. Berger 2015: 245ff.).

13. Cow sacrifices in the context of life-cycle rituals have become rare over the past 15 years or so. At the time of Podu's wedding, most young Gadaba would not have sacrificed cattle but only goats for their weddings.

BIBLIOGRAPHY

Bailey, F. G. 1981. 'Spiritual Merit and Morality.' In *Culture and Morality: Essays in Honour of Christoph von Fürer-Haimendorf*, edited by Adrian C. Mayer, 23–41. Delhi: Oxford University Press.

Banerjee-Dube, Ishita. 2001. 'Issues of Faith, Enactments of Contest: The Founding of Mahima Dharma in Nineteenth-Century Orissa.' In *Jagannath Revisited: Studying Society, Religion and the State in Orissa*, edited by Hermann Kulke and Burkhard Schnepel, 149–177. New Delhi: Manohar.

Baum, Robert M. 1990. 'The Emergence of a Diola Christianity.' *Africa* 60(3): 370–398.

Beltz, Johannes. 2007. 'Contested Authorities, Disputed Centres, and Rejected Norms: Situating Mahima Dharma in Its Regional Diversity.' In *Periphery and Centre: Studied in Orissan History, Religion and Anthropology*, edited by Georg Pfeffer, 79–104. New Delhi: Manohar.

Berger, Peter. 2002. 'The Gadaba and the 'Non-ST' Desia of Koraput.' In *Contemporary Society: Tribal Studies*, edited by Georg Pfeffer und Deepak Kumar Behera, Vol. 5, 57–90. New Delhi: Concept Publishing Company.

———. 2010. 'Assessing the Relevance and Effects of "Key Emotional Episodes" for the Fieldwork Process.' In *Anthropological Fieldwork: A Relational Process*, edited by D. Spencer and J. Davies, 119–143. Newcastle upon Tyne: Cambridge Scholars Publishing.

———. 2014. 'Dimensions of Indigeneity in Highland Odisha, India.' *Asian Ethnology* 73(1–2): 19–37.

———. 2015. *Feeding, Sharing, and Devouring: Ritual and Society in Highland Odisha, India*. Boston/Berlin: de Gruyter.

———. 2016. 'Liminal Bodies, Liminal Food. Hindu and Tribal Death Rituals Compared.' In *Ultimate Ambiguities: Investigating Death and Liminality*, edited by P. Berger and J. Kroesen, 57–77. New York: Berghahn.

———. 2017. 'Feeding, Sharing and Devouring: Alimentary Rituals and Cosmology in Highland Odisha, India.' In *Highland Odisha: Life and Society Beyond the Coastal World*, edited by B. Pati and U. Skoda, 71–106. New Delhi: Primus.

———. 2018. 'Millet, Rice, and the Constitution of Society in Central India.' *Paideuma: Journal of Cultural Anthropology* 64: 245–264.

Cannell, Fanella, ed. 2006. *The Anthropology of Christianity*. Durham: Duke University Press.

Engelke, Matthew. 2004. 'Discontinuity and the Discourse of Conversion.' *Journal of Religion in Africa* 34(1–2): 82–109.

Eschmann, Anncharlott. 1978. 'Mahima Dharma: An Autochtonous Hindu Reform Movement.' In *The Cult of Jagannath and the Regional Tradition of Orissa*, edited by Anncharlott Eschmann, Hermann Kulke and Gaya Charan Tripati, 375–410. New Delhi: Manohar.

270 *Peter Berger*

Fortes, M. 1969. *Kinship and the Social Order: The Legacy of Lewis Henry Morgan.* London: Routledge.

Fox Young, R. and J. A. Seitz. 2013. 'Introduction.' In *Asia in the Making of Christianity: Conversion, Agency, and Identity, 1600s to the Present,* edited by R. Fox Young and J. A. Seitz, 1–26. Leiden: Brill.

Fürer-Haimendorf, C. von. 1974. 'The Sense of Sin in Cross-Cultural Perspective'. *Man* 9(4): 539–56.

———. 1984. 'Bondo and Gadaba Revisited.' In *Anthropology as a Historical Science,* edited by M. Bhuriya and S. M. Michael, 73–78. Indore: Sat Prakashan Sanchar Kendra.

Geertz, C. 1973a. '"Internal Conversion" in Contemporary Bali.' In *The Interpretation of Cultures: Selected Essays,* 170–189. New York: Basic Books.

———. 1973b. 'Religion as a Cultural System.' In *The Interpretation of Cultures: Selected Essays,* 87–125. New York: Basic Books.

Gellner, David. 1999. 'Religion, politics, and ritual. Remarks on Geertz and Bloch.' *Social Anthropology* 7(2): 135–153.

Gooren, Henri. 2014. 'Anthropology of Religious Conversion.' In *The Oxford Handbook of Religious Conversion,* edited by Lewis R. Rambo and Charles E. Farhadian, 84–116. Oxford Handbooks Online.

Gustafsson, U. 1989. *An Adiwasi Oriya-Telegu-English Dictionary.* Mysore: Central Institute of Indian Languages.

Guzy, L. 2002. *Baba-s und Alekh-s – Askese und Ekstase einer Religion im Werden. Vergleichende Untersuchung der asketischen Tradition Mahima Dharma in zwei Distrikten Orissas (Dhenkanal und Koraput)/östliches Indien.* Berlin: Weißensee.

———. 2007. 'Negative Ecstasy or the Singers of the Divine': Voices from the Periphery of Mahima Dharma. In *Periphery and Centre: Studied in Orissan History, Religion and Anthropology,* edited by G. Pfeffer, 105–30. New Delhi: Manohar.

Hefner, R. W. 1993. 'Introduction: World Building and the rationality of Conversion.' In *Conversion to Christianity: Historical and Anthropological Perspectives on a Great Transformation,* edited by R. W. Hefner, 3–44. Berkeley: University of California Press.

Mahapatra, K. 1985. 'Desia: A Tribal Oriya Dialect of Koraput Orissa'. *Adivasi* 25: 1–304.

Malten, Thomas. No date. 'Desia Dictionary.' Unpublished manuscript.

Meyer, B. 1998. '"Make a Complete Break with the Past." Memory and Post-Colonial Modernity in Ghanaian Pentecostalist Discourse.' *Journal of Religion in Africa* 28(3): 316–349.

Obeyesekere, Gananath. 1980. 'The Rebirth Eschatology and Its Transformations: A Contribution to the Sociology of Early Buddhism.' In *Karma and Rebirth in Classical Indian Traditions,* edited by Wendy D. O'Flaherty, 137–164. Berkeley: University of California Press.

Otten, Tina. 2006. *Heilung durch Rituale: Vom Umgang mit Krankheit bei den Rona im Hochland Orissas*. Berlin: Lit.

Pfeffer, Georg. 2001. 'A Ritual of Revival Among the Gadaba of Koraput.' In *Jagannath Revisited: Studying Society, Religion and the State in Orissa*, edited by H. Kulke and B. Schnepel, 99–124. New Delhi: Manohar.

Reithofer, Hans. 2006. *The Python Spirit and the Cross: Becoming Christian in a Highland Community of Papua New Guinea*. Göttinger Studien Zur Ethnologie, Bd. 16. Münster: Lit.

Robbins, J. 2004. *Becoming Sinners: Christianity and Moral Torment in a Papua New Guinea Society*. Berkeley: University of California Press.

———. 2009. 'Conversion, Hierarchy, and Cultural Change: Value and Syncretism in the Globalization of Pentecostal and Charismatic Christianity.' In *Hierarchy: Persistence and Transformation*, edited by K. M. Rio and O. H. Smedal, 65–88. New York: Berghahn.

Sahlins, M. D. 2005. 'The Economics of Develop-man in the Pacific.' In *The Making of Global and Local Modernities in Melanesia: Humiliation, Transformation and the Nature of Cultural Change*, edited by J. Robbins and H. Wardlow, 23–43. Burlington: Ashgate.

———. 1965. 'On the Sociology of Primitive Exchange'. In *The Relevance of Models for Social Anthropology*, edited by M. Banton, 139–236, London: Tavistock.

Strathern, Andrew J. and Pamela J. Stewart. 2009. 'Introduction: A Complexity of Contexts, a Multiplicity of Changes.' In *Religious and Ritual Change: Cosmologies and Histories*, edited by P. J. Stewart and A. J. Strathern, 3–68. Durham: Carolina Academic Press.

Vitebsky, P. 2017. *Living without the Dead: Loss and Redemption in a Jungle Cosmos*. Chicago: The University of Chicago Press.

———. 2008. 'Loving and Forgetting: Moments of Inarticulacy in Tribal India.' *Journal of the Royal Anthropological Institute* 14(2): 243–61.

Afterword

India Seen from Amazonia

Aparecida Vilaça

Precisely 10 years ago, the Melanesianist anthropologist Joel Robbins declared his surprise at being invited by Robin Wright and myself, two Amazonianists, to write an afterword to the book we had edited on the Christian conversion of native peoples of the Americas (Vilaça and Wright 2009). A scholar of the Urapmin, a native group of Papua New Guinea, more specifically a specialist on the experience of this group with a Pentecostal version of Christianity, the author found himself faced with articles concerning an ethnographic area about which he had little information, and with Catholic and non-Pentecostal Evangelic versions of Christianity, quite distinct, therefore, from the kind adopted by the Urapmin. The strangeness served as an incentive, leading him to write a text in which the Amazonia–Melanesia comparison occupied a prominent place, coinciding with the intention of the editors (Robbins 2009).

I find myself now in the exact same position as Robbins. For 30 years I have carried out research with an Amazonian indigenous group, the Wari', who converted to Evangelical Christianity through the action of American and Brazilian missionaries from the New Tribes Mission. The difference between my own experience and the Indian cases related in this book could not be greater. India's distinguishing feature is its caste hierarchy and while there do exist indigenous Amazonian groups with some type of internal hierarchy (particularly in Northwest Amazonia), these involve a configuration very different to the Hindu caste system. The majority of the Amazonian groups are egalitarian, some of them, like the Wari', even unfamiliar with the notion of a chief.

Also, unlike the Indian case, the indigenous peoples of Brazilian Amazonia, though incorporated into the nation-state, secular in principle, are in many cases not considered to be regular Brazilian citizens but 'indigenous', that is, persons with distinct rights and their own cultures, which must be respected by the national constitution. Furthermore, the missionaries, who first reached the indigenous population five hundred years ago, threatening, very often successfully, their cultural diversity, are exclusively Christian – Catholic or Evangelical, with a Pentecostal minority among the latter. There are no Islamic or Buddhist Amerindians, religious options rare in Brazilian society as a whole,

Afterword **273**

while the disputes and conflicts with non-Amerindians, frequently bloody, do not play out through religious language, at least nowadays. For the missionaries and for some of the Brazilian population, the Amerindians have no religion and conversion involves moulding shapeless matter; for others, shamanism, which presumes contact with spiritual entities via specialists, is the mark of indigenous 'religion', associated with animism.

We are dealing, therefore, with a panorama radically distinct from the one presented to us in this book, which explores forms of religious agency in different parts of India. To read it, an Amazonianist such as myself needs to read Dumont (1980) again and his *Homo Hierarchicus*, as well as access more recent information on the caste hierarchy and the notion of *dharma*, and on the nomenclature referring to outcastes, known as untouchables or Dalits, today referred to as Scheduled Castes. The latter, along with the groups outside the caste system, classified as Scheduled Tribes, are the protagonists of the episodes of conversion related in the book.

To do justice to the editors' probable intention when inviting me to write this afterword, I shall adopt a tone of estrangement about the complex processes of change and religious conflicts experienced by different sectors of the Indian nation, as well as the tribal peoples some of whom do not conceive themselves part of the latter. In so doing, I situate myself on the epistemological continuum formulated in the book's final chapter by Peter Berger (Chapter 10), which is organised around three different perspectives on the adherence to Hindu reformism by some of the tribal peoples of Highland Odisha, namely those of the converts, the traditionalists, and the anthropologist/author. Continuing this distancing of perspective, here I look to offer an even more distant viewpoint, that of an anthropologist trained in another continent.

With its 10 chapters and an introduction, *Godroads* is a book surprisingly rich in historical and ethnographic data, collected by different specialists: anthropologists, sociologists, historians and theologians. Although it is the theme of most of the chapters, Christianisation is not the only form of 'conversion' (a term rejected by the majority of authors) discussed in the book, which also examines 'conversion' to Islam and to Hindu reformism. Past and present, anthropology and history, Hindus and animist tribal peoples, alternate in a fascinating exploration of Indian diversity. Among other questions, the authors seek to explain the reasons for conversion to Christianity, Islam or Hinduism by some sections of the population (castes or tribes) and their rejection by others, as well as questioning the very concept of conversion and the idea of sudden change it suggests. In most cases, they show that it involves a slow process in which aspects of Christianity tend to be indigenised, at the same time as social life transforms radically.

274 *Aparecida Vilaça*

In Chapter 1, Oddie describes the conversion of the Shudra of Hyderabad, in the south of India, by Methodist missionaries in the first half of the twentieth century. Seeking additional information, I learnt that the Shudra comprise the lowest segment of the caste system, a position related to their mythic origin and to the manual work they perform, considered polluting (less, however, than the work of the outcasts or Scheduled Castes). The notions of purity and pollution, related to the professions and to the objects that people handle, define this social hierarchy, which imposes strict rules of contact and caste endogamy. Nevertheless, due to the professions and specific types of work performed by each caste, their economic and ceremonial interdependence is a central aspect of the system's operation. As we learn from Dumont, caste hierarchy is only comprehensible through the notion of totality on which the society is conceived.

According to Oddie (Chapter 1), the Methodist missionaries who arrived in India at the end of the nineteenth century initially tried to convert higher castes. They were unsuccessful, though, which seems to have been a common experience in diverse parts of the country. Even the Shudra only became interested in Christianity after being impressed by the progress of the local outcasts who had converted and, in the process, obtained access to medical resources and schooling.

This is one of the book's recurrent themes: conversion to Christianity is usually limited to the lower castes and outcastes, for whom the egalitarian discourse of the missionaries offers a chance to escape discrimination, abusive treatment and forced labour. In diverse cases, like the one related in Oddie's chapter, they were relatively successful, even provoking revolt in the higher castes who saw themselves threatened by the rise of those they considered inferior but on whom they depended in every sense. In response, as Sahoo (Chapter 9) shows us in his study of conflicts between Hindus and Christians, religious language began to be used to legitimise war and the imposition of Hindu nationalism. In some cases, awareness of discrimination was facilitated by the prior action of communist organisations, which opened up ideological space for Christianity, as occurred with the Dravidapuram, in Guntur, Andhra, southern India (Kumar, Chapter 2).

One of the reasons for the success of Methodists (Chapters 1 and 7) and other missionary groups was the combination of their anti-hierarchical discourse, encouraging interaction between castes, with their openness to local culture, including its rituals and festivals, which facilitated the integration of the Christians. Another more significant reason, in this and other examples of missionary action, was the capacity to cure associated with medications. In the case of the Shudra of Hyderabad, during the cholera, bubonic plague and smallpox epidemics of the 1920s, the Christians had a higher survival rate due to their access to vaccines and hospitals. For the tribal Naga of Angami, in northeast

India, studied by Joshi (Chapter 6), not only was the effectiveness of the medications essential to their adoption of Christianity, the traditional curers themselves appropriated modern medicine, creating a bridge between traditions, much to the missionaries' displeasure. Fascination with the medications brought by the colonisers was evinced in many parts of the world, Amazonia among them, where the antibiotics distributed by missionaries to cure epidemics – caused by themselves in the expeditions to contact 'remote' indigenous populations – proved a decisive factor in their acceptance. Not just acceptance of the missionaries but so too of their God, whom they invoked at the moment of administering the medications, insisting that the cure would be impossible without divine intervention.

Jones (Chapter 7), who also examines the activities of Methodists in the nineteenth century, in this case in northern India, once again links the decision of the low and untouchable castes to adopt Christianity to their wish for better living conditions. The chapter's focus, however, is on the difference between the missionary and Indian narratives on conversion, the former concentrating on the idea of rupture and the denunciation of the earlier religion, the latter dwelling on the idea of continuity. The case explored in the chapter of an Indian man called Haqq, who became a successful Methodist leader due to his capacity to translate Indian traditions into the Christian idiom, illustrates the notion of continuity developed by the author.

The dynamics between continuity and change permeates the different chapters of the book, and most of the authors look to focus on continuity, which allows them to oppose the current notion of conversion as rupture and sudden change, associated by several of them with the approach taken by Robbins (2004) to the conversion of the Urapmin of Papua New Guinea. In my view, however, Robbins's work sometimes functions as a kind of straw-man, since the Melanesianist author's analysis in fact displays a much more complex idea of rupture (Robbins 2007). As Berger (Chapter 10) shows, continuity and change are above all perspectives, attributed differentially not only to diverse actors, such as missionaries and natives, but internally to the natives themselves, when we take into account different practices and spheres of action of sections of the population. In the case of the Urapmin, for example, the divinatory practices conducted by women were maintained within Christian practice, as well as diverse other aspects of social life. From this perspective, there is continuity. However, Robbins shows us that native discourse emphasises the rupture with the past, realised, among other means, by the destruction of images and objects connected to traditional divinities, preventing any kind of revival of the rituals associated with them. Additionally, Robbins offers us an original analytic perspective by focusing on change in the sphere of values, based on the Dumontian

276 *Aparecida Vilaça*

notions of hierarchy and encompassment, originating precisely from the Indian universe. Only on this basis is it possible to comprehend the native perspective of radical change, since individualism, previously a value encompassed by relationalism, becomes the dominant value in the Christian Urapmin world, generating a deep moral conflict that the Urapmin seek to resolve, always in a temporary form, by performing new rituals, such as the ritual of collective possession by the Holy Ghost in an ambient of dance and music called 'spirit disko'.

In the case of the Wari' and various other Amazonian groups that I analysed in an ethnographic book (Vilaça 2016), the dynamic between continuity and change takes on a different form. It is not simply a question of the indigenisation of Christianity by native peoples, nor an idea of radical rupture or an inversion of values. Diverse Amazonian societies like the Wari' conceive themselves to be in a constant process of change, with Christian conversion being just one more instance. The centrality of processes of 'opening to the other' identified by Lévi-Strauss (1995) as a characteristic of these peoples allows us to situate the missionaries as one more kind of 'other' in continuity with the animal spirits and enemies. The central question in Amazonia is that transformations are, in principle, reversible, following the model of the transformation of shamans into animal spirits, ideally temporary.

The model that I proposed to think about the conversion of the Wari' was alternation, where two perspectives, traditional and exterior (which includes Christianity), are distributed in distinct contexts (such as the church and everyday life), such that they can even coexist in a single context through translative works, which enable access to the traditional universe of practices and values through specific terms preserved by the native language (see too Barker 1993). This is the case, for example, of the terms for 'to love' and for God. In the Wari' language there is no positive term for the act of loving, which was translated as 'not-dislike' and employed in this form in Bible translations. Not-dislike, even when uttered in a Christian church service, refers to the Wari' and Amazonian notion of a primordial world marked by difference and alterity, the world of enemies and spirits, which people 'dislike', and through which relations of proximity or kinship, those associated with 'not-disliking', should be produced. In the case of God, the term chosen by the Wari', who had no kind of gods in their cosmology, was 'the truly invisible', highlighting the absence of God's body, to which they attributed his power of omnipresence and his encompassing perspective. In Amazonian worlds, it is the distinct bodies that produce differentiated perspectives, whose totalisation is impossible. In sum, if continuity and change are above all perspectives, without the comprehension of less evident aspects, like translative details, they can become invisible, leading the anthropologist or historian to a partial view.

The idea of an encompassing perspective, characteristic of the Christian God insistently present in the scriptures, brings us to an important difference between the Indian universe, on the one hand, and the Melanesian and Amazonian universes mentioned above, on the other. As I said, the strangeness of the God presented by the missionaries for the Wari' was related especially to his omnipresence and omniscience, given that they live in an essentially open universe where perspectives are incessantly negotiated. This is an ontology diametrically opposite to the notion of a whole that founds Hindu cosmology and social life (as well as most tribal cosmologies, in contrast to the gathering-hunting bands). In Melanesia, although this idea of unlimited opening to alterity does not apply, neither do people conceive themselves as part of a whole. As Robbins (2004) and other authors (Strathern 1988; Wagner 1975) show us, the Melanesian world is conceived as an intricate web of relations to be made and unmade by the agents, who thereby continually define variable positions within this network.

It may be that the absence of narratives on the impact of this unique and totalising God in the chapters of the present book is related precisely to the prior existence of this notion of a whole in Indian thought, which was not, therefore, impacted by the strangeness of this alien God, unlike what happened in the Amazonian world. God came to occupy perhaps a higher level on the pre-existing hierarchical scale, just as seems to have occurred in some areas of Africa where he assumed the position of more encompassing traditional gods without affecting the existence of local divinities (Hefner 1993; Horton 1975).

The chapters by Kumar (Chapter 2) on the relation between communism and Christianisation and Pool (Chapter 3) on Islamisation explore two other central themes for thinking about the adoption of Christianity: the importance of egalitarian values and the idea of moral reform (here associated with Islam), a topic also addressed in Berger's final chapter. Christian egalitarianism, which, as we have seen, explains the much greater success of Christianity among the most disadvantaged groups, is amply thematised in the book, but its correlate, individualism, lacks the same centrality in the exploration of the changes brought about by Christianity. Its analysis is limited to the introduction by Berger and Sahoo, who take individualism and the notion of the self to be a consequence of the modernisation brought by schooling and new employment opportunities, which enabled the social improvement of those who became Christian. As a process out of Hinduism, implying a rejection of social hierarchy, Christianisation creates individuals who no longer perceive themselves as part of a whole, ceasing to make ritual prestations, like funerals, which leads to the marginalisation and expulsion by their families.

278 *Aparecida Vilaça*

Since Mauss (1999 [1950]) and Dumont (1983), we have known that the notion of the individual, which implies a conception completely different from the multiple and relational person prevailing in diverse modern non-Western societies, is not only a lateral consequence of the Europeanisation and modernisation of the new Christians but is found at the heart of the Protestant Christian message faced by the former Hindus analysed here. The God of Luther and Calvin is personalised, that is, he exists within persons and relates to each of them individually. For this relation to be possible, an interior or core of the person, the self, previously inconceivable in several non-Western cultures, needs to be constituted. This was the case of the Wari', among whom the traditional notion of heart, the locus of feelings and thoughts that were necessarily open to others, was transformed by the Christians into a secret place accessible only by God (Robbins, Schieffelin and Vilaça 2014: 576). Among the Bosavi of Papua New Guinea, Christianity made it necessary to encounter a place inside the body to situate feelings, which previously had not been localised (Robbins, Schieffelin and Vilaça 2014: 571). Obviously, this involves versions of the individual very different to those found among ourselves, including because, as Robbins showed for the Urapmin, the relational values remained present, albeit encompassed. It is through the introduction of other factors, such as schooling and monetarisation, both frequently associated with missionary activity, that this individual acquires the features known among ourselves. As I sought to show for the Wari' (Vilaça 2018), the valorisation of the unit(y), the 'one', associated with the Christian God and the individual, benefitted from another context for its propagation. In contrast to the notions of solitude and lack attributed to the one by the Wari' and many other Amazonian groups, this idea acquired, through the teaching of mathematics in schools, a positive connotation that converges with the propagation of individualism as a central value.

Pool (Chapter 3), in her study of Islamisation, centres on the question of moral reform associated with religious change, suggesting that conversion should be conceived more as an ethical renewal rather than through the lens of religion. Berger (Chapter 10) also shows how excessive drinking and the conflicts associated with it comprise one of the reasons for the conversion to Hindu reformism by some members of the tribal community he studied in Odisha. This is also a theme common to studies of religious change and social revolutions, examined by Robbins (2004) through Sahlins's notion of humiliation and by other authors in the form of messianic movements (Carneiro da Cunha 2009 [1973]; Amaral 2014; 2019; Hugh-Jones 1994) and cargo cults (Wagner 1975; Lattas 1998). The consciousness of inferiority, based on access to an outside view of the self, stimulates an urgent desire for change, whether through the adoption of a new religion or through assimilation of the practices and customs of those

Afterword **279**

seen as superior, generally speaking the colonising Europeans, represented by the missionaries. In diverse cases, like some of those related here that stress the effectiveness of the new medications, moral consciousness may be a direct result of the collective physical deterioration provoked by epidemics.

Two other chapters of the book generate some interesting parallels with Amazonia: Heidemann's on the conversion of the Badaga of the Nilgiri Plateau by missionaries from the Basel Mission (Chapter 4) and Angelowa's on the conversion of the Sumi Naga of Nagaland (Chapter 5). In the first case, my attention was drawn to the information – absent from the other chapters – that eating with the missionaries was a central and irreversible factor in conversion. The author attributes this data to the notion of purity that informs the Indian relational perspective, and observes that converts were expelled from the group, conversion being expressed as a 'break up with the caste'. In the case of the Naga (Chapter 5), a tribal group, conversion took place collectively, led by chiefs and elders who took their entire family with them, or even their clan and village. The success of conversion was due precisely to the process taking place through the kin networks. Christians formed new villages and used the new religion as a form of identity in opposition to Indian nationalism.

These two points, conversion via kin networks and identity via commensality, are absolutely central to thinking about Amazonia, even though the Hindu notion of purity is absent there. In this ethnographic area, eating together is the most effective way of constituting identity, just as its opposite, devouring – of prey animals or enemies via cannibalism – is the privileged way of marking difference. Here we are in a world where humans and animals do not differ a priori, since both can assume the role of predators or prey, equivalent to humanity and animality, respectively. Marking differences to those from whom you wish to separate and similarities to those with whom you wish to live is a daily and primordial activity, one essential to survival. Thus, eating like and with white people is an important means of becoming similar to them. Differently to India, however, the idea of reversibility is central to thinking about Amazonian transformations. As I observed earlier, the latter are by principle reversible and, in this sense, equivalent to those promoted by new relations in Melanesia. For the Wari', eating strange food with the missionaries was a way of becoming similar to them, and certainly an important avenue for comprehending their message about God. However, just like the notion of dividual described for Melanesia (Strathern 1988 [inspired by Marriott 1976]; Mosko 2010; Vilaça 2011; 2015), its traditional component was not lost, but simply eclipsed, capable of becoming visible again through the activation of new relations and the sharing of food with other people. We are very far from a pre-totalised world, formed by

280 *Aparecida Vilaça*

parts with well-defined attributions and characteristics, where ambiguity seems to have no place.

This explains the place of kinship networks in the expansion of Christianity in the Amazonian world. Kin are by principle those with similar bodies, constituted through mutual care, exchanges and sharing of food. Conversion in Amazonia does not generally occur individually but collectively, as in the case of the Naga and mentioned also in studies of the Tamil and Toda. Among the Wari', a converted man tends to take his entire family and gradually his more distant kin. The new perspective on the world afforded by Christianity, one that fixed the Amerindians in the position of humans (who learnt by hearing about the divine creation narrated in Genesis; see Vilaça 2009), has no effect if it is not shared by kin.

One of the book's chapters, the study by Kannan (Chapter 8) of transformations in southern India at the beginning of the twentieth century, is extremely interesting, even though it is located somewhat on the margin of the book's general discussions. It focuses neither on missionary action nor on the conversion to Christianity, Islam or Buddhism, but on a subtle aspect of the construction of Hindu nationalism, which became almost invisible in the face of the violent religious wars that characterised the construction of an idea of the nation. Kannan shows us that the national movements produced radical transformations in the musical and performance arts, creating an idea of sacred national art through a radical selection of its component elements. As a consequence, some dances and music became legitimately Hindu, while others became forgotten by ceasing to be performed.

As I stated at the outset, this is an extremely rich book of major interest for scholars working in India and students of the movements of conversion to Christianity not only in India but also in other parts of the world. To conclude, I wish to return to the Afterword by Robbins (2009) for our book on Christianity in the Americas with which I began this text. Robbins drew our attention to a specific point, which at that moment did not – for me, as editor and researcher – amount to a central concern. This was the lack of dialogue between most chapters of the book and the literature produced thus far in the area of the anthropology of Christianity. In our book, we downsized any direct debate with the literature, arguing that we wished to offer an 'inside view' that sought to show above all the transformations that the indigenous systems of thought, values and ritual instilled in Christian practices. In other words, our focus was on the indigenisation of Christianity, which led us to pay less attention to the transformations provoked by Christianity in these same systems. The present book, with the exception of its dense introduction, dedicated entirely to connecting the chapters to more general issues and to authors working on the anthropology of Christianity, takes, in my view, a similar path. Aside from the omnipresent discussion on the 'radical rupture', referenced primarily to the texts by Robbins (2004) on the Urapmin and Meyer (1998; 1999) on the Ewe from Gana (Africa), who on converting sought to 'make a complete break with the past', the recent copious literature on the anthropology of Christianity is not consistently addressed in most of the chapters.

Obviously, selections need to be made when tackling a theme as complex and broad as religious change, and we should also recognise that *Godroads* is not only about Christianity, but also about Islamisation, Hinduisation and 'conversion' to communism. Readers may benefit from a discussion of more recent works from this literature, such as those on linguistic ideology (given that the missionaries were generally English-speaking), a topic central to the processes of transmitting a religious message of external origin (Handman 2015; Hanks 2010; Keane 2013; Schieffelin 2007; 2008; 2014). As we observed in an article written by two Melanesianists and an Amazonianist (Robbins, Schiffelin and Vilaça 2014: 560), the anthropology of Christianity offers theoretical tools for reviving the comparative perspective that characterised anthropology at its outset. Christianity, even with its important internal differences and distinct expressions when adopted by different peoples, has an evident unity, related, among other things, to the almost ever-present activity of foreign missionaries, to monotheism, to moral reformism and to individualism. Added to this subjacent unity is the wealth of ethnographic data that we have available today on the Christianity of native peoples or sectors of the national population around the world, which allows well-founded comparisons free of the evolutionist and diffusionist tethers that characterised them in Victorian comparitivist anthropology.

As I mentioned, the introduction seeks to circumvent this problem, and indeed the editors' observations concerning the different chapters construct a bridge between them and the general questions of the anthropology of Christianity. I suggest the readers, while reading the chapters with their fascinating ethnographic data on many different areas, to always have in mind the debates addressed in the introduction.

BIBLIOGRAPHY

Amaral, Virginia. 2014. 'A caminho do mundo-luz celestial: o areruya e os profetismos kapon e pemon.' MA thesis in Social Anthropology, PPGAS, Museu Nacional, UFRJ.

———. 2019. 'Os ingarikó e a religião areruya.' PhD Dissertation in Social Anthropology, PPGAS, Museu Nacional, UFRJ.

Barker, John. 1993. '"We Are Ekelesia": Conversion in Uiaku, Papua New Guinea.' In *Conversion to Christianity: Historical and Anthropological Perspectives on a Great*

282 *Aparecida Vilaça*

Transformation, edited by Robert W. Hefner, 199–230. Berkeley: University of California Press.

Carneiro Da Cunha, Manuela. 2009 [1973]. 'Lógica do Mito e da Ação: O Movimento Messiânico Canela de 1963.' In *Cultura com Aspas,* 15–49. São Paulo: Cosac & Naify.

Dumont, Louis. 1980. *Homo Hierarchicus: The Caste System and Its Implications.* Translated by M. Sainsbury, L. Dumont and B. Gulati. Chicago: University of Chicago Press.

———. 1983. *Essais sur l'individualisme: Une Perspective Anthropologique sur L'idéologie Moderne.* Paris. Éditions du Seuil.

Hanks, William. 2010. *Converting Words: Maya in the Age of the Cross.* Berkeley: University of California Press.

Hefner, Robert. 1993. 'World Building and the Rationality of Conversion.' In *Conversion to Christianity: Historical and Anthropological Perspectives on a Great Transformation,* edited by Robert Hefner, 3–44. Berkeley: University of California Press.

Horton, Robin. 1975. 'On the Rationality of Conversion.' *Africa* 45: 373–399.

Hugh-Jones, Stephen. 1994. 'Shamans, Prophets, Priests and Pastors.' In *Shamanism, History and the State,* edited by Nicholas Thomas and Caroline Humphrey, 32–75. Ann Arbor: Michigan University Press.

Keane, Webb. 2013. 'On Spirit Writing: Materialities of Language and the Religion Work of Transduction.' *Journal of the Royal Anthropological Institute (N.S.)* 19(1): 1–17.

Lattas, Andrew. 1998. *Cultures of Secrecy: Reinventing Race in Bush Kaliai Cargo Cults.* Wisconsin: The University of Wisconsin Press.

Lévi-Strauss, Claude. 1995. *The Story of Lynx,* translated by Catherine Tihanyi. Chicago: University of Chicago Press.

Marriott, McKim. 1976. 'Hindu Transactions: Diversity Without Dualism.' In *Transaction and Meaning,* edited by Bruce Kapferer, 109–142, Philadelphia: ISHI Publications.

Mauss, Marcel. 1999[1950]. 'Une Catégorie de l'esprit Humain: La Notion de Personne, Celle de 'Moi'.' *Sociologie et Anthropologie,* 332–362. Paris: PUF.

Meyer, Birgit. 1998. '"Make a Complete Break with the Past": Memory and Postcolonial Modernity in Ghanaian Pentecostal Discourse.' In *Memory and the Postcolony: African Anthropology and the Critique of Power,* edited by Richard Werbner, 182–208. London: Zed Books.

———. 1999. *Translating the Devil: Religion and Modernity among the Ewe in Ghana.* London: Edinburgh University Press, for the International African Institute.

Mosko, Mark. 2010. 'Partible Penitents: Dividual Personhood and Christian Practice in Melanesia and the West.' *The Journal of the Royal Anthropological Institute* (NS) 16(2): 215–240.

Robbins, Joel. 2004. *Becoming Sinners: Christianity + Moral Torment in a Papua New Guinea Society.* Berkeley, Los Angeles, London: University of California Press.

Afterword **283**

———. 2007. 'Continuity Thinking and Christian Culture.' *Current Anthropology* 48(1): 5–38.

———. 2009. 'Afterword.' In *Native Christians. Modes and Effects of Christianity among Indigenous Peoples of the Americas*, edited by Aparecida Vilaça and Robin Wright, 229–238. Hampshire (England) & Burlington (USA): Ashgate.

Robbins, Joel, Schieffelin Bambi, and Vilaça Aparecida. 2014. 'Evangelical Conversion and the Transformation of the Self in Amazonia and Melanesia: Christianity and New Forms of Anthropological Comparison.' *Comparative Studies in Society and History* 56(3):1–32.

Schieffelin, Bambi B. 2007. 'Found in Translating.' In *Consequences of Contact: Language Ideologies and Sociocultural Transformations in Pacific Societies*, edited by Miki Makihara and Bambi B. Schieffelin, 40–165. Oxford: Oxford University Press.

———. 2008. 'Tok Bokis, Tok Piksa: Translating Parables in Papua New Guinea.' In *Social Lives in Language: Sociolinguistics and Multilingual Speech Communities*, edited by Miriam Meyrhoff and Naomi Nagi, 111–134. Amsterdam: John Benjamins.

———. 2014. 'Christianizing Language and the Dis-Placement of Culture in Bosavi, Papua New Guinea.' *Current Anthropology* 55(S10): S226–S237.

Strathern, Marilyn. 1988. *The Gender of the Gift: Problems with Women and Problems with Society in Melanesia*. Berkeley: University of California Press.

Vilaça, Aparecida. 2011. 'Dividuality in Amazonia: God, the Devil and the Constitution of Personhood in Wari' Christianity.' *Journal of the Royal Anthropological Institute (N.S.)* 17(2): 243–262.

———. 2015. Dividualism and Individualism in Indigenous Christianity: A Debate Seen from Amazonia.' *HAU: Journal of Ethnographic Theory* 5(1): 45–73.

———. 2016. *Praying and Preying. Christianity in Indigenous Amazonia*. Berkeley, Los Angeles, London: University of California Press.

———. 2018. 'The devil and the secret life of numbers.' *Hau. Journal of Ethnographic Theory* 8(1–2): 6–19.

Vilaça, Aparecida and Wright Robin, eds. 2009. *Native Christians: Modes and Effects of Christianity among Indigenous Peoples of the Americas*. Hampshire (England) & Burlington (USA): Ashgate.

Wagner, Roy. 1975. *The Invention of Culture*. New Jersey: Prentice-Hall.

About the Contributors

Iliyana Angelova is currently Departmental Lecturer in Study of Religion at the Faculty of Theology and Religion (Oxford) and Director of Studies for Theology at St Peter's College. She was trained as a social anthropologist at the Institute of Social and Cultural Anthropology (Oxford) and has held postdoctoral positions at the Department of Social and Cultural Anthropology, Tübingen (Germany) and the Department of Anthropology, Maynooth (Ireland). Her publications include articles in *The South Asianist* (2017), *Journal of the Anthropological Society of Oxford* (2015) and *Manas* (2015) and book chapters in *Nagas in the 21st Century* (2017) and *Passing Things On: Ancestors and Genealogies in Northeast India* (2015).

Peter Berger is associate professor of Indian religions and the anthropology of religion at the Faculty of Theology and Religious Studies (University of Groningen), where he was head of the department Comparative Study of Religion between 2014 and 2019. His areas of interest include the anthropology of religion, indigenous religions, theory and history of anthropology and the anthropology of India. He was a visiting professor at the University of Zürich in 2012 and a visiting fellow at the Centre for Advanced Studies at the University of Munich in 2015. His books include *Feeding, Sharing and Devouring: Ritual and Society in Highland Odisha, India* (2015), and he co-edited *Ultimate Ambiguities: Investigating Death and Liminality* (2016), *The Modern Anthropology of India* (2013) and *The Anthropology of Values* (2010).

Frank Heidemann is professor for social and cultural anthropology at the University of Munich. He has conducted ethnographic fieldwork on politics and religion in south India (especially in the Nilgiri Hills), Sri Lanka, the Andaman Islands, the Lakshadweep and in the Maldives. More recently, he wrote an introduction to ethnology (2019, in German) and co-edited *Manifestations of History: Time, Space and Community in the Andaman Islands* (2016), *The Bison and Its Horn: Indigeneity, Performance, and the State in South Asia and Beyond* (2014) and *The Modern Anthropology of India* (2013). His interests include social aesthetics, emotions, atmosphere and affect.

286 *About the Contributors*

Arun W. Jones is the Dan and Lillian Hankey Associate Professor of World Evangelism at the Candler School of Theology, Emory University. He works on the history of Christianity in South and Southeast Asia in the nineteenth and twentieth centuries. He has published numerous articles and book chapters on these subjects, as well as *Christian Missions in the American Empire* (2003) and *Missionary Christianity and Local Religion: American Evangelicalism in North India, 1836–1870* (2017). This latest monograph probes the connections between *bhakti* and evangelicalism in nineteenth-century north India.

Vibha Joshi has been a research fellow and lecturer at the Department of Social and Cultural Anthropology, Institute of Asian and Oriental Studies, University of Tuebingen, Germany, from 2013 to 2019, and is a research affiliate of the Institute of Social and Cultural Anthropology at the University of Oxford. She is the author of the research monograph *A Matter of Belief: Christian Conversion and Healing in North-East India* (2012) and the book *The Land of the Nagas* (2004). She has authored articles in peer reviewed journals and book chapters and has co-curated the international exhibition and co-edited the accompanying book (2008) of the same title, *Naga: A Forgotten Mountain Region Rediscovered*, at the Museum der Kulturen Basel (2008–2009). Her main research interests are religious conversion, healing, traditional and charismatic Christian healing, and Naga material cultural heritage and museum collections.

Ashok Kumar Mocherla is Assistant Professor of Sociology in the School of Humanities and Social Sciences at Indian Institute of Technology (IIT) Indore. Before joining IIT Indore in 2018, he was a faculty member at the Indian Institute of Technology Mandi for six years. He has earned his doctorate from the Indian Institute of Technology Bombay in 2011. His academic interests include, among others, sociology of religion, caste and Indian Christians, sociology of faith healing and public health and religion in higher education. He is currently working on faith healing among the tribes of central India.

Rajalakshmi Nadadur Kannan is a Project Assistant Professor at the Centre for Global Communication Strategies, the University of Tokyo, and is an affiliated researcher at the Faculty of Theology and Religious Studies at University of Groningen. Her research interests are religion, gender and migration. Her publications include 'Copyright, Capitalism and a Postcolonial Critique of Performativity in Karnatic Music' in FocaalBlog, 'Redefinition and Representations of Sex and Body in the Early 20th Century Public Sphere in South India' in *Anthropos*, and 'Displacement and Gender Violence of Devadasi Communities in the Early 20th Century South India' in *Sikh Formations*.

About the Contributors **287**

Geoffrey A. Oddie taught history for many years in the University of Sydney and is now an honorary associated with the same institution. He was a visiting fellow at the Australian National University in 1982, a Visiting Fellow at the Jawaharlal Nehru University, New Delhi, in 2007 and Visiting Professor at the United Theological College, Bangalore, from 2009 to 2011. His books include *Missionaries, Rebellion and Proto-Nationalism: James Long of Bengal: 1814–87* (1998), *Religious Conversion Movements in South Asia: Continuities and Change* (edited, 1997), *Popular Religion, Elites and Reform: Hook-Swinging and Its Prohibition in Colonial India, 1800–1894* (1995), *Social Protest in India: British Protestant Missionaries and Social Reform, 1850–1900* (1979) and *Imagined Hinduism: British Protestant Missionary Constructions of Hinduism, 1793–1900* (2006, Hindi edition, 2019). He is also the series editor of *Hinduism in India* (Sage).

Fernande Pool is a Marie Sktodowska Curie postdoctoral fellow at the International Institute of Social Studies (ISS, Erasmus University Rotterdam). Her current ethnographic research with Muslims in the Netherlands aims to destabilise hegemonic conceptualisations of religion and secularism, well-being and (human) development. Her PhD thesis, completed in 2016 at the London School of Economics and Political Science anthropology department, is titled 'The Ethical Life of Muslims in Secular India: Islamic Reformism in West Bengal'. Fernande co-founded Lived Religion Project and is the co-founder and co-director of action network AltVisions.

Sarbeswar Sahoo is Associate Professor of Sociology at the Indian Institute of Technology Delhi, India. He was Charles Wallace Fellow at Queen's University Belfast, UK, and Alexander von Humboldt Postdoctoral Fellow at Max Weber Kolleg, University of Erfurt, Germany. He received his PhD from the National University of Singapore. His research interests include civil society and democratisation, and sociology/anthropology of religion, especially Pentecostal Christianity. He is the author of *Civil Society and Democratization in India: Institutions, Ideologies and Interests* (2013) and *Pentecostalism and Politics of Conversion in India* (2018).

Aparecida Vilaça is Professor of Social Anthropology at the Graduate Program in Social Anthropology, Museu Nacional, Universidade Federal do Rio de Janeiro. Since 1986 she has been working among the Wari' Indians in Southwestern Amazonia, Brazil. She is the author of *Comendo como gente: Formas do canibalismo wari'* (second edition, 2017), *Quem somos nós: Os Wari' encontram os brancos* (2006), *Strange Enemies: Indigenous Agency and Scenes of Encounters in*

288 *About the Contributors*

Amazonia (2010), *Praying and Preying: Christianity in Indigenous Amazonia* (2016) and co-editor of *Native Christians: Modes and Effects of Christianity among Indigenous Peoples of the Americas* (2009).

Piers Vitebsky is Emeritus Head of Anthropology at the Scott Polar Research Institute, University of Cambridge, and Honorary Professor at the North-Eastern Federal University in Yakutsk, Russia. His books include *Dialogues with the Dead: The Discussion of Mortality among the Sora of Eastern India* (1993), *Reindeer People: Living with Animals and Spirits in Siberia* (2005), and *Living without the Dead: Loss and Redemption in a Jungle Cosmos* (2017). His current projects include an interactive dictionary of the Sora language and a study of Sora spiritual and political vocabulary.

INDEX

active appropriation of external elements,
24
Adivasis, 100, 129–154, 155–178,
222–245, 231, 234, 242n8, 246–272
affirmative action, 8, 35
agency, 19, 30, 88–89, 91, 97, 159, 266,
273
  autonomous, 11
  of Christian god, 122
alcoholism, 169, 254
alimentary practices, food, meat, alcohol,
249, 258, 262, 264–266
All India Congress Socialist Party
  (AICSP), 71
alternation model of conversion, 276
Amazonia, Amazonianist, 31, 34,
272–273
Ambedkar, B. R., 5–6, 78, 83
American Baptist missionary, 162
American Baptist Missionary Union, 132,
149n4
American evangelicalism, 188
American Methodist, 179–180, 187–188,
193, 194n3
  ecclesiastical hierarchy, 179
  spiritual narratives, 183–185
Animism, 31, 155, 158–161, 163, 232, 273
anthropology of Christianity, 280–281
anti-hierarchical discourse, 274
antimodern antithesis, 12, 87
apostasy, 156

Arundale, Rukmini Devi, 217
Asad, T., 90
ascetics, asceticism, 21, 33, 36, 192, 246,
251–253, 256, 265
assimilation, 278
authenticity, 15, 209, 213–214
authoritarian irrationality, 10
autobiography, 14, 23, 120, 179–180, 185
  American spiritual, 184–185
  Methodist spiritual, 184, 193
  Zahur-al-Haqq's *Autobiography*, 14,
    181–184, 186–192
autonomy, 9, 30, 33, 90, 93, 97, 125, 148,
157–158
Axial age, 160

backsliding, 137, 161, 164
Badaga, 8, 11–12, 15, 19, 21, 30, 109–128,
279
baptism of the Holy Spirit, 184, 191, 194
Baptist nation, 129
Basel Mission, 21, 109, 118–119, 279
Basel Mission Archive, 117
Baum, Robert, 16–17, 247–248, 261–262,
267
bhakti, 57, 185–187, 191–192, 194, 211
Bharatnatyam, 200, 218n1
Bhil, 235–236, 241
Bible, 54, 78–79, 85, 112, 116, 120, 122,
135, 138, 143, 149n11, 163, 172–173,
226, 237–238, 276

290 Index

Bible women, 48, 53–54, 58, 62
biomedicine (biomedical), 144, 155, 158–159, 161, 166–167
Bourdieu, P, 15, 20–23, 28, 200–201, 204, 206–207, 209
Brahmanical Hinduism, 5, 233–234
Brazilian missionaries, 272
break from the past, 160, 181
British Empire, 3, 201, 222–223
Buddhism, 5–6, 12, 70, 78, 157–158, 232, 280

cannibalism, 32, 279
capitalism, 10, 16, 23, 76, 92
cargo cults, 278
caste allegiance, 48
caste endogamy, 274
Catholicism, 4, 6, 157, 167
charismatic nature of missionaries-cum-prophets, 21, 38, 141–142, 169–171, 248
charismatic healing, 138, 142, 169
Charter Act of 1813, 3, 223
Chettiar, Dr Alagappa, 209, 214
Chettiar, Raja Sir Annamalai, 213
cholera, 11, 60–61, 274
Christendom, 225, 229
Christian Badaga, 8, 109–111, 114–115, 117, 121, 125–126
    rebellion, 1920–1945, 117–119
Christian missionaries, 3–4, 6, 10, 34, 71, 86, 136, 222–223, 225–228, 230–231, 233, 235–238, 241
Christian practices, 35, 68, 275, 280
Christian temple, 122
Christianisation, 125, 171, 234, 273, 277
Christians, 4, 8, 32, 49, 52, 54–57, 59–62, 64n14, 65n17, 69–70, 78, 80–82, 83n16, 109, 116, 119, 122–126, 131, 134, 136–138, 144–145, 147, 149n10,

150n17, 155, 161, 164, 171, 174, 183, 189, 191–193, 222–231, 233–238, 241, 248–249, 262, 265, 274, 278–279
Christward movement, 14, 37, 47
citizenship, 10–11, 88, 90
civilising/civilisation/civility, 3, 10, 93–95, 97, 102, 141, 159, 223, 227, 236
classical arts, 200, 208–209
classicization, 203
coercion, 224
Coleman, S., 144
colonial elites, 200–204, 206, 208–210, 216
colonialism, 10, 12, 14, 16, 24, 27, 39, 86, 93, 130, 144, 208
communal identity, 96
communal religion, 250
communism, 8, 68–69, 71–77, 79–80, 277, 281
community health, 167–168
confession, 112, 121, 173
congregations, 48, 54, 56, 58, 85, 110, 115, 117–119, 122, 124–125, 168, 237
conjugality, 215–216
consumerism, 156–157
continuity thinking, 14
conversion experience, 32, 47, 130, 138, 160, 180, 182
conversion movement, 47, 53, 70
conversion narrative, 179–194
conversion to modernity, 9–13, 87
conversion, concept of, 1–5, 36–38
    caste and, 227–228
    consequences, 101–103
    debates, 226–230
    definition, 37
    as narrative, 120–121
    politics of, 233–235
    as a process, 37

Index   291

as protest, 5–9
protest against, 5-9
scholarly debates about, 36
and society, 29
cosmology, worldview, 3, 5, 16–17, 19,
24–25, 30–31, 33–34, 69, 81, 102,
140, 148, 159, 175n1, 232, 252, 263,
266, 276–277
criminal tribe, 51
crypto Christians, 237
cultural appropriation, 24
cultural capital, 200–201, 204–205, 209,
212–213, 217–218
cultural diversity, 272
cultural processes, 16
cultural space, 159
cultural transformation, 199–218

Dalit liberation/Dalit liberationists, 8, 69
Dalits, 4–7, 10–11, 69–70, 77–78, 81, 223,
227–228, 239, 273. *See also* Harijans
death rituals, secondary funeral, 251,
256–258, 263
deconversion, viii
deities (gods), 11, 34, 55, 61, 64n15,
205–206, 233, 246, 249–253,
255–256, 259–261, 263–264, 266
democracy, 89, 94, 98, 103, 209
demons, 165, 250–251, 255, 267
Deoband, 22, 27, 85–86, 91–94, 99,
101–102
Derrida, J., 204
Desia (indigenous population of Koraput),
247, 252–253, 268n7
*devadāsi*s, 22, 36, 211, 214–217
devotion, 14, 28, 36, 135, 142, 185, 187,
189, 209–211, 213–214
dharma, 27, 89–90, 94–103, 239
Dhenkanal, 246, 252, 255, 266
Diola Christianity, 17

discrimination, 5, 27, 34, 59, 69–70, 77,
80, 83, 92, 227–228, 242n6, 274
divide and rule, 222
doxa, 20
Dravidapuram, 68–69, 71, 76–78, 80–81,
82n1, 83n16, 274
Dube, S. C., 55
Dumont, Luis, 6, 15, 18–19, 247,
273–275, 278

ecclesiastical hierarchy, 179
egalitarianism, 277
Eisenstadt, S. N., 160
emotional conversion experience, 47, 130
Empire. *See* British Empire
Encyclopaedia of the Nilgiri Hills, 110, 114
endogenous events, 16
enlightenment, 13, 111, 210
epidemics, 55, 61, 62, 122, 124, 274–275,
279
ethical transformation, 4, 12–13, 22, 27,
85–103
Europeanisation, 278
Evangelical Fellowship of India (EFI),
224
evangelising, 133, 138, 155, 161, 163, 166
evil spirit, 16, 61, 111, 133, 138, 140
exclusion, 87, 90, 92, 102, 117, 156
exclusivism, 226, 238
exploitation, 1–2, 6–7, 20, 23–24, 33, 56,
58, 71–73, 76, 80, 232

fieldwork, 12, 33, 82n1, 87, 110, 120–124,
131–132, 158, 249, 259, 268n5
based interpretations, 120–124
forgiveness of sins, 8, 11, 112, 120–121,
173–174, 184
freedom of conscience, 228, 230, 239
Freedom of Religions Act, 229, 239
Frykenberg, R. E., 3

292 *Index*

Fuller, Chris, 4
Fürer-Haimendorf, Christoph von, 250, 261

Gadaba (ethnic group), viii–ix, 19, 21–22, 30–31, 37, 246–267, 268n2, 268n10, 268n13
Gaidinliu, Rani, 171
Geertz, C., 22, 262
God's body, 276
gospel (Christian), 59, 109, 111–114, 133–135, 138, 143, 163–165, 188, 191, 207, 223, 236, 242n4
gradual transformation, 47
Graham, Billy, 144, 169
group conversion, 70, 279
gurumai (ritual medium), 252–253, 255, 260
Guzy, Lidia, 252

habitus, 15, 20–23, 28, 96
Harijans, 4, 228 (see Dalits)
harvest, 115–116, 137, 163, 225, 254
healing, healers, 12, 60, 136, 138, 140, 142–143, 147, 155–159, 161, 164–166, 168–175, 210, 250–251, 255, 257, 259, 268n11
heathen, 116–117, 137, 147, 155, 166, 175n2
Hefner, Robert, 29, 88, 131, 247, 267, 182–183
hegemonic discourse, 37, 200
Hellenistic world, 182
hereditary chiefs, 132
hierarchy, 4–8, 14, 48, 50, 55, 73, 78, 93, 139, 179, 181, 189, 227, 272–274, 276–277
High God, 136
Hill Reddy (ethnic group), 250
Hindu caste system, 10, 232, 272
Hindu iconography, 217

Hindu mainstream, 231–233, 249, 267
Hindu morality, 223
Hindu nation/Hindu nationalism/Hindu nationalist, 2, 8–9, 36, 199, 223–228, 230–231, 233–238, 240–241, 241n3, 242n9, 274, 280
Hindu reform movement, 19, 21–22, 28, 31, 37, 246–267
Hindu reformism, 86, 273, 278
Hindu–Christian conflict, 222–241
Hindu–Muslim conflict, 222
Hinduisation, 231, 235–236, 281
Hinduism, 5–6, 8, 10, 36–37, 38n2, 68, 70, 110, 157, 186, 199–200, 203, 211, 218, 223, 227–228, 232–235, 238, 241, 242n9, 251, 273, 277
historicity, 180
History of the Basel Mission (Wilhelm Schlatter), 116
Hockings, P, 110, 112, 116, 122, 124–126
holism, viii
Holy Ghost, 276
Holy Spirit, 141–144, 165, 169, 184, 191, 193–194
hope, 1–2, 7, 15, 116, 120, 133
humiliation, 13, 23–25, 27, 33, 38n4, 92–93, 249, 268n4, 278
hyper-feminine, 215

ideology, 6, 26, 30–31, 34, 37, 71–72, 75, 77–82, 82n1, 83, 95–96, 98, 100, 199–200, 233, 238, 265, 281
identity politics, 8, 110, 199, 200, 204
immorality, 10, 101, 215
Indian National Congress (INC), 71, 199
Indian religiosity, 181
indigenisation, 16–17, 24, 34–35, 58–60, 93, 252–253, 261, 267, 276, 280
indigenous belief/indigenous religion, 16, 19, 29, 31, 158, 164–165, 246–267

Index 293

individual conversion, 70

individualism/individual rights, 10, 18, 31, 33, 87, 159, 276–278, 281

inducements, 158, 228–230, 234, 238, 242

inside view, 280

intellectual voluntarism, 88, 91

intellectualist, 88, 129–130, 147

interpersonal sociality, 31

inversion of values, 264, 276

iron deity (Durga), 255, 263

Islamic exceptionalism, 86

Islamic Mission Schools, 94, 103n2

Islamic reformism, 13, 37, 85–90, 93–95, 98–99, 101–103

Islamisation, 277–278, 281

Jagannath cult, 233–234

justice (social, economic), 6, 11, 13, 74, 89, 94–95, 102–103, 267, 273

Kandha–Pana relations, 231–233

karma and rebirth, 5

Kaviraj, S., 75

Kerala Christians, 4, 228

kingship, 202, 210

kinship, 33–34, 36, 77–78, 110, 132, 139, 276, 280

Koraput (Odisha), 21, 246–272

Latin Christian, 4

Levi Strauss, C., 32, 276

liberation, 6, 8, 69, 71, 185, 251–252, 266

lifestyle, 11, 19, 21–22, 24, 33, 36, 47–48, 85, 111, 130, 140, 148, 159, 216, 249, 252, 260, 262–267

liminal spaces, 1

Lingayat, 111, 115, 120

liturgy, 117–118

Lutheran missions, 51–52

Lutheranism, 77–78, 80–81

Madiga, 7–8, 11, 50–51, 53–55, 65

Maharana Pratap, 236

Mahima Dharma, 246, 248, 251–253, 256, 266. *See also* Olek Dormo

Mala, 7–8, 11, 50–51, 53–57, 71, 76–78, 80

Manusmriti, 211

marginalised/marginality, 4, 6–7, 12, 22, 24, 38, 69, 93, 124, 155, 200, 202, 205, 207, 211, 213–218, 227–228, 231–233, 236, 238, 277

marriage, wedding, 4, 11, 79, 115, 118, 121, 125–126, 168, 180, 192, 223, 249, 251, 253, 258–260, 266–267, 268n13

mass movement, 53, 69–71, 133–141, 147

Mass Movement Commission Report of 1918, 58

master narrative, 110, 124, 222

material progress, 8, 11, 13

materialism (materiality), 207, 209, 211, 215

Medak seminary, 53

medicine, 11–13, 51, 54, 60–62, 140, 155, 157–159, 161, 163–169, 236, 275

Melanesianist, 272, 275, 281

merit, 163–164, 250–251

Messianic movements, 278

Methodist, 7, 11, 14, 37, 47–51, 53–54, 57–62, 179–185, 187–194, 233, 274–275

Methodist mission, 11, 14, 37, 47, 51–53, 59–62, 179–180, 185, 187, 190–191, 194n5, 233, 274

Mewar Bhil Corps, 236

Meyer, Birgit, 13, 28–29, 39n6, 281

middle class, 22, 85, 203, 215–217

millets, 249

Mirabai, 192

mission schools, 22, 62, 85–86, 94, 111, 124, 132–136, 139–140, 145, 230, 234, 237

294 *Index*

missionisation, 3
modernity/modernity paradigm, 1–2,
    4–6, 9–13, 22, 24, 36–37, 87–90,
    97–98, 111, 126, 130, 139–140, 147,
    155–159, 161, 171, 174, 204, 249
moral reformism, 281
morality, everyday morality, ritual
    morality, 31, 92, 98, 100, 102, 130,
    137, 215, 223, 228, 250, 262, 265
multinaturalism, 34
multiple modernities, 88
Mutiny, 23, 192
mythographies, 1

Naga (ethnic group) viii–ix, 9, 12, 14, 20,
    27, 30, 125, 129–154, 155–178, 229,
    274, 279–280
Naga Mission Movement, 136, 143, 145,
    172
Nagaland for Christ, 9, 144–147, 171
nation-building process, 201, 204, 218
nationalism (national identity, nationalist
    movements), 22, 171–173, 199–200,
    215–216, 218, 224, 233, 274, 279–280
nationhood, 145, 148, 157, 161
native peoples, 272, 276, 281
New Tribes Mission, 272
Nilgiri Hills, 11, 109, 111, 119
Niyogi commission, 229
null hypothesis, 14

Olek Dormo, Olek, 19, 21, 28, 37,
    246–249, 251–253, 255, 257,
    259–267. *See also* Mahima Dharma
open captivity, 120
original religion, 240–241
orthodoxy, 142, 186, 212
other-worldly, vii
outcastes, 7–8, 11, 47, 50-51, 53–62,
    64n15, 112, 137, 190, 273–274

pagan, 4, 159
Pariah, 5–6
Parnami/Pranami, 186, 195n15
Partition, 222
patronage, 202–203, 209–210, 215
pedagogy (arts), 203, 212–214, 218
performance arts, 12
    contemporary south Indian classical,
        199
    dichotomy between sacred and profane,
        207–211
    institutionalizing and standardization
        of, 211–214
    patronage, 202
    changing spaces and context, 202–204
    of marginalizing communities,
        214–217
    sacralising, 205–207
    theoretical framework, 204–205
    transcendental power of, 206–207
persecution, 7, 9, 48, 56–57, 65n17, 137,
    157
personhood, 10, 37, 87, 89–90, 95–98,
    101, 103, 148
Phulbani Kui Jankalyan Sangh (PKJS),
    232–233
Pickett, J. W., 53
piety, 94–95, 160
politicisation, 131, 144–147
polytheism, ix
priest, 10, 19–20, 33, 38n3, 79, 81, 122,
    124, 159, 169, 224–225, 236–237
primordial world /activity, 276, 279
propagation, 229, 278
prophet, 20–21, 23, 38n3, 133, 143, 147
proselytisation, 34, 86, 91, 101, 120, 135,
    159, 161, 176n4, 223, 225–226, 231,
    242n9
Protestant Christian self, 10, 48, 146, 181,
    278

The Protestant Ethic and the Spirit of Capitalism (Max Weber), 10

pure gaze (Bourdieu), 206–207

radical change, 13, 17–18, 55, 182, 247–248, 267, 276

radical discontinuity, 130, 147, 160

Rajasthan Religious Freedom Bill, 230, 239

Raje, Vasundhara, 239

Rashtriya Swayamsevak Sangh, 218, 224

rationalisation, 10, 13, 88

reconciliation, 155–157, 161, 170–175

reconversion/*shuddhikaran*, 17, 36, 226, 235, 240, 242n9, 247–248

reference point, 18, 183, 247

reincarnation, 206, 250

religious field, 20

religious freedom, 69, 226, 241
  versus force and inducements, 228–230
  politics of, 233–235
  in Rajasthan, 235–240

religious transformation, 13, 15, 25–27, 29, 33, 37, 81, 130–131, 136–137, 140, 147–148, 182

Religious Transformation in South Asia: The Meanings of Conversion in Colonial Punjab (Christopher Harding), 47

renaissance, 199, 203, 209

reservation/affirmative action, 8, 35, 240
  benefits, 228, 232, 234
  politics of, 233–235

Retroversion, 16–17

revivalism (Christian), 169

rice, 74, 137, 246, 249, 258–261, 267

ritual status, village sacrifice, ritual cook, 19, 22, 28, 31, 55, 164–166, 173, 180, 223, 232, 246, 249–253, 255, 257–261, 264–267, 268n13

rituals
  of annual cycle, 249, 259
  Gadaba rituals, 247, 264, 266
  of healing, 12, 60, 136, 138, 140, 142-143, 155–158, 161, 165–166, 168–170, 172–175, 210
  of life-cycle, 249, 256, 258, 268n13

Robbins, Joel, 13–15, 16–19, 25–27, 38n4, 121, 129–131, 140, 147, 155, 160, 175, 247–248, 263, 272, 275, 277–278, 280–281

Robinson, Rowena, 4, 37, 78

Rona (ethnic group), 252–253, 260, 264

rupture, 246–267, 275–276, 281

Sabbath, 137

sacralisation (sacralised land), 24, 36, 199, 205–207, 216

sacrifice/sacrificer, 22, 55, 165–166, 173, 180, 223, 232, 249, 251, 253, 257, 259–260, 264–265, 267

Sahlins, M., 15–21, 23–24, 27–28, 30, 92–93, 249, 268n4

salvation, 1, 20, 31, 135, 140, 146, 166, 185, 187, 251

sanctification, 184

Sangh Parivar, 226, 241n3

Saraswati, Swami Lakshmanananda, 230–231

Sarna [indigenous] belief, 16

savagery, 164

Second World War, 21, 62–64, 74, 156, 159–160, 162, 167

secular modernity, 12, 22, 87, 90

secularisation/secularism, 4, 90, 94, 98–99, 102, 227, 240

secularisation theory, 9

self-definition, 183, 247

seminary, 53, 86, 117, 168

Seventh Day Adventists, 162, 248

296 Index

Shamanism, xi, 31, 273, 276
Siberia, ix, 31
sin, 31, 121, 124, 184, 186, 191, 250-251, 260
slaves, 5, 39n5
social order, 6–7, 32, 34, 249–250
social revolt, 6, 227
Sora, viii–x, 23
sorcery, black magic, *nosto* ('destruction'), 186, 250, 254, 256–257, 266
soteriological ideas, 250
soul, life-force, 173, 184, 186–187, 189–190, 193, 206, 217, 250, 256, 258, 264, 266
sovereignty, 157, 171, 202
spirit disko, 276
spiritual, 17, 28, 60–62, 92, 95, 111, 118, 130, 140–141, 143, 147, 156–160, 166, 179–180, 183–187, 189–191, 193, 205, 207, 209, 215–217, 228–229, 250–251, 258, 264, 266–267, 273
spiritual autobiography, 179–180, 183–184, 187, 193
Staines, Gladys, 226
Staines, Graham, 226–227
subaltern identity, 4, 24
subjective risk, 19–20
Sufi, 158
superstition/superstitious, 5, 116, 518–159, 267
sutok sorani (Gadaba name giving ritual), 256
syncretism, 17–18
Syrian Christian, 4, 78

teleological inevitability, vii
testimony, 52, 58

tolerance (tolerant), 158, 170, 173, 223, 226
totalisation, 276
traditional healers, 12, 155, 158, 161, 168
transcendent, 39n6, 160, 208

United States Commission on International Religious Freedom (USCIRF), 223–224
untouchables, 5, 7, 34, 69, 180–181, 193, 232, 234, 241n2, 273, 275
Urapmin (ethnic group), Papua New Guinea, 18–19, 25, 160, 248, 272, 275–276, 278, 281
utilitarian, 11, 121, 129–131, 140, 147

values(s), ideas and values, 11, 13, 16, 18–19, 24, 31, 54, 94, 98–100, 137, 140–141, 253, 263–265, 267, 275–278, 280
vernacular, 89–90, 95–96, 99–101, 135
violence, 1–2, 21, 27, 35–36, 62–63, 73, 91–93, 141, 156, 162, 170–172, 174, 192, 216, 222, 224–226, 228, 230–231, 234–241, 262, 266–267

Wari' (ethnic group), 30–32, 34, 39n8, 272, 276–280
Weber, Max, 10, 20, 38n3, 261
Wesleyan Methodist Missionary Society, 49
Western modernity, 12, 24, 139–140, 147

Yihovah, 138–140, 148, 150n17

Zahur-al-Haqq, 14, 21, 28, 179, 181
  Autobiography, 14, 181–184, 186–192
zamindari system, 73, 202